This book shows how the modern-day Sudan has been haunted by the distant past and presents the voices of two hundred peoples of South Sudan, a region which according to some "has no history." Many societies, worldwide, particularly those which have been non-literate, possess oral histories reaching back many centuries. They possess long memories, especially about wars and events of great trauma. Labeled "blood memories" in this book, the author presents a pre-colonial history of Southern Sudan. Beginning in the fourteenth century, the book follows the region's largest ethnic group today, the Dinka, from their original homelands in the central Sudanese Gezira between the Blue and White Niles, into their more recently adopted homelands in Southern Sudan. The book demonstrates how fierce wars, ethnic struggles and expansion shaped the "inner" history of the South today. External slave trades by Muslim cattle nomads from West Africa, the Baggara, further shaped the socio-political and military culture of the region. The book ends at the dawning of the Egyptian colonial era in 1821. Then, by way of an epilogue, it demonstrates how these earlier pre-colonial stresses have come to play a critical role in modern-day South Sudan, in what has since become the world's longest civil war, presently fought externally against the fundamentalist Islamic Northern Sudanese government as well as internally within the South itself.

SUDAN'S BLOOD MEMORY

ROCHESTER STUDIES in
AFRICAN HISTORY and the DIASPORA

Toyin Falola, Senior Editor
The Frances Higginbotham Nalle Centennial Professor in History
University of Texas at Austin

(ISSN: 1092-5228)

*Power Relations in Nigeria: Ilorin
Slaves and Their Successors*
Ann O'Hear

Dilemmas of Democracy in Nigeria
Edited by Paul Beckett and
Crawford Young

*Science and Power in
Colonial Mauritius*
William Kelleher Storey

*Namibia's Post-Apartheid Regional
Institutions: The Founding Year*
Joshua Bernard Forrest

*A Saro Community in the Niger Delta,
1912–1984: The Potts-Johnsons of
Port Harcourt and Their Heirs*
Mac Dixon-Fyle

*Contested Power in Angola:
1840s to the Present*
Linda Heywood

*Nigerian Chiefs: Traditional Power in
Modern Politics, 1890s–1990s*
Olufemi Vaughan

*West Indians in West Africa, 1808–
1880: The African Diaspora in Reverse*
Nemata Blyden

*The United States and Decolonization
in West Africa, 1950–1960*
Ebere Nwaubani

Health, State, and Society in Kenya
George Oduor Ndege

Black Business and Economic Power
Edited by Alusine Jalloh
and Toyin Falola

Voices of the Poor in Africa
Elizabeth Isichei

*Colonial Rule and Crisis in
Equatorial Africa: Southern Gabon
ca. 1850–1940*
Christopher J. Gray

*The Politics of Frenchness in Colonial
Algeria, 1930–1954*
Jonathan K. Gosnell

*Sources and Methods in African
History: Spoken, Written, Unearthed*
Edited by Toyin Falola and
Christian Jennings

*Sudan's Blood Memory: The Legacy of
War, Ethnicity, and Slavery in Early
South Sudan*
Stephanie Beswick

SUDAN'S BLOOD MEMORY: THE LEGACY OF WAR, ETHNICITY, AND SLAVERY IN EARLY SOUTH SUDAN

Stephanie Beswick

R UNIVERSITY OF ROCHESTER PRESS

First published 2004
by the University of Rochester Press

The University of Rochester Press
668 Mt. Hope Avenue, Rochester, NY 14620, USA
and at Boydell & Brewer, Ltd.
P.O. Box 9, Woodbridge, Suffolk 1P12 3DF, UK
www.urpress.com

ISBN 1-58046-151-4

Library of Congress Cataloging-in-Publication Data
Beswick, Stephanie.
  Blood memory : the legacy of war, ethnicity, and slavery in early south Sudan / by Stephanie Beswick.
     p. cm. — (Rochester studies in African history and the diaspora, ISSN 1092-5228 ; v. 17)
     Includes bibliographical references and index.
     ISBN 1-58046-151-4 (hardcover : alk. paper)
     1. Southern Region (Sudan)—History. 2. Southern Region (Sudan)—Ethnic relations—History. 3. Slavery—Sudan—Southern Region—History. I. Title. II. Series.
  DT159.6.S73 B47 2004
  962.9'023--dc22

                                                                    2003016697

British Library Cataloguing-in-Publication Data
A catalogue record for this book is available from the British Library

Designed and typeset by Straight Creek Bookmakers
Printed in the United States of America
This publication is printed on acid-free paper

To my parents Douglas Beswick and Stella Beswick-Boyd—
if you hadn't been there, I wouldn't have been there!

CONTENTS

MAPS

PREFACE

In 1996 when I visited the war zones of the African territory of South Sudan my goal was to understand the causes and complexities of what had become one of the world's longest civil wars. I anticipated writing a history that would begin in the mid-twentieth century, one that would mirror many others in the continent of Africa where the legacy of colonial rule has often led to postcolonial disasters. What I discovered however, upon inteviewing numerous South Sudanese (including Dinka, Nuer, Shilluk, Luo, Bari, Azande, Balanda, Latuka, Atwot, Acholi, Fertit, and Yibel) were answers that delved far beyond the twentieth century. I uncovered issues far more complex concerning the last forty years of the modern civil war than those presented in the popular media who argue that the conflict, in simple terms, can be reduced to that of an "Islamic North" versus a "Christian South."

It is evident that many of South Sudan's problems today—including civil war with Northern Sudan and the intense hatred of those Islamic peoples on their northern frontier, the desire to have separate nation status from the Islamic Northern Sudan, disagreements over the official geographical boundary and definition of "South Sudan," intense intra-South Sudanese ethnic conflict, the continued and preferred reliance on the pastoral economy of raiding and its concomitant conflict, perceived ethnic expansion and dominance by one ethnic group, the Dinka, over all other South Sudanese peoples, the continued problem of Northern Islamic slave raids, the persistence of the Nilotic philosophy of fission politics, the importance of communal religion, and the centuries-old male forms of dominance over women—all have their roots in the older precolonial history of South Sudan. This book, therefore, presents a history of the formation of a precolonial stateless society in what is politically known today as "South Sudan" (in the colonial era it was Southern Sudan) and shows how these early stresses have since come to play a pivotal role in one of the world's longest civil wars.

This region has been especially important to study because there has been a perception in the community of historians and scholars that vast expanses of Africa, which have not hosted great or even small states and empires, must be devoid of any history worth knowing. Yet this territory today, which encompasses one third of a million square miles within the

largest nation in Africa, and which is largely peopled by historically stateless societies, has evolved, over time, into one of the most troubled places
on earth. In the process of writing this book I conducted approximately
two hundred interviews with South Sudanese peoples on three continents
in six countries including South Sudan, Kenya, Egypt, England, Canada,
and the United States. When I visited South Sudan in 1996 to conduct
field research it was not my first experience in Africa or this country. I was
born in Khartoum, the present-day capital of the modern nation of Sudan
and spent my first ten years in various points of central and Southern Sudan.[1]
I visited Sudan again in 1988 prior to the political coup of 1989. From
1992 to 1995 I interviewed Sudanese refugees in Britain, the United States,
and Canada. In 1996 I conducted research in Kakuma Refugee Camp in
northwest Kenya near the Sudanese border. Kakuma gave shelter to forty-
thousand Dinka peoples who had fled the civil war (and today this "temporary" camp houses 110,000 refugees from the Horn of Africa). I then visited the war zones of South Sudan and conducted research at the towns of
Akot, Nyabagok, Yambio, and Nazara and their surrounding areas, basing
myself, in between, at the transit town of Lokichoggio in northwest Kenya
on the borders of South Sudan. Following my research in South Sudan I
interviewed a number of South Sudanese in Nairobi and its environs. In
1997 I collected oral histories from a number of Dinka exiles in Egypt.

My methodology for the structure of this book has been to document
the history of the largest and most centrally located ethnic group in South
Sudan, the Dinka. I then compared and reconstructed their historical relations with all those with whom they came in contact. In this fashion, many
other multiple ethnic groups of South Sudan have come into historical
focus.

This study is among the first of its kind for this region of the continent. From an academic viewpoint, this book, in the tradition of Jan Vansina,
represents one of the very few "longue-duree" historical studies for

---

1. From 1947 my father, Douglas Beswick, worked for the Sudan Plantations Syndicate in the southern
Gezira at Fahal. In 1953 he was then hired by a Sudanese business man, Abdel Hafez Abdel Monheim,
to manage the giant twenty-thousand-acre cotton scheme in the southwestern Gezira at Goda on the
White Nile adjacent to the Abialang Dinka town of Geiga. In this region, along with the Dinka peoples
there were Selim Baggara. In 1956 he was employed by Sayed Mohammed el-Khalifa Sherif to manage
the cotton scheme at Zuleit on the west bank of the While Nile forty miles south of Kosti. Here there
were many resident Western Nilotic Shilluk, Kawasaba Baggara, and Ja'ali peoples. In 1961 we transferred to a large cotton scheme on the eastern banks of the Blue Nile thirty miles north of Roseires in
the Southern Gezira on the borders of Ethiopia, called Bunzega. It was in Ingessana territory. Lastly the
family moved to Khartoum, the nation's capital, where one of my numerous nannies was a Dinka lady,
Toma. We left the Sudan in 1963.

precolonial Africa. Such other seminal studies have included, for example, David Beach's *The Shona and their Neighbours* (Blackwell 1994), Robert M. Baum, *Shrines of the Slave Trade: Diola Religion and Society in Precolonial Senegambia* (Oxford 1999), and Timothy Cleaveland's *Becoming Walata* (Heinemann, 2001). Up to now, because of a long civil war (the first conflict dated from 1955 to 1972; the second from 1983 to the present), the region remains understudied. In a scholarly sense, South Sudan has been almost exclusively the domain of anthropologists. Very few precolonial histories of the entire South Sudanese region exist, with the exception of those written by twentieth-century missionaries such as Stefano Santandrea and J. P. Crazzolara, who concentrated primarily on limited geographical regions of the territory or on specific ethnic groups.

African history is still dominated by an historiography that is heavily oriented towards the European colonial era. Histories of African communities where the European presence is absent are few. Precolonial histories of stateless African societies are even rarer. Thus, this volume on the one hand contains discussion of the various possible methods of recovering the history of stateless precolonial African societies and aims to be useful for scholars of all disciplines as well as those interested in an earlier African era, particularly of Northeast Africa. On the other hand, this book is also important for scholars more concerned with modern-day events in Africa insofar as it contributes to an understanding of the many civil wars and conflicts that plague the continent today. The concluding chapter shows how the past is very much a factor of the present. It is no coincidence that most secessionist wars in recent decades (including the Biafran war in Nigeria, that of the Oromo of Ethiopia, the continuing conflict in Somalia, and the longest of them all in South Sudan) are essentially spearheaded by formerly stateless peoples in nations that have been independent for half a millennium.

Stephanie Beswick

Ball State University

ACKNOWLEDGMENTS

During the research for and the preparation of this book many people gave freely of their time, friendship, and advice. My profound and special thanks to the following: Dr. Roger Winter of the U.S. Committee for Refugees, Washington D.C., John Prendergast (formerly of the Center of Concern) Washington D.C., Reverend Roger Schrock, formerly of the New Sudan Council of Churches, and Angela Raven-Roberts. I also thank the Africanist members of Michigan State University's Department of History: my former advisors, the late Harold Marcus, Elizabeth Eldredge (particularly for urging me to acquire and document precolonial history), and David Robinson.

Special thanks to the following South Sudanese scholars and friends, presently or formerly resident in the United States who have given me much support: the late Dr. Damazo Dut Majak, Dr. Ambros Beny, Dr. Julia Aker Duany, Dr. Michael Wal Duany, Dr. Abannik Hino, Dr. Sam Laki, Dr. Yongo Bure, Dr. Lual Deng, Margaret Deng, and Dr. David Chand. Since my days as an undergraduate Dr. Mom Kou Nhial Arou has mentored me in the Dinka language and given me consistent unwavering support and encouragement through my dissertation-writing phase; to him I offer very special thanks.

In Africa, for support and aid in my field research at Kakuma Refugee Camp, Kenya, special thanks to Robert Koepp, Eric Watts, and Alice Chege of the Lutheran World Federation and the United Nations High Commission for Refugees. At Kakuma my sincere and profound thanks to Mr. Deng Dau Deng, Chairman of the Dinka at Kakuma, without whose support and encouragement my rich data collection among the major Dinka groupings would never have been possible. Many people also supported and aided me in my research at Kakuma, including Ayuel Parmena Bul, Sister Mary Ellen, Sister Nikki, Sister Carolyn, Sister Maureen, Yilma Teferi, Nuwa Senkebe, Zaka Kuawogai, Simon Sael Lomoe, Helen Ajode, and Nazir Mohamed Fara. I also thank Cesar Pastor Ortega, Sally Bernheim, and Phillip O'Brien at UNICEF Nairobi, and Pagan Amun and Arthur Achuien Chol, formerly of the SRRA in Nairobi and the SPLM/A, for support and permission to conduct research in South Sudan. At Lokichoggio I thank David Kagunda, Howard Meredith, and Moses Hixhanga. In South

Sudan I am profoundly grateful to all those who aided me with my data collection. In Akot my special thanks to Raphael Ngei Mutiku of Oxfam as well as Jok Ayom Majak, Stephen Anyaak Chol, Dut Malual Arop, and Paul Mayom Akec, who encouraged many to talk to me. In Nyabagok my thanks to Bruce Menser and Rob Jenkins of World Vision and Victor Majok Amecrot, Matthew Mathem Daw, and Napoleon Adok Gai. In Yambio I thank Walter Baumgartner, Timothy Chomba, and Samuel Juma Abende of UNICEF and Bangasi Joseph Bakosoro, Bandindi Pascal Uru, Samuel Abujohn Kbashi, and Bishop Daniel Manase Zindo. Very special thanks also to Lual Benjamin and Simon Malual Deng for their aid and support with my research in Nairobi.

During the period of archival research I obtained support from many. Special thanks to Dr. Rex O'Fahey for kindly allowing me use of his personal (and very rich) library at the University of Bergen as well as Leif Manger and Terje Tvedt at the Center for Development Studies, University of Bergen, Norway. Special thanks also to Jane Hogan at the Sudan Archives Durham, England, Father Eppink at the Mill Hill Mission in London, and Reverend Andrew Wheeler at the archives of the New Sudan Council of Churches in Nairobi. Since my undergraduate years I have been also given strong support and encouragement for my study of the Sudan by those at the Sudan Studies Association, U.S.—special thanks to Drs. Carolyn Fluehr-Lobban, Richard Lobban, John, and Sarah Voll and Nelson Kasfir.

Many people read this manuscript in its various phases of development and gave valuable advice for which I am most grateful; they include Dr. Fred Suppe of Ball State University, Dr. Harold Marcus, Dr. Jay Spaulding, Dr. Walda Metcalf, Douglas Beswick, Stella Beswick-Boyd, and the readers for the University of Rochester Press. I also thank Connie McOmber, cartographer, Ball State University, for her arduous work on my maps.

Last but not least, this volume would not have been possible without the support of my husband, Jay Spaulding, for whom I offer my profound gratitude and warmest thanks. It is also unlikely I would have possessed my enduring interest in the Sudan had it not been for my parents, Douglas Beswick and Stella Beswick Boyd, who spent years in the country both during and after the colonial era; to them I offer my profound thanks for their support and encouragement over the years. I also thank my stepfather Tony Buzzelli and my sister Yvonne Reinecke. As a pilot for American Airlines she aided me in the early years of my field research by providing discount airline tickets.

A NOTE ON ORTHOGRAPHY AND LANGUAGES

For all the African languages as well as Arabic I have adopted a transliteration without diacritical marks. Well-known place names such as Khartoum, Sinnar, Kosti, Bahr el-Ghazal, etc. appear in their most common (although less technically correct) Anglicized forms. Place names of administrative posts in South Sudan are given as they are found on most English speaking maps. Other place names mentioned in the text are transcribed according to the pronunciation given by the numerous informants. When writing common South Sudanese group and individual names I have used their written Anglicized form.

As many of the informants were Dinka, an explanation of this language is given. There are a number of systems of orthography for the Dinka language currently in use in Sudan, derived primarily from those developed by different Christian missionaries and agreed upon at the Rejaf Language Conference of 1928. For the purposes of this volume I use the orthography presented in Father A. Nebel's *Dinka Dictionary with Abridged Grammar*[1] (Rek/Malwal dialect) and the Summer Institute of Linguistics in Nairobi's 1996 *Language Learning Dinka Rek* by Lino Kiir and John Duerkson.[2]

Field research has revealed that the Dinka language is divided into approximately four major dialects (Bor, Agar, Rek, and Padang) and numerous sub-dialects, according to the historical background of a Dinka person. I also noted a difference between Rek and their close neighbors the Malwal, for the latter use some Arabic because of a close historical relationship for centuries. Difficulty can occur if a Dinka informant hears a researcher use a "neighboring term" or a different dialect from another region. The informant may possibly become a little annoyed that the researcher has apparently spent more time learning "another" dialect, or perhaps more

---

2. Father A. Nebel, *Dinka Dictionary with Abridged Grammar* (Verona: Missioni Africane, 1936).
3. Lino Kiir and John Duerkson, *Language Learning Dinka Rek* (Summer Institute of Linguistics in Nairobi, Dinka Literature Production Team, July 1996). It was written for the Dinka Course at the University of African and Asian Studies, Khartoum.

time in another region. Simple phrases such as "thank you" change from one region to the next and will be followed by a "correction" and a "repeat after me," if used in the wrong district. For example, *incalec aret* is "thank you" in the Agar district but *incalec apath* is used in the Rek district. Goodbye is *ok abi ben yok* in Agar, Bor, and Western Ngok but *ook abi ben yok* in the Rek dialect. In this instance the short *ok,* if heard among the Rek, is said to be insulting. As the Dinka language becomes more unified it is hoped that researchers will not offend their future Dinka informants.

Other difficulties can occur because of the tensions inherent in present-day politics of South Sudan between the Bor Dinka of the eastern Nile, those with the most political power, and other Dinka groups, particularly those west of the Nile who resent the power of the east. One western Dinka claimed: "The Bor are not true Nilotes but are Nilo-Hamites, and have Bantu in them [a Mundari admix]; even their language, if they want to, cannot be understood by other Dinka." The Bor Dinka dialect, however, reveals a large correlation with that of others, though localized words are in use, much as with many other Dinka peoples. Hello or *kudwal* is universal among the Dinka but "how are you?," for example, is not *ci yi bak* as in much of Dinkaland but rather *pwol gwop* in Bor Dinka country. Those Dinka on the Kir/Bahr el-Arab River today in the northwestern Dinka territory, adjacent to the Islamic Baggara , tend to use some Arabic words interspersed with the Dinka, for they have been exposed to the Arabic speakers for centuries.

As with the English alphabet, that of the Dinka consists of regular vowels that include "a" (pronounced as in *father*), "e" (as in *ape*), "ɛ" (as in *eh*), "i" (as in *see*), "ɔ" (as in *caught*), "o" (as in *over*), "e" (as in *set*) and "u" (as in *cool*). Some Dinka vowels are pronounced with a "breathy" sound. In Dinka orthography, breathy vowels are marked with a dieresis (two dots) above the vowel. For the ease of the reader only key consonants will be explained. The letter "c" is pronounced as "ch" in Dinka. The letters "ny" at the end of the word have a similar pronunciation to the "ñ" in Spanish. The letter "ng" has no corresponding sound system in English but is similar to "ring."

A NOTE ON SOURCES

This book presents the viewpoints, historical memories, and voices of many present-day South Sudanese. Because of the large number of personal interviews presented and the extreme length of many of the African names used, those not actually cited by name in the text are listed in the endnotes. I have used the abbreviation "PI" for personal interviews, followed by a number. A full listing of those interviewed, their interview number, their clan and ethnic association, and the place and date of the interview are listed at the beginning of the bibliography. The numbers are not always in sequence, since not all those interviewed have appeared in this book. Informants cited before a quotation in the text are not cited again in the endnotes, although the particulars of their interviews can be found in the bibliography.

A number of personal interviews or oral histories used in the text were conducted by others. These have included scholars, missionaries, former British District Commissioners, other personnel working in Sudan in the twentieth century, as well as letters and notes written to me by South Sudanese. Please see the general bibliography for these particulars.

Map1. Present-Day Sudan in Africa

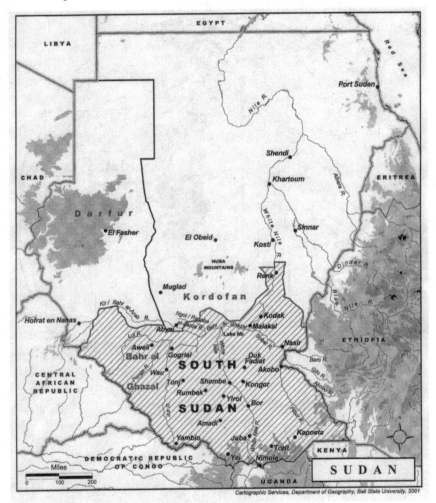

Map 2. The Present-Day South Sudan

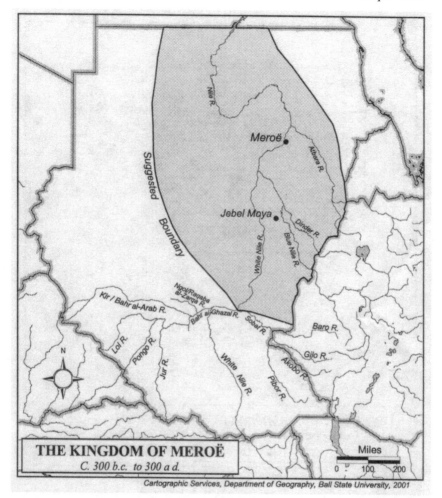

Map 3. The Kingdom of Meroe (c. 300 B.C. to 300 A.D.)

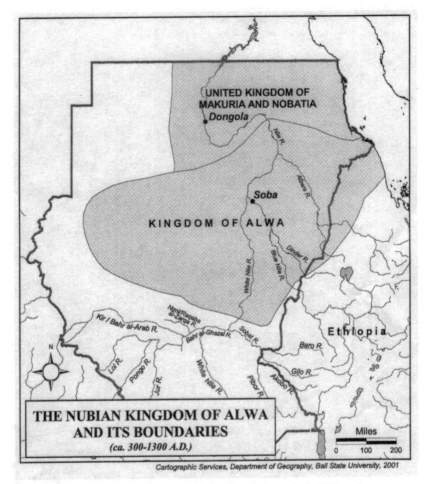

Map 4. The Nubian Kingdom of Alwa and its Boundaries (c. 300–1300 A.D.)

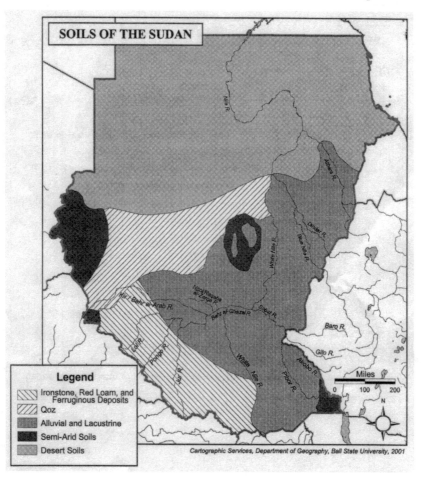

Map 5. Soils of the Sudan

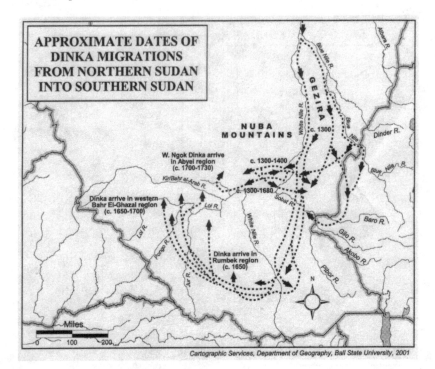

Map 6. Approximate Dates of Dinka Migrations from Northern into Southern Sudan

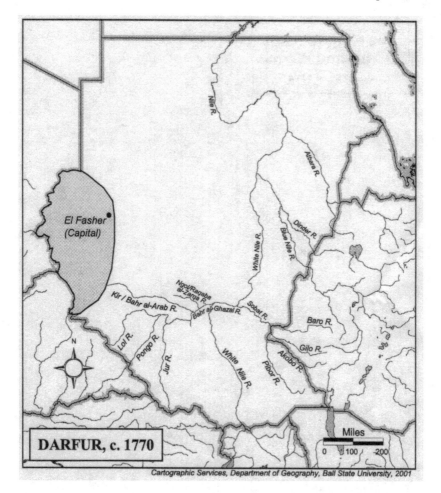

Map 7. Darfur (c. 1770)

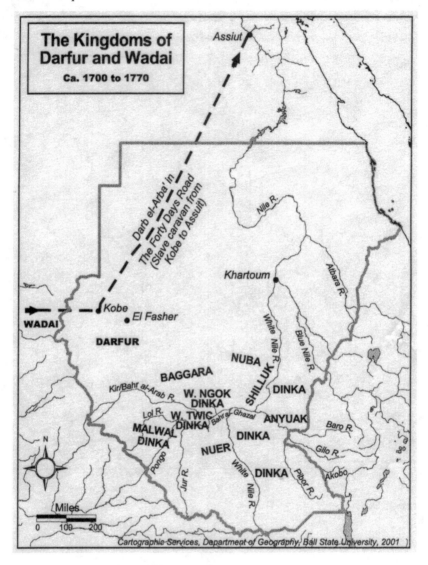

Map 8. The Kingdoms of Darfur and Wadai (c. 1700–1770)

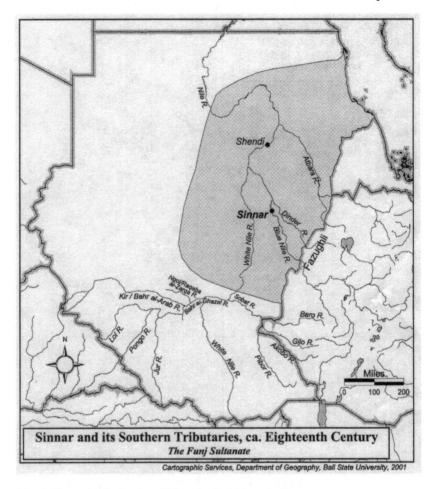

Map 9. Sinnar and its Southern Tributaries (c. 18th century)

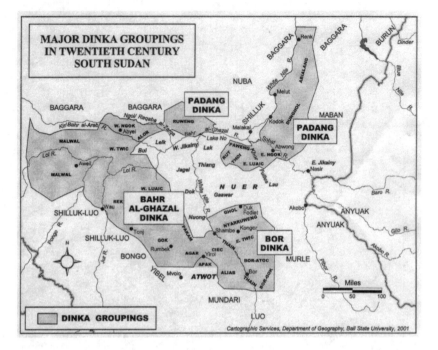

Map 10. Major Dinka Groupings and their neighbors in Twentieth-Century South Sudan

1

INTRODUCTION

Many societies today, worldwide, possess oral histories that reach back many generations. Those that are stateless and fall into the lineage category of society possess even longer memories, particularly for wars and events of great trauma. In this book I have allowed the "voices" or oral histories of numerous peoples—their "blood memories"—to present a precolonial history of Southern Sudan. I also show how certain key themes have continued to dominate from precolonial to modern times.

The older histories of central and northern Sudan have been much studied. Yet, beyond the early nineteenth century, little is known of Southern Sudan. Indeed its inhabitants, who have primarily been stateless, have been deemed to be a people without history. This book begins in the fourteenth century and shows how fierce wars, ethnic struggles and expansion, and external slave raids shaped the sociopolitical and religious culture of the region. For political reasons today, the residents of the geographical region of Southern Sudan, since 1983 have preferred to refer to their homeland as "South Sudan." For purposes of clarity, therefore, I refer to the region as "Southern Sudan" only when discussing events which pre-date 1983.

I suggest a number of theses in this volume: that the geographic cradleland of East Africa's Nilotic peoples is the central rather than Southern

Sudan; that this Nilotic frontier has been shifting southwards for centuries; and that the Western Nilotic Dinka were the last of the Nilotes to migrate out of the central Sudan into Southern Sudan. Since this time, the northern frontier of the Western Nilotes has historically been a boundary of stress and predation in the remembered history of many in the region. As they migrated into Southern Sudan the Dinka introduced a hardier variety of cattle and sorghum into the region. In time they underwent massive ethnic expansion (by marriage), coming to geographically dominate much of the central Southern region. Their routes of migration, however, were often dictated by soil types and water availability. The Western Nilotes, and particularly the Dinka, relied heavily on their religion, a communal and Olympian type of belief system that suggests they were in close contact with the ancient central Sudan kingdoms of the Nile. I further suggest that slave raids into what is now the Southern Sudan began in the latter eighteenth century and not in the nineteenth, as has been previously argued. The theme of ethnic conflict, a key and relevant theme in the history of this region since the precolonial era, is a factor both of economics and totemic closeness to one's neighbors. The concomitant "blood memories," or long historical memories of wrongdoing by other Southern peoples over the centuries, have tended to dominate particularly among and within the Western Nilotic societies of Southern Sudan. The latter form the numerical majority of the region. Because these "blood memories" have tended to prevail throughout the generations this volume shows how these early stresses have since come to play a critical role in what has become the world's longest internal and external civil war in Sudan.

Methodology and the Challenge of Using Oral Source Materials

Methodologically this study was conducted by following the Western Nilotic Dinka, historically, out of the central into Southern Sudan. As there were many wars between the Dinka and those in Southern Sudan during this migration, a comparison of oral histories was possible. In the meantime, the Dinka became the largest and most centrally located ethnic group, and thus oral histories of others with whom they came in contact have allowed a reconstruction of events in precolonial Southern Sudan. Because the Dinka expanded quickly against many other ethnic groups and were and are today bordered by much of the populace of South Sudan, it has been possible to include numerous other ethnic groups in this history.

Today there is a debate in the scholarly community as to whether verbal traditions are historical documents, or whether they are sources for merely discerning contemporary social arrangements and cultural statements. The main weakness of oral narratives is that to reach the present, they must be remembered and retold numerous times, reducing their reliability and accuracy because of accretions, transformations, and falsification of the original events. Hence, most scholars are aware that they are not completely accurate as indicators of the past; some writing South Sudanese history today refuse to use oral data.

Many believe, however, that oral histories are very useful, even critical for scholars. Jan Vansina, for example, points out that all narratives have an internal structure, that is, plots, sequence of events, repetitions, and so on, which may distort their content, but that the historian, armed with an understanding of the dynamics, can separate the historical message from the literary expression. Robert Harms argues that by tracing the changing relations within and between institutions in a temporal sequence one may reveal a "structured history because the links among institutions and sequence of change lie at the heart of the analysis." This methodology is especially appropriate for writing a history from broad, shallow data without precise chronological events. Thus, a number of scholars believe that oral traditions/histories contain "nuggets of meaning" preserving parts of the past in the present. Understanding the historical messages, however, requires an awareness of the indigenous system of thought as well as of the basics of the social structure. For example, Robin Horton suggests that a system of thought seeks to explain the disorder of experience by the use of abstract models. They are not intended to provide accurate chronological information or abstract quantification but rather are products of oral historians' attempts to make sense of the past.[1] Thus, intermingled with other data these accounts contain accurate historical facts which are corroborated by other forms of evidence.

Drawing, then, upon the major authorities in the methodology of oral history as presented above, this volume traces out what Vansina and other scholars call the "converging lines of evidence." I compare the South Sudanese histories of one ethnic group to that of the others (from different geographic regions). Among the Dinka, who presently comprise twenty six major groupings, the oral data of one major clan group is compared to that of another or others. Also relying on Vansina's methodology, I have crosschecked the oral data above against oral histories collected by British administrators, missionaries, and other scholars, as well as against nonverbal evidence, including primary and secondary source materials and cross-disciplinary sources. These sources include studies of linguistics and archaeology, historical weather patterns, the history and archaeological studies of animals and plants, hydrology, twelfth and thirteenth century Arab/Nubian geographers' accounts, Northern Sudanese genealogical texts and histories, and foreign travelers' accounts.

Finally, within the scholarship of South Sudan, regarding the value of oral evidence Dinka scholar Francis Deng notes that it is necessary to counter the denigration of oral literature and the overemphasis on written, mostly published sources, in order to understand the culture of a predominantly preliterate society.[2] Deng has been one of the few to present, in his ethnographies and histories, the voices of South Sudanese within the body of his work. In that spirit, this volume also allows the voices of many to be presented.

I begin this account in the prehistorical fourteenth century approximately when the forefathers of the Western Nilotic Dinka, still living in central Sudan, began to forge out of their original homelands between the Blue and White Niles commonly known today as the Gezira (island in Arabic), into what is now the heartlands of Southern Sudan. I end it in 1821 at the dawning of three subsequent colonial periods: the Turco-Egyptian (1821–1885), the Mahdist (1885–1898) and the Anglo-Egyptian Condominium (1898–1956). These periods represent the better-studied historical era of Sudan.

Because the concept of time in South Sudanese communities differs from that of a Western dating calendar, positioning historical events accurately has been a challenge. During the process of interviewing, it was necessary to ask the informant to give me the names of each of his ancestors up his/her lineage line so as to calculate, approximately, the numbers of generations that an event took place. In estimating historical events I used the conservative estimate of a thirty-year time span for each generation; that is, unless another formally dated event could be pegged to each account.

Theoretical Approaches

It would be difficult to reconstruct Southern Sudanese history without referring to scholarly theories, and those not specifically mentioned in the text include those of the *Annales* school and Peter Schmidt. The history in this volume follows the "longue duree" perspective of the Annales School in France which dates to 1929. Here historians of the movement regarded orthodox history as too concerned with events, too narrowly political, too narrative in form, and too isolated from neighboring disciplines. Annales scholar Fernand Braudel further argued that "traditional history" on the whole is often centered on the drama of "great events" conceptualized in a short time span. On the other hand, an historical study based on events over a long time span could allow the historian to note economic, social, and political cycles over time. The "longue duree" approach for this volume, therefore, has proven the most useful in observing the history of precolonial Southern Sudan. Peter Schmidt has suggested that the marriage of archaeology and oral histories has great value to the modern historian. During his early field research in Eastern Africa he acquired histories dating back numerous centuries. Against all expectation, the oral data was generally accurate, suggesting that oral histories passed down for many generations can still have great value. With Schmidt's experience in mind, I have found my own collected oral data to have a similar worth.[3] Because the oral histories of this volume primarily comprise those of clan peoples, a definition follows.

Lineage/Clan Group

There is no agreed definition of the term "clan" today in the scholarly literature. I therefore rely on that suggested by John Middleton and David Tait, who note that a "clan" is a longstanding term generally used to refer to a unilineal descent group, especially when it is exogamous consisting of several lineages which may be segmented. It is usually believed to have a single founding ancestor.[4] For the purposes of this book, a Western Nilotic lineage group or section is thus an association of stateless subclans with the addition of individuals or families who have attached themselves by marriage. The Western Nilotes of South Sudan have periodically become centralized. Thus, a definition follows for the early state.

The Early State

In Southern Sudan I suggest an inchoate early state evolved on the northern frontier. For the definition of the latter political entity I rely on that suggested by Henri Claessen and Peter Skalnik. In the various societies that can be classified as early states, the degree of complexity, the extent of the territory, the size of the population, and the degree of power of the central government may differ considerably. The inchoate early state is found where kinship, family, and community ties still dominate relations in the political field; where full time specialists are rare; where taxation systems are only primitive and ad-hoc taxes are frequent, where social differences are offset by reciprocity, and where there are close contacts between the rulers and the ruled.[5]

The Means by Which History is Stored and Remembered in South Sudan: The Case of the Dinka

Wars and critical historical events, particularly of a religious nature are often preserved in songs of all Southern Sudanese peoples, particularly the Nilotic peoples of Eastern Africa. These are handed down for numerous generations. Malwal Dinka, Kawac Makuei Mayar states:

> Our history is kept in these songs. In defiance of the Rek, we have a song of the Malwal people when we started to fight. We also sing that the Arab [the Dinka refer to all their enemies in northern Sudan as "Arabs," although they are in fact, Muslim Africans] is to make room for us. We keep our history in songs and count back numerous generations. Many Dinka claim to have songs of migrations which include details about past wars or how totems were acquired. There are long-remembered political songs. All people may create songs but it is believed that some are endowed with special knowledge and hence, they become the special poets in the community. There are also Dinka songs which record the exact geographical areas that the ancestors moved into after migrating from other areas.

Beyond songs, since historical times the Nilotes, for example, have developed another means by which to remember their histories. According to Rek Dinka Bona Acuil:

> We used to have sacred sticks in our house. Thirty sacred sticks were bunched together and the gnarls on the wood represented events in history. They are made from a tree called Akoc [a *Nihyalic* tree and very sacred]. We never burn this tree but just put it in the sun to dry and each notch in the tree represents an historical event and this is passed on down the generations. Only the eldest children acquire this information and it is only the men not the women. For example when the *beny biths* [priests] have had a meeting they go home, tell their sons of the history and he must remember. If you don't remember you are not a man's son. Not everyone kept sticks with these knobs. There were only three families who kept these sticks in our area.

Most Western Nilotes have an intimate knowledge of their familial backgrounds for, according to lineage systems worldwide, and according to

Paul Macuer Malok, "If a Dinka does not know his background he is not a Dinka and he will have difficulties in life." Among the Dinka it is important to remember one's ancestry for up to a dozen generations, although some claim to remember as many as twenty. Among other lineage societies in South Sudan the length of remembered ancestry varies.

Overview

This volume is broken into three parts: the ethno-historical formation of Southern Sudan; the ascendancy of the Dinka in Southern Sudan; and the dawning of foreign intrusion and its consequences. The methodology of recovering this history has been to follow the Western Nilotic Dinka from central into Southern Sudan. The events which occurred because of their arrival have formed the body of this book.

Chapters 2 and 3 outline the geography and a brief history of Sudan. In "The Ethno-Historical Formation of Southern Sudan," chapters 4 through 8 cover the oral histories of a residence in central Sudan followed by the migrations of the forefathers of the Dinka, from their ancestral land in what is now central Sudan and specifically the Gezira (between the Blue and White Niles), into Southern Sudan. From the time the Dinka arrived in the Southern Sudanese region of the Sobat/Nile rivers junction in the fourteenth century they warred with numerous peoples, including the Funj, the Shilluk, the Murle, Luo, Yibel, and Luel. Their migrations and continued wars with other ethnic groups concern chapters 5 through 8 and are presented in the form of micro-histories derived almost entirely from oral sources from many South Sudanese peoples as well as the Dinka.

In "The Ascendancy of the Dinka in Southern Sudan," chapters 9 through 14 show the success of the Dinka in migrating into key regions was directly related to an economic system of grain agriculture and cattle, both of which were superior to those then in the region. Their migrations were also dictated by appropriate soil types. Chapters 10 through 12 cover the religion and practices of the earliest forefathers of the Dinka in Southern Sudan and show how these migrants relied heavily on their beliefs in nature, the ancestors and their priests. Religion also played a large part in the psychological expansion of these Nilotes because of their economic security during severe ecological stress.

Notwithstanding the Dinka military success in acquiring new homelands in the central heartland regions of Southern Sudan, from this time onwards they came to absorb most of their surrounding neighbors ethnically. Chapters 13 and 14 explain this phenomenon, for during these stressful times in Southern Sudan, the Dinka were able to marry numerous non-Dinka women on their periphery, bringing a somewhat peaceful but rapid ethnic expansion throughout the region.

Chapters 15 through 17, "The Dawning of Foreign Intrusion and Its Consequences," cover and document the arrival of the eighteenth-century slave raiding Baggara, the chaos introduced by these external invasions, and the political changes which take place in Southern Sudan in response to these events. From this time onwards, the history of the region changed forever. External pressures exacerbated ethnic tensions and encouraged political centralization and stratification.

Chapter 18 gives a summary and comparison of the Western Nilotes of South Sudan today, and chapter 19 presents the legacy of the past in the present in modern South Sudan. It shows how many modern-day problems were born in the precolonial past. These "blood memories" have continued to predominate in the region and will have to be addressed if peace is to be accomplished in the future.

2

GEOGRAPHY AND BRIEF HISTORY OF SUDAN

The geography and climate of Sudan have had a profound effect on its history. Indeed, the migrations of many peoples have often been pegged to weather patterns and types and quality of soils. Additionally, the availability of water resources has also been an important factor in dictating the movements of peoples throughout Sudan's history.

Today, the modern nation of Sudan is the largest country in Africa; it is just over one quarter the size of the United States and the population in 2000 was estimated to be thirty million. The northern states cover much of the Sudan and include most of the urban centers. Most of the twenty-two million Sudanese who live in this region are Arabic-speaking Muslims, though the majority also use non-Arabic mother tongues (such as Nubian, Beja, Fur, Nuban, Ingessana, etc). The southern region has a population of approximately eight million who practice a predominantly rural subsistence economy. The lingua franca is English and there are numerous indigenous languages.

Geographically, Sudan lies immediately south of Egypt and extends over a distance of fourteen hundred miles from north to south and twelve hundred miles from east to west, comprising approximately one million square miles. It borders Libya and Egypt in the north, Eritrea, Ethiopia, Kenya, and Uganda in the east, the Democratic Republic of the Congo in the south, and the Central African Republic and Chad in the west.

Topographically the terrain of Sudan is generally flat, consisting of a featureless plain, with mountains in the north and west. Its lowest point is on the Red Sea; its highest is at Mount Kinyeti in the south, which rises to 10,456 feet (3,187 meters). Its greatest natural hazards are dust storms.

Sudan can be geographically divided into three regions. The first is the desert north of latitude nineteen degrees north. The rain fall is infrequent due to the prevailing of the dry northerly winds throughout the year. The second region is the typical tropical continental climate south of latitude nineteen degrees north, which is dominated by the movement of the inter-tropical convergence between the dry northerly and moist southern winds. The rain fall ranges from less than one hundred millimeters in the desert to fifteen hundred millimeters in the high-rainfall Savannah and mountain rain-forests of the subtropics in South Sudan. The third region is the Red Sea Coast and eastern slopes of the Red Sea Hills in the east of Sudan where the northerly winds prevail throughout the year, though the climate is modified by the maritime influence of the Red Sea. Other regions of specific local climate are Jebel Marra in the west in modern-day Darfur province, the eastern and southeastern uplands and the arid southeastern plains.

Sudan's temperatures and precipitation vary. The north is hot and dry with temperatures reaching 120°F (49°C) in summer. Rainfall is heaviest in the south where 50 inches (1,270 millimeters) may fall in a year. The north receives too little rainfall to allow farming without irrigation. The rainy season is from April to October.

Rivers have been historically important in Sudan and its most important physical feature, the Nile River, flows the length of the country from south to north. All perennial flowing streams of significance in Sudan are part of the Nile system. The White Nile (known as the Bahr el-Jebel in the south) receives much of its water from the Lake Plateau of East Central Africa (Kenya, Uganda, and Tanzania are riparian states) and originates in Lake Victoria. The Blue Nile rises at Lake Tana in the Ethiopian Highlands and makes its way through the mountains for about five hundred miles before entering Sudan. At Sudan's capital, Khartoum, the two rivers meet. The majority of Sudan's river channels are concentrated in the southern, northcentral and northeastern regions. In the south the major river systems are the Bahr el-Jebel, the Bahr el-Ghazal, and the Sobat. The numerous rivers and streams of South Sudan are thus fed by the White Nile, and, as it wends its way northwards into central Sudan, much water is lost in one of the world's largest swamps, the *Sudd*, or "barrier/dam" in Arabic. Thus, whereas the Northern Sudan is poor in vegetation, Southern Sudan, because of its mass of rivers, embraces a swampy plain surrounded on all sides by higher ground and is canopied with tall grass and evergreen forests.The White Nile, Blue Nile, the main Nile, and the Atbara Rivers flow in northcentral and northeastern Sudan. There are also numerous *wadis* (dry river beds) or intermittent streams, which flow only part of the year. Some drain into the Nile during the rainy season, others drain into swamps, which have no outlet to a river, or disappear into the sands of an inland basin during the dry season. Some of these intermittent streams carry huge discharges during the rainy season and support local areas of agriculture (the Gash and Tokar deltas, for example). Of the other rivers in northcentral and northeastern Sudan, the Atbara, Rahad, Dinder, Gash, and Baraka all have their sources in these highlands, and Ethiopia is the source for all these waterways.

Sudan's soils are rich in certain regions. K. M. Barbour delineates natural resource regions according to the state of water and soil resources which include 1) northern Sudan, 2) eastern Sudan, 3) western Sudan, 4) the Central Clay Plains, 5) the Southern Clay Plains, and 6) the Ironstone Plateau. The first four of the regions are in Northern Sudan, while the last two are in the south.

There are five broad soil types: desert, *Qoz,* semi-arid, alluvial, and lateritic soils. The desert soils are found in Northern Sudan, eastern Sudan and in the semidesert regions. This includes part of the Sahara Desert. These soils are extremely thin and support very little plant life except for specialized vegetation.

The sandy soils in the semi-arid areas south of the desert in modern-day northern Kordofan and northern Darfur provinces support vegetation used for grazing. In the southern part of the these states and the western part of southern Darfur are the so-called *Qoz* sands. The *Qoz* or aeolian soils are a vast extent of now static billowy sand dunes in the central western region. These dunes absorb all the rain that falls and store it until exhausted by growing plants or until it escapes into underground channels. The *Qoz* sands are the principal areas from which gum arabic is obtained through tapping of the Acacia Senegal tree (known locally as *hashab*).

The semi-arid soils are also confined to the Jebel Marra region in the extreme west of the country, as well as the Nuba Mountains in the center, and the extreme southeast of South Sudan including the Boma Plateau. Rainfall is higher in these highlands than in the surrounding areas. The soils are fertile and well drained and provide good opportunities for specialized crops especially in the Jebel Marra Mountains.

The alluvial and lacustrine soils are the most widely distributed soils in the Sudan. The more extensive and more important alluvial soils are the clays that have been deposited by the streams from the uplands to the south and east of the country. In northcentral and northeastern Sudan they form the Central Clay Plains, which consist of limited areas of alluvial terraces beside the Blue and White Niles and their tributaries, together with the northern Gezira Plain. The area between the Nile's two main branches is Sudan's most fertile (known as the Gezira or *jazireh,* island in Arabic) comprising river valley soil. In central Sudan, the clays stretch from the Nuba Mountains to the Ethiopian foothills.

In South Sudan the clays are even more extensive. Known as the Southern Clay Plains, they occupy a vast triangle between Lake Rudolf in the south, Melut in the north, and Aweil in the west. The Southern Clay Plains consist of heavy, dark grey-to-dark chocolate clays that develop deep cracks in the dry season and expand in the wet season, becoming impermeable. The clay content and the fertility of the clay plains in general increases from north to south. All studies on the Southern Clay Plains agree that these soils are rich in fertility but characterized by drainage problems. The southern part of the clay soil zone lies in the broad floodplain of the upper reaches of the White Nile and its tributaries in southern Sudan, covering most of what is now upper Bahr el-Ghazal province. Subject to heavy rainfall during the rainy season, the floodplain proper is inundated for four to six months. The large swampy area of South Sudan, the *Sudd* is permanently flooded, forming the world's largest swamp, and adjacent areas are flooded for one or two months. When the latter problem is solved this region will be regarded as having one of the better agricultural soils in Sudan.

The laterite soils of South Sudan cover most of the western Bahr el-Ghazal region. They underlie the extensive moist woodlands found in the west and south of this region. Crop production is scattered and the soils, where cultivated, lose fertility relatively quickly. Even the richer soils are usually returned to bush fallow within five years. The lateritic or ironstone soil of the Ironstone Plateau of far South Sudan is covered almost the whole of its extent by hard red concretionary ironstone of lateritic type. These soils are generally thin and their agricultural potential is variable. The exception is the Ironstone Plateau region in the so-called "Green Belt," which consists of an area covering the extreme southwestern part of what is now Western Equatoria Province along with a similar area around the Acholi Mountains in the Torit District of what is now Eastern Equatoria Province. The soils in the Green Belt, much like the rest of the Ironstone Plateau, are deeper and agriculturally richer. In terms of soil quality alone, the best are the limited volcanic soils of the Jebel Marra and Boma Plateau regions, followed by the extensive clays in central and southern Sudan, the Ironstone Plateau, and finally the southern *Qoz.*[1]

Sudan's Cultural Heritage

The Sudanese people share a rich African cultural heritage rooted in the distant past. However, the diverse historical experiences of communities in several parts of the country have encouraged the adoption of different sets of customs and beliefs. In the northern and central parts of the country these cultural innovations often came from the Mediterranean or Arab world. For example, the religions of Ancient Egypt, Christianity and Islam have each in turn achieved great prominence.

Brief History to 1821

The written history of present-day Northern Sudan goes back to biblical times. The Egyptians called the land Kush, and added it to their empire. For about a century, however, the princes of Kush seized Egypt itself and ruled it as the twenty-fifth dynasty. When Egypt fell under foreign rule, the central Sudanese kingdom of Meroe (c. 300 B.C.E. to 300 A.D.) preserved the ancient tradition for most of a millennium. During the Middle Ages the Nubians established several new kingdoms and adopted Christianity (c. 300–1300 A.D.). At the dawn of the modern age in the early sixteenth century a new realm, Sinnar, was founded by a Muslim African dynasty, the Funj. The Funj sultans ruled large parts of central Sudan until 1821. Around 1780 Islamic West African slave raiders entered western Sudan from the east (from what is now Chad) and raided for slaves in the southern Sudanese and southern Nuba mountain regions. With the rise of the Islamic Sultanate of Dar Fur in the west, slave raids increased. In 1821 the country was conquered by the Turco-Egyptians, auguring a new era of foreign and colonial conquest until 1956. Since this volume presents a history of Southern Sudan, an explanation of names, specifically for the region's largest ethnic group, the Dinka, follows.

The Historical Origin of Names in South Sudan: The Example of the Dinka

Much like many African peoples, the present-day nomenclature "Dinka" is of foreign origin. Historically the Dinka have always known themselves as "*moinjiang*" much as their present-day Western Nilotic neighbors, the Nuer, actually know themselves as "*naath.*" But from an external view, in the early central Sudanese literature of the nineteenth century the Dinka and other southern peoples were also known, derogatorily, as "Zanj" or non-Islamic Africans.

It is not actually known whence the name "Dinka" derives; most likely it evolved from European or Arabic sources when, according to Victor Majok Amecrot, Matthew Mathem Daw, Deng Dau Deng, and Akol Ding Duot, some centuries ago a stranger approached the northern Dinka (now known as the Padang) looking for a Chief Deng. It is postulated that as the word "over there" is "*kak*," the term "*dengkak*" emerged (meaning "Deng is over there"). It is said that after a time all foreigners referred to these Nilotes as "*Denka*." Another explanation is offered by Musa Ajak Liol, who suggests that the non-Dinka peoples of the southern Gezira complained to foreign intruders that a people called "Dengkak" had attacked them, and "it is this word which became 'Dinka' today, which is now used to refer to the people of Chief Deng who chased them up to the Ethiopian border."

What is known is that the term "Dinka" existed in the precolonial era, for the traveler James Bruce mentioned the "Dinka" in the latter eighteenth century. Some time later, in 1857, missionary A. Kaufmann used the term "Dinka" only to refer to the northern Padang who resided north of the River Sobat, east of the Nile in the Gezira. Elsewhere he referred to these Nilotes only by their major group names such as Ciec, Bor, and so on. Thus, evidently, the word "Dinka" originated first among the northern Padang, or northern Dinka as they are often termed, adding some support to the oral histories presented above.[2] It was only during the colonial Anglo-Egyptian Condominium period (1898–1956) that the Dinka eventually came to identify themselves by this term.

The individual names by which the major Western Nilotic-speaking peoples in South Sudan as well as the Dinka are known are often those of animals, or they may be derived from peculiarities of the country or even from history. For example, according to Abraham Mayuom Mangok, the major Dinka group, the *Aliab*, derived their name from a time in the past when two major clan groups "agreed to be one." According to Paul Manhom Mading, the literal meaning of the word *Agar*, one of the largest of the Dinka groupings, is "someone left by his people." The term *Bor*, which represents the most politically powerful Dinka section in modern times, refers to their land and means "flooded" because their country is largely under water in the wet season. The large Dinka group in the northwest, the *Malwal*, claim their name is derived from a time in history when "we followed the same pass made by the buffaloes; it is called '*Malwal*.'"

3

THE CHANGING NILOTIC FRONTIER

"We see a similarity between the Dinka and the ancient culture of Egyptians."
Samuel Bulen Alier, a Bor-Atoc Dinka artist

Archaeological studies strongly suggest that the most populous Nilotic culture of present South Sudan, the Dinka, did not arrive in the region until the fourteenth to fifteenth centuries. Yet, it has long been held by some older scholarship that all the Western Nilotic peoples originated in Southern Sudan. The Dinka, who comprise the largest population of Western Nilotes in Sudan today, however, support the archaeological studies and possess oral histories that their forefathers once lived much father north. Many suggest, for example, that they originated from the land between the Blue and White Niles, the Gezira. Others claim an ancient origin even closer to Egypt. What follows is a comparison of Dinka oral histories and myths cross-checked with linguistics, and Nubian geographers and travelers' accounts. Many East African Nilotic peoples possess a common myth/history which may hold a key to their origin.

Histories and Myths of a Central Sudanese Homeland

Within the Western Nilotic Dinka, Luo, Shilluk, Anyuak, Nuer, and Atwot are myths concerning migrations from a large body of water. For example, the Atwot remember that before they lived in Southern Sudan: "[A]ll Dinka, Nuer and Atwot came from a place known as *adekdit*, a body of water so vast that a bird would be unable to cross its expanse without dying." An Eastern Twic Dinka, Ayuel Parmena Bul, states: "It is said we came from the north, possibly from Egypt and the Mediterranean. There are two reasons for this: our people picture a river where a bird can fly until it gets so tired it falls in the water, but there is no river in our area like that. Yet the Dinka terminology for this body of water is *abab dit* [ocean], a river with no shore. We think that this story refers to the Mediterranean or the Red Sea and so we believe we come from the north."[1] Yet no scholar has been able to place this mythical "sea" geographically.

Pertaining to Dinka connections to Egypt, Samuel Bulen Alier, a Bor-Atoc Dinka artist states:

> We see a similarity between the Dinka and the ancient culture of Egyptians. Their drawings show canoes, spears and ivory very similar to our own. Arabs always use swords and Africans use spears, yet we note hieroglyphics in Egypt show shapes of spears and sizes of sticks attached to them which are similar to ours. They used the same small spear with identical teeth; long in the middle with thick or thin sticks. Our ancient Dinka burial practice was to bury the dead kneeling and their way was similar. Also our way of hunting birds and fishing is similar. Their pictures show ancient Egyptians hunting birds using a stick with a small flat iron object or heavy soil or metal on soil as a slingshot to make it travel to kill the birds. Our way today is similar. The way they dress, use skin of animals and the beads they put around their waists and necks are similar to ours. We also note they have similar names, and wonder whether it is coincidence. We believe we left with the formula and that ancient Egyptian civilization is also ancient Nilotic civilization.[2]

A present-day analysis of material culture between the South Sudanese Nilotes and Egypt indicates certain correspondences, as in stool design, traceable to Egyptian prototypes. An Egyptian hieroglyph for Zeti (the earliest name of Nubia) shows the ceremonial use of a Nubian bow, which is almost identical to that carried by Dinka religious leaders and currently used in dances by their linguistically close neighbors, the Nuer, at weddings. The practice of artificial deformation of the horns of cattle, a typical Dinka and Nuer practice today, is recognized by some scholars as being of ancient Egyptian origin (Fifth Dynasty, c. 2500–2350 B.C.E.). The Dinka note similarities between their language and that of ancient Egyptian. Eastern Twic Dinka Phillip Aguer Panyang states: "I counted twenty seven [Dinka] names that are similar to Egyptians', including Tut, Tap, Diing,

Aman, Mun, Lual, Acol." Additionally, the present-day Dinka custom of beer drinking while sowing seed was also practiced by ancient Nubians within the kingdom of Alwa in the Gezira.[3]

Oral Histories and Myths of Towns, Geographical Place Names, and the Sinnar Sultanate

The majority of Dinka today claim they once lived in central Sudan. Many claim the city name "Khartoum," now the capital of Sudan, located at the junction of the Blue and White Niles, originated from the Dinka language and means "meeting place of two rivers," that is, *kir* for river, and *toum* for meeting. A number of Dinka claim that the town of Shendi, north of Khartoum, was named after an historical Dinka figure, a Chief Shendit, who settled there and later migrated south. According to the early fifteenth-century traveler, David Reubeni, there were two rulers in the Kingdom: Abu Akrab near Shendi and the "great chief" at Ataqqi. In later years Shendi was a metropolis of commerce and the largest town in eastern Sudan; the people grew *dhurra* and possessed many fine cattle as do the Dinka of today. It is estimated that this city's kingship began in the sixteenth century and that prior to this time no central political control existed. The ancient residents of Shendi, the Nubian Ja'aliin, claim an historical relationship with the Dinka. One published Ja'ali oral history actually claims that all the branches of the Ja'aliin are from one man and "our dear Dinka and Watawit are from the Ja'aliin."[4] A Ja'ali scholar, Malik Balla, states that a number of his people concur with this ancient belief while Bor Dinka Manyok Akuak Geu states: "My people migrated from Khartoum. There is a group called Ja'ali . . . in a place called Shendi. They said they are our ethnic group and that my people defected from them."

Problems occur in the Ja'ali/Dinka connection, however, because Dinka informants, while strongly insisting they resided in an ancient Northern Sudanese homeland, including the Ja'ali region of Shendi, disclaim any knowledge of a connection to those modern-day "Northern" Sudanese who claim ancient connections. For example, Agar Dinka Stephen Anyaak Col recounts: "I had a Nubian professor and he told me that the Dinka and Nubians share many words such as *acak, cak* [donkey, shoulder]. Additionally, the Ja'aliin claim we are their cousins. The Ja'alis say they come from Arabia and met the Dinka and intermarried with us and they call us 'the sons of Abbas' but we do not believe this."[5] The antipathy towards any historical connection to Islam, as expressed above, may well stem from the postcolonial policies of various fundamentalist Northern Sudanese Islamic governments that have attempted to thrust Islamic law on the non-Islamic Dinka and Southern Sudanese in modern times. Thus, the Dinka do not wish to acknowledge any connection to the Ja'ali.

Along with a belief of an ancient residence in regions whose modern towns have the name of Shendi and Khartoum, Mourwel Ater Mourwel states that other geographical names exist today, remaining "from the time when we lived in the region. For example, *Arashkol* [Bad Sun] which today is a mountain in the center of Sudan. We also note *Aliab*, [the name of a major Dinka grouping in South Sudan on the Nile] in Northern Sudan, and Karakoj [which in Dinka means branch of the *Koj*], near Khartoum."

The Dinka also claim that long ago they resided in places that have now been renamed by the present residents of central Sudan; for example, Omdurman. This neighboring town of Khartoum is known to the Dinka today as *wut/wad durman* (brothers crying for their mother); the Gezira towns of Kosti and Wad Medani are claimed to have been previously known to the Dinka as *wunthow* and *wet badek* respectively.

As for the Gezira (the land between the Blue and White Niles), there are a number of Dinka histories and myths concerning the Sultanate of Sinnar that arose in the early sixteenth century. Located on the Blue Nile, this sultanate was ruled by an elite people known as the "Funj." This expanding political entity now evolved into the Islamic Nubian successor state to the medieval kingdom of Alwa. Although officially born in 1504, a nascent Funj Sultanate began political centralization in this region perhaps two centuries earlier; the first merchant from southern Nubia to enter the historical record was Al-Hajj Faraj al-Funi, listed as a Muslim Funj trader. He exemplified the increasing involvement of southern Nubians in international commerce during the fourteenth century. Throughout its history, not all aspects of which are presently fully understood, the Sultanate of Sinnar struggled to control the Nuba Mountains, the southern Gezira, and the White Nile valley as far south as the Sobat River.[6] Today, the Dinka claim ethnic connections to the Funj of the Gezira. For example, Bor-Atoc Dinka, Col Mayen Kur recounts: "When we left Shendi, Chief Ajak was a king by then and remained in Sinnar as *Melek* [king] and the rest of us left southwards. These people got assimilated and now there are people in Sinnar who still call themselves people of Ajak although they are Muslims and Arab. We found the Funj in Sinnar and fought with them, but they were not Muslim at that time; Islam had not reached the area. They had totems but no Islam or Christianity." Western Twic Dinka Michael Angok Malong adds that present-day Funj peoples on the Blue Nile in the Gezira still claim to be Dinka: "In 1985 I ran into some Funj Dinka in the southern

Blue Nile region south of Kurmuk. They were a Funj section called Mapou and they were originally Dinka. They still speak Dinka today, and they have the same physical features of Dinka and claimed to have been there a long time. They told me that when the people dispersed and the Dinka left the area, that they remained with the Funj. They had owned cows but were looted by the Arabs and now owned pigs and goats and cultivated a lot of dhurra." Dunghol Dinka informants also support this assertion: "Regarding the 'Funj Dinka' near Kurmuk, these are people in the Funj area from the Ager Dinka section. They have been with the Funj a long time and those still there know the Dinka language, although it is fading away. The clan within the Ager Dinka today called Kiel are related to those in Kurmuk who say they used to be Dinka a long time ago."[7]

The Dinka claim of having resided in central Sudan is supported by oral histories of other Nilotic peoples. Nineteenth-century oral histories collected in the Southern Sudan by a missionary, G. Beltrame, record a central Sudanese (Gezira) residence for the Dinka. He wrote that the Nuer and Shilluk complained that the Dinka had "long ago invaded their land from the north." Other southern peoples reported to Beltrame that the true speakers of the Dinka language lived in the Gezira; that they were the "true tribes, the Dunghol, the Angarquei and Abuyo Ageer (Agier) and Abialang."[8] Other twentieth-century Dinka and non-Dinka oral accounts support missionary Beltrame. In the early 1950s the Agar Dinka told British District Commissioner Brian Carlisle that their ancestors came from Northern Sudan. Further, the late Luo/Malwal Dinka scholar, Damazo Dut Majak Koejok, who collected two hundred Malwal Dinka histories in South Sudan produced similar accounts.[9] According to the grandparents of Southern Sudanese Luo, Albino Ukec Simon, all the Nilotes originated from the southern Gezira region: "We Shilluk-Luo came from the far east in southern Blue Nile at a place called 'Tindil' close to the Ethiopian border. It is believed that this is where all mankind came from and dispersed, and a man called 'Cai' moved with his people west and settled . . . east of the Nile." A Tanzanian Maasai (linguistically classified as Eastern Nilotes) claims his people "originated in North Africa. Many centuries ago we migrated and followed the Nile River upward to where we are now."[10]

Dinka histories also recall that their ancestors, at one time, en route from the north, resided in the Ethiopian borderlands, at or near the Blue Nile. For example, Malwal Dinka Lawrence Lual Lual Akuey states "we were on the borders of Ethiopia before we crossed westwards." Supporting this idea Bor-Atoc Dinka, Mom Kou Nhial Arou muses that within the Dinka language is the word for "mountain" (*pan-nhial*) yet present-day

Dinkaland is entirely flat, suggesting a former homeland in a different topographical region. Many Dinka today bury people with their heads facing east because ancient migration myths claim that they came from the direction of Ethiopia.[11] The above myths and oral historical accounts, although numerous, would be difficult to take at face value alone without the support of linguistics, archaeological studies, and other written histories.

Linguistics, Archaeology, and Travelers' Accounts

Linguistically, Christopher Ehret and Lionel Bender classify "Nilotic" as Eastern Sudanic which in turn is part of Nilo-Saharan. Nilotic is divided into three: *Eastern Nilotic* (comprising Bari and Lotuko/Ongamo-Maa [Maasai]); *Southern Nilotic* (comprising Kalenjin [Nandi, Sebei, Dorobo] and Omotik/Datoga); and *Western Nilotic* (comprising Jieng [Dinka], Naath [Nuer], Burun, Anywa [Anyuak], Colo [Shilluk], and Acholi/Southern Lwo). Linguistic studies such as those by Ehret suggest that the cradleland of all Nilotic languages lies north of the Ethiopian border between the Blue and White Niles in the Sudanese Gezira, specifically in the present-day homeland of the Burun. Nicholas David adds that a dialect chain of western, eastern, and southern branches of Nilotic languages diversify from a more northerly part of the Gezira in a southerly direction suggesting the language began in what is now the central Sudan and then spread south. Clarifying the puzzle, William Y. Adams argues that the original homeland of any language family emanates from that area where the various member languages have the widest diversity; in this case the country of the Burun west of the Ethiopian highlands in the Gezira. Thus, the cradleland of all Nilotic people, according to linguistics, was the Gezira.[12]

Adding further evidence and looking back at the ancient linguistic history of the Nilotes, Ehret suggests the material culture of the Nilotes in the Gezira took shape during the Aquatic period around 9000–6000 B.C.E. The ancestral Nilotes took on a distinct identity from 6500 to 550 B.C.E. approximately, and as the *Sudd* shrank to modern proportions from 2000 to 1000 B.C.E. at the end of the Saharan wet phase, some of the Nilotes expanded southwards as far as Lake Turkana. They primarily followed the higher ground along the western edge of the Ethiopian escarpment which stood above the still-swampy lowlands. Their descendants, for the most part, are found there in the western borderlands of Ethiopia today. One group, now classified as Eastern Nilotes, the Ateker, were present in the Lake Turkana area by 1000 B.C.E. In 1000 B.C.E. the future Southern Nilotes split off from the older community (which now became the "Eastern Nilotes") and began their move south into Kenya from the Lake Turkana area. Some of the future Western Nilotes, known as the Jii, began their initial expansion southward out of the old homeland area in the Gezira. In the meantime the ancestors of the Dinka remained in the old homelands. Around 1400 A.D. the Dinka began their expansion out of the Gezira while the modern Luo speakers of all descriptions were pushed southwards to various peripheries.[13] Within South Sudan today there are only Western- and Eastern-speaking Nilotic peoples. As the former are the numerically dominant, much of this volume is devoted to their histories in the region. Other recent scholarship also shows that the Dinka language has a close connection to classical Nubian of central Sudan.

The Dinka/Nubian Linguistic Connection

Many Dinka claim an ancient historical connection with the Sudanese culture and kingdoms of Nubia; according to Bor-Gok Dinka Michael Alier Agou "we are all brothers." Bender lists Nilotic and Nubian as Eastern Sudanic languages and linguistic studies conducted by Robin Thelwall suggest an unexpected degree of similarity in vocabulary between Dinka and the modern linguistic descendant of classical Nubian, *Nobiin*. Thelwall compared Daju, Nubian, and Dinka and wrote: "The inter Daju-Nubian comparisons give a spread of ten to twenty-five percent. . . . However, the check of Dinka gives one comparison (with Nobiin [the classical language of Nubia]) of twenty-seven percent . . . and this stronger link to Dinka than to Daju implies that it was in close contact with Dinka." In his first interpretation of this linguistic evidence, Thelwall attributed these similarities to a loaning process of historical interaction between speakers of classical Nubian and their Dinka contemporaries. The plausibility of this interpretation has more recently been enhanced by the demonstration that numbers of the modern Arabic-speaking peoples of the central Nile valley Sudan previously spoke a Nubian language more closely related to *Nobiin* than to the modern-day Nubian language of *Kenzi-Dongolawi*. In the recent past Nubian speakers were widely distributed extending up the Nile as far as modern-day Khartoum and over much of the Gezira.[14] The far southern Nubian kingdom was Alwa and, if the subjects of this kingdom spoke classical Nubian, as seems likely, they had at least a millennium in which to interact linguistically with the Dinka who claim to have resided in the same region. Archaeology also supports the Dinka claims of a central Sudanese homeland.

Archaeological Studies from Northern Sudan

Archaeological studies suggest a Nilotic presence in central Sudan many centuries ago. During the Meroitic period (c. 300 B.C.E. to 300 A.D.) the plains between the White Nile and its tributaries were rich corn-growing regions; the most fertile was that between the Blue and White Niles, the Gezira. It was covered with a dense forest of mimosa thorn and plentiful in rain. In this region 270 kilometers south of present-day Khartoum (at the confluence of the Blue and White Niles) there is archaeological evidence at Jebel Moya (in the center of the Gezira) of the Nilotic trait of evulsion of the lower teeth practiced by 12.8 percent of the males and 18.1 percent of the females. Evulsion, or removal of the lower incisors and sometimes of the upper is a custom practiced in the ethnographic present overwhelmingly by all the Western Nilotic people (Dinka, Nuer, Shilluk, etc.). Lipstuds, another Jebel Moya trait, are also worn by some Nilotic peoples today.[15] More persuasive are a number of archaeological studies from the Southern Sudan strongly supporting the view that the Dinka culture was not indigenous to this region.

Southern Sudanese Archaeological Studies

North of the Sobat which is now home to the northern Padang Dinka, an archaeological study conducted by Else Kleppe at Debbat Bangdit located near the White Nile south of Renk found evidence of a mound-building culture, quite different from that of the Dinka. Evidence supports the view that this region in the southwestern Gezira was home to a mound-building culture prior to the middle to late first millennium A.D.[16] and may have represented the remnants of an older far-southern Nubian peoples of the Gezira.

Fewer archaeological studies have been conducted east of the Nile in South Sudan. The first site to have been excavated was Nyany, located thirteen kilometers east of Jonglei on a ridge of high ground. It was at one time home to the Dinka and more recently their close neighbors the Nuer. Prior to the arrival of the Dinka and the Nuer, however, this region was home to a culture termed the "Turkwel" by archaeologists whose material culture most resembles the modern-day Eastern Nilotic Turkana peoples of western Lake Turkana in Kenya.[17]

Archaeological research in the present-day Dinka homeland west of the Nile, known as the Bahr el-Ghazal at such towns as Wun Rok, Dhang Rial, Rumbek, Jokpel, Ngeni, Bekjiu, Kat, and Na'am show that the previous residents of this land had a radically different culture from that of the Dinka. Rather, in early times this region was home to both the Turkwel and the non-Nilotic Luel. Studies conducted by Peter Robertshaw, et al., and Jonathan Kingdon have found that the Turkwel culture lived in the region of Ngeni, near present-day Rumbek in the latter first millennium A.D. The Luel were also ancient residents of the Southern Sudan; studies by Robertshaw suggest a culture of peoples similar to the latter existed here from the eighth to the thirteenth centuries prior to the Turkwel. Possibly central Sudanic speakers, the Luel unlike the Dinka herded humpless cattle, fished, hunted, made bone tools, wore and made iron jewelry, and did not practice dental evulsion. Nicholas David argues that archeological evidence shows that the Dinka migrated to their present territory of Rumbek west of the Nile in the Bahr el-Ghazal only within the last five hundred years.[18]

Further northwest in the northern Bahr el-Ghazal (west of the Nile), archaeology supports the view that the Western Twic Dinka territory was also once home to the Luel. Studies of numerous village mounds around Wun Rok (160 kilometers north of Wau, the capital of the Bahr el Ghazal Province) and Dhang Rial (nine degrees north and twenty-eight degrees east) reveal that hump-backed cattle (introduced by the Dinka) entered the region only within the last five hundred years. The earlier inhabitants herded humpless cattle, fished, hunted, made bone tools, and wore iron jewelry, suggesting they too were Luel. In fact, excavations suggest that the Luel were the ancient residents of most of Southern Sudan prior to the arrival of the Western Nilotes. The mounds of the Luel were first noted in 1923 by British administrator Titherington and several new sites were located in 1979. Referred to by the Dinka today as *tethony* (places of potsherds), many can be found around the town of modern-day Nyamlel.[19] This data along with linguistic studies is the strongest evidence supporting Dinka claims of a more recent arrival in Southern Sudan from a homeland in central Sudan. Written historical sources from Central Sudan add to these claims.

Historical Sources: Geographers, Scholars, and Missionaries

Other data supporting Dinka oral histories of a central Sudanese Gezira homeland include written historical sources from the Nubian period (c. 300–1300 A.D.). The dominant power in the region was the far southern Nubian kingdom of Alwa. A number of differing ethnic peoples resided on the periphery of this empire in the Gezira and during this time Arab travelers and geographers noted the larger ones, some of whom bear a great resemblance to the modern-day Nilotes of South Sudan. In the tenth century Arab geographers recorded a people called the *Damdama* or *Damadim* (plural), possibly the forefathers of the Dinka and/or Shilluk. Ishaq an-

Nadim specifically wrote that their speech resembles a mumbling sound. Because Western Nilotic people practice dental evulsion (and archaeology supports that they have done so in the past) their language sounds muffled to the uninitiated ear and thus it is possible the *Damadim* were of Western Nilotic origin. In the thirteenth century Al-Harrani placed the *Damadim* peoples geographically further southwest at the River Sobat, describing them as having a large population. Today the Dinka represent the largest Western Nilotic peoples in Sudan and aside from the Shilluk, who are presently a considerably smaller group but in the precolonial era were much larger, they are the only Western Nilotes who claim en masse to have resided both throughout the entire Gezira as well as near the Sobat River prior to the sixteenth century. This further suggests that the *Damadim* may well have been the forefathers of the Dinka or the Dinka and the Shilluk who are Western Nilotes. During this same time period Arab geographers and travelers Abu'l-Fida and Ibn Sa-Id al-Andalusi wrote that the *Damadim* were at war and killed many: "Among the towns of the Blacks [as-Sudan] located in this fourth Section [juz] there is *Dumdum,* whence the *Damadim* people set out against the Nuba and the Habasha [Ethiopians] in the year 1220 A.D. [617 hijra] at the time when the Tatars [at-Tatar] invaded Persia. For this reason the *Damadim* are called 'the Tatars of the Sudan.'"[20]

These accounts make clear the *Damadim* were also based in the southern Gezira as well as near the Sobat and that they waged war with their neighbors on both the Blue and White Niles. These written accounts correlate somewhat with Dinka oral histories. For example, Abialang Dinka Musa Ajak Liol states: "We chased the Funj [the former residents of the Nile/Sobat junction] all the way up to Omutholwi, east of Renk, then up to Parmi, now called Gospami, and then chased them all the way to the Ethiopian border, called Jebel Toktok and left them there."

It has been fairly well established that during the Nubian period (c. 300–1300 A.D.) a people called the Funj resided near the junction of the Nile and Sobat rivers as well as throughout the Gezira; indeed the sultanate of the same name emerged in the sixteenth century.[21] Dinka oral histories recount meeting the "Fung" people as they forged south up the Nile. Abialang Dinka Musa Ajak Liol states: "We found Funj in our areas and we fought with them and defeated them." In their travels south the Dinka remember many wars with the Funj which are noted in detail in the next chapter.

A number of written accounts suggest the Dinka are closely related to the Nubians. They are derived from both the precolonial and colonial Sudanese periods and, at the very least, suggest that the Dinka resided in central Sudan. Early in the eighteenth century two manuscripts (one which claims to date back to 1738) and another by the Northern Sudanese writer, Muhammad walad Dolib the younger, both quote the thesis of the four-teenth-century North African traveler Ibn Khaldun that the Dinka were ancestrally connected to the Danagla (Nubians). Harold MacMichael's vol-ume *A History of the Arabs,* comprising oral data collected from various Northern Sudanese peoples asserts that the "Gankay are Anag from among the Zing." I interpret "Gankay" as Dinka, and indeed in much travel litera-ture they are referred to as Ganka, Janga, Jonga, and so on. Further, "Anag" in Sudanese literature refers to Nubian peoples and O. G. S. Crawford also suggests that the Anag ("Anak") are Nubian fugitives who fled before the onslaught of the Arabs after the destruction of the far southern Nubian kingdom of Alwa (also referred to as Soba).[22] This account corresponds with Dinka oral histories which claim that they fled south out of the Gezira many centuries ago to escape slavers, and corresponds to the older Nubian geographer's accounts mentioned above.

Another manuscript collected by MacMichael refers to the medieval period of the Funj Kingdom of Sennar (1504–1821) in the Gezira. Here there is evidence that the Dinka and Shilluk remained a strong presence within the kingdom's periphery. Dekin, an early Funj sultan (1562–1577) claimed that his brothers were "Shilluk, Dinka and Ibrahim."[23]

The nineteenth-century genealogies of the Hameg, the successors to the Funj sultans at Jebel Gule in the Gezira, mention Shilluk, Dinka, and Kira (the ruling elite of the Sultanate of Dar Fur in the far west) as having a common ancestor with the Funj, the ruling elite of the Kingdom of Sinnar. This ruling elite was of Nubian ancestry.[24]

British administrator Sir James Robertson collected oral histories of the late Funj period where it was claimed that the people of Abu El Dugu in the Gezira were indigenous and that "the *mek* [king] is always chosen, usually by heredity, from some eight families of Dinka who are said to have come from Teifa." It is recorded that early in the Egyptian colonial period (1821–85) the Hameg, Dinka, and Hudur quarreled about the kingship of this region. However, the Dinka won and with the Hudur sat together as rulers in Abu El Dugu in the Gezira.[25]

Conclusion

This chapter suggests that the original homeland of the East African Nilotes is the central Sudan between the Blue and White Niles in the Gezira. The largest of the Western Nilotic peoples in Sudan today, the Dinka, recount histories of migrations from north and south of the confluence of the Blue and White Niles, the modern-day capital of Khartoum, southwards into their present homelands in South Sudan. Thus, evidently, around the fourteenth and fifteenth centuries they were the last Nilotes to leave central Sudan. Empirical evidence in the form of linguistics and archaeology in both central and Southern Sudan and historical accounts further support the above data. This includes Arab and Nubian geographers' and travelers' accounts of the eleventh to the thirteenth-century Nubian period along with more recent Northern Sudanese manuscripts and oral histories from the Gezira. As the forefathers of the Dinka migrated out of the central Sudan into their new homelands further south and southwest, however, they faced an onslaught of military resistance.

The Ethno-Historical Formation of Southern Sudan

4

SLAVE RAIDS, WARS, AND MIGRATIONS

"The Dinka and the Nubians have a connection; we are all brothers. They were our neighbors and we left them behind."
Bor-Gok Dinka Michael Alier Agou[1]

The ancient homeland of the Nilotic Dinka was the central Sudan and by all accounts they were the last Nilotic people to leave the region. As the forefathers of the Dinka moved south and southwest with their cattle they became embroiled in a series of major wars with other Southern Sudanese. Some of these conflicts were so bitter they lasted into modern times.

Why the Forefathers of the Dinka Migrated South

Dinka oral histories suggest that their early forefathers left central Sudan many centuries ago because of military stress, slave raids, and droughts. Thus, their forefathers fled southwards from their original homelands in the central Sudan. For example, according to Ciec Dinka Gordon Matot Tut: "We moved from Khartoum south via the Blue Nile towards Ethiopia, while others followed the White Nile mostly because of desertification but also because of wars." Historical events depicted in a number of scholarly accounts of the thirteenth-century Gezira support these historical accounts. In the tenth century, the main town of the far southern Nubian kingdom of Alwa, Soba, located near the Nile confluence, was the most important in the Sudanese region south of the Christian kingdom of Dongola. It included some of the richest grazing lands and was heavily infiltrated by nomadic peoples who migrated south between the eleventh and fifteenth centuries. The catastrophic decline of this kingdom after 1208 was followed by an increase in slavery and slave raids. Further, the cordial relationship existing after 1250 between the southern Nubian kings of Alwan successor states and the Mamluk sultans of Egypt was motivated by a strong commercial interest in slaves.[2]

Early evidence of contempt and negative Muslim attitudes towards non-Islamic peoples of the southern and central Gezira is illuminated by the fourteenth-century geographer, Abi Talib as-Sufi Ad-Dimishqi: "Beyond the Alwa country there is a land inhabited by a race of Sudan who go naked like the Zanj and who are like animals because of their stupidity; they profess no religion."[3] Evidently these non-Islamic peoples of different cultures and religions in the Gezira were viewed as fair game for slaving expeditions for centuries; a twelfth-century geographer, Tahir al Marwazi, wrote:

> Cunning merchants visit the places [of those Zanj] to kidnap their children and boys. The merchants go out to the grazing lands [of the Zanj] and hide in swamps covered with trees, carrying with them dry dates which they throw in the playground of the boys, who scramble to pick them up, find them good and ask for more. On the next day, the merchants throw the dates to them in a place further than the one of the previous day and so continue to go further. The boys follow . . . and when they are [sufficiently] far away from the homes of their fathers, the merchants rush on them, kidnap them and take them to their home countries.[4]

Along with Dinka oral histories of slave raids when their forefathers lived in central Sudan are traditions of drought during this era. Supporting evidence of severe ecological stress is offered by various scholars who note that the climate from the seventh to the twelfth centuries was fairly stable. After this time however, severe droughts plagued Eastern Africa at intervals from the thirteenth to the late fifteenth centuries. In 1201, for example, famine killed one third of Egypt's population.[5] Thus, in the thirteenth century famine and war struck simultaneously in the Gezira. Thus, on the basis of available evidence, it appears that the forefathers of the Dinka, who formed part of the slaving classes in the region, began to migrate southwest out of the Gezira in or after the thirteenth century—a date coinciding with the fall of Alwa. These migrations did not take place immediately and many clans remained in the Gezira for centuries. One other factor, however, was critical to the earliest Dinka migrations.

The Mechanism for Migrations

The forefathers of the Dinka could never have left their wealth, cattle, in the Gezira had it not been for the import of a new breed of this animal into Sudan a few centuries earlier. H. Epstein argues that the Western Nilotic people acquired Sanga and Zebu hump-backed cattle from what is now the northern Ethiopia borderlands sometime around or after the year 1000. From this era onwards these Nilotes possessed a great advantage, for this new breed was better suited to long distance transhumance patterns and less affected by drought. Upon the adoption of these cattle the Dinka acquired a mechanism to flee away from the populous central Sudan region southwest into the lowlands of Southern Sudan.[6] This topic will be covered in more detail in chapter 9.

The routes traversed by the various Dinka clans to their respective modern-day homelands were various; the Dinka claim to have songs of these migrations. Oral histories remember that they preferred to follow water and evidently many followed the White Nile southwards to the Sobat River region and then to various points of Southern Sudan. Others followed the Blue Nile south into Ethiopia. From there many then forged west towards the Nile and Sobat confluence. Skeletal remains discovered in the Fazugli region of northwest Ethiopia are believed to be of Western Nilotic (Dinka, Shilluk, Nuer, Luo) or Burun (pre-Nilotic people who remain in the region) origin supporting Dinka oral accounts.[7] The pursuit of new and safer homelands, however, was hazardous, for every step of the way was fraught with military conflict.

Wars and Southern Migrations

Missionary Stefano Santandrea recorded that as the Dinka sought new homelands they "wrung piece by piece most of their territory from its former inhabitants."[8] However, for most of their migrations southwards into what later became the Southern Sudan the Dinka were on the defensive, militarily. It is only with the Funj and Luel, at the beginning and end of their journeys, respectively, that the Dinka definitively became the aggressors. Their first remembered wars took place with the Funj.

The Dinka Wars with the Funj (Thirteenth to Seventeenth Centuries)

With the fall of the kingdom of Alwa in the thirteenth century and the beginning of the great Dinka migrations south, many clans arrived at the junction of the Sobat and Nile Rivers and displaced and warred with, and absorbed, a new people. On the evidence of their settlement mounds, pottery and construction in red brick, this particular culture was the "Funj" who represented the far-southern remnants of an older culture of the Gezira. These folk were also members of the central Sudanese cultural tradition that included ancient Meroe and medieval Nubia and thus they were, in reality, ethnically Nubian. Dunghol Dinka, Cok Kuek Ywai who resides in this former Funj region, notes that even today there are non-Dinka pots to be found in his homeland: "According to my grandfather . . . we met the Funj going southwards and fought with them. Today around Renk there are artifacts that used to belong to the Funj. When you dig in the ground you step on pots made of mud that were burned and do not perish; these are Funj pots. Every section of the Dinka has its own decoration and its own size, and we always know our own pots."[9]

Although these wars took place centuries ago, the memory of them has been preserved in Dinka oral histories. Abialang Dinka Musa Ajak Liol states: "When we killed the Funj the women made pots and cut off the heads of the Funj and put them in pots and buried [them]." A similar oral history is remembered by Eastern Ngok Dinka, Simon Ayuel Deng: "When we moved east of the Nile we found Funj and we fought them. We overtook this place and took their land and came and settled in our present location. We pushed the Funj to the Blue Nile."

In the early days of the thirteenth- and fourteenth-century migrations the Dinka who arrived at the junction of the White Nile and Sobat Rivers found a land that was sandy to the north of the Sobat and even less hospitable to its south; it was constantly flooded and provided poor grazing, forcing the Dinka to move. According to oral histories, over time, as Dinka populations increased many chose to migrate west across the Nile to the lands south of the Nuba mountains, leaving a skeletal population at the Sobat. The reasons for this decision may well have been ecological. In the early fifteenth century, rainfall in Sudan and Ethiopia was above normal, causing the waters in the White Nile to back up and forming huge swamps south of the Sobat in the Southern Sudan region.[10] This barrier would have made a southern migration into the heartlands of these swamps, particularly with cattle, very hazardous. Thus, many forged west and crossed the Nile.

With the rise of the sixteenth-century Sultanate of Sinnar many Dinka clans still resident in the Gezira became embroiled in a series of bitter wars as this kingdom expanded. It further created pressures for those clans who were migrating south along the Blue Nile. In the previous chapter a number of Dinka oral histories concerning the Funj Sultanate were presented; pertaining to migrations south Agar Dinka Paul Manhom Mading asserts: "We were taking the west bank [White Nile] and the Funj were on the east bank [Blue Nile] and those Dinka following the eastern Nile [Blue Nile] fought with the Funj."[11]

Meanwhile, northeast of the Sobat/Nile junction during the latter sixteenth and early seventeenth centuries Sultan Dekin of the Funj Sultanate was still expanding throughout the central Sudan. In this period many other Dinka clans still residing in the Gezira fled southwest in a steady stream following in the footsteps of those who had left centuries earlier. According to a number of Dinka the Western Nilotic neighbors of the Funj at the Sobat, the Burun, a separate pre-Nilotic ethnic group indigenous to the southwestern Gezira region, fared somewhat better. The Dinka recount: "When we came, the Burun were already there. We think they were part of the Funj at one time. When the Dunghol people fought with the Funj, the Burun didn't take sides, so when we chased the Funj from the area the Burun remained our neighbors."[12]

Perhaps for ecological reasons of flooding mentioned earlier in this chapter, around the latter fifteenth and early sixteenth centuries another Western Nilotic group, formerly resident further south in the heartlands of Southern Sudan, now moved north. Six families of Shilluk, led by their culture hero Nyakang, arrived at the junction of the Sobat and White Nile Rivers. Soon, they also began a long series of wars with the Dinka.

The Dinka Wars with their Nilotic Cousins, the Shilluk

The Shilluk also speak a Western Nilotic language and their oral histories recount that their previous homeland, Dimo, was located far to the south of their present-day residence. Upon arrival in their new homeland the Shilluk fought a series of battles with sedentary peoples they called Apfuny, Obwongo, and/or Dongo (terms interpreted by scholars today as "Funj")—the same people who had previously warred with the Dinka. Over time the Shilluk displaced and absorbed these Funj peoples, some of whom relocated north of the Sobat around the modern-day town of Wau. There is only minimal mention of the Dinka at this juncture of Shilluk history and it must be assumed that most Dinka clans had migrated west and/or south beyond the Sobat.

In the seventeenth century, however, Shilluk oral histories record that they came under severe military pressure on their northeastern frontier. In this era an increased number of Dinka clan groups, described by the Shilluk as "hordes," fled southwest out of the Gezira away from the rapidly expanding kingdom of Sinnar. Weather patterns had reverted from the previous centuries and this region now witnessed severe droughts and, according to the Funj Chronicle, hit the Gezira during the reign of Sultan Badi II's nephew, Unsa walad Nasir. "It was he during whose reign there appeared the year of 'Umm Lahm.' That was a year of famine, and of a plague of smallpox. It is said that the virulence of the famine was such that people ate dogs." In this same time period another source for history is the *Tabaqat* which notes drought and the death of a *shaykh*: "He passed away at the age of 91 in the year 1094/1682–83 and in 1095/1684 'Umm Lahm' began." The *Tabaqat* also lists droughts in 1686–87 and 1696–97.[13] Thus, drought in the latter seventeenth century is well documented in Sudan; it appears, once again, that more Dinka clans were forced to flee the Gezira both because of drought and war in search of their extended families at the junction of the Nile and Sobat Rivers and beyond.

As the Shilluk forcibly tried to stop these new Dinka migrants from settling in their land, violent and bitter wars broke out. The Shilluk king list is very important to historians of Southern Sudan and unique for these folk are the only ones among the Western Nilotes in Sudan who politically centralized into a state. The latter king list notes all of its kings, the approximate lengths of their reigns, and the wars fought since the sixteenth century. Using this list as an approximate dating system, scholars postulate that the Shilluk began to centralize during the first set of wars with the Dinka under Reth (king) Ocolo (Odak Ocwalo) from 1600 to 1635. War intensified during the reign of Ocolo's son, Duwat.[14]

Ironically, around this time in the Gezira some Dinka clan groups and the Shilluk actually united when Sinnar annexed the seventeenth-century successor state to the fallen Nubian kingdom of Alwa, Fazugli, to its south. This kingdom lay beyond the borders of the southern Gezira in what is now modern-day Ethiopia and the invading Funj Sultanate faced intervention from these Nilotes who, it was claimed, were formidable fighters. Their "citizenry at arms" far outnumbered the small professional armies of the Funj. Oral histories collected by a British administrator claim that the Dinka leader, Aiwel Longar, invaded the Funj Empire and that he and his son, Akwaj Shokab (Cakab), pursued the enemy as far as the Shidra Mahi Bey. This correlates with the Dinka oral histories of wars with the Funj, and the belief that "The Padang [Dinka] went from Nasir up to the borders of Ethiopia. We were led from west to east by Ayuel (Aiwel) Longar, leader of all the Abialang."[15]

Between 1635 and 1650 Funj Sultan, Badi II attempted to drive a wedge between the Dinka and the Shilluk and formed an alliance with the latter's leader, Reth Duwat (Duwad). The latter's combined efforts succeeded in partially containing the Dinka; nevertheless, the latter contested the Funj hegemony in this region into the eighteenth century, carrying their raids to the gates of Sinnar itself. Over time the wars with the Funj Sultanate declined and it is recorded that units of Dinka mercenaries began to serve the *makks* (kings) of the southern Funj provinces. Dinka merchants became important suppliers of the slave trade of Sinnar.[16] Thus, those Dinka in the Gezira came to terms and adapted to the new power in the region.

At the Sobat in the seventeenth century however, Dinka/Shilluk tensions were again heightened. Along with those fleeing out of the Gezira from the northeast away from the expanding Funj Sultanate, Shilluk oral histories also record that in the early seventeenth century (1600–1630) a second front of Dinka clans appeared on their southwestern borders. Described once again as moving in "hordes," these Dinka clans comprised those who had centuries earlier crossed the Nile westwards towards the southern Nuba mountains and the Lake No area. Eastern Ngok Dinka Simon Ayuel Deng states that many of these Dinka retraced their steps in a bid to reach the eastern bank of the Nile because of severe and prolonged droughts. These Dinka/Shilluk oral histories of wars and droughts are further supported by R. S. Herring who suggests that the period 1587–1623 was one of almost continuous low rainfall punctuated by total crop failures.[17] When the Dinka began to cross the Nile river from west to east the Shilluk blocked further movement. Thus, according to Simon Ayuel Deng, the Dinka attempted to buy permission to pass the river with a gift of a daughter of a prominent Dinka priest. Each Dinka leader/priest disagreed over the issue of whether a Dinka girl should be given to the Shilluk chief and this dispute led to a split within this major Ngok clan of the Dinka and a number of clans now returned west in protest.

Throughout the reigns of Shilluk kings Reth Boc (1650–60), Reth Abudok (1660–70), and Reth Tokot (1670–90), these Nilotes were still at war with the Dinka as the latter struggled to cross the Nile from west to east, southwest of the Shilluk territory. This steady population movement compounded competition for available resources and intensified ethnic stress. Soon after this period, however, the balance of military power shifted unequivocally in favor of the Shilluk when the latter made a trade alliance with the Muslim Nuban king of Tagali giving the former access to a reliable source of iron for weapons. At this point the Shilluk became even more politically centralized because of an extensive trade network which developed and allowed the war against the expanding Dinka to be resolved in favor of the former.[18]

Thus, although the Dinka were by now numerically stronger than the Shilluk, the latter predominated over this region of the Nile/Sobat confluence ruling as far north as El Ais. By 1799 traveler W. G. Browne observed that the Shilluk had dominion of the White Nile and conducted a "ferry" service. In the meantime Shilluk traditions recount that after numerous wars the Funj moved north of the Sobat. The leader of the Dinka, on the other hand, Dengdit, retreated to its southern banks. As late as the early Egyptian colonial period (1821) Dinka/Shilluk wars continued to erupt particularly during the reign of the Shilluk Reth Akwot (1825–35). Another battle with the "Dinka hordes" represented the last large Dinka migration from west to east across the Shilluk country to the eastern banks of the Nile. At this juncture, those Dinka living on the right (east) bank of the lower Sobat river had been driven inland by the Shilluk. During this period it is remembered that every Shilluk at that time had a Dinka slave girl and a Dinka cow from the booty of Reth Akwot.[19]

From the sixteenth to the eighteenth centuries Dinka clan groups had increased on the eastern banks of the Nile as well as south of the Sobat and the land had rapidly become overpopulated. They were unable to migrate east because of tsetse fly.[20] Nor could they move north because of the Shilluk or northeast because of the Funj Sultanate, nor return west because of the fear of constant droughts. Thus, many now forged further south up the Nile, only to be embroiled in more conflict.

The Murle-Dinka Wars

During the sixteenth-to-eighteenth-century era of early migrations up the eastern banks of the White Nile beyond the Sobat River into the heartlands of Southern Sudan, many Dinka clans had come to reside in an arc from what is now Akobo near the modern-day Ethiopian border towards the modern-day town of Bor on the White Nile. From the mid- to latter eighteenth century, however, a martial pastoral non-Nilotic group, the Murle, arrived from the east. They originated from the modern-day Didinga territory near what is now the Ugandan border and their language has been classified as forming part of the Surma language family. They are remembered in old Dinka songs as the "Bier."

Murle oral history recounts that they forged north under pressure from the Jiye and Topotha. Migrating from Kathiangor Mountain to the Maruwa

Hills, they reached the valley of the Lotilla near southeastern Ethiopia around 1780. They then migrated west into what had become Dinka territory.

The Murle now militarily forced those Dinka residing in the east, westwards towards the Nile. The latter were thus left on less fertile lands, which flooded regularly. Dinka oral histories recount: "We had to abandon the good agricultural areas in the far east because of the Murle threat." The modern-day town of Bor today is named after the Dinka word for "flood" and came to represent the far southern extent of the Dinka confederation.[21]

Throughout the world, pastoral lineage societies customarily rob and pillage their pastoral neighbors. This is largely because the observance of peaceful relations diminishes wealth within these types of nonstate societies. Because the non-Nilotic Murle were pastoralists, relations from the outset between these two groups were marked by constant raids for cattle and women.[22] The military events of this era set off a continuous chain-reaction of wars between the Dinka and the Murle primarily east of the Nile that have continued into modern times. The best remembered is the battle of Anyidi. This famous conflict exploded sometime in the Egyptian colonial period (1821–85) when the Murle raided a Bor-Gok Dinka cattle camp at Manjongo. The latter defeated the former, however, and captured war weapons, spears, shields, and a series of "beautiful hats" made of animal skins. That evening as the Dinka celebrated their victory dance in Anyidi the young warriors sought the advice of their priest (the *Beny Bith*). According to Bor-Gok Dinka informants: "We asked if the priest could make the Murle attack again so that we could acquire more of the beautiful animal skin caps, weapons and spears." Shortly thereafter their wish came true and the Murle attacked. However, the event did not bode well for the Dinka as they were totally defeated and acquired no booty whatsoever.[23]

Populations increased in the eastern banks of the Nile at what is now the modern town of Bor, where the poorer soils, which were often flooded, could not support the increasing numbers of Dinka migrants. Further south of this region, their particular grain agriculture was not successful. This event encouraged many to cross the Nile to its western banks into what is now the twentieth-century Bahr el-Ghazal province of South Sudan and soon more conflict followed.

The Dinka Wars West of the Nile

When the Dinka initially crossed the Nile to its western banks they found a territory, unlike that of the region of the eastern Nile, which they considered to be the richest soils yet found. The land was particularly hospitable to their favorite genus of *dhurra* known to them as *kec*. There were also rich grasslands with salt licks (*bar*) for their cattle, and thus many Dinka clans now crossed the Nile. A testimony to the fertility of this soil was recorded in 1857 by Catholic Father Beltrame who noted that these Dinka produced large quantities of *dhurra* without cultivating much land.[24] Over time those who crossed the Nile followed the limits of the clay soils in which their grain agriculture could be successfully grown and in time forged three hundred miles in a northwesterly direction, then stopped.

The region west of the Nile, however, known since the twentieth century as the Bahr el-Ghazal, was not empty when the Dinka arrived. The former residents of these rich grasslands were Luo, Luel, and more recently Yibel, and in the more distant past the Turkwel. The Dinka remember that their chief, Juet, fought a people whom they believed to be Luo and who later migrated south. (Luo and Dinka relations will be covered in chapter 14.)

Dinka/Yibel Relations: War and Peace

There are a number of oral histories concerning Dinka-Yibel (sometimes referred to as Jurbel or the Belli) relations. The latter are now presently located south of the Agar and Gok Dinka and southwest of the Ciec Dinka. The Yibel claim to have originally come from West Africa in the seventeenth and eighteenth centuries and reached the Nile, inhabiting the modern-day areas of Yirrol, Rumbek, Tonj, and even Bor, on the eastern banks of the Nile, just before the arrival of the Dinka. Soon after this time they were pushed south and west by the Dinka and today reside in Cuebet and Mvolo. The Yibel were hunters and farmers and prior to this period most of their former historical conflicts had taken place with other closely related non-Dinka peoples. According to Yibel Ruben Macier Makoi, who is now an Anglican Bishop:

> Usually we call ourselves Yibel. We have similar [language] words as the Bongo people, the Mvolo and Mavocodor of Madi as well as the Beridi and Baka tribes. We comprise one section with our own language. Our most famous chief, Awat, was a great warrior. He used to fight . . . the Bongo and other Jur-Bel. Our other famous chief, Maciek was also a warrior and people talked of him as a spiritual man, a rain-maker. Up to one hundred years ago we were iron workers. We used to make spears and bows and . . . we had our own poison for arrows.

The Yibel present proof of a former more northern residence by citing present-day non-Dinka place names in Dinkaland such as "Paneka" which they claim is of Yibel origin. Peter Robertshaw's research supports this assertion; he writes that several mound sites in the present-day Agar Dinka town of Rumbek have possible Yibel names, including Bekjiu.[25]

The Dinka still remember early wars with the Yibel. According to Agar Dinka Gabriel Mathiang Rok:

> We crossed the Nile and found Jurbel there (on the western bank). We had skirmishes with them and assimilated and intermarried some. To cement the deal, a lady, Lietakun Buol, was given to the Jurbel. After this many girls were given to the Bel and now there are no more wars. This land was good for grazing cattle and the Jurbel did not need this land because they do not keep cattle.

Agar Dinka Simon Adel Yak and Paul Manhom Mading state: "When we came we did fight them but the Jurbel people are not cattle owners and the Dinka animals would go into Jurbel farms to eat their crops. So they moved away from us. We are now about twenty miles from them." Other oral histories recount even more intense wars with the Yibel and evidently the Gok Dinka pushed the residents of this region south. Paul Macuer Malok states: "The Gok [Dinka] were sitting in Jurbel territory and they fought very hard wars with them. The [region of the] town of Rumbek at one time was inhabited by the Jurbel. Then the Kuei [Dinka subsection of the Gok] bought the land. A girl called Akon Buol was given to the Jurbel. Today another word for Rumbek is Akon Buol in memory of this girl." One section of the Gok, the Ayiel, derived its name from the Yibel word for "dirt surrounding *dhurra* supplies which is stored [*ayiel*]." Apparently the Yibel initially named the Gok as such and the latter adopted it.[26]

Along with the Yibel, it appears that the Southern Sudan had become home to numerous other migrants by the eighteenth century including the Luo, Bari, Murle, Balanda, Bongo, Moru, and Fertit. (The last major grouping to arrive in southwestern Sudan were the Azande who migrated into the region in the latter eighteenth century). With the first arrival of the Dinka the more ancient residents of Southern Sudan, the pastoral Luel, began a series of violent wars against these new migrants.[27]

War with the Luel: the Ancient Residents of South Sudan

Oral histories of Dinka wars with the Luel, the early residents of the Southern Sudan, are plentiful. As mentioned earlier archaeology suggests that the Luel culture prospered in Southern Sudan from the eighth century onwards. From the time the Dinka migrated to the western banks of the Nile

(c. sixteenth century) they were at war with many Luel clans. Anthropologist Godfrey Lienhardt noted one oral history of war between two Dinka clans when a number of newly arrived Twic Dinka stole Ciec Dinka cattle after a fight and then fled in a northwesterly direction. Soon they met a mound-building people called the Ber Ajou and stole their cattle and went on until they reached the country near Meshra el-Req.[28] (My subsequent field research reveals that the Ber are a subsection of the Luel, suggesting that along with the Yibel, Luel peoples were also present when the Dinka first arrived on the west banks of the Nile.)

The close Western Nilotic cousins of the Dinka and Shilluk, the Shilluk-Luo, had preceded the Dinka by a generation or more into the region. Their own oral histories claim to have migrated south from the main body of the Shilluk at the Nile/Sobat confluence and then crossed to its western banks in the sixteenth century. They then forged northwest for some distance.

The Luo had been unsuccessful militarily against the Luel and retreated westwards. Some time after their defeat a clan of Dinka, the Rek (Areik) arrived from the southeast. Initially the Rek were also repulsed after much heavy fighting, largely because the Dinka spears were no match for the Luel's poisoned arrows, darts, spears, and clubs. While the Luo had accepted defeat and moved beyond the cattle country, the Dinka made ox- and buffalo-hide shields and attacked the Luel again, this time successfully. Driving them beyond the present-day River Lol, the Dinka captured sheep, cattle, women, and children, and forced many Luel to flee as far north as the Bahr el-Arab River. Known to the Dinka as the *Kir,* this waterway follows westwards from the White Nile and today is the approximate political dividing line between the Islamic Northern and non-Islamic Southern Sudan.[29]

Forging northwest, shortly thereafter other Dinka clans arrived from the southeast and found more Luel peoples near the banks of the Kir/Bahr el-Arab river. Further wars resulted. These Dinka are today known as the Malwal. Akot Ajuou Majok states: "We found these Luel here and we displaced them. They were cattle owners and my great-great-grandfather used to fight with these people at night which is when they attacked. He addressed the god of light [the star of Venus, *ciir*] asking it to 'light the way for my cows so that Luel people do not come and get me.' Later we adopted '*ciir*' as a totem."[30]

Lawrence Lual Lual Akuey recounts that when the Paliet Malwal Dinka arrived they also found Luel people in the area all the way up to the river Kir (Bahr el-Arab). A Chief Deng told the young men to fight the Luel and take their cattle: "so the young people pushed some of the Luel north, integrated with the others and acquired cattle. This is how our area was founded."

As the Malwal Dinka consolidated themselves they came to represent the far northwestern extent of the Dinka confederation in Southern Sudan.

The Malwal's neighbors to the east, later known as the Western Twic Dinka, had forged in a northeasterly direction from the Rek country into more Luel territory. Some of these former residents were driven out while others were assimilated. According to Western Twic informants: "They [the Luel] were red skinned and when we went into the area we fought and displaced many of them but also integrated with them by marriage." According to Luel oral histories collected by Father Santandrea, a Luel chief, Akangtok lived in a place called Rec, a hillock within the present-day Western Twic territory. He was defeated by two Twic sections, the Adiang and the Yol-Kuel who joined forces against him. At this point most of Akangtok's people fled west while the Luel chief was found dead after he had fallen to the ground in grief. Others however, remained and even as late as the 1950s discrete or unintegrated Luel clans known as the Gurmok and the Gumbek now resided within the Dinka community and still remembered their old Chief Akangtok.[31]

Archaeology provides a baseline for the earliest possible arrival of these Dinka in the northern Bahr el-Ghazal as 1500 onwards. Oral histories claim, however, that the Dinka followed the Luo after two generations and the late Dinka/Luo historian Damazo Dut Majak proposed that the Luo migrated into the Bahr el-Ghazal around 1600. British administrators, J. M. Stubbs and C. G. T. Morrison, however, suggest the Luo migrated into the region sometime between 1500 and 1620. Crosschecking these dates with the archaeological evidence it is reasonable to assume that the Western Twic arrived in this region sometime during the sixteenth and seventeenth centuries.[32]

The last Dinka group to settle in their present-day homeland was mentioned earlier in this chapter as being originally part of those Dinka peoples located south of the Nuba mountains who elected, during the bitter wars with the Shilluk on the Nile and Sobat Rivers, not to cross the river to return to its eastern banks. Rather, they returned to the west, south of the Nuba mountains and slowly over many years their populations multiplied. Thus, they moved further and further west into even more inhospitable territory. Now known as the Western Ngok, these Dinka encountered peoples they called Begi who were either Luel or a closely related group. Once more, wars erupted. Much like their southern predecessors in the Bahr el-Ghazal, many Luel/Begi were forced further north and west, eventually integrating with other non-Dinka peoples of the region. Those Luel who remained were either ethnically absorbed into Western Ngok Dinka society or remained in discrete unintegrated groups.[33]

The Ngok Dinka moved into a land plagued by the harshest climate in Southern Sudan. Known today as Southern Kordofan Province, they found that the region swung from desert in one season to swamp in another. The date of the arrival of the multiple Western Ngok clans to their final homeland, which represented the last major Dinka migration into Southern Sudan, is estimated to be the early eighteenth century.[34]

Conclusion

After the fall of the Nubian kingdom of Alwa the pressures of slave raiders coupled with droughts forced the forefathers of the Dinka to pursue new secure homelands farther southwest of the Gezira. The various Dinka migrations south along both the White and Blue Niles into Ethiopia and Southern Sudan respectively were fraught with wars that are still remembered in oral histories and songs. These conflicts can be broken down into five major events: 1) The first erupted with the Funj at the Sobat in the thirteenth century. 2) In the sixteenth century the rising Sultanate of Sinnar, also known as the Funj Sultanate in the Gezira, began to expand against those Dinka who had not migrated southwest. 3) In the same century there followed a series of wars with the Shilluk, who arrived at the Nile and Sobat rivers junction in the later fifteenth century, which lasted until the nineteenth century. 4) Many Dinka who had migrated south along the Nile were also displaced by a martial group, the Murle, in the eighteenth century. 5) In the meantime the former inhabitants of much of the Southern Sudan, the Luel, also began wars with the Dinka in the sixteenth and seventeenth centuries when the latter crossed the Nile to its western banks. Limited wars with a newly arrived people from West Africa, the Yibel, which resulted in the latter being forced south and west. Limited wars also ensued with the newly arrived close relations of the Dinka, the Luo. Finally, as they continued to forge northwest, the Dinka found themselves under attack by increasing numbers of Luel. This final series of wars led to a definitive victory for the Dinka throughout the western Southern Sudan known today as the Bahr el-Ghazal and these Nilotes now came to permanently settle in their new homelands. Beyond wars, throughout their journeys, the varying Dinka clans retained the details of their clan migrations into Southern Sudan and over time they came to define themselves as three major groupings within the region itself. The first, the Padang, settled on the northern fringes of what is the Dinka nation today.

5

COMMUNITIES OF THE SOBAT/NILE CONFLUENCE: THE PADANG

In the previous chapter we saw how the Dinka confederation as a whole struggled militarily to find new homelands in Southern Sudan. This chapter is the first of four presenting the ethno-historical formation of central Southern Sudan. These histories offer an intimate view of the intensely complex structure of clan/lineage politics as the Dinka confederation moved into the heartlands of Southern Sudan and integrated with many other peoples. Further, these chapters suggest that the geographical position of the vast Dinka confederation was dictated by soil quality and type. This chapter specifically covers the formation of the Northern Nilotic frontier of the modern Southern Sudan including the Padang Dinka community. These histories also illuminate those other ethnic groups with whom the Dinka came in contact.

Today the Dinka comprise twenty-six major groupings, within which there is an association of numerous subclans. The males (and sometimes females) of these groupings mark their foreheads in a differing fashion to demonstrate the passage into manhood and to distinguish between sections. Each resides within in its own well-defined territory separated from each other by history and by natural boundaries such as rivers, swamps, and forests. Historically, these Nilotes came to be divided into three major geographical regions in Southern Sudan: the *Padang*, who reside at the borders of Northern Sudan and represent the far northern confederation of the Dinka; the *Bor* on the eastern bank of the Nile in southeastern Southern Sudan; and the *Bahr el-Ghazal* Dinka, who, as the numerically largest grouping, reside on the west bank of the Nile in the region stretching in an arc three hundred miles northwest to the Kir/Bahr el-Arab river in present-day Kordofan Province. In this volume, because of history and ecology, the latter group is divided into two; the northern Bahr el-Ghazal and the southern Bahr el-Ghazal.

The earliest Dinka clans to arrive in Southern Sudan were those known today as the *Padang* (in Dinka the "place/land of Deng") or "Northern Dinka." They initiated their migrations out of the Gezira in a southward direction following the Nile River between the period after the fall of the Nubian kingdom of Alwa in the thirteenth century and the arrival of the Western Nilotic Shilluk at the Nile/Sobat tributaries in the latter fifteenth century.

Presently, the Padang Dinka reside on the eastern bank of the Nile north and south of the Sobat, and also extend west across the Nile south of the Nuba mountains as far west as Abyei into modern-day southwest Kordofan province in what is now the Northern Islamic Sudan. The Padang can be broken into ten distinct groupings or sections and include, from north to south, the Abialang, the Dunghol-Aiwel, the Eastern Ngok, Eastern Luaic, Thoi, Rut, and the Eastern Ruweng (or Paweng of Paneru). West of the Nile the Padang include from east to west the Ruweng, the Alor, and the Western Ngok. Although the Padang were the first of the Dinka clans to arrive in South Sudan, the Western Ngok were the last to find a permanent homeland in the Southern region, finally settling in the early eighteenth century.

Dinka informants claim that the earliest Padang homeland in South Sudan was at one time located farther south of its present location. In the mid to latter eighteenth century the Bor Dinka grouping (now in the southeast and separated by the Nilotic Nuer) originally connected with the Padang, specifically the Eastern Ngok who now represent the southeastern limit of the Padang. The eastern expansion of the neighbors of the Dinka, the Nilotic Nuer, during the latter eighteenth and nineteenth centuries, however, split these groups in two, forcing some north and others south.[1] Below are the ethno-historical micro-histories of the major Padang clan groupings along with the histories of those with whom they came into contact.

The Abialang Dinka

The name *Abialang* is derived from a tree called *long* and the Dinka word for following, *abia*. As the people migrated southwards up the White Nile they followed this tree, which had edible fruits to sustain them during their long journey. In time the people came to be known as the people following the *long* tree or *Abialang*. There are four main subsections of the Abialang—the Kwac, Banweng, Togmac, and Abweng—all of which are referred to as the Giel clan. They are also the original four sections of the priest, Lul Dengkak. The Abialang claim that they migrated from further north of their present-day country on the right (eastern) bank of the Nile north of the Sobat, and numbers of clans settled in what is now the modern town of Renk under a priest named Areng, for whom the area is named today. Shortly thereafter, another part of the clan moved further south to Wunkur (Wunapur) under Priest Ager, settling in what is now Melut and giving birth to the section today known as "Ager" while other clans accompanied Priest Ager's sons migrating still further south. Areng's father, Aiwel, was also the father of Kak. While Areng remained in Renk, Priest Aiwel moved south with his son Kak and grandson, Dengkak. When Aiwel died Dengkak became the leader and within the Abialang chieftainship this family ruled until 1963.[2]

The Padang displaced and absorbed Funj peoples as they migrated into the region north of the confluence of the Nile and Sobat Rivers. Another nearby people, the Burun, however, escaped the wrath of the Dinka and, according to Dunghol Dinka Cok Kuek Ywai and Majak Col Mayiik, because these people did not war with the Dinka they "remained our neighbors." After fighting with the resident Funj, the Dinka pushed east of another group in the region, the Maban, into the Burun territory. This land, however, which is located southeast of the Ethiopian highlands, is a dry region with little *toic* (grasslands) and is heavily infested with tsetse fly. This factor discouraged the further eastern penetration of the Dinka cattlemen.[3]

To the south of the modern-day Abialang Dinka are the Dunghol.

The Dunghol Dinka

The Dunghol today count four sections within their group, including the Abialang, noted above, along with the Ager, the Nyiel, and the Dunghol-Aghol. The formal name of all these peoples is Dunghol-Aiwel. The Dunghol and Abialang are therefore very closely connected historically and much information regarding the former is therefore also considered to be the history of the latter. When the Abialang settled in modern-day Renk, the Ager and Nyiel made their homes farther south along the Nile and today they reside in modern-day Melut while the Dunghol-Aghol now locate themselves further south in Akoko town; all are contiguous to each other.

Historically, the Ghol (now part of the Bor Dinka group in the south-east) and Dunghol (now part of the Padang group in the far north) claim at one time to have been geographically connected and hence one people. But because of the expansion of the Nilotic Nuer in the eighteenth century the latter were pushed farther north of their former residences in Southern Sudan.[4]

To the southwest of the Dunghol are the Eastern Ngok.

The Eastern Ngok Dinka

Today the Eastern Ngok have eleven major sections: the Ajuba, Baileit, Ngar, Duot, Acak, Balak, Awueir, Adong, Deng, Abiei, and Dhiak. They are located today living along the River Sobat south of the Abialang and centered at Abwong (latitude 9 longitude 32). According to Eastern Ngok Dinka Sarah Nyanek Daac and John Deng Pur these folk left from a place called Deng somewhere in the north along the river Nile.

When these clans arrived at the Nile/Sobat confluence east of the Nile they found Funj peoples and also fought with them. Eastern Ngok Dinka Simon Ayuel Deng and Sarah Nyanek Daac states: "We overtook this place and took their land and came and settled in our present location. We pushed the Funj to the Blue Nile." Thus, in the past the Eastern Ngok claim that the region of the modern town of Malakal, which is now home to the Nilotic Shilluk, was part of Padang Dinka territory and stretched southeast to Nasir and eastwards up to the borders of Ethiopia.

The major dispute within this group however, took place when all of the Ngok had crossed the Nile and migrated beyond its western banks south of the Nuba mountains. The leader of all the Abialang, Aiwel Longar, had initially led the Dinka across the Nile from east to west. However, a century or so later an Ngok priest, Lual Ayak, decided to lead his people back to the Nile's eastern banks during a period of great drought. Eastern Ngok Dinka Simon Ayuel Deng states: "The real problem of the Ngok was in trying to cross the river, for the Shilluks stopped them. Lual Ayak . . . who was fighting with the Shilluk chief . . . selected a girl to bribe the . . . chief so we could cross the river. Then [chief] Deng Kuol said 'what you have done is not good because the leader of the Shilluk is going to put the girl in the water' [as a human sacrifice]. The girl belonged to Kuol." Each Dinka leader disagreed over the issue of whether a Dinka girl should be given to the Shilluk chief and this dispute led to a split within this major clan.

According to Simon Ayuel Deng, priest Lual Ayak, however, continued eastwards across the Nile, locating his people near the Sobat. These people today are known as the Eastern Ngok. The legend of Acai, who was the daughter of the disputing Dinka chief and who was possibly sacrificed to the River Nile in order to settle the latter dispute, is still remembered by many Eastern and Western Ngok today.[5] (A discussion on the sacrifice of Dinka women to rivers follows in chapter 11.)

In the process of relocating themselves on the eastern banks of the Nile Lual Ayak's clans ethnically integrated with other Nilotic peoples resident in the area, including the Western Nilotic Anyuak. According to Simon Ayuel Deng: "We were originally Anyuak and Shilluk. The Dinkas came from the west and the Anyuaks were in the area. The Anyuak and Shilluk are brothers of the Luo . . . in the Bahr el-Ghazal [western Southern Sudan] and in Kenya and they have common words."

In the meantime, those clans who had not crossed the Nile eastwards became disconnected from the main body of the Ngok Dinka. Deng Kuol's people retraced their steps westwards into what later became the modern-day province of Kordofan, eventually becoming the "Western Ngok" who are today located almost two hundred and fifty miles to the west of their former kin. The Eastern Ngok nevertheless still refer today to the Western Ngok as their own people although there has been little contact between the two for centuries. Simon Ayuel Deng states: "Our name 'Ngok' comes from all Dinka who come from the east. We came from the north, moved westwards and then returned to the east bank of the Nile."[6]

To the west and southwest of the Ngok are the Eastern Luaic.

The Eastern Luaic Dinka

Today the Eastern Luaic have six major sections: the Kuaac, Acuil, Koko, Mud, Alier, and Raac. These peoples claim they are connected to those of the same name (the Western Luaic) who migrated away from them generations ago into the Bahr el-Ghazal. In fact, Luaic clans can be found today all over the Southern Sudan. Some integrated into other Western Nilotic groups, for example, and today there are Luaic-Atwot peoples who consider themselves non-Dinka and who are located south of the Agar Dinka territory west of the Nile.[7]

According to Luaic Dinka Malwal Chan Gaac oral history largely parallels that of the Ngok Dinka: "We came with the rest of the Dinka from the north, beginning from Khartoum, then up to [what is now] Kosti.

We were led by Priest Adel Aguer." Originally all the Luaic had, like many other Dinka clans, migrated from the Nile/Sobat confluence in the east to the western bank of the Nile and south of the Nuba Mountains. But some people released their cattle into the bush for grazing and then discovered their animals had crossed back to the east. Under Priest Guat Lung Jook, certain people pursued their cattle eastwards again across the Nile and, according to Malwal Chan Gaac, "When we found our cattle in the east we discovered very good pastures so we came as far as Ayut."

Just to the west of the Eastern Luaic are the Thoi and the Rut.

The Thoi and Rut Dinka

The present-day Thoi and Rut Dinka, who used to be one group, reside just west and northwest and contiguous to the Eastern Luaic and west of a region known today as the Khor Fulus. Subsection information regarding the Thoi was not obtained but those of the Rut are the Pajut (or Panajuot), Cuei, Wau, Akok, Bior, and Palom. The parent group was the Thoi. According to Philip Thon Marol, "The name 'Thoi' comes from our great ancestor Athoi, eldest son of Mabek. Majak, the youngest son of Mabek was a trouble-maker so the father said to him: 'Leave us, you are too much like a winter wind [*rut*].' So the youngest son left and took some people with him eventually calling the clan the 'Rut.' This split took place around ten generations ago." However, another oral history maintains that Palom is the name of the greatgrandfather of one of the major Rut sections today. In turn his son, Ajuot gave birth to daughters who were impregnated by spiritual power; that is, they were candidates to become priests. According to Santino Malval Meet and Paul Dak Kachvol, the Rut were originally located to the south of their present homeland but forced north some generations later by their Nilotic neighbors, the Nuer: "We settled in Ayut (today's Gawar Nuer territory) and the Nuer came in big numbers. We fought them and were pushed north to our present position at Khor Fulus." The Rut and Thoi are not contiguous to their western Dinka neighbors, the Ruweng today, because the Western Nilotic Nuer and Shilluk peoples now separate them.[8]

The Ruweng Dinka

The first clan group of the Ruweng was the Kwil (Quil) whose first priest-leader was Makuac. The Kwil subsequently proliferated considerably and over time gained the name *Ruweng* which means "to remain by night" and may have been associated with pastoral practices of these Dinka. Today the Ruweng claim they have three major subdivisions, the Kwil (which has ten subsections), the Awet (which has three subsections), and the Alor (which has six subsections). The last is treated as a separate group today. There is also a fourth Ruweng group east of the Nile called the Paweng which today is also recognized as a separate grouping. Among the subdivisions of the Kwil are the Buka. Buka clans are also found within the Paweng east of the Nile (hence one is a Buka of Bul or a Buka of Angau).

The Ruweng at one time were also joined to the major grouping the Nyarruweng, now resident among the Bor Dinka in southeastern South Sudan. During the mid to latter eighteenth century (1730–80) a substantial population of Ruweng occupied the entire northern rim of what is now Nuer territory. However, the eighteenth and nineteenth-century Nuer expansions east and northeast forced the Ruweng northwards, separating them from other close members of their group who moved south. Those in the north remained as "Ruweng" while those to the south became "Nyarruweng." In sum, today the Ruweng (proper) comprise two main sections, the Kwil and Awet, who remain in the far west.[9]

The Paweng or Paneru (Eastern Ruweng) Dinka

As a whole the Eastern Ruweng are also known as *Paneru,* or *Paweng* (the original name of their homeland) and they were once part of the greater Ruweng Dinka confederation located farther to their west. According to one oral history, when these Dinka moved east to Fanjak they were on a raiding expedition and the name *Paneru* came to mean "people leaving that got delayed." Eastern Ruweng Dinka Daniel Dok Manyang states: "We left and came to Panthiang and from there crossed the Nile to where we are now. Then we moved to a place between Khor Fulus and the Sobat. We settled temporarily then moved to Atar near the Sobat and the Nile. We are south of [the modern town of] Malakal and neighbors of the Shilluk, Thoi, Luaic and Rut [Dinka]. Today we have clear borders between east and west Ruweng: it is Alela." The Paweng also claim their real name is *Ajuba,* there being an eastern Ajuba and a western Ajuba. In more specific terms these Dinka clan groups are located between the Khor Fulus and Bahr el Zeraf contiguous to and north of the Rut and Thoi Dinka. The western subsection of the Paneru is located in the Fanjak district while the eastern Paneru now locate themselves within the Eastern Ngok territory, calling themselves the *Weny.*

Another oral history exists for this section of the Dinka. It is claimed that a female priest called Atiam led some Ruweng clans from the west to the eastern banks of the Nile during the wartime Mahdist period (1883–98). Crossing the Nile with six sections, (the Bugo of Bol Piok, the Thiong, the Tungdiak, the Aniek, the Jueng, and the Palei) these clans then settled in a place called Atar. At this time Atiam was around forty years old and she ruled as a priest and leader of these Dinka into the British period (1898). At her death a member of her family continued as priest and leader of the Paweng.[10]

Far to the west of the Paweng is another closely related Ruweng group, the Alor.

The Alor Dinka

The Alor are closely related to their parent group, the Ruweng to their northeast. Today they comprise six subsections, the Mijuan, Amal, Abang, Ngokciel, Thingyier, and Mandeng. Alor history recounts western migrations across the Nile from the Paneru region on the eastern banks of the Nile to present-day Bim-nohm in the west because of a fight between two sub-clans, the Mijuan and Diar. The split also came about because of the need for better land and pasture. Alor Dinka William Mayar Dau states: "We are generally called Ruweng but when we left Paneru, our name came from when the remaining Ruweng used to call us 'Alor Piny' meaning people who have left or gone away. Later it was reduced to 'Alor.'" Kur Kuol, the original leader of the Alor was then succeeded by his son, Col Kuot who, in turn, was succeeded by Ajuang Col Kuot, all ruling family members of the Mijuan subclan of the Alor.

Some informants still consider this group of Dinka as an integral part of the Kwil section of the Ruweng; others suggest that they are not culturally separate from the parent group but were only physically separated from their larger family member, the Ruweng, during the nineteenth century. Although today the Alor and Ruweng are described as culturally one and the same people, during field research in Nairobi in 1996 the author was informed by the Minister of Culture and Information of New Sudan, Pagan Amun, and the secretary of the Sudan Relief and Rehabilitation Association, Arthur Akuien Col, that the paramount chiefs of the Alor strongly insisted they be considered as "separate" and independent from the main body of the Ruweng, suggesting that these clans are following the typical fission politics of pastoral stateless clan peoples worldwide.[11]

To the west and northwest of the Alor are the Western Ngok. While partly emerging from the original Eastern Ngok east of the Nile on the Sobat, they are also composed of a number of Alor members. This is feasible considering the two lived in close proximity for centuries.

The Western Ngok Dinka

Today the Western Ngok have nine sections, the Abyor, Mannyuar, Anyiel, Mareng, Diel (Dil), Acueng, Acak, Bongo, and Alei. According to missionary Stefano Santandrea the Alei clan were originally non-Dinka people who were later ethnically integrated into the larger body of the Ngok, and the word in Dinka means "strangers." He notes that long ago they were remembered to be shorter than the Ngok Dinka and reddish in color and suggests they were Luel in origin. It is remembered that they were helped by the nineteenth-century Abyor leader, Arob Biong, who "gathered [them] in one place and offered them a land to live in by themselves." When Chief Arob Biong died in 1903 their Ngok neighbors evicted many from the region. However, another more Dinka-ized section of these peoples remained permanently in the land, having renounced their former language and culture. Another history states that it is only in the last few centuries that the Mareng and the Anyiel have been considered separate sections, for at one time they were under the suzerainty of the powerful Mannyuar.

As mentioned earlier, prior to the arrival in their western homeland, all Ngok peoples (this includes the Eastern Ngok) resided east of the Nile but at some point they crossed the Nile and headed west. Western Ngok Dinka, Maguith Deng Kuol and Agoth Alor Bulabek state: "We branched from [what is now] the Eastern Ngok whose great-great-grandfather was Dombek. The area of the Eastern Ngok today is a lowland that used to be flooded so our people broke away to look for better land."

The Eastern Ngok (mentioned earlier) recount a number of clan histories for the Western Ngok. One recounts that when these Ngok peoples moved from the east, the region from which all the Padang migrated, the Western Ngok comprised a number of people who later formed the Ruweng. Ruweng Dinka John Biem Ngok Bilkuai claims: "We are related to the Ngok of Abyei. In the old days the Ngok were called Jok and were part of the Ruweng. They eventually came to be called Ngok (Abyor). In the past we had the same totems; the Ngok and Ruweng share the Lion, Cobra and the Python." They then proceeded further west with some members of the Alor/Ruweng group. At this juncture the Ngok now came to call themselves the "Jok" while the Alor maintained their own name. The Jok eventually acquired the clan name of "Abyor" which, according to Western Ngok Dinka Ring Deng Biong, means a place which has steam coming from hot water: "We acquired the territory because of wars and then acquired the name."

Another history claims that two of the nine present-day major sections of the Western Ngok, the Abyor and the Dil clans, were united at one time under one leader, Tiing Luoth. When these peoples initially crossed the Nile they split in two. Thus, today, within the Abyor and the Dil there are clans people of the Pajok family. Further, there are Pajok clan members within the Eastern Ngok as well as those among the Western Ngok.

Another history recounts that prior to the arrival of the large clan of the Pajok, now known as the Abyor, the first Dinka clans to actually arrive in the entire region of what is now southwest Kordofan were the Alei clan. Of interest here is that missionary Santandrea wrote that a number of these peoples were non-Dinka. Western Ngok Dinka Abyei Kon states that they approached from the east and forged north of what is now the Western Ngok homeland and came to reside along the River Ngol in the latter seventeenth and early eighteenth centuries. They later spread as far north as Muglad.

A few decades later the Pajok/Abyor and another powerful clan, the Mannyuar, approached this region from much farther south. Other oral histories and a number of scholars estimate that around 1740 the first clans under a priest, Kwoldit of the Abyor, moved north across the Kir/Bahr el-Arab river. These peoples were ostensibly in search of wider grazing areas.

Of all the nine major sections under the Ngok, the Abyor have maintained the most extensive histories, thanks in large part to the Abyor Ngok scholar, Francis Deng. The Abyor count their leaders back nine generations ago from Francis Deng beginning with Dumbek, followed by Monydhang, Alor, Biong, Arob Biong (nineteenth century), Kuol Arob (twentieth century), and Deng Majok, whose son is Francis Deng. However, of importance here is that prior to the nineteenth century the most prominent leader of all the Ngok peoples in the area was a member of another powerful clan, the Mannyuar. Connected to the Alor family, his name was Alor Adjing. With the coming of the nineteenth-century Egyptian colonial period the nine major clans, each of whom possessed its own priest-leader, were forcibly united under one. When Alor Adjing refused to collect Egyptian taxes, the Egyptian administration recognized instead Arob Biong of the Abyor clan as the major representative of all of the Ngok peoples in the region. Arob Biong's responsibility towards the colonial government was to collect taxes in the form of cattle. From this time, the Abyor have predominated in the region.[12]

Located three miles north of the Kir/Bahr el-Arab river, the center of the Western Ngok homeland came to be known as *Abyei*. This region has two source of water, the Kiir/Bahr el-Arab River and the Nyamora River, which flows from the Nuba mountains into the Kir/Bahr el-Arab to its south. (As this large Dinka section has been the most studied by other scholars, I have devoted chapter 17 to the ethno-politics of this region.)

Conclusion

This chapter has presented the ethno-histories of the "Northern" or Padang Dinka, who are located in the far north of today's Dinka confederation. These Dinka remember wars with the Funj peoples, formerly resident at the Nile/Sobat confluence. A number of closely related clans split at the Nile, and the one conflict that stands out is that within the Ngok, which broke into two leaving one group hundreds of miles to the west of the other. Ethnically, these Padang appear to have primarily absorbed Funj, Anyuak, and Shilluk peoples in the east and to a much lesser degree the Luel/Begi peoples in the west. Otherwise the Padang clans appear to have remained fairly heterogeneous. There are few histories of wars between the various Padang Dinka (unlike those to their south), suggesting they have remained closely related. The land these Dinka migrated into was not particularly rich and did not support huge populations. Thus, many east of the Nile began to migrate south. These clans later became known as the *Bor*.

6

COMMUNITIES ON THE EASTERN NILE: THE BOR

While many Dinka clans remained near the Nile/Sobat confluence in the sixteenth century a number forged south beyond the Sobat River. Some migrated as far as the modern-day town of Bor on the eastern banks of the Nile. Others had also located themselves southeast of the Sobat River towards the modern-day borders of Ethiopia. The Dinka of the Eastern Nile from south of the Sobat River to Bor town are today referred to as the Bor Dinka. This confederation possesses six major groups including, from north to south, the Ghol (or Hol), the Nyarruweng, the Eastern Twic, the Bor-Atoc, the Bor-Gok, and the Thain. Today the Bor are separated from their northern Padang neighbors by the Nilotic Nuer (see chapter 16).

The Ghol (or Hol) Dinka

There are four major sections among the Ghol: the Nyiel, Pathal (Patel or Pathien), Angac, and Duor (or Aduor). Oral histories claim that centuries ago after these Dinka left the junction of the Blue and White Niles (at what is now the modern capital city of Khartoum in Northern Sudan) some Dinka arrived in Renk and settled. This region later became Padang Dinka country. Others over time filtered further south up the Nile. Ghol recent history claims that they are related to the Ador, one of the two big sections of the Ciec Dinka, who now reside west of the Nile. According to Barnaba Wuor, Samuel Majak Piok, and Deng Malwal Mabur Mahboub: "We fought with the Ciec . . . and then we crossed back towards the eastern bank of the Nile. This split among the Ador (Aduor) came about because we quarreled over grazing land. So we left under the leadership of Thorcok Ring who was a powerful magician [priest]. Before we left we killed a bull and we were given a thigh bone, *ghol.* After we left we maintained this name *Ghol* for our people and we are the Ghol-Ador [Aduor] people."

Another variation of Ghol history recounts that the Duor who crossed the nile from west to east had been accompanied by three other Dinka clans, the Nyiel, Angac, and Patel. The Nyiel had been part of the Angac at one time west of the Nile and originally occupied the area around Lake Jur west. Later they came to reside in the Ghol country in the geographic area up to Khor Fulus. They migrated east across the Nile away from Ciec-Aduor (Ador) territory sometime before 1800. Oral histories recount that they were displaced by other Ciec clans when they were pushed south by the Nuer. Upon arrival on the eastern banks of the Nile (in the region now known as Duk Fadiet), the three clans (Nyiel, Patel, and Angac) combined with the resident Duor of a previous migration and agreed to unify by making a pact promising that they would not separate for any reason. To seal the agreement they killed a cow and did not break the thighbone, the *ghol,* taking this word as their group name. Ghol Dinka Isaac Lat states: "Today when we eat cows we never break the thigh bone or we will die." In the precolonial period the Ghol's most famous war leader was Kucayom who led many Dinka against the Nuer in a series of later wars.

When these Dinka clans migrated back across the Nile to the eastern banks they used two major crossing points that had been used by the early Ciec Dinka settlers when they initially crossed to the west. The Ghol came to settle in a region south of and adjacent to what was then Thoi Dinka territory. Ghol migration histories of the movement east recount that one of their major sections, the Duor [Aduor] of present-day Duk Fadiet, initiated the first migration and soon thereafter was at war with a non-Nilotic people who had recently arrived from the east, the Murle. The Dinka were soundly defeated and all but one Duor clansman, Fadiet Agoth, lived. Today the place name, Duk Fadiet is taken from this one Duor survivor of this Murle war. Within the Nyarruweng who are the southern neighbors of the Ghol there are, according to Lazarus Leek Mawut, Duor clan peoples who are direct relatives of the Nyarruweng: "We see the Duor and Nyarruweng as one." Thus, a number of Duor apparently also migrated further south beyond the Ghol region.

In the meantime, other Duor folk still located west of the Nile and who heard of the war, crossed the river to the east to aid their fellow clansmen. In the meantime the Nile was very wide and it was difficult to cross. Thus, the people decided to traverse the river near the modern-day town of Yirol. To ensure that the men crossed safely the daughter of a priest, Aluo, was sacrificed to the river (see chapter 11). To cross rivers the Dinka typically put reeds together and float along with them while others hold onto the tails of their cows, who can swim.

The approximate dates of the Ghol crossing from west to east can be determined because of a history of these Dinka published by a German missionary, A. Kaufmann. He worked among the Ciec Dinka west of the Nile in the 1850s and produced the first, if incomplete, map of the White Nile Dinka within the Southern Sudan (although each White Nile Dinka group is clearly marked on this map those of the Bahr el-Ghazal in the west are only vaguely located). It primarily illustrates in detail those located on both sides of the Nile and specifically noted a Dinka group, Arol, northwest of the Ciec who were the ancestors of the modern-day Ghol. Before 1857, missionary Beltrame noted that these Dinka were still west of the Nile (west-northwest of the Ciec).

On the other hand, while some Ghol clans migrated into their present-day homeland by crossing the Nile to the east other clans did not cross the river but rather, moved westward in the opposite direction. Some traversed hundreds of miles towards the northwest, eventually reaching the modern-day far-western region of the town of Gogrial in Dinkaland. These clans are still identified today as belonging to the Ghol east of the Nile.[1]

To the south of the major Ghol grouping are the Nyarruweng.

The Nyarruweng Dinka

The Nyarruweng are divided into two broad divisions, the Ager and the Athon (also known as the Aborom). Each have two sub-divisions: the Ager comprise the Bikar and the Abiok; the Athon includes the Nyaying and the Kumas.

Historically the Nyarruweng claim they came from the north passing from the region of Khartoum and initially settling in present-day Duk Fadiet beyond the Sobat and Nile confluence. Eventually all Nyarruweng came to settle between Bor and Pibor at a place called Macdol. Deng Malwal Mabur Mahboub states that after migrating south along the eastern banks of the Nile, groups of Luo peoples who were previously resident in the region became assimilated into the migrating Nyarruweng. Thus, according to Lazarus Leek Mawut the Nyarruweng are not a single group of people: "We also have Luaic clans (from the major Padang Dinka group in the north) who are now integrated into our larger Nyarruweng lineage."

All informants agree that the Nyarruweng are related, from a much older historical time, to the Ruweng Dinka, now part of the Padang Dinka group in the north and that: "We are still related to the Ruweng but because of grazing we separated. We were all along the Nile from Renk down to Bor and this was our area but when the Nuer came they fought and cut us in two. Now the regions around Waat, Ayot and Fanjak are Nuer territory."

One important factor that may have affected migrations is that the soils of the Ghol, Nyarruweng, and Twic on the east banks of the Nile are better than those of the modern-day Ruweng in the north, composing a mixture of deeper clay and sand. The Nyarruweng settled on the highest ground, while their southern neighbors the Twic and Bor were left with lands at lower elevations, which periodically become flooded.

The Nyarruweng also claim that centuries ago their former more easterly residence away from the Nile some distance inland possessed even better soils for grain cultivation. The arrival of the Murle around 1780 however, forced these Dinka westward to the eastern banks of the Nile. Thus, today the Nyarruweng boundaries, according to Lazarus Leek Mawut, are as follows:

> Our northeastern boundary is with the Lau Nuer at Ayuai river. Our boundary with the Ghol is the highland mid-way between the two Duks. Our southern boundary with the Twic is at Nyaken where there is a well called Padarkok. To the east are the Murle people but between these people and the Dinka the land is uninhabited until forty miles east of Duk to a place called Pac Markol. Our western boundary goes up to the main Nile river at Nyam. We border the Ciec Dinka, west of the Nile but because of the *toic* [watery grasslands within the Nile] we have little contact. In 1952 when the river was very low young men crossed up to Shambe by canoe where they bought tobacco because Ciec tobacco is highly prized by the eastern Dinka.

"Nyarruweng" means literally "Nyar," the period when the cattle are released before being milked and then brought back around nine a.m. Some Nyarruweng claim this name was also derived from the saying "other Dinka milking cows in the early morning"—that is *weng acinyar,* which was later modified to Nyarruweng. Today Nyarruweng informants say they have the same lineage as Aiwel Longar, the legendary leader of the Dinka centuries ago, and claim to be "brothers of Aiwel."[2]

To the south of the Nyarruweng grouping are the Eastern Twic.

The Eastern Twic Dinka

There are four major subsections among the eastern Twic: the Lieth, Nyuak, Adjuong, and Paker. The Lieth (Liet) are located in the north. The Nyuak and Adjuong are located in the center of Eastern Twic territory. The Paker (Faker) are located in the far south, bordering the Bor-Atoc Dinka.

Tor Deng Lual and John Majok Deng state: "We were in Khartoum but we are cattle people and the area was too dry for cows. So we moved south looking for pastures and cultivatable areas. Then we migrated [first from east to west and then] across the Nile from the west back to the east under the leader Ayuel. We left part of the Dinka west of the Nile."

Oral histories I have collected suggest that part of what became the major Twic grouping migrated southwards out of the region of the Eastern Ngok territory near the Sobat River and arrived after the eighteenth century Murle wars. Supporting these ethno-histories, Eastern Twic Dinka Diing Akol Diing states: "My family came from the Padang region nine generations ago and Chief Padol led us out of the Ngok region as we migrated south." Certain Twic clans had been west of the Nile and south of the Nuba Mountains (in modern day Ruweng territory) when Ajak Amot and another priest, Ngok Keny, led these folk eastwards across the Nile and then south along the banks of the river to their present territory.

Historically, like many other clans the Twic are a combination of many Dinka and non-Dinka peoples, the majority of which arrived ten or eleven generations ago. The original inhabitants of what is now Eastern Twic territory spoke different languages. Philip Aguer Panyang states: "My clan is composed of ancestors who have been in the region only seven or eight generations. When my great-great-grandfather came, the Dinka told stories of non-Dinka who had been here originally and disappeared." Hence, when the various Dinka clans arrived they apparently displaced a number of peoples and also absorbed others. Non-Dinka place names such as Dorkolong and Kolmerak are believed to be Bari (now resident in the far southeastern Sudan). Other Dinka histories note that just to the east of the original Dinka settlement there was a pastoral group called the Loki (or Lau) believed to have been Luo who later moved north. These folk knew how to preserve water, a skill unknown to the Dinka. Philip Aguer Panyang states: "Our fathers told us this area belonged to the Luo people. There is a place near our home of Paliou called Loki and this is a Luo name. Today we still know it as the home of the Loki. These Loki(o) people are now part of the Nyarruweng." These Dinka arrived also finding other Dinka clans, including the Leek, and settled with them in the present-day Kongor area.

Another history recounts that the Leit (Leith) section of the Twic who, it is claimed, were originally a "foreign element," crossed from the west bank of the Nile near Shambe, about twenty miles south of Lake Jur into Eastern Twic territory. When the Murle, remembered by the Dinka as a hostile non-Nilotic people, later arrived from the east, they also displaced some of these people, many of whom migrated north and south. Dinka informants also suggest that their non-Dinka neighbors, the Lau Nuer, are "newcomers to the area" who may also have been of former Luo extraction.

When the differing clans of what became the "Twic" Dinka grouping arrived in their present territory, two priests who were brothers came to predominate, Atwic Ariem and Yiep. Yiep assigned all the people to their various geographical locations and determined that the whole clan should take his name. However, Atwic, who was the senior brother, disagreed and insisted that the people be called Twic after him. Ultimately, it seems that Yiep assigned the names of the various subsections before dispersing the people at Patundur. For example, Yiep brought forth cows with the color *lieth, Paker,* and *Adjuong.* He assigned the former people this name and sent them north to what is now the present-day region of Kongor. The Paker were sent southwards and those remaining acquired the name Adjuong because they remained. In the meantime all of the clans as a whole became known as the Twic Dinka.

According to Bul Awuol Ayuel, at some point a large number of Twic clan groups split away from the main group, crossed the Nile to its western banks and migrated hundreds of mile in a northwesterly direction to the Kir/Bahr el-Arab river north of the Bahr el-Ghazal province to what is now the northwestern periphery of the Dinka confederation. These Twic clans, hereafter referred to as the Western Twic today use a similar nomenclature and both Eastern and Western Twic peoples share the same religious symbols. When these early clans left the area of the eastern Nile they were given cows and a bull was killed to mark the ceremony of their departure. Thus, no battle marked the split of this group but rather many left because of the need for new pastures and grazing lands.[3]

South of the Twic are the Bor-Atoc and Bor-Gok Dinka.

The Bor Dinka

The Bor are divided into two main sections, the Bor-Athoc in the north and the Bor-Gok in the south. Both groups encompass four subsections. The Bor-Atoc comprise the Angakuei, Pathuyiei, Juet, and Abuoudit Alian clans. The Bor-Gok divide into the Abiei, Hol, Palek, and Koc. Most believe that the latter acquired their name from a forest of trees in their region which the Dinka call Gok. Likewise, the Atoc settled in a region of trees known as *Athony,* also giving rise to the section name. Most believe the origin of their larger section and region name *Bor* was derived from the word floods [in Dinka, *Abor*] which plague the region frequently. Thus, over time surrounding Dinka called these residents the "people of the flooded area" the Bor.

Ethnically the Bor comprise multiple Dinka clan peoples. Certain Bor clans were originally part of the Padang group who later migrated south of the Nile/Sobat confluence, crossed the Nile to its western banks near the modern-day Shambe area, and then later still recrossed the river back to its eastern banks, settling in their present-day position. Ancient priests Aiwel Pagangdier and Alier Ngeth are remembered to have led the Dinka south into the Bor country from the Sobat. The Bor Dinka clan, the Palek, for example, trace their descent to an Aliab Dinka man from west of the Nile called Agwer, who married a Bor woman, Gop.

Bok-Gok Michael Majok Bor states that many people today calling themselves Dinka or Bor are also, in reality, descended from peoples of different ethnic origin who had migrated from the south of the present-day Bor Dinka community, including the Eastern Nilotic Mundari. Bor-Gok Dinka Abed Nego Aciek claims that numbers of people who migrated north into the Dinka amalgam had also migrated from as far away as the modern-day town of Kapoeta in the far Southern Sudan and had been part of the Eastern Nilotic Toposa "because smaller groups get absorbed into larger ones. . . . My section migrated [farther] north into Bor to our present-day location."

The approximate date when many Dinka clans of the Bor region reached their present position migrating from the north as well as the south can be crosschecked with the oral histories of the Bari. These non-Dinka Southern Sudanese Eastern Nilotes reside far to the south of the Dinka today. In 1857 they informed missionary Kaufmann that they had more recently migrated from south of their present homeland six generations ago in a northerly direction from what is now Uganda. Other oral histories, however (supported by linguistics), claim an ancient central Sudanese origin. Counting thirty years for each generation, it is probable that the Bari arrived in their present-day territory around the mid 1600s or early 1700s. As some Bari place names exist in southeastern Dinkaland today, it must be assumed that the Dinka arrived shortly after this time, dominated the area, absorbed some Bari and either stopped the larger Bari advance north or pushed the Bari southwards.

The above ethno-histories suggest that the Bor have a very diverse background. Today the largest admixture of different cultures is most pronounced in the southern section of the Bor confederation among the Bor-Gok. The Bahr el-Ghazal Dinka who are today resident west of the Nile claim that the Bor have a large Mundari admixture (the Mundari primarily reside today south of the Aliab Dinka west of the Nile although some of their related folk also lived on the eastern banks) and that their language is sometimes not understood by other Dinka peoples. Bor-Atoc Dinka Mom Kou Arou admits that his people speak Dinka with an admixture of other languages. It is also believed that the Adul clan of the Bor has assimilated many Luo groups.

The Bor remember many wars, not so much with other Dinka but with the hostile non-Nilotic Murle who arrived from the east in the eighteenth century sometime after the Dinka. The pastoral Murle are located east of the Dinka and conquered their present-day territory from the latter and the Western Nilotic Anyuak. The previous chapter covered wars with the Murle and this theme has historically dominated relations between the Dinka and Murle.

Periodically, however, truces have also taken place between the Dinka and Murle, resulting in peace and ethnic integration. Eastern Twic Dinka Diing Akol Diing states: "The Murle were our friends to the South of Bor and many of these [Bor] Dinka are believed to be of [former] Murle ancestry. In the Southern Bor region many kept cattle together and intermarried and there was only minor raiding between both. Other Murle immigrated and become Dinka, and adopted our culture and became assimilated. . . . This situation can happen for a number of reasons: if you commit a crime you have to flee to another area and also hunger drives people into foreign lands, if their crops fail."[4]

Murle/Dinka integration was also encouraged in the early nineteenth century when an earthquake hit the borders of the Murle/Bor region at the end of the mountains in a place called Macbol. Bor-Gok Dinka informants recount that "People were dancing and then the earth opened and swallowed them up. The people in this place were Duor Dinka." Fearing the place was cursed, the Duor migrated further into the Murle area and eventually became Murle while those closer to the Bor region migrated into Anyidi (Dinka territory) becoming Dinka. Compared to the Dinka, however, whose population by the early twentieth century numbered in the hundreds of thousands (and possibly even a million), the Murle only numbered around twenty to thirty thousand. The oral histories above suggest that many diverse peoples migrated into what is now the Bor Dinka region and over time the Dinka socio-economic and political culture prevailed.[5] Another group of people located on the Nile today and claiming to be Dinka are the Thain.

The Thain Dinka

In 1857 missionary A. Kaufmann noted that between the Ciec, Ghol, Twic, Bor, and Aliab Dinka on both sides of the Nile small settlements of poor nations supported themselves by fishing and blacksmithing. They did not make their living by pastoralism, although some owned cattle which they left with their wealthier Dinka neighbors who pastured them. Kaufmann wrote: "Because they are poor they are regarded with contempt by their neighbors although they live more pleasurably than the herdsmen." These Thain peoples claim to be Dinka today; whether they were always Dinka, however, is debatable and it is more likely that they were originally of Luo or Mundari origin.

In 1934 the Thain numbered approximately 1,164 and were located on the river banks between the Mongalla boundary and Jonglei under seven chiefs. British administrators presumed them to be of common origin with the Bor and Aliab Dinka, the various Dinka clans of which claimed overlordship over them. It was noted by British administrator, R. T. Johnston, for example, that "the Pariak Thain belonged to the Abiiy Dinka clan, the Malek and Malwal Ayuit to the Ghol Dinka, the Malwal Cat and Gweleik to the Paleik Dinka clan, the Mading to the Koic Dinka, the Malith to [the] Baidit (Angakwei) Dinka, the Anganya to the Juet Dinka and the Jonglei to the clan of Dinka Chief Majok Ajak." Although these Thain were "despised" by their cattle-owning Dinka neighbors, they also provided "cheap women" for marriages. These fisherfolk departed from the usual Dinka philosophy of not becoming blacksmiths, for within their polity there were many who practiced this skill.[6]

Conclusion

In this chapter we have seen the formation of the southeastern Dinka grouping later known as the Bor. This confederation, unlike the Padang, initially comprised multiple ethnicities. First there were numerous different Dinka clans who converged on the area east of the Nile. Those formerly resident on the land prior to the Dinka arrival, including Luo, Mundari, and possibly Bari, were either absorbed ethnically or fled north, south, and east. Additionally new clans arriving from the south, some from as far away as the Toposa, who presently reside on the modern-day borders of Sudan and Kenya, also became part of this confederation in southeastern Dinkaland. As the region became crowded many were forced to cross the Nile to its western banks. Today, those who migrated west form the largest Dinka grouping in Southern Sudan and are known as the "Western" or Bahr el-Ghazal Dinka.

7

COMMUNITIES IN THE SOUTHWEST: THE SOUTHERN BAHR EL-GHAZAL

The land east of the Nile could not accommodate the growing populations of Dinka clans, and thus many crossed the Nile at what is now the modern town of Bor over to its western banks, while others crossed from a point further north. Some settled immediately on the opposite banks of the Nile while other clans then forged northwest, some as far as three hundred miles. Today all of the Dinka west of the Nile are known as the *Bahr el-Ghazal* (named after the modern-day province) or "Western" Dinka and they comprise ten major sections, the Ciec, Aliab, Apak-Atwot, Agar, Pakam, Gok, Western Luaic, Rek, Malwal, and Western Twic. The Dinka of this vast region can be broken into two groups; the Southern Bahr el-Ghazal and the Northern Bahr el-Ghazal, the dividing line being the types of soils and land into which these various clans migrated.

The land in the southern Bahr el-Ghazal is by far the richest in the whole Dinka confederation, and thus more wars and less ethnic integration of "foreign" peoples (with the exception of the Aliab who are not in such rich territory) mark the history of these peoples. In specific terms the fertile soils afforded these Dinka the opportunity to grow large quantities of their favorite crops much coveted by other Dinka. Thus, by today's standards these Dinka are considered the richest of the whole confederation. Those groupings living in the southern territories are from east to west the

Ciec, Aliab, Apak-Atwot, Agar, Pakam, and the Gok. The Ciec territory was the first land into which those from the east migrated.

The Ciec Dinka

Today the Ciec reside on the western banks of the Nile near the modern towns of Shambe and westwards toward Yirol. They comprise two major sections, the Ciec-Lou and the Ciec-Ador. These folk claim that, en masse, they acquired their name from the Dinka word for "bee," for in the region of the Lou (Pagarou) there were many of these creatures. They believe that their ancestors resembled bees for they "were unified in searching for their own food." The Dinka claim that the ancient father of all of the Ciec Dinka clans was Manyiel Tiop (*tiop* means the land where one is buried).

The Ciec estimate that they initially arrived west of the Nile around the latter seventeenth century and migrated under the leadership of two priests crossing the Nile at two points. The first, Juet, arrived at Cuei, which is located at the modern-day town of Shambe. The crossing of the river was named after this priest-leader and today it is known as Cuei Malwal Juet. This group settled north of today's Ciec Dinka territory and established themselves in a place called Palual (which could be interpreted in Dinka as "place of Luel" or "Lual"). Later these Ciec Dinka were forced south during the phase of Nuer expansion to Lake Jur sometime before 1800.

The second prominent leader to cross the Nile with his people, Jokom, was closely related to the people of Ciec leader, Juet. He crossed the Nile at a place remembered as Paneka (north of the modern-day town of Bor) to its western banks. This clan migrated further south beyond the Juet's Ciec people into what is now the Aliab Dinka region. Soon after this they fissioned into various groups. Those that stayed became part of the Aliab Dinka grouping while other clans migrated west into the modern-day Rumbek area, becoming Agar. A third group, it is claimed, migrated south into what later became the non-Dinka Nilotic Atwot territory and over time changed their ethnic identity. Some, in smaller clan groups, also migrated hundreds of miles far to the northwest to the present-day Tonj and Gogrial areas, eventually becoming Rek and Western Twic Dinka.[1]

The land into which these initial Dinka had migrated was far richer than that east of the Nile. Further, it had sod and natural salt or *bar* for the animals, and thus they found they could grow more food crops than in their previous homelands with far less effort. In 1857, for example, missionary Beltrame noted that these Dinka produced much *dhurra* (grain) without cultivating large tracts of land.

Thus, the land was hotly contested by others. Ciec Dinka Gordon Matot Tut states: "Juet protected our land from the [non-Dinka Western Nilotic] Luo, who then left. Then the [non-Dinka Western Nilotic] Nuer tried to occupy the land, he resisted. Then the [non-Dinka non-Nilotic] Murle crossed to the west of the Nile and he fought them off too, pushing them back to their territory on the eastern banks." Thus, all other intruders were repulsed. Juet, in protecting this rich red soil (*lual* in Dinka) named the region Palual Juet, which retains this name to the present day. Although in the nineteenth century the Ciec were forced further south of their initial homeland, the land was still rich, and thus these clans acquired much wealth "because people acquire cattle by bartering their *dhurra* grain crops."

A description of the Ciec major sections, subsections, and clans is typical of the bewildering ethnic complexity of nonstate lineage societies and offers a window into the Dinka politics of fission, historically. The Ciec-Lou have six subsections: the Kuacdit, Kuacthi, Ajak, Pajook, Padiet-Anion, and Padongluel. Along with those of ancient Dinka ancestry, these groups comprise peoples of Luo and possibly Mundari ancestry. The major subclans of the Kuacdit are the Pajiek, Pakol, Jaar, Alieb, and the Cuajak (or Atoc), who are a fishermen section, possibly of Luo rather than Dinka origin. The Ajuong (or Ajong), also not of original Dinka ancestry, are possibly of Mundari origin and are a blacksmith section, a practice historically shunned by mainstream Dinka society. The Kuacthi major clans comprise the Nam, Alico, Nyueny, Kun and lastly the Beciec who are also a small section of fishermen most likely of Luo origin. The Ajak (or Ajiek) comprise the Duor and Panalak (also called Pannyigeng) both of which originated from one lineage. The Pajook, Padiet Anion, and Padongluel are also derived from one lineage group and are also known as "Ciliic." All the above sections are today further subdivided into clans or sub-subsections headed by clan (*gol*) leaders. These Ciec-Lou peoples are geographically located in the west and north of the modern town of Yirol.

Although we do not have a detailed account of the political and ethnic complexity of the Ciec-Ador, it is known, for instance, that the Ciec Ador has two major subsections today: the Gok and Ajak. Each in turn has eight subsections. Geographically the Ador are today located east of the modern town of Yirol, north of the Nilotic non-Dinka Atwot and adjacent to the Nile south of Shambe.

Of importance to Southern Sudanese ethno-history is that the northern Nilotic neighbors of the large Ciec Dinka grouping, the Western Nuer, also have Lou and Ador sections, suggesting that these clans were historically one people. This is feasible considering that numerous Dinka changed their ethnic identity with the onslaught of the Nuer expansion east in the latter eighteenth century (see chapter 16).

Further, it is known from the oral histories of other southern peoples that the Ciec Dinka displaced a number of non-Dinka groups previously living in this territory. Atwot Napoleon Adok Gai and Ciec Dinka Gordon Matot Tut state: "The Yirol region was originally inhabited by the Luo, for it is remembered that Chief Juet fought a people who later migrated southwards towards the Nile." Yibel (Jurbel) elders (now presently located south of Agar Dinka territory far to the southwest) also assert that at one time large densities of their people resided in the present-day Ciec Dinka territory of Shambe and were displaced. For proof, they claim that Yibel place names in this area are still extant, for example *Paneka*. Although there are no oral histories obtained from the Mundari, who now reside to the south of the Aliab Dinka beyond the Ciec, the presence of isolated non-integrated clans of former Mundari peoples within the Ciec (who now claim to be Dinka) suggests that this culture may also have been residing in the region prior to the Dinka arrival.

The splintering of the various Dinka groups in the Ciec territory is a key example of how the Dinka have fissioned and sometimes later fusioned politically over the centuries. For example, one Ciec informant stated: "I'm from the Paleu subsection of the [Ciec] Ador and about five generations ago because of tribal fighting the Paleu split into different directions. We have little sections of Paleu people as far north as Tonj town. We also have Paleu people in the non-Dinka Atwot area among the Ror-Kec." The initial split of Jokom's people is estimated to have taken place somewhere between the seventeenth and eighteenth centuries.

Directly to the south and contiguous to the Ciec is the large Aliab Dinka grouping.

The Aliab Dinka

The Aliab comprise four major sections: the Akuei in the west, the Apuk in the northwest, the Bulok in the southeast, and the Akeer in the north. The Aliab clans migrated from the Padang territory of the present-day Eastern Ngok Dinka region, proceeding southwards largely because of the need for good *toic* (grasslands) for their cattle. They found Bor Dinka already residing on the east bank of the Nile in their present position and following the Ciec they crossed the Nile westwards. Soon the four different sections of Aliab arrived in their present territories south of the Ciec.

Each Aliab section was named after an event in history or by those who led them. After they had crossed the Nile, Bulok was the first to lead his section in a southern direction after a disagreement with his father, Apuk. He was followed shortly thereafter by another brother, Acol Bohn [Boon], whose section acquired the title *Akeer* because in Dinka, *akeer* means "behind" other peoples. These clans settled in what is now northeastern Aliab territory and oral histories corroborate the Ciec belief that these Dinka clans were also following the clans of the latter and the non-Dinka Atwot.

The third Aliab section, the Akuei, and the fourth, the Apuk, became closely allied. The former clans crossed the Nile westwards from Bor under their leader, Nyinger Apac Adier. They too claim to have been following the Atwot, who had left earlier and who initially migrated into the present-day Aliab country. At this juncture they met the last Aliab section to settle, whose leader was Apuk, to which the section was later named. He had also led his people from the north of the Western banks of the Nile after crossing the river at different places. Upon reaching the western banks of the Nile, Apuk temporarily chose to join the Akuei people under their leader Nyinger. The latter priest was remembered as a "terrible priest/magician" whose prophecies (good or bad) never failed and whom the people greatly feared.

The Apuk and Akuei initially moved together into an area today called "Pap" and upon arrival found a number of peoples, the most threatening of which were the forefathers of another powerful Dinka clan grouping later known as the Agar. The latter had migrated before the Aliab and occupied the land. Under the two Aliab leaders, Nyinger and Reng Apuk, the Akuei and Apuk went to war to evict the Agar from the territory. Ultimately the latter were forced west. Aliab Dinka Edward Ngong Deng and Abraham Mayuom Mangok recount: "We had one big battle and the Agar rushed in a horde westwards creating a pass as they fled for their lives. In later years it became a river bed and we remember this trench today as 'Digar'— that is, the Digar river bed where our great-great-grandfathers pushed the Agar west."

Along with the Agar there were also other groups living in the region before the various Aliab clans arrived, among them the Eastern Nilotic Mundari who, according to Bor-Gok Dinka informants, speak Bari. These non-Dinka residents were raided because they had better grazing areas and eventually they were militarily pushed southwards or partially absorbed into the Dinka amalgam by intermarriage. Anok, the son of Aliab leader, Nyinger, eventually led the Akuei peoples to their present-day homeland in the Digar region.

The Aliab soils were not as rich as those of the Ciec to their north or the non-Dinka Western Nilotic Atwot to their west, who grew their favorite Dinka *dhurra* grain, *kec*. However, the clans that collectively became known as the Aliab were able to grow more than enough to survive and prosper. While *kec* prefers sandy soils the Apuk Aliab found they could grow another type of *dhurra*; *rapjiang*. Those Aliab in the far south however, were forced to settle in soils that could only grow an inferior crop, *calla*, which grows in muddy regions. It is also grown by their southern neighbors, the Mundari. Because the soils improved as one migrated in a northwesterly direction of the Aliab, Dinka migrations to the south halted.

From this point on the Aliab represented the far southeastern extent of the Western Dinka confederation. They controlled the region by raiding the Mundari to their south and sealing off their areas from migrating Bor-Gok Dinka east of the Nile, who attempted to cross the river west. Today the Aliab claim that the collective name is derived from the word "mixed" because, in reality, this group is recognized as being composed of a number of different ethnic peoples, including Dinka and Mundari. Much like the history of many other Dinka clans and sections, migrations continued and some Apuk-Aliab Dinka can be found today hundreds of miles to the northwest in the Rek and Western Twic Dinka country near Gogrial.[2]

West of the Aliab and southwest of the Ciec are the Atwot.

The Western Nilotic Atwot (Non-Dinka)

Western Nilotic Atwot migration histories corroborate many Dinka accounts and thus will be included here. Today there are three major groupings around the modern-day town of Yirol west of the Nile. The Ciec Dinka are in the north, the Aliab Dinka are in the south, and the Atwot (some of whom claim to be Dinka and others do not) in the southwest. This town represents the northern limits of the Western Nilotic Atwot, whose major sections are the Apak, Ror-kec, Akot, Jilek, Luaic, and Kuek. The ancient ancestor of the Apak subsection came from Yei while the ancestors of one of the latter's smaller components, the Aper, come from east of the Nile. On the western boundary of the Atwot is the Rok-Kec section, which is contiguous with the non-Nilotic Yibel peoples of southern Movolo. The Kuek section occupies the eastern boundary of the Atwot and is contiguous with the non-Dinka Mundari.

Much like the Dinka the Atwot did not migrate into empty space but warred with and displaced or ethnically absorbed the previous residents.

J. M. Stubbs and C. G. T. Morrison suggest that the Luo migration into the Bahr el-Ghazal coincided with that of the Atwot moving into their new homelands between 1500 and 1620. Atwot informants claim that when their ancestors arrived from points further north into their present homeland they found non-Nilotic pottery. Akec Nyatyiel Nar states: "We found fisherman when we moved to Atwot territory as well as Mundari where, at certain places, they were together with Bor Dinka people." It is remembered that others were pushed south to the Mvolo area. However, some Atwot cattle camps also have Bari names, indicating that at one time this territory may have also been home to these non-Dinka non-Atwot southern neighbors. The Bari kingdom, which reached its greatest prominence in the mid eighteenth century, was located north of the modern-day boundary of Uganda primarily east of the Nile but its many conquered subjects also resided on both sides of the Nile, acquiring the Bari language. Atwot oral histories claim that upon arrival in this new territory the previous residents were hunters, trappers, fisherman, and iron workers.[3]

Although not as rich as the Ciec territory to their north the land the Atwot claimed was still very good, of a mixed sandy and clay composition in which *kec dhurra* could still be grown. Thus, the Atwot, over the centuries, have been able to acquire wealth. Of all the major Atwot sections today, the Apak in the north claim actually to be Dinka while all the others claim to have been of former Nuer ancestry (see chapter 16 for an extended discussion on this topic). To be covered in the next section, therefore, are the oral histories of the Apak-Atwot. Although the greater confederation of Atwot claim that they reached their territory before the Apak, this assertion does not comply with Apak mainstream history.[4]

The Apak (Atwot) Dinka

Today the Apak are often thought of as more Dinka than Atwot and informants claim their subsections are composed of people from many places. According to David Deng Athorbei the Apak reside between the Atwot (proper) to their south and the Ciec Dinka to their northeast. They comprise eight subsections: the Aper, Aciek, Pakuac, Palual, Aparer, Rir, Guer, and Awan. The Awan includes clans claiming agnatic heredity from the Atwot ancestral figure Reel as well as from peoples who migrated into Apak country from the eastern Nile Bor Dinka region and the Yibel country to the south. The Aper subsection of the Apak comprise those who migrated from the Aliab Dinka territory to the east and historical songs of these migrations still exist. Additionally, the Aciek and Pakuac comprise those who migrated from the Ciec Dinka land while the Palual comprise those who migrated from the Agar Dinka homeland. Concerning the Aparer, Rir, and Guer, some oral histories note that they were in place before the arrival of the Awan clan, many of whose members migrated into this region from the far south. Thus, it is likely that these clans were of original Luo, Luel, Mundari, or Bari ancestry.

Today the Awan subsection of the Apak is the largest. Apak informant David Deng Athorbei is the great great-greatgrandson of the original leader of the Awan whose name was Guaji (Kwaji) and who, as a non-Nilotic Kakwa prince, migrated north from Yei near the borders of modern-day Uganda:

> My great-great-grandfather in the seventeenth century followed the Yei (Payii) river ten generations ago after he left his home village at Yei. He was a Kakwa and migrated north after a dispute as to who should inherit spiritual leadership within the clan. My ancestor was the youngest in a chiefly family and thus, had to leave and establish his own chieftaincy. He left Yei alone going from place to place performing magic until he reached Payii opposite the modern-day Apak area. He was a powerful spirit-healer and as he moved he gathered many people to him during which he acquired a wife. He was received by the Guer people who were already resident in the region.

Much like many other Dinka clans migrating into Southern Sudan, Guaji and his followers found others residing on the land when they arrived. David Deng Athorbei adds:

> One "Apak" group, the Guer, although speaking Dinka today do not practice Dinka pastoralism but rather are blacksmiths and animal trappers and work for other Atwot. It was these Guer people already resident in Apak country who received and accommodated the Chief from Yei, Guaji, whose family began to multiply and expand very quickly. Eventually they [Guaji and his people] chased other Atwot to the east and pushed the Ciec northwards. Guaji remained with the Guer and at his death he was succeeded by four sons. Mel (which means someone who never goes back on his word), Akot, and Kuc (later known as Kaker). Mel acquired the chieftaincy and shortly thereafter amalgamated what had become eight sections in the region into the modern-day Apak. At a ceremony he killed a bull which was colored "*Mapuor*" and pronounced [to the people] "from now on you will all be called Apak" meaning "to get together." After this point he began fighting the other Atwot in the region expanding in all directions. Initially we were in the center but then we fought the Agar, the Ciec (Ajak section), the Atwot

specifically the Luaic section who, among the Atwot were the majority. The Luaic were annihilated and now they are a smaller section within the Apak-Awan. Now Kuc took over because he was the youngest and had many children, and introduced arrows, a skill brought from [what is now] Equatoria. This made us powerful because my family had an intimate knowledge of poisons which contributed to our technological superiority allowing us to expand against the other Atwot. Today we have songs which document our history.

As the above account suggests the ancestors of certain Apak-Atwot peoples were originally from differing ethnic groups throughout Southern Sudan, who migrated into the region over time and became integrated into the larger Nilotic Atwot amalgam. Others, however, were already resident prior to the arrival of Guaji and were likely of Luo, Mundari, or Bari origin. John Burton suggests that having established some number of cattle camps in what is now Atwot country, indigenous blacksmiths and trappers became Atwot through intermarriage. In the meantime the region also became home to numbers of other migrating Dinka clans from the north who integrated themselves into the larger Atwot amalgam. Some informants claim that the Apak dialect today is an admixture of Mundari, Moru, Dinka, and Atwot; others state the Apak-Atwot speak Dinka and other Atwot do not.

The method of choosing leaders among the Apak however, did not follow that of mainstream Dinka society. Among the former, the first war-leader, Mel, was not a priest; nor was the Apak leadership passed down by primogeniture (succeeded only by the sons of chiefs). Mel was succeeded by a relative, Ayol Ngong, who was followed by Piny Deng. Succeeding generations of chiefs were Dhieu Alam, Apugi Alam, Macar Ijong, Mayar Macar (Ijong's son), and Kon Mayar, the present chief. The last two chiefs acquired their posts by election while their predecessors acquired the chieftaincy only if they demonstrated superior military skills and leadership.

The historical migrations of the Atwot-Apak have left a legacy of closeness with their northern neighbors, the Ciec Dinka. It is said today that the Ciec and Atwot are "one family" and that the boundary between the two is less defined than with other major Dinka groups. On the other hand, the Agar Dinka and Apak have a "strong border," leaving an empty area between the two because the former fought many battles with the latter over the centuries and are considered more "foreign." This legacy of closeness with the Ciec is a result of more of these clans-people being integrated into the Apak.

Although the Apak identify more with the Dinka than the Atwot proper to their south (they speak Dinka), during the Anglo-Egyptian Condominium period they were subsumed administratively under the Atwot, and thus today they are viewed as such. As Apak-Atwot Pur Ciengan states, major Dinka sections today resemble the United States: "If you move into an area of a major grouping, that is what you become. Now we are all Apak."[5]

To the northwest of the Apak and west of the Ciec is the major Dinka grouping, the Agar.

The Agar Dinka

The Agar today have four sections comprising the Rup, Kuei, Aliam Toc, and Pakam. Centuries ago the Agar migrated across the Nile from the east, some claiming to have come from as far away as Western Ethiopia, after forging south up the Blue Nile from central Sudan. Many of these folk eventually headed west and reaching the Nile crossed to its western banks where they then separated.

Two priests led the people to their present area in the Bahr el-Ghazal: Rok Korec and Malwal Arop. The land was not empty and, according to the non-Nilotic Yibel, the heart of this Dinka territory (Rumbek) was at one time inhabited by their ancestors. Supporting these claims, Agar histories note that centuries ago, they pushed into this land to the limits of *kec*-yielding soil. Now the Yibel could only grow *nyandok,* a less popular form of *dhurra* which the Dinka claim does not taste so good and is only eaten when the people are really hungry.

Yibel elders including Ruben Macier Makoi claim that their population used to be far larger but that many died of disease; mostly malaria and sleeping sickness. Today the Yibel in South Sudan number approximately forty to fifty thousand. Yibel Simon Malual Deng states: "On our east are Dinka Apak, on our north are Dinka Agar, while on our west and south are Moru people. We are not Nilotes but come from west central Africa and we understand that the Moru are our brothers." Sudanese Luo Albino Ukec Simon states: "We know the Jurbel (Yibel) as 'Wira' after the name of one of their leaders. The people were called 'Wir' all the way up to Uganda and their country was known as Pawir. As people moved they carried the name. Bel is the name of millet."

Although the Dinka fought wars with the Yibel, other oral accounts also remember little conflict and that a peaceful compromise was reached with the Yibel. This corresponds to Yibel Ruben Macier Makoi's assertion that his people have been a very peaceful. Michael Manyiel Col adds a note concerning Akon Buol, the woman given by the Dinka to the Yibel to end the wars between the two: "The chief took the girl and told his people to move, leaving the land for the Agar. So the land today is called the land of Buol:" After this time it is remembered that much assimilation began between the Yibel and the Agar, with Akon Buol representing the first to intermarry. However, today there is less intermarriage because the Yibel have no cows to marry a Dinka girl (brideprice is around thirty to forty cows); they only have honey, goats and hoes."[6]

According to Agar Dinka Julia Benjamin the Yibel were iron makers who made bows and arrows and possessed a knowledge of poisons which even today makes the Dinka fear them. During the colonial Anglo-Egyptian Condominium (1898–1956) one British administrator reported that within the Yibel territory there was an absence of cattle because of tsetse fly. He noted, however, that the Dinka attributed this to the malevolence of the Yibel, that the Dinka were frightened of their magic, and expressed anxiety over the number of Dinka affected by it. This *akwel* (magic) was worked by means of a small bean which was retained by the Yibel practitioner but invisible to the human eye. When he wished to, the bean could be propelled from his eye and strike his victim in the forehead.[7] It appears that this knowledge of poisons was the one major defense against the Dinka.

But despite the wars between the two peoples centuries ago, more recently the Agar have helped the Yibel, leading to geographical integration. Yibel informants claim: "We are in the same area, Rumbek, and our people used to produce honey to sell to the Dinka" and "in the Agar Dinka town of Rumbek some families known as 'Agar' are actually Yibel in origin." Likewise in present-day Yibel country in the Amadi district south of Malou (Billing) and between the River Naam and Toinya Road, the Dinka residing in this area have become ethnically mixed with their non-Dinka neighbors.

An example of Dinka/Yibel ethnic integration is observable with the genealogy of Ruben Macier Makoi. His father, Makoi, and grandfather, Awat, both have Nilotic names. His great-grandfather, Lu, and his great-great-grandfather, Girnga, however, possess non-Nilotic names. Allotting twenty-five to thirty years per generation (Ruben Macier is perhaps fifty years old) it can be estimated that around a century or more ago this Yibel family adopted Dinka identity. This would correspond with the unstable era of the Egyptian and/or Mahdist slave-raiding invasions into Southern Sudan (1865–98) when many fled into Dinkaland for safety. The Yibel have evolved a myth to explain their close ethnic connection with the Dinka: "The creator produced two sons, the elder of which was the ancestor of the Yibel and the younger that of the Agar Dinka."

The origin of the name *Agar* is connected to history. First it is claimed that the name derives from the father of the original settlers in this region. On the other hand, the literal meaning of the word *Agar* is "someone left by his people," because Marol was powerful but not a magician (priest) and his family abandoned him. Thus, the Agar believe: "Today we are called 'Agar Marol' and this is how the word 'Agar' was born." Informant Agar Marol states: "Marol was the chief's name while the Agar were his people."

Other Agar explain a myth that the major Dinka groupings, Luaic, Rek, and Gok, as well the Nuer (who are not Dinka), are derived from daughters of Agar Chief Marol. "Marol is the grandfather of our grandfathers. These various daughters gave birth to four groups. Amou Marol gave birth to the Rek people, Nyantoc gave birth to the Nuer, Acuei gave birth to two sons, one of which gave birth to the Gok and the other to the Luaic." The Agar believe that the Malwal and Western Twic also originated from Agar territory. This is supported by the latter's own oral histories. Thus, what is clear from crosschecking other Dinka accounts with that of the Agar is that many of the northern Bahr el-Ghazal Dinka passed through the Agar territory and, en route to their modern-day homelands, acquired some Agar clans on their travels.

Many regions of the Agar territory possess very rich soils and thus, much like the Ciec before them, this land was hotly contested. Agar Dinka Michael Manyiel Col states that the people of his section, the *Kuei* ("eagle" in Dinka) founded the region of the modern-day town of Rumbek: "We were very martial and we defended our land." Because the land, like that of the Ciec Dinka territory, yielded a variety of crops it gave rise to a burgeoning population. It is recounted that there was plenty of food and that, in the old days, women regularly gave birth to up to fifteen children. Today, the Agar occupy the center of *kec dhurra* territory. When they have good harvests they sell their grain to surrounding Dinka and acquire more cattle.[8]

In the far north, the Pakam Agar section possess a very different history and is therefore treated as a separate Dinka grouping.

The Pakam (Agar) Dinka

Today the Pakam number approximately one quarter of a million people and comprise five subsections: the Gak, Lith, Manuer, Akok, and Niel-Niel. The section name *Gak* means "to quarrel" in Nuer. The Pakam are today adjacent to the Nuer and this section of the Agar was originally Nuer. According to Stephen Anyaak Col:

Five generations ago, two [Nuer] brothers, (one of them called Thian) killed another man, and to escape revenge he hid in the garden while their houses were burned. The attack took place in Nicong Ganylul in Nuerland. Their mother advised them to go to the *Djiang* (Dinka) area, and so they moved [with their followers] into the Dinka region that is north of present-day Agar territory and camped. Eventually the two brothers split. Moving near to Rumbek, numbers of other [Nuer] followers chose to remain near the border of Nuerland farther north. Eventually Thian was given a Dinka girl, Aruai, in marriage and so they produced a son, Wuol, who later became a famous Dinka chief and war leader.

The first prominent Pakam leader, Wuol, eventually became one of the best known "Agar" Dinka leaders of the nineteenth and twentieth centuries, becoming a paramount chief during the British colonial period (1898–1956). After having established himself in Agar territory, he fought wars with his Dinka neighbors to his east and west, establishing a sovereign territory for the Pakam. He and his progeny are considered great heroes to the Pakam people and his divine powers were said to increase as he got older. His ancestors continue the chiefly line in modern times.

Thus, the ancestors of the Pakam, who were Nuer, fled their former homelands into their present territory by design rather than accident. Over time they intermarried with their Dinka neighbors. Because the land was rich they acquired cattle and unexpectedly became very wealthy.

Although the Pakam are today still thought of as Nuer by some Dinka, they are located in Dinka territory and have become sociopolitically and economically incorporated into the larger Agar Dinka amalgam. Stephen Anyaak Col states: "If you migrate to Dinka territory, you become Dinka. But when I'm with my paternal uncle I'm a Nuer. Even today, some Dinka call me 'Nuer' even though I am Dinka. I am a doctor and one day I visited a lady and she claimed ,'You Nuer, you don't treat wives well.' When I go to the Nuer country, people recognize me and I attend funerals. However, I was raised by my maternal Dinka uncles so I identify with being Dinka."[9] In Dinka society the maternal uncle has more control and responsibility for his nieces and nephews than does their father. Maternal aunts also tend to predominate in the hierarchy of Dinka family relations.

To the west of the Agar reside another major Dinka grouping, the Gok.

The Gok Dinka

Today, geographically, the Gok are located between the Western Luaic Dinka to their north, the Pakam-Agar to their northeast, and the town of Rumbek thirty miles directly east. To their south are the Yibel. Rivers demarcate most of the Gok sections as they do for most other major Dinka groups. Thus, more specifically, the Gok's eastern boundary is the river Aber, their western boundary is five miles east of the town of Tonj, their northern boundary is the river Tonj, and their southern boundary lies near to the border of the modern-day town of Maridi.

Although the Gok Dinka today are administratively part of Agar territory, they claim a different ethno-history for their ascent, and their naming of trees is different. Further, as a Dinka grouping they have been historically separate from the Agar. Some oral histories recount that the Gok Dinka clans originally migrated from the Ciec territory adjacent to the west bank of the Nile. Other accounts, however, suggest that they are primarily related to the Agar. The first Gok leader in early times was Ater Malwal from the Kabek clan. He led the Gok people to their present position and is remembered as being very courageous and having special spiritual powers.

Gok clan history, like many others, is very complex. Initially the Gok had two major sections, the Langdiing and Macar. The Langdiing today comprise the Ayiel, Joth, Pathiang, Pagok, and Kongor subsections. The Macar comprise the Waat, Akony, and Panyar subsections. The Panyar subsection has become further subdivided into four subsections: the Kongor, Amal, Yiep, and Amel. Before the Langdiing split into its various subsections the people were living east of the Nile in a place called Waat, in the *toic* (grasslands) area. Because of drought the clans of both the major groups mentioned above started moving south and then crossed the Nile. Soon after they began to fission politically. These new clans evolved into the Panyar who moved to present-day northern Gok territory. The Waat clans followed them. The Akony moved west, the Ayiel to the center (Cuibet town), and the Joth and Pagok clans moved east along with the Pathiang, who today border the Agar. In the meantime wars took place between various clans of the Agar and Gok Dinka peoples who now shared east/west borders. The Gok were led by their prominent military leader, Dut Raac.

With their neighbors, the Yibel, however, along with war, much peaceful integration also took place. The Pathiang remember meeting the Yibel who were in a place called Aguguang. However, everyone was hungry so they moved south until they reached Aluai, the area of the Yibel. When they moved into this territory the Yibel leader Dier Yai welcomed them and said "you will be our people." He bestowed on these Dinka their name saying "you will be called Pathiang Dier." This is not a Yibel name but may represent a Dinka derivative of his name. Much as with the Agar, over time some Yibel became cattle owners and began to marry Dinka women and today many Yibel have adopted Gok Dinka culture. Yibel age sets now mark their foreheads in the specific Gok fashion and Dinka men marrying Yibel women pay a brideprice of ten cows. The Yibel still maintain a strong independent culture, however, and separate ethnic identity. Although the Yibel have similar religious symbols to the Dinka, for example the python, unlike many Dinka groups the Yibel do not observe the incest laws of their neighbors wherein it is forbidden to marry close kin.

Dinka relations with the non-Nilotic Bongo peoples to their south and west, on the other hand, differ from those with the Yibel. The Bongo were once a large nation of hunters (they seldom cultivated the land) and were located some distance away from the Gok Dinka near the modern-day Rek Dinka town of Tonj. The Gok only met the Bongo during hunting expeditions in the forest. As hunters the Bongo historically sold dried meat to the Dinka. Initially the Bongo were unable to marry Gok women as they did not possess cows. Recently however, Bongo men have begun acquiring cattle and marrying Dinka women, paying a brideprice of twenty to thirty cows. The Dinka presently pay a brideprice of approximately ten goats to acquire Bongo wives. Although the Bongo nation today is considerably smaller than a few centuries ago, unlike the Yibel, they have remained separate and adopted very little Dinka culture.

Agriculturally, much like the Ciec, Agar, Pakam, and Apak Atwot homelands the Gok territory is very rich and more productive than other regions of Dinkaland. Most importantly, these Dinka are able to grow the much coveted *kec* grain which they sell to their less fortunate Dinka neighbors. Thus, the Gok are among the richest Dinka people today and possess more cattle than their Dinka neighbors to the northwest.[10]

Conclusion

In this chapter we have seen how the Western or Bahr el-Ghazal Dinka of the southern region came to settle on the richest lands of any of those Dinka within the entire confederation of Southern Sudan. In consequence, these populations proliferated considerably becoming the most dense of the Dinka confederation. There are histories of many wars with many peoples, Dinka and non-Dinka, over the land. These include conflicts with the Murle, Mundari, Nuer, Luo, Yibel, and Atwot. To their north beyond the rich *kec*-yielding soils are the northern Bahr el-Ghazal Dinka groups.

8

COMMUNITIES IN THE NORTHWEST: THE NORTHERN BAHR EL-GHAZAL

North and northwest of the Gok and Agar is the vast expansive homeland of the northern Bahr el-Ghazal Dinka. These Nilotes discovered, as they forged northwestwards into their new homelands because of the increasing shortage of lands, that these soils were not as rich as those from which they had migrated. Unlike those of the southern Bahr el-Ghazal, lack of rich soils encouraged faster geographical expansion and hence, faster ethnic integration with many "foreigners." Thus, the topography of the land dictated the history of the peoples of this region, for these Dinka were forced to fight more battles against formerly resident peoples in order to survive and to support their increasing populations. The northern Bahr el-Ghazal Dinka comprise the Western Luaic, the Rek, the Malwal, and the Western Twic; their northern frontier was the Kir/Bahr el-Arab River. (It is *Kir* to the Dinka and Bahr el-Arab to the Islamic central Sudanese).

The Western Luaic

The Luaic Dinka are split into two widely separated groups today: one in the Upper Nile Province, which is now part of the Padang group (the Eastern Luaic), and the other residing in northern Bahr el-Ghazal Province and known as the Western Luaic. There are also Luaic clan-peoples within the non-Dinka Atwot amalgam far to the southeast forming a subsection of the same name, although some of these Atwot peoples today disclaim any historical connection to the Dinka. The Western Luaic has six sections: the Abuong, Kuok, Pariak, Rubar, Wunthuc, and Kongor all with subsections.

Historically the Luaic clans forged south from their parent Padang group in the north and crossed the Nile from east to west from the region of the modern town of Bor. It is remembered that the Atwot preceded them and settled in their present homeland. Other Luaic clans, however, continued migrating northwest with the Agar, Gok, and Rek Dinka, apparently leaving some of their clan members en route as others found new homelands. Makuac Majok Mangeng states: "We were moving with our cattle and goats and then eventually the Gok people settled. Sometime after the Rek clans had settled in their new homelands the Luaic then settled to their east led by a priest, Makol Thokeor, who led a number of Luaic clans to their present location in [what is now] the Bahr el-Ghazal."

The Luaic clans were also migrating along with the Twic Dinka who had left their parent group on the eastern bank of the Nile. Within Luaic territory today there is a pyramid of stones known as *Alel* which is reputed to be the burial place of the great Twic leader and priest, Kuol Alel. Having led his people across the Nile and many miles northwest into the Bahr el-Ghazal he suddenly died in what subsequently became Luaic territory.

Although it is probable that the origin of the word *Luaic* was carried by those who migrated away from the parent body in the Padang Dinka territory, certain informants believe the name was acquired after the original peoples' long trek northwest through the Bahr el-Ghazal. Having reached their modern-day territory these Dinka told their fellow clans people "you can go ahead, we are exhausted." In Dinka, the word for tired or exhausted is *Luaic*. People made fun of them and thus they acquired the name. Today the boundary between the Luaic and their Dinka neighbors, the Rek, to their west and northwest is Loupaher and Ador Bac. On their far northern borders are the Western Twic and on their eastern borders are the non-Dinka Nuer; to their south are the Agar-Pakam Dinka.

In terms of Dinka intergroup relations the Luaic believe that their western neighbors, the Rek-Tek Dinka, are their brothers, and hence they quarrel rarely. The same is said of the Gok Dinka to their south who are also referred to as "brothers"; relations are cordial because "Gok is the son of our aunt (Gok Acuei) and the Luaic are also called Luaic Acuei." However, with the Agar to their southeast there are sometimes more serious wars, because there is deemed to be no family relations between these two large Dinka groupings.

The Western Luaic believe their land is quite rich, although *kec* does not grow in this region. In the past they mobilized all family members to acquire enough *dhurra* grain for food-selling in order to buy more cattle.[1]

To the west and northwest contiguous to the Western Luaic are their close relations, the Rek.

The Rek Dinka

The Rek are the most numerous of all major Dinka groups in Southern Sudan today, comprising three main sections. The Kuei reside from the modern-day towns of Tonj to western Gogrial. The Apuk reside from Tonj to east of Gogrial and the Ngok reside in the town of Gogrial. These three main sections above are further subdivided: the Apuk have three sub-divisions, the Gier, Joweer, and Padoic; the Kuei have five major sub-divisions, the Kuac, Thiei, Akop, Aguok, and Anaiatak; and the Ngok have two divisions, the Awan and Ngok. Each division is further sub-divided into smaller clan groups.

The Rek, unlike the Gok, Agar, and Luaic Dinka above remember much harder-fought battles with the former residents of their homelands to acquire their lands. Chapter 4 provided a detailed report of the Rek arrival in their new homelands and the wars with the former residents of the land, the Luel. Oral histories recount that the Rek originated from far in the southeast (east of the modern town of Rumbek), having previously crossed the Nile from east to west. Much like the Shilluk-Luo who had preceded all of the Dinka into the western Bahr el-Ghazal, these Dinka were initially repulsed by the Luel. After much heavy fighting, however, they forced many of these non-Dinka pastoralists to flee to the Kir/Bahr el-Arab River far to the north. As the Dinka forged along the River Lol they were joined by the Shilluk-Luo (now known as the Nirdimo). The latter had been militarily beaten by the Luel and fled west. As the Dinka appeared to win the wars with the Luel these Luo folk joined their closely related Nilotic cousins in battle.

Many other oral histories of Rek migrations exist. According to Dinka Victor Majok Amecrot and Matthew Mathem Daw: "Many generations ago we migrated to Aliab country after crossing the Nile from the east settling at a place called Angac in Yirol country. From there we moved west. We left the Agar, the Ciec and the Atwot. There are Ciec in Angac and in Rumbek. However the Rek continued migrating northwest settling in Thiet along the River Tonj up to a place called Payuel as well as up to the River Gogrial. However, the water was not sufficient so the Rek moved again." Rek Dinka Gabriel Awec Bol presents another oral history: "Our great-great-grandfather, Parek, gave birth to the present Rek. We came from the east and passed through Ethiopia to Pibor [east of the Nile] and then we crossed to the west of the Nile to Shambe then to Meshra and from there some proceeded onwards and the Rek settled around the Tonj and Gogrial areas."

A number of histories concern female leaders. During the Anglo-Egyptian colonial period British administrators reported that the Dinka of the Northern Rek District stated they were descended from a female, Areik. She and her people had migrated from east of Rumbek. In another history a smaller Rek section known as the Riny Tiik (Tek) proceeded under a male war chief, Makol Thogor, settling in Gogrial. For a time this section had resided within the vicinity of another female leader, Acol, in Meshra er-Rek. This same woman and her people later settled in what became the modern town of Gogrial. As an "executive chief" she had the power to decide on the direction of migrations and eventually came to command the area of present-day Wau. The Dinka claim that she is the one who chose this position for settlement and that the name of Wau today is derived from the Dinka name, Wauacol. Some difficulty in dating exists here, for Nyarruweng Dinka Lazarus Leek Mawut states Acol lived before the Turkish period, but the traveler G. Schweinfurth notes a female Rek chief also called Col at Meshra in the 1860s who was later murdered by slavers.

In terms of politics the three major sections of the Rek Dinka (Apuk, Akuei, and Ngok) came into being shortly after these clans arrived and settled. The Apuk was formed when other Dinka sections began wars with them. All but one Apuk warrior was killed and hence, the victors decided by consensus that he should be allowed to survive to compensate for all the others killed (*apuk* in Dinka means "compensation"). This surviving man married and eventually gave birth to this section. The section *Kuei* (eagle) is derived from the name of the bird native to this area. The Ngok section of the Rek acquired its name from a deadly fish of the same name.

Although the Rek tend to shy away from discussions of absorption of "foreign" peoples, it appears that this group ethnically absorbed more non-Dinka than all other groups. Among the Rek today are many of former Luo and Luel ancestry. (This topic is covered in greater depth in chapter 14.)

Agriculturally, Rek Dinka territory is not as fertile as that of the Agar, Ciec, and Gok to their south and southeast. At best the soils are muddy. *Kec* stops growing well at the southwestern limits of this territory and only a grain, *jiang*, can be cultivated. Thus, these Dinka found they needed to cultivate a larger geographical region to grow enough food to survive.

Other ecological factors also affected the Rek particularly around what is now the modern-day town of Thiet. Here the people were forced to expand quickly because of insufficient water. Even today when the Dinka in Thiet run out of natural resources they move to areas such as Nyabagok, joining other members of their family with better access to this vital resource.[2]

Hence, the Rek Dinka needed to geographically expand more quickly to both feed themselves and graze their cattle. This factor in turn encouraged more militant behavior among these people as everyone struggled to acquire more land and vital resources. As the Rek were forced to quickly expand geographically they gave birth to a major new grouping on their northern periphery; the Malwal.

The Malwal Dinka

In the British colonial era (1898–1956) the vast area of the Malwal Dinka was broken into four administrative districts and major sections. The Malwal-Malwal became located in the northwest, the Abiem-Malwal in the northeast, the Palyoupiny-Malwal in the southwest, and the Paliet-Malwal in the southeast. The Malwal and Abiem are located north of the river Lol, the others reside to its south. The Malwal-Malwal have four subsections, the Malwal-Abiem have six, the Palyoupiny-Malwal have five, while the Paliet-Malwal have four.

On the other hand certain informants do not recognize the British colonial structure but rather believe the Malwal are divided into two rather than four: those north of the Lol river called Pajok-Malwal and those to is south called Palyoupiny. Others claim, confusingly, that there are twenty-four (rather than nineteen) subsections in total. To the north are the Payweng, Duliet, Athiou, Korok, Ajuong Dit, Ajuong Thiei, Duliet Kuany Ngor, Apoth Yol, Akany Jok, Wundiing, Lou Agueir, Wut Anai, and Makuac Athian. To the south are the Guom Jueir, Cimel Kuac, Ajuet, Celkou, Ajak Akol, Ajak Wek Ateny, Buonycuai, Kongder (Aweil), Mading, Aweil, and Raja (which is also the name of a river that divides Lol-Ayat).

The Malwal evolved from the giant grouping of Rek to their south. According to Rek Dinka Matthew Mathem Daw and Victor Majok Amecrot: "The Malwal were Rek but the people became many and fission took place." Rek Dinka Gabriel Awec Bol states: "A Rek Chief, Longar, became powerful, overshadowing his brother Ariath who then became jealous and both quarreled. So Ariath left so [that] he could be an independent *beny bith* (spear master) accompanied by his younger brother Malwal. Eventually Ariath settled north of today's Gogrial area while Malwal, the younger brother accompanied Ariath, becoming the great-great-grandfather of the Malwal of Aweil." The Malwal and Rek parted ways near Apuk in Gogrial and the former headed northwest, eventually taking their position in the far northwestern corner of Malwal-land, leaving the Apuk (Rek) Dinka in their present position. The Abiem section of the Malwal evolved from a Rek group, some of whose clans members remained in the modern-day Tonj region and reside there today. Pertaining to the Paliet, Lawrence Lual Lual Akuey states:

> The Paliet-Malwal group also migrated from Rek territory, near the modern day town of Gogrial and were led westwards by my great-grandfather, Wek Deng, five generations ago. . . . He was told by his father: "Deng go west because the young people will die, because they are constantly hunting buffalo and will be killed by them." His own father was a spiritual leader based at Mariel (not the town near Tonj). What he meant by this statement was that it was bad that people hunted buffalo in large hunting parties. . . . He believed that one day the buffalo would kill them all. So he wanted us to leave the life of hunting, get our cattle, and settle down as herdsmen.

A number of informants remember that several chiefs led the Malwal migration northwards. Among the Palyoupiny-Malwal, Chief Kuac Kuac, Chief Ding Lual, Chief Autiak Akot, and Atuojong Anyuon are remembered. Among the Abiem it is Chiefs Kuol Makuac and Malong Yor who are renown. Among the Paliet it is Chiefs Ariath Kon and Week Atuong.

Generally, all the Malwal state that centuries ago their forefathers migrated south along the eastern banks of the Nile: "We dispersed in a place called Cuei (Angan)." Sometime after, they crossed the river. Two famous priests, Deng Dit and Ariath Makuei, led the people to the western banks of the Nile. They then migrated in a northwesterly direction.

The direction of the Malwal migrations in the Bahr el-Ghazal was related to the search for animals and eventually yielded the name of this large Dinka confederation. The northwestern Malwal-Malwal (bordering the Kir/Bahr-el-Arab river region) arrived because they were following the buffalo: "When we left from Angac to our present area we followed the same pass made by the buffaloes which is called 'Malwal following' and from this time we were called *Malwal.*" A variation of this history is that the Malwal followed a certain buffalo for some distance with a view to killing it. When they did, they acquired the name "people following the buffalo" also known as *Malwal.* Another history states that the group name *Malwal* was acquired by the people when they left the Rek area with red bulls which they slaughtered to ensure their new home was holy. In Dinka *malwal* is also the color of a red cow.

The three other major Malwal group names (Abiem, Palyoupiny, and Paliet) are also derived from history. The Dinka section name *Palyoupiny* is said to have come from those migrating into the region who settled in a place with many Lulu trees (*Rak* in Dinka), from which oil is derived. It is said that when people eat this oil they get fat and become "palyoupiny." The Malwal section name *Paliet* (whose people reside in the southeast of the Malwal amalgam) was acquired when these particular clans failed to come to the aid of their neighboring Dinka, who frequently fought wars with the Islamic Baggara pastoralists to their north (who arrived in the latter eighteenth century). Rather, they remained "idle" or just looked on, which in Dinka is *liet*, hence the name "place of the idle ones" or Paliet. These Dinka objected to being called by this name but over the years came to accept it because all their neighbors kept referring to them as such. The group name *Abiem* was derived from a clan who still reside in the Rek region of Tonj.

During the migrations of the Malwal into their present-day homelands there was much conflict, specifically with the former residents, the Luel. However, not all these folk were driven off the land, for in the twentieth century there still existed many unintegrated Luo and Luel clans within the Malwal amalgam. Further, the Malwal have also absorbed some non-Dinka Nilotic Shatt peoples. These groups now live in the modern town of Aweil, north of Wau.

The land that the Malwal Dinka migrated into was even less fertile than that of the Rek country and it flooded for much of the year. Unwittingly, these Dinka clans had moved beyond the clay plains into the agriculturally poor Ironstone Plateau. However, these migrants were able to grow enough to survive, including short growing *dhurra* varieties known as *anyan* and *jiang* as well as millet. Because the soil was poor for cultivation of grain agriculture these Dinka, therefore, did not expand further northwest. Father Santandrea proposes that the Malwal Dinka arrived in their present land around 1700.[3]

To the northeast and east of the Malwal are the Western Twic, who moved into their land sooner than the Malwal and whose territory is far richer.

The Western Twic Dinka

There are four major sections of the Western Twic along with their respective subsections. These include the Akwar, Amol, Adiang, and the Thon. All four are north of the modern town of Gogrial and are located from east to west respectively.

Western Twic Dinka oral history recounts that the various clans are related to those of the same name residing today in the southeastern Dinka confederation on the eastern banks of the Nile in the Bor region. At some point a number of Dinka clans split from the parent group, migrating across the Nile in a northwesterly direction. Oral histories record that the groups divided peacefully at Patundur and from here many clans migrated as far as three hundred miles northwest into today's northern Bahr el-Ghazal province. No wars or battles are remembered; rather, many left because they needed new pastures and grazing for their cattle. Even after centuries of separation a similar nomenclature exists between both groups: the Eastern Twic claim that those in the west now call themselves Twic Mayardit, a name also existing among those on the eastern banks of the Nile. Additionally, within the Western and Eastern Twic there are Kuac clans which are both part of the Adjuong subsections. Lastly, both groups share the same totems. The Western Twic version of their migrations is similar to that recounted by their eastern counterpart. According to Michael Angok Malong:

> When we were east of the Nile the Twic were one people but some of us crossed the Nile and migrated to our present region. When we were east of the Nile there was a chief called Atwic Arem, who was the father of the Twic, and when we crossed we took the name with us . . . and so we are brothers with the Eastern Twic. This is confirmed because of sub-clans in the Eastern and Western Twic of the same name: Kuac, Adiang, Hol, Payeth, and Aweng, Wunrok, Akoc. We crossed the Nile under the leadership of Ayuel and Garang [two different priests] and then [we were led by] Bol Nyuol, who was a *beny bith* (spear master). We had no quarrel but left because there was not enough land.

Those Twic who crossed the river do, however, remember battles with other Dinka as well as non-Dinka peoples. For example, after certain Twic clans crossed to the western bank of the Nile at what is now the modern town of Shambe, one subsection resided for some time among the Ciec Dinka. As mentioned earlier, scholar Godfrey Lienhardt noted oral histories recounting how the founding ancestor of the Twic Nyang clan, Ajing Anoi, and his people warred with the Ciec Dinka and then left the country taking many of the latter's cattle. As these Twic clans moved northwest they met a mound-building people called the Ber Ajou, a Luel clan, and also stole their cattle.

The Twic clans continued forging northward through what is today's Western Luaic Dinka territory in the northwest. In their migrations through the Bahr el-Ghazal, another Twic subsection reached the modern-day Western Luaic territory, remaining there for a period. As mentioned above, at this juncture the famous Twic Chief, Kuol Alel, died and was buried in a pyramid of stones. It is believed he died quite some time before the Turkiyya, which began in 1821.

Dinka Twic histories parallel that of their Rek neighbors. Missionary Santandrea reported that these Dinka remembered that as they migrated into their present-day territory (prior to the migration of the Malwal out of the Rek territory) they warred, once again, with the Luel, who were also resident in this region. It is remembered that some were driven out while others were assimilated. Western Twic informants state: "There were people in our region called Luel. They were red-skinned and when we went into the area we fought and displaced many of them but also integrated with them by marriage."

The sections of the Twic are named after historical events. The Akwar acquired their name when Chief Juk Ring and his people migrated to their present territory and settled, while many others kept moving ahead into what is now Nuer and Western Ngok Dinka territories. Chief Juk decided to encourage some of these peoples to return to his land "because his area comprised rich soils and grasslands." Hence, *Akwar* in Dinka means "someone who gathers people around him and unifies them into a collected group." Today there are twelve subsections of the Akwar.

The origin of the section name *Thon* parallels that of the Akwar but emerged into a different section. These peoples were also "brought back" (*thon*) by Chief Juk. Today the Thon section consists of four subsections.

The Adiang section of the Western Twic acquired their name from an historical incident concerning a powerful priest who specialized in solving problems. One day when the people visited him he failed to wake up and so his wife donned his leopard skin and impersonated her husband. When the priest awoke to discover his wife performing his "miracles" he angrily accused the masses of having distorted minds. He asked "why did you accept her?" He then accused them all of being disturbed, stating "from today you are all *adiang*." He then collapsed and died. At present there are thirteen Adiang subsections.

According to Bol Bol Col the Amol acquired their name in the following way:

> There were two people in the cattle camp. Both were courting one girl and they applied to the father of the girl to get married. Many other people were also competing for this girl. The father of the girl told each of the two men to bring [many] cows. All the men came and had a meeting and said this man [the father] is trying to joke with us. It is better to kill the girl. So they called

her and then killed her. The father asked them "Why did you kill the girl if you wanted to marry her?" All the men said it was better to kill her because all of us cannot marry one girl and it would be no good to give her to one person. So we will all go without her. Then the father said "If that is what you did you are all mad people (*amol* in Dinka)." So . . . this section became Amol.

The Amol section has six subsections.

The land the ancestors of the Twic migrated into was of far better quality than that of their later western neighbors, the Malwal, for it was still within the region of clay soils and lay adjacent to the Bahr el-Ghazal and Kir/Bahr el-Arab Rivers, benefitting from the riverain soils. They discovered their *toic* (grassland) was among some of the best in the region, yielding much food for their cattle. Over the centuries other Dinka and Nuer groups vied for these rich grasslands but the Twic clans repelled them. Although not able to grow *kec*, they were able to grow a variety of other *dhurra* crops, including *athial.* Because of their rich soils they became a wealthier people and claim to have always commanded higher brideprices for their women than the Rek, Malwal, and Luaic. It is estimated that the Western Twic came to settle in their new homelands in the latter seventeenth and early eighteenth centuries.[4]

Conclusion

The northern Bahr el-Ghazal Dinka have much in common with the Bor east of the Nile in that their land was, for the most part, of poorer quality than those to their south. Thus, they needed to cultivate more land to survive and therefore fast geographic expansion was followed first by wars and then (as with the Bor) by a greater absorption of non-Dinka peoples than either the Padang or those of the southern Bahr el-Ghazal. Of the northern Bahr el-Ghazal Dinka the Malwal were the last to settle, although the Western Ngok to their north within the Padang group were, overall, the last major Dinka grouping to move into their present homeland. At this juncture the Dinka confederation formed a complete circle around the swamplands, today known as the *Sudd*, occupying a large region in the central heartlands of the Southern Sudan. Encapsulated within this large Dinka amalgam was a different ethnic but Western Nilotic culture, the Nuer. Throughout their migrations into the heartlands of Southern Sudan, soil types and access to water were paramount in choices of migration routes. Ultimately, therefore, it was the Dinka grain and cattle that influenced migrations in Southern Sudan and allowed this quickly expanding confederation to survive.

The Ascendancy of the Dinka in Southern Sudan

9

GRAIN, CATTLE, AND ECONOMIC POWER

"Land is very important to the Dinka; we slaughter gifts to our grandfathers and like to remain on the land of our ancestors."
Rek Dinka Victor Majok Amecrot and Matthew Mathem Daw

The greatest advantage possessed by the Dinka and their priests in their
quest for geographical, religious, and political sovereignty in Southern Sudan
was their economic advantage in the face of ecological turmoil. From the
fourteenth to the seventeenth centuries much of the Sudan was subjected
to intense periods of drought and famine. These weather patterns, perhaps
more than any other factor, changed the course of history in the precolonial
Southern Sudan. As the Dinka forged south into their new homelands they
carried with them new strains of grain crops, or *dhurra,* known today as
caudatum sorghum. It was not formerly grown in much of Southern Sudan
but, nevertheless, grew well in certain harsh environments. They also possessed a hardy variety of cattle which were capable of long distance migrations and of surviving severe droughts, which also, as yet had not been
introduced into Southern Sudan. Both of these items greatly facilitated
Dinka migrations, allowing them to move into various points of the South
in a relatively short period.[1]

Caudatum Sorghum

The Dinka have often been viewed merely as pastoralists. Grain agriculture, however, has always been very important to their livelihood and economy. Caudatum Sorghum agriculture is related to Nilotic folk movements, and by the year 1000 it was already grown in many parts of Africa in the savanna belt, stretching from the eastern shores of Lake Chad to southwestern Ethiopia. Of importance here is that this type of grain agriculture is drought resistant and produces well with very little care. Its limitation is that once used to a particular soil, the seeds of the grain do not travel well.

During their migrations into Southern Sudan the forefathers of the Dinka first settled in those territories whose soils were similar to their previous homelands in the Gezira and were thus also favorable to their crops. They specifically sought land rich in alluvial and lacustrine soils. Over time, they came to permanently reside in the region surrounding the vast Southern Sudanese swamp, one of the world's largest. Known today as the *Sudd,* it is located in the central heartlands of Southern Sudan. They avoided migrations far onto the Ironstone Plateau, which rings the far southern and western Sudan region, because these soils were not favorable to their particular crops. Further, the presence of tsetse fly and trypsanomiasis here killed their cattle.[2]

Archaeologists suggest that those agriculturalists and pastoralists formerly resident in the Southern Sudan prior to the Dinka arrival, particularly the Luel and the Luo, did not possess this hardy variety of *dhurra.* Oral histories support this assertion and suggest that in the face of serious droughts many former residents of Southern Sudan were forced to relocate southwards into the Great Lakes region and beyond. This included numerous agricultural and pastoral Luo communities who, for example, from 1382 to 1409, from 1436 to 1463, and from 1587 to 1652 (a period remembered as the "Great Famine" or the "Nyarubanga famine") migrated south into what is now the modern country of Uganda and points beyond (present-day Kenya and Tanzania). For those who did not migrate out of the Southern Sudan region during these droughts, the only option, if one's crops had withered, was to accept service among their incoming wealthier agro-pastoral neighbors;[3] in this case the Dinka.

The tendency of the Dinka to rely heavily on agriculture has existed for centuries. This is proven by the fact that a high percentage of Nilotic-speaking peoples, although they drink milk, are lactose malabsorbers. Thus these Nilotes could never rely too heavily on dairy products.[4]

For the most part, having planted their crops in their new home-lands, the Dinka were reluctant to move away from land they now considered their own. According to Rek Dinka Victor Majok Amecrot and Matthew Mathem Daw:

> Movement away from a compound only takes place if people die; in this instance a place is believed to be unhealthy. Further, if a region is infertile people will also move. Otherwise Dinka families often have two fields. We have "gor," this means fields that are far away . . . they are the fields of the young men. . . . The majority of Dinka depend on cultivation for food while wealth is represented by cattle and it is a condition for marriage . . . you must be a cultivator and have a house . . . without this you can be rejected.

In modern times the Dinka continue to place much importance in their agricultural activities.

Modern-Day Agricultural Practices

Present-day practices yield a window into the past and in modern times the Dinka continue (notwithstanding the modern-day civil war of 1983 to the present) to rely heavily on agriculture for their food supply. In Dinka culture both genders are involved in cultivation, and on big farms the women brew beer and everyone is involved. Prior to the civil war each household cultivated an average of two acres of sorghum around their homestead along with other crops.[5] It is estimated that 87% of total calories and 76% of protein by weight are provided by crop production compared with 13% of calories and 24% of protein derived from livestock produce. Today, 83% of all available labor is estimated to be employed in agricultural activities compared with only 17% in livestock husbandry.[6] In recent times, poor or cattleless Dinka have even farmed the land of their non-Dinka neighbors. According to Balanda Bandindi Pascal Uru: "The Dinka are good cultivators; they cultivate slowly but surely for hours. When the Dinka leave the business of cattle they take the hoe very seriously." Perhaps the most important reason to practice agriculture is that it is a means by which to acquire cattle.

Agriculture, Trade, and Cattle

Because of the variety of crops grown by all Southern Sudanese a lively intraregional trade has existed for a long time and many Dinka acquire cows in exchange for food items from their neighbors. For example, the

Eastern Luaic Dinka trade grain and fish to the Nuer for cows. Western Luaic Dinka Makuac Majok Mangeng states: "There are times when if you mobilize all members of the family you can acquire enough grain to sell. We sell grain for cattle, which is our medium of exchange."

Kec, the most favored of all sorghums grown by the Dinka, grows only in the Bahr el-Ghazal in the southern regions among the Ciec, Agar, Apak, and Gok. Hence, those sitting in *kec*-producing areas are the richest of all Dinka peoples. Agar Dinka Samuel Aru Bol stated: "The wealthiest people today are the Gok Dinka [who] are expanding faster than any other group because they have much land and good soils and sell much *kec* along with such items as tobacco."[7] Even more important is the connection of agriculture to marriage.

Agriculture, Economics and Marriage

In modern times the connection of agriculture and economics to Dinka marriage is important, yielding another possible sociocultural window to the past. Grain as well as cattle have been and continue to be used in both bartering and bridewealth payments. Wealth is acquired when a man and his family produce a small surplus of crops which they convert into a more stable and valuable resource, cattle. In turn, this enables a man to acquire more wives, more children, and thus more economic and political power.[8]

In Dinka society cattle acquired by the wealth yielded from agriculture are considered a more stable form of "property." If a Dinka man and woman divorce the cows given as bridewealth may be returned to the former husband. Rek Dinka Victor Majok Amecrot and Matthew Mathem Daw state, however, that those Dinka male members of a clan who possess animals bought with grain, rather than acquired by way of marriage payments, are more honored and given more respect because their wealth is perceived as being more stable. Thus: "this cattle is not returnable and does not have external links and cannot be taken back easily, for example, by divorce. It therefore represents 'pure property' derived from labor and this kind of man has much more stable wealth and is more honored. However, no one has all cattle that are free of ties." Because of the link between agriculture, wealth, and marriage the Dinka grow a wide variety of crops.

Crops Grown by the Dinka Today

Today the Dinka continue to practice considerable agriculture, which is critical to their economy. Along with sorghum they grow a variety of items including ground nuts, simsim, different types of beans, maize, tobacco, *mermedi,* pumpkin, okra, water melons, cassava, millet, and cow peas.[9] Sorghum, however, has always been the favored crop. The Arabic term for sorghum, *dhurra,* is today often interchanged with their own local names for the various types grown. For example, in Abyei, in northern Dinkaland, home to the Western Ngok Dinka, *ruth* is grown. The Rut Dinka east of the Nile grow *jak,* which survives best in desert areas. The Ciec Dinka west of the Nile in southern Dinkaland occupy very rich land and their sorghum, *kec,* the most favored among all Dinka, is grown. Further south in the Aliab country, *rapjiang,* also known as *nyithien,* is grown. The Pakam Dinka (north of the Agar in the Bahr el-Ghazal) also grow *rapjiang* while their Western Nilotic neighbors immediately to their north, the Nuer, are able to grow only short term varieties of sorghum. To the northwest the Rek Dinka also grow a variety known to them as *luel, anianjiang, jang, mahar,* and *aer.* Some in the south are also able to grow some *kec.* From the Rek Dinka country to the Western Ngok in the north the soil is much the same and *rapjiang* is grown by all in these regions. To the northeast of the Rek are the Western Twic, whose sorghum is known as *athial,* which has a short growing season because of flooding. In northwestern Dinkaland to the west of the Twic are the Malwal, who have less fertile soils and an even shorter growing season—here *anyan* and *jiong* are grown. In the Bor Dinka territory, east of the Nile, the Dinka claim to have red Indian *dhurra* corn. According to Nyarruweng Dinka Lazarus Leek Mawut:

> The Nuer corn is the same as ours. This type of *dhurra* came from Ethiopia or India. In addition there is white and yellow *dhurra.* White dhurra is the fast growing and then there is the yellow which takes longer. . . . We don't have the long growing *dhurra* because our soil is mixed. We have deeper clay soil and sandy soil in the Duk area and this is the same as that of the Twic to the south. The Bor [Dinka] have poorer soils which do not produce well. The Twic, Ghol, and Nyarruweng land is good for *dhurra* cultivation.

All of the sorghum grains mentioned above have one thing in common however: once planted in a particular soil they do not travel well.

Thus, centuries ago, the introduction by the Dinka of caudatum sorghum into Southern Sudan gave them an economic edge against other resident communities who were suffering from drought. However, they possessed yet another valuable resource as they migrated into Southern Sudan. Cattle may have been even more historically important for Dinka migrations, for they provided the initial mechanism for movement out of the central Sudan.

Hump-Backed Cattle: The Next Best Thing to a Camel

As mentioned previously, prior to the year 1000 people throughout the Sudan region were limited to short-distance migrations because their cattle could not withstand long-distance travel.[10] After this period, however, the Sudanese in the Gezira, including the Western Nilotic Dinka, acquired Sanga and Zebu hump-backed cattle from the Ethiopia borderlands and moved south. Hump-backed cattle were considerably stronger than the resident breeds in Southern Sudan and capable of long-distance transhumance patterns. Even more important, they were less affected by drought. The Western Nilotic Luo, who predated the Dinka in their migrations into Southern Sudan, did not possess these cattle, for this breed was introduced into Southern Sudan only four to five hundred years ago, which correlates with the approximate time when the Dinka migrated into this territory.

Conversely, archaeology suggests that the previous settlers (the Luel, Luo, and Turkwel cultures) of what later became Dinka territory herded a humpless breed of cattle that was more vulnerable to droughts.[11] Thus, Luo oral histories recount their mass migrations out of the Southern Sudan towards the Great Lakes during the years of the "Great Famine."

The long series of droughts that plagued Southern Sudan during this time period intensified the reliance on cattle for all concerned, since livestock are indispensable in bad years when crop failure occurs. The introduction by the Dinka of this new breed was a significant causative factor in the spread of modern patterns of Nilotic pastoralism in Southern Sudan. Eventually these cattle replaced all of the humpless varieties. Ultimately the domestication of caudatum sorghum grain along with the hardier breeds of cattle introduced into this region of Southern Sudan an economic system of the greatest efficiency in Sudan and East Africa. These integrated systems were able to support population increases in the Bahr el-Ghazal and later expansions towards the west.[12]

Conclusion

On entering the Southern Sudan the Dinka possessed economic and technological advantages not known to those then residing within the region. When the Dinka acquired hump-backed cattle they possessed the much needed mechanism to flee the instability of their former homelands in Central Sudan. These cattle, unlike the non-humped variety, could withstand the strain of long-distance migrations. Further, archaeology supports the view that the Dinka introduced this hardy variety of cattle into Southern Sudan, for these animals have been in the region for only approximately four to five hundred years. Over time they replaced all other humpless varieties. This was important in light of the series of droughts in the region from the fourteenth to the seventeenth centuries. Furthermore, the Dinka food supplies were bolstered by possession of a particularly hardy form of grain agriculture, caudatum sorghum, which they discovered would grow well in harsh conditions and droughts and which previously they harvested in their former northern homelands. The domestication of caudatum sorghum grain coupled with ownership of well adapted breeds of hump-backed cattle created an economy far more efficient than any other in Sudan or East Africa. In turn, this greatly enhanced Dinka migrations into much of Southern Sudan, giving them a military and political edge over all other communities in the region. Further, this wealth, combined with the religions of nature aided the Dinka on their travels.

TOTEMIC RELIGION

"Earth always had people but we descended in a boat to earth (my clan believes) at Patundur, which is where the Twic started to fission."
Atem Garang Deng and Deng Kuek Atem, Eastern Twic Dinka

"Totems are most powerful and created by the creator for our protection. All clans have some symbols of protection and power."
Bona Acuil, Rek Dinka

Today, as in historical times, all Southern Sudanese are highly religious, practicing simultaneously their ancient religions alongside newly acquired Christianity, and to a far lesser degree, Islam. One of the most important aspects of Dinka cosmology is observance of totems. This aspect of their religion is only one in a pantheon of ideas about the world of nature around them. The most powerful Dinka spirit in their belief system is that of "Deng," who was once a great living leader. Col Mayen Kur states:

> We came with our god, Deng, and also Garang and a stone called Kur, these were our gods. This Deng is the god of all of the Dinkas. Christianity and Islam differ from the Dinka in that when we go to our god, Deng, we kill a bull or a goat for him but when you pray to Christ or Muhammad, you pray without killing anything. When there is drought we ask Deng to make rain

98

and it will fall. Christianity and Islam do not make rain fall. We can go to Deng and ask him to stop rain from falling. . . . There is a stage where if there is too much rain, the grain will get spoiled. Our own religion heals people. Deng is more powerful for curing cows than Western doctors. We bring out a ram, we kill it and ask Deng to cure our cows.

Most prominent in Dinka oral migration, histories, however, is the observance of clan totems along with the acquisition of new ones along the way as symbols of protection.

Totemism

Within the Dinka culture and history totems are very important. These Dinka "symbols of protection" aided in wars against hostile neighbors, cured the sick, and protected the people from the elements. Ultimately some totems could also bring great wealth.

In scholarly terms, totemic consciousness among peoples and the processes that give rise to it have occurred widely in precapitalist Africa and there are a number of theories explaining, in more specific terms, the place of totems in these societies. David Conrad suggests that "totem" as a term often refers to an animal or plant that is regarded as the protector of a particular clan, lineage, or branch thereof. These beliefs are supported by legends telling how the animal or tree, for instance, once saved the life of an ancestor or performed some other critical service. Hence, the ancestors' descendants are forbidden to kill that creature or plant which is the totem of their clan. Similarly, Radcliffe Brown suggests that animals and plants are used as totems not merely because they are symbols of social groups but that the relationship of the aborigines to their environment is a special one, conditioned by their dependence on the hunting of wild animals and collections of wild plants. Hence, the acquisition of a totem is connected with the relationship to a particular environment.

There has been some confusion on the part of Western scholars in regard to understanding the meaning of totems in regard to Dinka cosmology. According to Nyarruweng Lazarus Leek Mawut: "Totems are separate from divinity, but are representative of a particular concept, for example, the python, cobra, lion, and rain. These are 'divinity' represented by a totem, but we worship the spirit *within* the snake. The missionaries tried to put it the other way around." Rek Dinka Bona Acuil explains the meaning of totems in the Dinka culture in even simpler terms: "Totems, as you refer to them, are symbols of protection and all [Dinka] clans have some symbols of protection and power." Totems could also take on special meaning when people migrated into different ecological zones.

Totems and Migrations

Peter Freuchen observed that when the Greenland Eskimos migrated into strange new environments that required different technologies they tended to acquire new totems. Similarly, the observance of totems from the old homelands along with the acquisition of new ones aided the Dinka in their migrations and constant struggles against hostile peoples and the environment. For example, almost all Dinka sections revere snakes that prevail in much of both Southern and Central Sudan. Ruweng Dinka John Biem Ngok Bilkuai states: "The foreign environment encouraged the observance of clan totems. We don't remember how totems were chosen but it must have been fear. If you make it your god it will not attack you and be peaceful. If you make friends with snakes they will not attack people." The Abyor section of the Western Ngok Dinka revere *nyiel* (the python), *koor* (the lion), and *ring,* a small thin red snake that "only appears if you believe in it." An adjacent section, the Bongo, revere *bok* (a snake). Other Dinka clan groups revere *biar/magak* (the cobra) and *anyak* (the viper), as well as small animals such as *gong* (a porcupine) and *nyang* (the crocodile). Many sections have *koor* (lions), *akohn* (the elephant), and *kwac* (the leopard) as totems. Rek Dinka Mel Anyar Aduol claims that these animals can neither be eaten nor killed, for "if you eat hippopotami it will poison you; you will start to crack."[1]

Many Dinka keep wild animals and snakes as pets. For example, Gok-Toc Dinka Lual Wuol Nhiak's totem is *Agany,* the alligator. Western Luaic Dinka Makuac Majok Mangeng states that during drought some Dinka groups go singing and dancing to *biar/magak* (the cobra), which is housed in the *luak* (a large structure for keeping milking cows) of a prominent individual in the village; in so doing the cobra will "play among the people, for it responds to the music." Then a bull is brought out and killed and cooked. Then sometimes rain falls immediately or later. Rek Dinka Mel Anyar Aduol claims "if you . . . select a cow or goat and give it to your totem it will protect you from disease and bad luck." Hence, the Dinka offer milk to snakes and crocodiles in the hopes that these creatures will remain in their houses to protect them, a practice they claim to have observed for centuries. According to Rek Dinka Bona Acuil: "The Pathian people do not kill certain snakes. We feed them milk and they stay in the *luak* when people pray. The name of our symbol of protection is a snake called *athian*. When people were created our protection was these snakes; they killed other people and protected us and other snakes kept away."

Totems serve as medical helpers in Dinka society. For example, women will sacrifice animals to their totem if they are failing to have children. Bona Acuil states: "One man was crippled for a year and when he put the *athian* (snake) on his lap, after a day he could walk. The snake cured him. I saw it with my own eyes!" Totems also play an important role in protection during conflicts with hostile neighbors.[2]

Dinka Totems—Protection in Wars

In Dinka society new totems came to provide protection against hostile neighbors throughout their long perilous journeys into Southern Sudan. According to Makuac Majok Mangeng the western Luaic Dinka also claim that *mac* (fire) is an important totem. It was "inherited from the great-great-grandfathers" and is also important in wars. Undoubtedly, however, *mac* has been revered from earliest times in a former homeland. Certain Malwal Dinka clan sections revere a star, *Ciir* (Venus), which provided illumination for their ancestor, Makuac Athian, when he migrated into what is now the northwest Bahr el-Ghazal region. Today *Ciir* is a Malwal totem. The Western Ngok say that one of their totems is the spirit of Acai, the daughter of a prominent priest reputedly sacrificed to the river Nile during the early migrations of the Dinka.[3]

Among the Bor-Atoc another war totem, *Mangok,* comes from a piece of wood derived from a tree growing in the Agar Dinka territory. Abdulla Ayom Kuany states: "When we are going to fight any section, we go to this totem. A bull is killed and we ask the totem 'we are going to fight section x or y.' If the totem gives us a green light we know we are going to defeat these people. But if it says 'no' we suspend the battle."

The Bor-Gok Dinka today revere *Bar,* an ancient drum three meters long and three quarters of a meter high, which, thirteen generations ago, came floating down the Nile river from what is now Juba. Drums have historically been a means by which the Dinka communicate, particular during war, and today *Bar* is considered sacred as a war totem. The Dinka claim a stick came attached to this drum and that "it can beat itself alone; the stick will move and beat the drum" and that it has been reputed to "talk within the wall of a house." Further, when *Bar* is transported from one place to another "it shakes people to and fro." Bulls are sacrificed to this drum and Bor-Gok Dinka Johnson Kuol Kur asserts that before war one must "kill a bull by night, which is eaten by night. If there is any left it should be hidden so that the sun does not get to it. The meat is finished the next night and then the men go to war." Today *Bar* is owned by two clan sections, the Koc and Atet, who are "brothers," and recently it "resided" in the house of a man, Kwol Atiel. The Bor-Gok also possess a spear which protects and provides wealth.[4]

Sacred Spears: "Lierpiou," and the Mahdi's War Spears

One spear among the Bor-Gok Dinka is believed to have more power than all totems combined, the sacred spear of Lierpiou. According to Bor-Gok Dinka Deng Acuoth, a descendant of the family who originally possessed the spear:

> When the people migrated from the South we moved to the west of Terkaka in the Mundari area to a place called Karcum in the Gualla region on the eastern bank of the Nile. This spear Lierpiou was the sacred spear of [a man called] Ajak. Ajak was accompanied by his Mundari wife and when he settled he married a Dinka woman, Adic. The first wife, Nyariang, gave birth to a son called Rith, who was born blind. Then all her subsequent children died. Ajak's second wife gave birth to Kut. He was perfect.
>
> Convinced that it was Ajak's spear that killed her children and angry with it, Nyariang disposed of it in the forest. Adic, however, believed the spear was a symbol of good power, retrieved it and escaped with it into the bush, fearing the wrath of the first wife. . . . When a Dinka man passed by she begged him for water. He obliged her and she told him her story. She was alone with the spear and her son Kut.
>
> Soon thereafter she moved to a place called Angakuei. In the meantime her husband remained with his first wife. Some people, however, decided to follow her and this is how the two groups of people divided. When she [Adic] migrated with the spear she arrived on the eastern side of Angakuei village and went to buy a bull. As time passed this spear became special and Adic became rich as people went to "Lierpiou" to get healed and to beg for rain. The spear sometimes spoke through people, spoke alone, and would periodically bend of its own accord. People discovered that if they wanted to acquire property they could walk around with the spear to collect cows and goats.
>
> One day the Gualla people got word of this spear and Ajak, the original owner, desired to reacquire it. He approached the Angakuei town by the western side and went to Adic's house. He then stole the spear by cutting a hole into her back wall behind her dwelling. He then returned to his own village via the western side of Angakuei. After he had returned home to

Karcum he sent word to Adic stating, "We have the spear. You can try and steal it back and when you take it we will not prevent you. But let us agree to share it every four years." So Adic stole it the same way four years later. The stealing of Lierpiou has become ritualized over the centuries and every four years when the Angakuei people want it they go east. When the Gualla people want the spear they go west.[5]

By the time of the British colonial rule in Southern Sudan, Adic, the second wife of Ajak, was recognized as the ancestral mother of all of the Abuor people in Angakuei. This era, however, still witnessed tensions between Adic's descendants and the descendants of Ajak and his first wife, Nyariang, known today as the Gualla. Around 1945 Lierpiou was implicated in the death of a paramount chief, Joseph Maciek, by the descendants of Nyariang. Bor-Gok Dinka Wuut Mac and Wec Col (Bor-Gok) state: "This spear was suspected of masterminding the chief's killing and was taken to Khartoum and put in detention in 1945. In 1973 President Nimeiri gave it amnesty and returned it to the Bor Gok people."

Today, Lierpiou reputedly still has powers. Bor Gok Dinka Wuut Mac and Wec Col claim that when both the spear and its scabbard are placed individually on a wall, the former will put itself into the latter independently: "it fits itself together by itself." If the spear is transferred from place to place the spear may refuse to move. If people are moving and Lierpiou wants to rest it will suddenly stop so that the people have to rest. The metal part of Lierpiou is one half meter of white iron and it is two meters long (seven to eight feet) and according to Bor-Gok Dinka, Johnson Kuol Kur, Lierpiou is now a totem for war and for peace: "Whatever you want, Lierpiou will bring it to you. I saw it and gave it a cow. It is a spear one half a meter long and it is flexible. If you touch it and injure it, it will bleed blood. If it is transported it can refuse because the scabbard and spear are kept separately and if it does not want to move, it refuses to fit the scabbard. Once the spear moved itself into the scabbard. It will make a sound like a thunder storm and people will be unconscious for some time. It can glitter and shine."

In recent times Lierpiou "sits" in the house of a woman, Aguet Deng Nyok, whose duty it is to clean the house and be responsible for the upkeep of the spear. An American, Reverend Marc Nikkel, claims that after the 1994 Bor Massacre by the Nuer, Lierpiou was destroyed when a Dinka evangelist had it beaten publicly and broken into four pieces and then put in a well, never to be retrieved. Nikkel stated the Dinka wanted to destroy its power as it no longer served the people.[6] On the other hand, Dinka I interviewed in 1996 still believed it thrived.

Other sacred spears have come into existence: some evolved in the colonial period when the Malwal and other Dinka made agreements with the Northern Sudanese holyman, the Mahdi, in the early 1880s. Lawrence Lual Lual Akuey states: "The Mahdi gave us Dinka war spears. They were holy . . . and we were told that when we wanted to fight the enemy with these spears they would be conquered. . . . All the Dinka representatives came back [from the Nuba Mountains and] these spears became famous later among the Malwal as totems. We kept them in the *luak* because they were sacred and the people held great reverence for them. We have one at home now in our *luak*. You can never point this spear at people or they will die." Along with their symbolic importance for war, totems have also become important for coping with extreme weather conditions.

Veneration and Protection Against Extreme Weather

Much like the Eskimos of Greenland and their acquisition of new totems as they moved into new homelands, the Dinka have also acquired totems to aid with unpredictable weather patterns. According to Mom Kou Nhial Arou the Bor Atoc Dinka revere a divinity, *Reo,* a tornado. "Once a year people come home to celebrate its existence at a feast called the 'Reo celebration' where every daughter has a bull for *Reo.*"

During droughts the Ciec Dinka also pray to a totem, "Kajok Mit Mabor Ayual." Today bulls are sacrificed, the people dance and pray for rain, and this totem may appear in the physical form of a spirit of a ram grazing at the ponds during a rainbow or as lightning. Today, when the rain falls and the crops have grown successfully, the seeds of the harvest are taken to the *luak* of a prominent priest where a celebration occurs as a thanksgiving for the rain. Totems also represent a respect for nature, in and of itself.[7]

The Veneration of Trees and Plants

To many Dinka certain trees and forests are sacred; within these regions no Dinka may cut the trees. For example, Gok-Toc Dinka Deng Nhial Diek and Agar Dinka Paul Macuer Malok state that the large sacred tree, *Rual,* is a totem. "It is a nice shape and is believed to be strongly spiritually powerful and assumed to be inhabited by Gods." Comboni Missionary Father Mattia, who presently works in the Rek country, states that a sacred tree of the Rek Dinka, *Kou,* grows in the forest. "They put beautifully carved sticks near the tree poles to make their sacrifices and we put a stick on top to make another alta for mass. Those that have converted to Christianity also put crosses on the tree."

Trees are also considered to "give birth" to people. According to Malwal Dinka Lawrence Lual Lual Akuey, the sacred tree *Rual* possesses a spirit:

> My great-great-grandfather is said to have been found in the hub of this [*Rual*] tree in the forest where no people live in the dry season, only insects (*kom*). He was therefore considered to be very holy and named Mayual Cikom because the people believed he had been an insect which formed into a human being and that his father was the sacred tree, *Rual.* When he was old he left the people and said "I'm going away" and he disappeared into the forest and was never seen again. This was eleven generations ago. I'm a direct descendant. All of this took place in the east on the borders of Ethiopia before we crossed to the west.

Trees have become sacred as objects for remembering history. Bona Acuil states: "To remember our history we used to have sacred sticks in our house . . . made from a tree called *Akoc* (a nihyalich tree and very sacred). We never burn this tree but just put it in the sun to dry; each notch in the tree represents an historical event and this is passed on down the generations." Among the Rek Dinka, there is also a certain type of grass, *ariec,* which is sacred and never burned but rather brooms are made out of it.[8]

Thus, nature is venerated and represented by totem plants. Birds also have a special place in Dinka religious culture.

Birds as Totems and Messengers

According to Agar Dinka Michael Manyiel Col most people in his home region possess bird totems, in this case the *Akuei,* the eagle: "We believe we have a connection with the eagle which is a powerful bird. The people of Kuei founded Rumbek. They were very martial . . . and good fighters." Even in modern times, birds are considered sacred and one Eastern Twic Dinka states: "Birds are considered messengers. In 1986 we were in Kapoeta [during the present-day second civil war] and we heard of lot of them chirping. We considered this as a warning of the enemy. If a bird flies to the trees and then flies back from where it has come, we believe it will repel the enemy. If it flies into the trees and then keeps going in the same direction, we know we will lose the battle. If you are in the forest and there is no water and you hear birds it means there is water in the forest."

The Dinka also call on other religious phenomena to aid them for protection.

Spirit Helpers

Within Dinka cosmology there are also spirits known as *jak* (singular *jok*), which are not related to specific clans but can be acquired from those possessing them to be adopted, tamed, and used for good. For example, Agar Dinka Gordon Muortat Mayen states: "If we want to go to war we call on 'Mayual,' our spirit, to protect us. He's a minor spirit and a war god and used by the special people [priests] who lead us and this is inherited by the ancestors. He is called upon when war is approaching to bless us. When our clan fights and is blessed with Mayual we will succeed. . . . No other section of the Agar Dinka have Mayual as a spiritual presence."

As in other cultures, the Dinka practice a form of astrology. According to Eastern Twic Dinka Atem Garang Deng and Deng Kuek Atem:

> The Dinka name the stars—for example, "Orion" is called "Wathal Jook." Orion is a hunter in Greek mythology but Wathal Jook (dogs) are hunters also. The constellation of the scorpion, in Dinka, is called *Cuur,* which is a type of fish that looks like a scorpion. We believe these mythologies may connect us with others in the east. In our religion the mythology of Ayueldit recounts he was looking for external life and said "the son is eternal." So they looked for the food of the sun and sent his messengers west cautioning them "go where the sun is every evening."

Also within the Dinka culture the dead often visit their living relatives in dreams. A visit from an ancestor can presage sickness because the latter is angry. On the other hand, if one becomes sick and is visited by an ancestor the next day the person will become well. Sometimes, a visitation from an ancestor is followed by the acquisition of a fortune.[9]

Conclusion

In the course of their migrations, the Dinka were forced to come to terms with new and very hostile environments, unpredictable weather conditions and dangerous animals and snakes. In so doing they drew on their religious beliefs to facilitate safe movement and settlement into these strange new homelands. They possessed specific totems to preside over them during migrations. To protect and heal the people when diseased they relied on snakes. For defense in war they used *mac* (fire) and various drums. In some cases totem objects have provided great wealth, such as the sacred spear of the Bor-Gok, "Lierpiou." Today as in the past, totems, which can comprise animals, plants, trees, spirits of ancestors, spears, drums, and other objects are regarded by the Dinka as protectors of a particular clan, lineage, or branch thereof. Beyond totems, the Dinka also came to rely on other key aspects of their religion to protect them during their travels, including human sacrifice.

11

HUMAN SACRIFICE, VIRGINS, AND RIVER SPIRITS

"For the Dinka there is a pride for those who offer their daughter. . . .
Only prominent priests can offer women for sacrifice."

Bona Acuil, Rek Dinka

Along with totems, the Nilotic Dinka relied heavily on other aspects of
their religion as they migrated south into uncertain lands, particularly the
practice of human sacrifice. There are a number of theories concerning
religion and human sacrifice in Africa today. C. G. Seligman, A. J. Arkell,
and Timothy Kendall point to the practice of human sacrifice among the
Nilotes of Southern Sudan and suggest that these modern-day societies
represent, in the ethnographic present, socioreligious cultures of the ancient Nile kingdoms of central Sudan. Even Nubian Sudanese archaeolo-
gist Ali Osman told me in 1998 in Boston, "as far as I am concerned the
Dinka are all Meroites," suggesting a close association with the ancient
Nile kingdom of Meroe. Further, other scholars hold that there is an essen-
tial similarity in the religious institutions of many sub-Saharan monarchies
and that these institutions diffused westwards and southwards from Egypt,
the eastern Sudan, and adjacent areas. Jan Vansina disagrees with many of
the arguments above, however, and suggests that religions do not recreate
themselves as blue prints when cultures move away from a religious center

to a periphery. Rather, over time they absorb other societies and religions.[1] In this chapter I will explore the validity of the arguments above to discover whether some aspects of religious practices of the ancient central Sudanese Nile Kingdoms appear to have been transported culturally by the Dinka in their migrations from central to Southern Sudan.

Religious Practices of Ancient Nile Kingdoms and Western Nilotes

Among the causes of human sacrifice in world history have been population control, meat hunger, state terrorism, and religious rites. Marvin Harris suggests that human sacrifice was a practice closely connected to early state formation as new rulers consolidated control over their emerging kingdoms.

King-Killing

Both ancient Egypt and the southern Empire of Meroe (in what is now Sudan) observed the custom of king-killing wherein divine kings or godmen were ritually killed when their bodies showed premature signs of weakness or old age. Similarly, further south along the Blue Nile, king-killing was one special instance of a general feature of pre-Islamic ideology in the medieval sultanate of Sinnar.[2]

Historically as well as in the present day, many Dinka also believe that prominent priests, *beny biths* (spearmasters), should never die a natural death. Should this event occur their royal powers would not pass to their successors, and a great disaster would fall upon the people. Thus, the Dinka have put their priests to death "before their bodily vigors have passed away."[3]

Dinka oral histories contain legends of the premature death of their great culture hero, Aiwel (or Ayuel) Longar, the reputed ancestor of the Ric, Dwor, Nyarruweng, Rut, and Thoi Dinka, who died by live burial. One history, collected by British District Commissioner P. P. Howell, recounts that the moon took her fishing spear and, when she was within striking distance, thrust and skewered Aiwel to the ground through the crown of his head and his body. Aiwel was not killed and retained the power of speech and bid his people to remove the spear but they could not. He then bid them dig the ground under him but water rose where they dug and they could not remove the spear. Then Aiwel's sister addressed the people and told them that "it was no good doing anything more as he was bound to die" and with that, they piled earth over him forming a mound.

Out of the top of the mound stuck the man's spear. To complete the job they took Aiwel's drinking vessel and clapped it over the top of the mound. This pyramid exists today, with a spear protruding from its peak, and is now a spirit center situated at an old village site called *Pwom,* which is located between Paw and Tithbel inland from the Nile river. Howell, however, estimated it was built only in the early nineteenth century, a date too late to correlate with Dinka migrations. It stands about thirty feet high, but was obviously much higher in its original form. To one side is the reputed grave of Ayuel (or Aiwel) Longar.[4]

Another legend of the killing of Aiwel is recounted, mythically, by Eastern Twic Dinka Atem Garang Deng and Deng Kuek Atem:

> Aiwel Dit was looking for eternal life and said "the son is eternal." So they looked for the food of the sun and sent his messengers west cautioning them "go where the sun is every evening." After a long time they found the hiding place of the sun, said to be a sea without end. An old woman was sitting there serving the sun. The woman asked the messengers "what do you want?" They replied "we are looking for the food of the sun." She told them that everyone was looking for it. She gave them some food and they ate it but later the sun discovered some of his food was missing. So now the sun was looking for Aiwel Dit [Aiwel the Great]. When the messengers came they told Aiwel Dit to not go out into the sun. The sun was looking for him for centuries but finally the sun consulted the moon which had no light. The sun told the moon, "if you can find Aiwel Dit I will give you light." The moon said he is at his house every evening and I will kill him for us. So he was killed by the moon. So Aiwel had to die.

What is apparent in the above myth is that Aiwel is believed to have died a premature death and that his life had to end because of a higher cosmic responsibility.

Live Burials

But beyond myths, a more fundamental similarity exists between Dinka "king-killing" and that practiced centuries ago in central Sudan. Archaeological findings of the ancient Nile kingdom of Kerma, which date to about 1500 B.C.E, recovered one of the largest tombs in African history. Here, four hundred people were sacrificed by being buried alive with the monarch. The king lay in his grave on a bed, lying on his right side with the legs slightly bent at the knees, the right hand under his cheek, and the left hand on or near the right elbow. Many other bodies in this grave lay with their heads to the east.[5] There is an uncanny resemblance here with modern-day burial practices of the majority of Western Dinka priests who are also placed lying down in the exact same manner, often facing east. In this instance, when the priest declares he is ready to die he is given an *athiak pir*, a live burial. Rek Dinka Bona Acuil explains a modern-day live burial:

> The elders come out of the house after the priest has informed them he wants to be buried. The elders then instruct the young ones to beat the drums, which they do and the women start dancing and singing. The priest . . . is still in the house but nothing about the burial is said to anyone. Six people are selected by the *beny bith* [priest] to go and dig the grave. They dig a deep rectangle and then dig off to the side and create a burial chamber. Before he is buried people line up, both men and women, forming two lines from his house to the *luak* [large covered dwelling place where the milking cows are kept]. Then he is carried through the middle of this line of two rows of people on his *yaak* [sleeping mat] without the people seeing him. From there he is carried directly to the grave. The *yaak* is made out of special grass near the *toic* [grasslands]. The priest is usually carried on a chosen *yaak* and buried lying on it. He is also buried with a spear. Usually the oldest in the family covers him with leopard skins. The dancing then starts and everyone knows that the chief has been put in his grave alive but no one talks about it. The grave is dug in the direction of the east so that his head is facing towards the east. After they have filled in the grave they announce it and then everyone tells stories of his life.

The early twentieth-century anthropologists C. G. and Brenda Z. Seligman noted other burial details similar to the above account by adding that when Dinka priests are lowered into their graves they lie there for some time speaking to the people, recalling their past history and instructing them how to behave in the future. Towards the end of the day, when the priest has finished talking, he bids the elders cover him up by raising a spear. Earth is thrown into the grave and he is soon suffocated.[6]

Another version of the ceremony leading up to a live burial in the mid-twentieth century is given by British administrator G. W. Titherington, who wrote that among the Rek Dinka of western Bahr el-Ghazal, when a man who has "this right" is very old and his senses fail he feels death is near but is ashamed to die like a sick cow. Thus, he calls his sons around him and explains his wishes and makes them promise to carry them out. The news is sent around and parties come from all the clans to say farewell, bringing bulls and goats to slaughter at the funeral feast. A vast grave is dug in the priest's big cattle house (*mak* or *luak*) and at the bottom is tethered his favorite ox. At the other end of the grave the man is laid out on a sleeping skin with a pillow under his head, another under his feet, and a second skin placed over him to prevent earth falling into his eyes or ears. He is given a gourd of milk and a spear and then a stage is built across the grave and covered with grass. Dancing, singing, and drumming continues all night and the next day around the *mak/luak*. In the meantime someone watches the grave. If the priest pushes up the spear the earth is immediately filled in but if he does not the earth is filled in on the tenth day by which time he is dead. The ox generally dies in eight days. At a later date earth is taken from the grave and used to make the horned bull shaped tomb (*yik*) of the deceased.[7]

In Northern Sudan archaeological findings at ancient Kerma have revealed that many graves contained one or two sacrificed retainers. A parallel exists among the Dinka of modern times. According to Bor-Atoc Dinka Mom Kou Nhial Arou, prior to the British period (1898), the youngest wife of a priest was also sacrificed: "When the chief was about to die his favorite wife was buried with him along with a servant and a number of his precious belongings. The young wife was caught and her hands and feet were tied." According to a Western Ngok Bongo Dinka, Abyei Kon: "I was told that some people may voluntarily be buried with the chief so that when you die you accompany the spirit of the chief. But in the olden days it was voluntary. The Ngok did not do this but I heard that other Dinka groups would do this. In those days the people believed you would live somewhere else." Supporting this assertion British administrator Titherington also noted that periodically a young male was also buried along with a priest.[8]

In Northern Sudan ancient kings in Kerma and the Nile kingdom of Meroe were buried in L-shaped burial chambers. Similarly today the Dinka bury their priests in L-shaped graves with a burial chamber to the side. A skin is sometimes hung as a curtain, placed between the chamber and the main funnel of the grave so that soil does not get into the priest's eyes.[9] Thus, a partial correlation exists between the live burials of the ancient Nile kingdom of Kerma and modern-day religious practices of the Dinka. In Ethiopia, once also a temporary home to the Dinka who migrated out of the Gezira following the Blue Nile, there is also historical evidence of Nilotic human sacrifice.

Nilotic Regicide on the Borders of Ethiopia

Evidence exists of an ancient Nilotic presence in the Bela Shangul region in present-day Ethiopia, and this area still contains strong cultural influences from the Dinka as well as their close Western Nilotic cousins, the Shilluk. Historian A. Triulzi states that ceremonial regicide is the best example of such ritual syncretism and cultural miscegenation. E. E. Evans-Pritchard also reported an isolated tradition of ritual killing of rain-makers in the same region among the Bertha adjacent to the Beni Shangul region. It was a custom said to have existed in Fazogli, the successor state of Alwa, up until 1838, and may have been a Dinka-derived custom.[10] It is not only the Dinka among the Nilotes, however, who practice king-killing and human sacrifice, for their close neighbors, the Shilluk of the White Nile and the Luo of the western Bahr el-Ghazal, have observed similar religious rites.

King-Killing Among Other Nilotic Groups in Southern Sudan

The Shilluk also practiced human sacrifice of kings until recently. Shilluk kings were either strangled, clubbed to death, or walled up in their houses until they died. In the latter case, it was an old custom of king-killing that dictated that the Shilluk king, the *Reth,* prior to his death, would take one nubile maiden or possibly two to a specially built hut, the opening of which was then walled up. The inmates were left without water or food and died of suffocation and/or starvation. By the 1950s, however, king-killing among the Shilluk was said to have been given up some five generations ago. On other occasions, the *Reth* was killed by a spear or a club at the hands of his opponent or a pretender to the throne. In yet other instances a member of the non-royal Ororo clan was selected to kill the king; in this case, the *Reth* was taken to his hut and strangled. Following the death of a king further human sacrifices sometimes followed.[11]

The Western Nilotic Luo also possess divine kingship with sacrificial practices similar to those of the Dinka and the Shilluk. Their culture hero is Dimo, brother to Nyikango of the Shilluk. Among the Luo, great importance was attached to Dimo's spear, said to be in possession of the Wad el Maks (special prominent priests). They carried this spear, believed to have been inherited from Dimo, with them in their long wanderings throughout the Southern Sudan to their present homeland, southwest of the Dinka. Historically, when a chief was seriously ill and it was feared death would ensue, elderly relatives and counsellors were summoned by him to his own death bed. After a ritual address, in which he invited these men to help his soul to pass away in a manly fashion, they broke his limbs and then suffocated him. Afterwards his wives mummified the corpse by smoking it with a slow fire. At the earliest opportunity the dead Luo chief's body was carried to the burial ground of his forefathers. Along with the priest's corpse, which was placed in a skin bag, a bull and two "slaves" were likewise killed, representing a royal sacrifice to Dimo's spirit. These human offerings were placed under the dead chief's head as a royal pillow.[12]

Finally, the eastern neighbors of the northern Padang Dinka, the Burun, who live in the Gezira, also reputedly practiced live burials at one time. Today they are linguistically classified by some scholars as Nilotes and by others as "pre-Nilotes," a culture predating the Western Nilotic presence in the Gezira. This historical practice, however, suggests that this custom has existed for centuries in the central geographical region of Sudan, whence the Western Nilotic people most likely acquired it.[13] Along with human sacrifice other cultural practices from the central and northern Sudan have parallels with those of the Western Nilotes of the modern-day Southern Sudan—for example, the construction of pyramids.

Pyramids

Another correlation exists between the pyramids of prominent Egyptian and central Sudanese kings and revered Dinka priests. In Dinkaland there exist a number of mounds, described by the Dinka as "pyramids," which have religious significance to those who tend them. These mounds were built in the form of a cone and the material used was cattle ashes, cattle dung, cotton soil, clay, and debris. In all cases the history of the origin of each mound is connected to a prominent Dinka priest who ordered its construction by the people as a monument to his name. Other oral histories suggest that they are the tombs of the men who were buried in or alongside them, often alive.

The Pyramid of "Yik Ayuong"

In Padang territory in northern Dinkaland east of the Nile among the Dunghol Dinka and north of the modern-day town of Malakal, the pyramid of a great ancestor and prominent priest, Ayuong Dit, is located at the holy village of Rukcuk. It was constructed on the site of this priest's *luak*. The mound was built over the body of this priest who, with his wife and eight bulls, was locked up in their cattle byre by his express orders. District Commissioner Ibrahim Bedri who served during the British colonial period noted that this pyramid was seventy-five paces in circumference and twenty-six paces along the slope. During the harvest season of each year it was cleared of grass, more earth was added to it, and the surface smoothed by women who made stripes along the pyramid with large quantities of *dhurra* (flour). This was in preparation for the annual ceremony *yairunka baiet,* which took place at the pyramid. During the celebrations the people gathered together for communal offerings to the spirit of Ayuong Dit and a "new fire" ceremony was performed in which eight bulls were sacrificed to bring fertility to the women. Today this mound is known as *Yik Ayuong.*[14]

The Pyramid of "Pwom Ayuel" (or Aiwel)

Another pyramid, *Pwom Ayuel,* is reputedly the burial place of Ayuel, the culture hero of the Dinka (and referred to earlier in this chapter). It is situated in what has now become Nuerland on the southern part of an island formed by the Bahr el-Zeraf and Bahr el-Jebel Rivers. As recounted earlier in this chapter, some Dinka myths suggest that Ayuel was killed by external forces beyond his control. Aliab Dinka Parmena Awerial Aluong, however, recounts an oral history (similar to that collected by Howell) suggesting that the mound was built on the orders of Ayuel Longar himself. According to historical accounts there were many years of toil in the early days during which Ayuel, who had reached the Nile and Sobat Rivers, ordered his people to construct a large monument. Some people died in the building of this structure, their bodies adding to the rising edifice. Other versions of the building of *Pwom Ayuel* recount that human bodies were used as props in the scaffolding: the persons chosen for this "honor" were buried alive. Some Dinka even say this mound was built after Ayuel's death. Today the mound remains a center of great sanctity, but is no longer attended with communal gatherings and ritual operations.[15]

The Pyramid of "Luak Deng"

Another pyramid, *Luak Deng,* is the Mecca of the Dinka and Nuer people and contains the shrine of their deity (and possibly real historical figure) Deng Dit (Deng the Great). It comprises a palisade standing on higher ground near a picturesque pool of water surrounded by *ardeiba* and *suba* trees. This pyramid is connected in mythology with a chain of lesser shrines in the former Nyarruweng Dinka region in what has now become the Gaweir Nuer country. Around the shrine and within a few miles of it reside a small section of Rut Dinka who have crept back and live there by agreement with the Nuer to tend the shrine. *Luak Deng* (or *Luak Kwoth,* as the Nuer now call it) has become a shrine of great significance today for both Dinka and Nuer peoples.[16]

The Pyramid of "Alel"

A pyramid of stones known as *Alel* exists today in the country of the Western Luaic Dinka in a town called Makuac. This pyramid reputedly entombs the body of a prominent Eastern Twic Dinka priest named Kuol Alel who led his people across from the banks of the eastern Nile and in the process of migrating west died in this region. Every year there is a celebration held at Alel in honor of this prominent leader. The pyramid is located north of the Paliang region in the Bahr el-Ghazal, and local Dinka estimate that it pre-dates the Egyptian colonial period (1821) and hence is at least over two centuries old.[17] Thus, there is some correlation between the pyramid-building of the central and northern Sudanese and Egyptians and that of the Southern Sudanese Dinka.

In central Sudan there are also legends of prominent women who have been offered as sacrifices, specifically to appease the powers of the waters, and a correlation also exists here among the Dinka and to a lesser degree, the Shilluk.

The Sacrifice of Prominent Virgins and the Powers of the Waters

An important oral tradition of the central Sudanese successor state of the Funj Sultanate, the Hamaj kingdom of 1762, also has parallels with that of the Dinka. It is recounted that the daughter of a king, Om Nagwar, was selected to be sacrificed at Jebel Dali (in the Gezira) in honor of the "god of the waters" and the rain god. A very severe drought made it necessary that a virgin should be cast into one of the perennial rivers to drown and hence to become a bride to the deity. Unless this highly powerful entity was provided with such a bride annually, it was believed he would become angry and withhold rain.[18]

The Dinka have long believed that spirits inhabit waters and that sacrifices must be made to these entities. For example, the Bor Dinka observe one deity of the Nile known to them as *Aguar Uyerr*; it occupies all of this waterway and can be seen when foggy cold weather appears on its surface. British administrators reported that another Dinka group, the Niel, actually made annual sacrifices of animals to the "river people."[19] The Rek

Dinka claim that spirits of old people who died a long time ago remain alive in and are centered around the *nyin,* the eye of all rivers. According to Rek Dinka Bona Acuil: "This is the deepest part of the river; a place where no one can reach and where there are many rapids and the water is rotating. This eye is the secret part of the river and the people make sacrifices of bulls and sheep every year to it. Without these sacrifices, people crossing the river would be taken by the spirits."

Historically however, it was not only cows that were sacrificed to rivers but also people. Dinka oral histories remember that as their forefathers migrated into various parts of Southern Sudan it was necessary to sacrifice the virgin daughters of prominent priests to large rivers in order to traverse them. For pastoralists, the fast moving Nile River was dangerous to cross. An eyewitness account of the extreme hazards of this operation with livestock was recorded by Emil Ludwig in the early twentieth century:

> Getting across rivers is a hazardous business. The Dinka men cross the river in a few hollowed tree trunks. They drag a few calves into the water with ropes, the lowing of the frightened animals attracts them so others . . . follow them half swimming and finally the bulls follow the . . . cows. The sheep are carried over the Nile in boats, the dogs swimming alongside heedless of danger. Thus the livestock is ferried across the Nile by families in two days and the medicine man, smeared with ashes, stands on the bank and exorcises the crocodiles who snatch their booty all the same.[20]

One of the best-known accounts of a woman sacrificed to a river during the earliest era of Dinka migrations was that of Acai of the Ngok Dinka. However, various differing accounts of this woman's premature death exist. Western Ngok Ring Deng Biong states: "When we came west we found a river in front of us; a river so big we could not cross it. There was a priest called Longar Jiel and he suggested the girl be sacrificed. Her name was Acai. She was decorated [laden down with stones] and sacrificed to the river. After this the people crossed the Nile." Former British District Commissioner P. P. Howell collected yet another version of Acai's sacrifice, noting that the Ngok lived in the east but were forced to move west because grazing was poor and their country was subject to floods. He recorded that their leader was Jok, who had four sons—Ayuel, Bulabek, Dhion, Biar—and a daughter, Acai. On their way west they came face to face with a river that they feared to cross. Jok then pushed his daughter into the river and she was seized by the water spirit. In return the latter caused the waters to part and the people marched across dry shod.[21] Western Ngok Dinka Abyei Kon states that Acai was a member of the Abyor clan of the Pajok family.

Supporting the histories above he states that three clans, the Abyor, Dil, and Acueng, were all attempting to cross the river at once and the actual sacrifice took place near the Nile at what is now the modern town of Bentiu at the junction of the Jur river near Lake No:

> At that time the Mannyuar [clan] had the power, though through time the Pajok gained power. The Nile was very big and in those days if you came to a river it was a holy place and you had to make a sacrifice. We made sacrifices everywhere we went to help us stay there. . . . During sacrifices the *beny* [priest] must call God and he will help us. The *Kir* [Nile River] was flooding and they felt there was something unusual and that they had to make a sacrifice. . . . The girl was from the Pajok family and a daughter of a *beny bith.*

On the other hand, Eastern Ngok Simon Ayuel Deng states that the sacrifice of Acai took place centuries later, after the Dinka had crossed the Nile from east to west. It brought about the split between what eventually became the Eastern and Western Ngok who are separated today by hundreds of miles, for the choice of woman to be sacrificed was in dispute:

> Lual Ayak of [what became] the Eastern Ngok, now called the Ngok of Ayak, was fighting with the Shilluk chief who would not let us cross the river. We selected a girl to bribe the Shilluk chief so that we could cross. . . . Then Deng Kuol of [what is now] the Western Ngok said "what you have done is not good because the leader of the Shilluk is going to put the girl in the water" [sacrifice her]. The girl belonged to Kuol. They . . . disagreed over the issue of whether the girl should be given to the Shilluk chief and this is why both split. Lual Ayak of the Eastern Ngok then crossed the river and went east.

Suggesting a more personal view of the ceremony leading up to a prominent virgin's sacrifice, Western Ngok Dinka Raphael Abiem claims that Acai was actually the daughter of a priest, Jok: "It is the custom to sacrifice the most beloved child of the chief. She would not be married. She is convinced that she is saving the whole community and is sacrificed in a ceremony, during which the people play drums, slaughter bulls, and create an atmosphere of ecstacy to induce the spirits to help the people, so that the woman meets her demise in a state of euphoria. The ceremony would last some time, for the Dinka would not quicken someone's death."

Another history of a woman sacrificed to a river is remembered by the Ghol Dinka. Originally resident in the Bahr el-Ghazal adjacent to the Ciec Dinka, members of this large clan recounted as recently as the mid

1850s that they were migrating in large numbers across the Nile from west to east and that a woman, Aluo, was sacrificed to the river. According to Ghol Dinka Isaac Lat: "She was a very beautiful girl and afterwards the people crossed the Nile to what is now Duk Fadiet. Instead of dropping to the bottom, however, as she should have done because she was heavily loaded down, her body floated to the Shilluk territory in Panikany near Fanjak on the Zaraf river. Because her body was in such perfect condition the Shilluk believed she had religious power and buried her beneath a pyramid." Other histories of sacrificed women in Dinka history exist among the Malwal Dinka, including another called Acai. As late as the early twentieth century a Malwal woman, Acol, the sister of the prominent Dinka priest and leader, Ariendit, was sacrificed to a river.[22]

Myths and oral histories also exist for the sacrifice of women during severe droughts in Dinkaland, which also correlate with the Hamaj tradition mentioned above. Ciec Dinka Madol Cuot Cep, who is descended from a prominent line of Ciec priests, recounts an old clan history of a prominent priest, Nyang, who had a beautiful daughter called Yirol. Yirol was sacrificed to a well because of drought. Later this well became a large body of water known today as Lake Yirol, which is reputed to have been named after the sacrificed woman.[23] In very recent times Dinka informants state that women in Dinkaland are no longer sacrificed to rivers.

Notwithstanding the parallels between central Sudanese and Dinka culture, it must be noted that there is also much divergence. Dinka culture has grown and expanded to incorporate many different ethnicities over the centuries. Thus, as Jan Vansina has argued, Dinka religion has absorbed many foreign elements over time and undergone much change.

The Point of Departure from the Ancient Central Nile Kingdoms

A comparison at this point between recent Dinka religious customs and those of ancient cultures and kingdoms in central Sudan shows much correlation. Nevertheless, Jan Vansina's argument, that religions do not recreate themselves as blueprints as people migrate to a periphery, prevails. Many religious practices within Dinka historical culture have no parallel with the ancient kingdoms of central Sudan. Rather, they more nearly resemble historical societies of other parts of Africa. For example, Rek Dinka Bona Acuil states that live burials occur in modern-day Zambia. In this case, two young men are also buried with the priest before he dies, which suggests that the religious culture of live burials may not be purely a Nile corridor phenomenon. Further, Dinka burials in the past have varied greatly.

Historically, not all Dinka "king-killing" has followed the live burial paradigm of the historical central Sudan. The earliest documented account of a Dinka burial is given in 1821 by the last Sultan of Sinnar, Badi VI (1792–1799 and 1805–1821), who noted that the Dinka bury their dead in an upright position, rather than lying down. During the British colonial period administrator Ibrahim Bedri reported on the killing of a prominent priest and noted that when the elders of a section decided to kill their *beny riem* (literally priest of blood) or when he himself made the request, a different scenario than those so far mentioned took place. All the warriors who were initiated by him were summoned. They arrived in dancing attire, circled around his hut, and sang songs in his honor. Then the elders entered the hut and killed the priest, usually by suffocation; one man held his wind pipe and the other his nose. They then covered the body with butter from a sacred cow and broke the priest's joints; sometimes they were broken before death and sometimes the elders vigorously stretched the priest's legs and penis and squeezed his testicles. His death was then announced to the warriors, a sheep was sacrificed and thrown to the birds, and then the priest was buried secretly by night, usually in the bed of a *khor* (the Arabic word for a dry river bed) in the forest; thus nobody else would know his resting place. The grave consisted of a deep hole in which the body of the priest was placed seated in front of *indarab* stakes and bound with hide to keep him upright. His *mendyor* (spear) was put into his hand pointing in the direction of his enemies. Then the body was covered with grass from the river bank and the grave was filled. If an enemy interfered with the grave or the position of the body, it was believed that it would bring misfortune to the section. This practice does not correlate with that of the central Sudan but rather resembles numerous sub-Saharan burials, for example the Zulu of South Africa.[24] On the other hand it does resemble Shilluk king-killing practices and to an even lesser degree, those of the Luo.

There are other examples that do not correlate with central Sudanese ancient customs. As previously mentioned in this chapter, around the turn of the century prominent priest Ayuong Dit of the Dunghol Dinka was built into his barn with his first wife and his favorite bull and left to die of starvation. In other cases priests have been suffocated to death before actual burial and among the Padang, women have also played a part in the sacrificial process. In 1948, for example, the eldest wife of a prominent priest, Run Deng of the Niel Dinka clan, killed her husband as part of the ritual of king-killing. She is reported to have depressed his diaphragm and held a cloth over his mouth and nostrils. In central Sudan historically, women are not reported as being involved in the killing of their husbands for ritually religious purposes. There is, however, some correlation with the Shilluk practice where special stress is laid on the maintenance of high standards of sexual activity. In these instances, the king's wives are at liberty to strangle or choke their husbands to death.[25]

Certain historical burial practices of the Dinka in no way resemble the "typical" Dinka live burials more prominent in modern times. For example, according to Bona Acuil: "a long time ago we looked for caves called *haal,* the area where the elephants dig a hole and we buried our chiefs there." These forms of human sacrifice do not correlate well with those of the Nile kingdoms of Egypt and central Sudan.

Illustrating Vansina's argument that socioreligious cultures change with migrations over time in more recent years, the Bahr el-Ghazal Dinka have also adapted the king-killing practice to serve other needs. Rek Dinka Mayar Mayar Mareng states that in the early 1880s a prominent priest who was in perfect health offered to be buried alive to save the Dinka from the encroaching slave-raiding armies of the Egyptians in the 1880s:

> Our regions had become totally depopulated so Chief Mayen Deng, a Rek-Kuei Dinka and a prominent *beny bith* [priest], called together all the religious leaders of the Rek, Western Twic, and Malwal. When all the people had assembled he said, "We have to help ourselves out of this situation." After some discussion, it was agreed these Dinka should militarily confederate to fight the Turks [the colonial Turco-Egyptians of 1821–85]. We had a meeting for seven days among all the *beny biths* of the areas during which one religious leader stated "I will be buried alive and take the message to God." Then others also offered to be buried alive. Eventually it was decided that Chief Ajing Dit would sacrifice himself for the cause. Shortly after a Dinka military confederation came into being under the command of Malwal Chief Mayen Deng (Mayendit), who commanded all three big sections along with various other sub-commanders. Every group chose a distinct sign for identification; for example, one group killed a white bull and wore its skin around their necks. Another did the same with the skin of a red bull. The idea was to unify all the groups in a bid for military resistance. When all these signs had been distributed to the Malwal, Twic, and Rek we moved forcefully against the Turkish administrators within their home territories and ended Turkish administration and slavery in our areas.

By the twentieth century in certain parts of Dinkaland live burial represented nothing more than a political coup. For example, among the Agar Dinka of the Bahr el-Ghazal, an unpopular priest, Jokom, was buried against his will when his son, accompanied by the Pabuong clan, pushed him into a grave with a bull and then hurriedly buried him with wood and earth. It is reported that it took five days before the priest and the bull stopped bellowing. Lienhardt collected this oral history but does not give a clear date for this event; the context however, suggests it took place at the beginning of the twentieth century.[26]

At least one priest changed his mind about his "sacrifice" at the last moment. In the Padang region in the British colonial era, after announcing he was ready to die and his wives came to kill him, the priest suddenly acquired a new spurt of life, went "crazy," and broke through the side of the ashhut. His wives had to finish killing him outside. British administrator Titherington also reported that one priest, upon burial, changed his mind and was thereupon retrieved. In the early part of the twentieth century a British administrator arrived in the nick of time to "rescue" a recently buried Western Ngok priest, Arob Biong. After being retrieved from his grave this prominent leader recovered and had four more sons and several daughters in his remaining few years.[27]

One may note a syncretism between Christianity, introduced initially in the Southern Sudan in the nineteenth century, and more modern live burials, particularly in the western Bahr el-Ghazal. Western Twic Dinka Archangelo Ayuel Mayen states that in the late 1940s, his uncle, a prominent priest, Cyer Dit, was buried alive: "With Cyer Dit when he was dying we put him in a grave with milk and a goat. Like Jesus he was buried and the wind and the rain came and later we looked and there was no body. The wind came and took him to heaven."

During the British colonial period (1898–1956) live burials changed and adapted because ritual killings were outlawed. Thus, over time new covert forms of killing prominent leaders emerged. In the early part of the century among the Bor-Atoc Dinka east of the Nile a prominent woman, Yom Dieo, requested that she be sacrificed; she was one hundred years old and felt no need to keep on living and ordered her family to give her an *athiop*, a choking ceremony. Bor Atoc Dinka Mom Kou Nhial Arou states: "She was carried to the middle of an area on a bull's hide and then the people celebrated by dancing around her, kicking up so much dust she was choked to death." After this time, similar ceremonies for prominent priests took place all over Dinkaland. In 1922 Bor Dinka priest, Byordit, who had chronic bronchitis, was killed in this fashion.[28] This form of sacrifice, also termed *tuur,* continues in modern times.

Yet, the older historical practice of king-killing by live burial has also endured. According to Rek Dinka Bona Acuil, a series of prominent Rek-

Kuac priests in the Bahr el-Ghazal have received these burials in recent times, including "Madut Nyok, who was buried in 1957, Nyok Amet (1963), and Ayok Nyok (1969). In 1988 Aguer Adeldit, a priest of the Western Luaic who, it was reputed, was one hundred and twenty years old, received a live burial. The oldest male member of his family buried him with his sacred spear soon after he was lowered into the grave."

Thus, certain Dinka religious practices of the past as well as present times have little or no correlation with that of the ancient Nile kingdoms of the north, while others bear an uncanny resemblance.

Conclusion

The religious and cultural beliefs and practices of the modern-day Dinka show much continuity with those of the ancient central Sudanese kingdoms, a fact that adds further credence to Dinka oral histories of an ancient central Sudanese residence. Jan Vansina's suggestion, however, that religious cultures change as they move towards a periphery and absorb other ethnic socioreligious cultures, also holds in this case, for Dinka priestly sacrifices appear to have undergone change over time. Further, Dinka religion does indeed appear to have a history, which counters the suggestion of the anthropologist, Godfrey Lienhardt, who argued that these Nilotes lacked any tradition of historical development.[29] Although the act of human sacrifice, particularly, represented a critical factor in Dinka migrations, oral histories suggest that the roles of religious leaders, the Dinka priests, were in fact the most important.

12

PRIESTS, POLITICS, AND LAND

Although the act of human sacrifice was deemed critical to the survival of the various Dinka clans as they migrated into Southern Sudan, oral histories suggest that it was the religious leaders, the priests, who played the most crucial role during these journeys. They spearheaded migrations, legitimized control over those foreign territories into which the people migrated, and capitalized on their knowledge of statecraft to gain control over the previous residents of the land. Scholars suggest that weak political systems coupled with ecological crises allow external control by religious leadership.[1] I believe that Dinka priests did indeed follow this model as they led their numerous clans deep into the heartlands of Southern Sudan.

Aristocratic Clans and the Role of Priests in Dinka Migrations

Since the earliest arrival of the Dinka in Southern Sudan there has developed two classes of people: the aristocratic and the commoner clans. The former, believed to represent those original Dinka who migrated from central Sudan, claim that their first priest/leader was Aiwel. He is believed to have passed on his "divine" powers to certain members of his descendants by way of the divinity or *Ring* (flesh).

In modern times Ghol Dinka Barnaba Wuor and Samuel Majak Piok explain how a person becomes a priest:

> Spiritual power begins when power falls on a person. He will call on people and tell them his prophecy and when it happens he is considered to be endowed with this power. For example, he may say "in a few days an elephant will come. Prepare yourself." Then the elephant comes. Then a few days later another problem comes true and the people are convinced he has power. Or if a person is sick, he says God is unhappy, you must do so and so. . . . They do [it] and get well and the person is then considered powerful. But he cannot kill anyone with magic.

However, the priest himself always has a warning that he has received power from his ancestors and in Dinka culture dreams have paramount importance. They are often the first step to recognizing one's priestly prominence. According to Eastern Twic Atem Ayiik, there are two types of people: those whose dreams become a reality and those whose dreams do not:

> If you dream something that a person is going to die, you must tell the parents and a bull or a goat is sacrificed to avert this event. If you dream and prophesize on authority, after a time a ceremony is performed for you and you become a priest. During this ceremony the people gather together and a bull is brought out and killed. Later on the skin is removed and you are covered with it. You come out with a lot of stories to tell and you will be talking while you are under the skin. Sometimes you will need to select a translator as you will speak in jargon and it needs to be translated. You speak different languages.

The spiritual power of these sacred priests, or *bany*, resides in their spears, used for sacrificial killing and thereby also to preserve life. Hence, their special religious functions are symbolized by the sacred fishing spear, the *bith* from which their full titles *bany-bith* are derived. Over the centuries, Dinka priests have "inherited" their religious powers only when a special divinity has "chosen" them specifically from within one of the aristocratic clan families. If the divinity within them proves to be particularly strong they will become well known for their powers. All other non-aristocratic Dinka clans, however, are recognized as the *kic*, or "commoners," who have no special hereditary religious and political function in Dinka society and thus could not ever become prominent priests.[2]

Priests historically have fulfilled numerous roles in both Dinka and Luo society. As mentioned in the previous chapter these religious leaders along with the Shilluk kings (the *reths*) are believed to be divine; their physical and ritual well-being ensure the prosperity of the whole land.[3] As rainmakers, they not only fulfill roles as priests who "create" rain but they also mediate and represent life to their people. Centuries ago, they also spearheaded the migrations of the various Dinka clans into Southern Sudan.

Today, as in the past, priests function in multifaceted roles, from war leaders to initiators of peace. It is claimed that a *beny riem* (chief of blood), another term for a *beny bith,* possesses powers to kill anyone outside his/her section. To do this the priest builds a clay image of a person and then pierces it with a small spear, resulting, it is claimed, in instant death. Funj Sultan Badi IV was reputed to have practiced a similar act during the Ethiopian invasion of Iyasu II in the eighteenth century. It is believed that some Dinka priests shed blood in their tears, as did, for example, Deng Wol, father of the chief of the Nyiel Dinka during the recent British colonial period (1898–1956). Dinka priests also have other wider influences and authority: for instance, they are the only persons to wage or restrain war against the enemies of the clan or group. They are not allowed to join or witness a fight personally because, it is believed, they have sufficient power to kill anybody while sitting in their homes. When a priest sends the people to war he leads them out of his village, gives them his blessings, and retreats to pray for their victory. Dinka priests also play a mediating role in society at large; as the major representatives of their clans they are responsible for officially ending wars and conflicts and handing over the blood cattle payable in mediation after wars. Finally, it is the priests who arrange the necessary sacrifices for maintaining peace.[4]

The role of "priest" has not always been represented by men. In Dinka history there are at least two cases where female religious leaders have led their people into new homelands. According to Col Macar Dau, during the Mahdist colonial era (1885–98) a female priest and leader, Atiam, led six clans of what later became the eastern Ruweng from west of the Nile to the east. Here she presided over the creation of a new Dinka grouping known today as the Paweng. Another female priest, Acol (or Shol) of the Rek Dinka, is credited with leading her people into the region of the modern-day town of Wau in the Bahr el-Ghazal in the mid-nineteenth century. Today, according to Lazarus Leek Mawut, the Dinka still call it Wande Acol (town of Acol). Accumulating immense wealth, Acol gained further political power in the 1860s when she became one of the most influential personages at Meshra er Rek among the neighboring Lao Dinka. Advanced in years when the traveler Georg Schweinfurth, met her, Acol played an important role as a chief in the region. Her immense wealth of at least thirty thousand head of cattle would have made her prey to the Nubian slavers of the first nineteenth-century colonial period in Southern Sudan, had it not been for their need of a convenient and secure landing place for their boats. Thus, she reached a deal with them, allowing them to leave their boats unhindered at the Meshra during the rainy season. For the favor of protecting the boats, she was ensured of not being robbed nor her people enslaved. The situation did not last, as later she was killed by slavers.[5] Rek Dinka Gabriel Awec Bol states that Acol was considered to have great spiritual powers and made decisions of migrations for the Rek Dinka. Still, notwithstanding Atiam and Acol, most priests have been male.

Both Dinka priests and Shilluk kings have historically embraced political centralism; yet the former society has been described, perhaps incorrectly, as historically stateless.

Dinka Religion: Residence on the Periphery of a State?

While historians acknowledge that the Shilluk have represented the only Western Nilotic centralized state or kingdom in Southern Sudan since the sixteenth century, the Dinka collectively have always been assumed to be stateless. For example, previous scholars have written that Dinka leaders did not command any form of tribute, judicial authority, or military power. Oral histories of the functions and practices of Dinka priests in recent years as well as in the more distant past, however, suggest that these Nilotes possess a socioreligious culture derived from an historically more politically centralized society. This is best demonstrated by understanding the typology of religion that the Dinka collectively practice. Anthony Wallace proposes that there are four main religious types in world societies: shamanic, communal, Olympian, and monotheistic. He further suggests that each of these types of religions corresponds to a key level of political centralization.[6]

The two religious typologies presented by Wallace pertinent to the Dinka are communal and Olympian (the shamanic religion is most commonly the domain of hunting and gathering peoples). Communal religions are predominantly associated with stateless pastoral communities. Here, African societies outside of the central African kingdoms and Muslim North Africa have maintained communal cults emphasizing severe puberty rituals for young men and girls. All major economic enterprises are associated with a significant degree of uncertainty and are thus carried out with the aid of secret knowledge believed to have been handed down from the ancestors of prominent priests. Thus, the task of priests is to communicate with the spirits of the dead. These ancestors continue to maintain control over matters of conception and other elements in society and must be remembered and praised. Communal cults embrace a pantheon of major deities controlling departments of nature, either presently or in the past. Rituals are performed in which many lay persons also actively participate. Most of this applies to the Dinka religion, even in modern times.

But the Dinka, Shilluk, and Luo and, to a much lesser degree, the Western Nilotic Anyuak, who also reside in Southern Sudan today, also practice an Olympian typology of religion, as described by Wallace. This is more representative of early state societies such as Dahomey in West Africa. Olympian religions contain a variety of ecclesiastical institutions, including the "Great Gods Cult," which has many of the features of an established church, since this pantheon is divided into sub-pantheons. The deities in each pantheon are related, genealogically, by the creation myth. Each deity is responsible for a major department of nature and each pantheon is associated with a separate religious order. Within the Dinka religion, a study of the female deities alone suggests a closeness to the Olympian religious model. For example, among the clans of the Bahr el-Ghazal in western Southern Sudan, Abuk is believed to reside in heaven and represents a god-like figure who is the mother of Deng, the Dinka counterpart to Adam; thus, she is the creator of men. Among the Ciec Dinka of the White Nile she is believed to be the mother of the supreme culture hero, Aiwel Longar, the first spiritual-political leader of the Dinka. Aciek, another female cosmic entity predominant in the Dinka belief system, represents an alternative female manifestation of the original High-God, Nhialic, in this sense meaning "Creator." To the pastoral Dinka and Nuer, Abuk (*Buk* to the Nuer) is the custodian of the waters, rivers, and lagoons, and when people fish in protected waters without her permission evil befalls them. Thus, her importance as the custodian of waters is paramount in Nilotic spiritual life. Nuer Wal Duany states, "when the people go fishing a bull or a goat is slaughtered for 'Abuk' who lives in the water."[7]

It is only within the domain of Wallace's Olympian typology of religious societies that the sacrifice of humans as well as animals is commonly practiced. The Dinka today continue to sacrifice animals and, as discussed in the last chapter, human beings. Further, scholars suggest that the practice of human sacrifice often indicates a society that is undergoing an early phase of state formation. As the Dinka, Shilluk, and Luo have sacrificed priests, kings, and virgins, their religions can be described as embracing both the communal and the Olympian typology as laid out by Wallace.

As Olympian religious societies are more commonly associated with state societies, Dinka religion therefore, it can be argued, possesses within it remnants of an historical exposure to a centralized state society in the past—in this case, prior to migration into Southern Sudan. Christopher Ehret has recently demonstrated that certain cultures become politically decentralized during the migration process and the Dinka appear to fit this model.[8] Knowledge of statecraft, therefore, supported by their charismatic religious authority appears to have aided many Dinka priests as they led their people into various regions of Southern Sudan. The two best-known priest/leaders in Dinka history are Aiwel Longar and Deng Garang. A close study of the oral histories below suggest that the former was shifting from a leader to a ruler of an early state.

Aiwel (Ayuel) Longar and Deng Garang

Many oral histories recount that the first Dinka master of the fishing spear was Aiwel (or Ayuel) Longar, the great culture hero who "was the first to be created after coming from the land of divinity." Aiwel's birth is described in a myth about the old days when the Dinka were in the Bor area on the east bank of the Nile (prior to the great migrations west). A very old woman, after bathing in a river, suddenly felt she had become pregnant from the river spirits. After seven years she delivered a male child with adult teeth and named it Aiwel. The ability to lead the people in times of crisis and provide for them is often the mark of a powerful leader. Aiwel is remembered in myths for fulfilling this role during periods of severe droughts by performing miracles. According to Rek Dinka Gabriel Awec Bol:

> Longar was the most powerful of all chiefs for when drought came and the water dried at the cattle camps, he looked for a particular variety of grass (*awar*), and when he pulled it out of the ground water appeared and people and cattle drank from it. . . . If you are hungry and go to his home he has a small gourd and takes it near the river. He addresses his god and comes back with it [the gourd] which is full of milk but when he took it, it was empty. If you drink this milk it never runs out. It is a bottomless gourd until you are satisfied and you leave the gourd with milk in it. The people wondered how he did this as the gourd was rather small. His prayers were powerful and truthful enough to maintain the fertility of people, livestock and land.

Thus, over time the people acknowledged Aiwel as their savior and leader and suffixed *dit* (great) to his name, and he is now remembered as

Aiwel Dit.[9] Aiwel, however, in other myths and histories, becomes more than just a leader.

Scholars suggest that the perception of possession of religious power allows small incoming communities to dominate more populous resident peoples in situations when weak political authority is appropriated by supernatural consocation.[10] These theories are highlighted in the Dinka case by the existence of another "Dinka" leader and hero of the past, Deng Garang or Deng Dit. Some oral histories claim this leader accompanied Aiwel Longar from the north and traveled far south into Twic Dinka (eastern Dinka) country, east of the Nile. Other histories claim that Deng met Aiwel when he arrived from the north. Perhaps of most importance is that oral histories describe Aiwel as politically dominating societies into which he and his people migrated, including the territory presided over by Deng. In the case of Deng Garang, power was evidently willingly yielded. Oral histories recount that:

> Among the northern Dinka, Aiwel appeared mysteriously and after performing miracles, took over the supremacy of the people. The leader of the commoners, Ding . . . who was believed to be the first ancestor of the Dinka and Nuer and Aiwel's foster father, surrendered his position to him. The agreement between them resulted in Aiwel being acknowledged as leader and "savior" and given many wives. His foster-father asked only that he and his descendants should be recognized as landowners. Each of Aiwel's sons together with their people was allocated by Aiwel a different territory over which he was placed as religious and temporal head.[11]

Yet, if Deng Garang was also a Dinka leader, this account reveals little. On the other hand, if Deng was ethnically Nilotic, but not Dinka—perhaps Luo, for example—the history above reveals a more significant event in the Southern Sudanese Nilotic past. It would explain how the many Dinka clans, led by Aiwel, who arrived in Southern Sudan some generations after the Luo, gained political control over recently acquired Luo territory, particularly if drought conditions persisted.

Other oral histories on the relations of Aiwel and Deng may shed some light on the background events of these two revered historical figures. A similar version of relations between Aiwel and Deng was collected by British administrator, P. P. Howell who recorded that the prominent Chief Deng (Diing) considered it the proper time to speak to Aiwel and therefore summoned all the notables and elders of the country. In their presence he abdicated his chieftainship. He then renounced all his and his descendants' rights to any power, giving it to Aiwel Dit and his descendants, though requesting that he and his descendants always be recognized as "the owners of the land." This was their covenant and today, this agreement is still in force in eastern Padang Dinka territory. Whenever a member of the Diendyor (the people of Aiwel) quarrel with the *kic* (the people of Deng and the original land owners) the latter always reminded him saying "*piny piny Diing*" (this land is the land of Diing [Deng]).

Of importance here is that the term *kic* also denotes the "commoner" Dinka clans, or those who were not originally from the north but, rather, resident on the land when the forefathers of the first Dinka clans arrived. Oral histories gathered by Per Sofholm among the Northern Dinka support the view that the *kic* clans in recent times claim to be "indigenous" (those people who were present before the arrival of the various Dinka clans) and that they yielded their land to "outsiders," that is Aiwel and his Dinka migrant followers. Today, Deng is believed to be the spiritual leader of certain Dinka groups, particularly among the Padang in the north; Dunghol Dinka Cok Kuek Ywai and Majak Col Mayiik claim that Deng Dit was the god of their people.[12] Even more important is the suggestion in myths and histories of Aiwel that expand his role from priest/leader to ruler.

Oral Histories of Aiwel Longar as King and Administrator

The oral histories of Aiwel's early exploits suggest that having acquired preeminence over many into whose lands he had migrated, he then began a loose administration of the territory. Later he distributed administrative control of the land among his seven sons. They in turn became the masters of the fishing spear, the *bany bith,* or the religious/political leaders who then led the various clans and subsections in their extended migrations to their present-day homelands within Southern Sudan. In the meantime it is remembered that Aiwel remained "like a governor [General]" on the east bank of the Nile while his relatives were dispatched "like provincial governors," indicating the responsibility of the descendants of Aiwel.[13]

The western Dinka however, claim that Aiwel Longar actually took them across the Nile and helped them found their communities. Malwal Dinka Lawrence Lual Lual Akuey states: "Longar is the spiritual leader who took the people west of the river Nile. He was a warrior, a judicial and spiritual leader, and possessed the spirit of *Rual* which also possesses certain Malwal clans."

Even more important in studying early Dinka leaders are the myths/histories depicting Aiwel Longar as a man attempting to build a kingdom or a politically centralized early state, for he is very often described as a dictator or harsh ruler, rather than just a leader. For example, one version of the mythology/history connected with Aiwel's mound at Pwom on the east bank of the Nile suggests that it was built specifically on his orders. There were many years of toil, for which the reward of some people was death (human sacrifice), their bodies adding to the rising edifice. Another history recounts that human bodies were used as props in the scaffolding, the persons chosen for this honor being buried alive. Another ancient story recounts that Aiwel was with the Dinka in the Upper Nile region in a place called *Deng Dit,* suggesting a location formerly under the control of the leader of the same name. Nyarruweng Dinka Lazarus Leek Mawut states that Aiwel had made a *luak* composed of people—"he made short people into women and tall people into a scaffold." As he continued to collect people to hold up his *luak,* many became annoyed and, voting with their feet, departed, crossing the *toic* (grasslands). Other histories concerning Aiwel's *yik* (shrine) remember that from this spot he speared in the head those who crossed the river Nile.[14] The above accounts/myths suggest that Aiwel, as the recognized Dinka leader of many migrating followers, was attempting some sort of political centralization. In turn, it was apparently resisted by most of his Dinka constituency who fled. These histories and myths are important, for they support the historical tendencies of certain Dinka leaders toward political centralization as demonstrated in Dinka religious and political culture. But they also suggest that the leaders' ambitions towards political centralization were thwarted as their constituents disapprovingly voted with their feet.

The Luo, Shilluk, and Anyuak

Of other Nilotic peoples in Sudan, it is only the Shilluk who have become so politically centralized as to be led officially by a king. Dinka myths and histories suggest that there has been a tendency towards political centralism which has been only partially successful. To a much lesser degree the Anyuak and the Luo in Southern Sudan also follow this model. The Luo of the western Southern Sudan, who are recently descended from the Shilluk of the Nile, also have practiced human sacrifice. Neither the Nilotic Nuer, Atwot, nor Anyuak have ritually killed their priests, although the Anyuak have tended toward more political centralization than the Nuer and Atwot.[15]

Conclusion

Dinka religious leaders played a crucial role throughout the Dinka migrations into southern territories. Myths and histories handed down over the centuries have significant political implications and, with much other data, support the view that although the Dinka fought many wars in the south, there was also a degree of peaceful integration because of the perceived power of Dinka religious leaders, particularly that of Aiwel Longar. Anthony Wallace's typology of religion juxtaposed with Dinka oral histories of the most prominent priest-leaders, Aiwel and Deng, suggest that the former attempted some form of political centralization but was unsuccessful. These attempts, however, would correlate particularly with Marvin Harris's argument that human sacrifice (see chapter 11) is often connected to early state formation. In this case, practices historically inherited from central Sudan were followed, with migrations southwest, by political decentralization as people were no longer limited to a proscribed homeland. Economics, however, also played a critical role in the success of Dinka priests and their migrations. The political power and economic advantage of the Dinka was to have a large impact on the central Southern Sudanese region in terms of ethnic expansion.

13

ETHNIC EXPANSION BY MARRIAGE

"We can only marry foreign people, we can never marry our relations."
Samuel Aru Bol, Agar Dinka

"'We the Dinka' are a group of people that have all been assimilated .
. . and the Atwot are the latest to be absorbed."
David Deng Athorbei, Apak Atwot, whose
great-great-grandfather was a Kakwa prince

Today the Dinka are the largest ethnic group in Sudan. The size of their
population centuries ago as they migrated into their present homelands is
difficult to estimate. The only historical clue is given by the oral histories of
the seventeenth-century Shilluk who describe the Dinka as moving along
their borders in "hordes," suggesting a sizeable population relative to their
own. Dinka oral histories, however, support the view that they acquired
much of their population after reaching the South by way of massive ethnic
absorption of non-Dinka peoples. By the twentieth century Dinka ethnic
expansion in Southern Sudan was such that their ethnic circumference was
one thousand miles. Yet, in the South today one cannot easily "become
Dinka." It is only by marriage that a person and his/her children can be
ethnically integrated into the community. Sandra Greene suggests that gen-

der studies and ethnicity in precolonial Africa cannot be understood in isolation,[1] and I believe that this argument also applies to the history of Southern Sudan.

The Difficulties of "Becoming Dinka"

With few exceptions, adopting Dinka identity outside of marriage has been extremely difficult both in the past as well as in the present day. On the other hand, it is far easier to adopt the identity of the close neighbors of the Dinka, the Nilotic Nuer. In modern times ethnic incorporation into the latter society has been accomplished by means of a ritual of sacrifice.[2] For the Dinka, however, there is no such cultural act or ceremony available for incorporating foreigners into their amalgam. Nor do the Dinka fully accept, in a social or political sense, non-Dinka peoples living in their midst. According to Ciec Dinka Gordon Matot Tut: "Nuer law [and custom] is different from Dinka law. . . . The Nuer have one thing that differs from the Dinka. When you are among them you are not discriminated against. They take you wholly . . . and even if others may discriminate against you . . . they will protect you. This does not happen in Dinka society." Dinka law makes it difficult to acquire "citizenship" by merely residing within a Dinka community. There is only one exception to this rule, however: the Western Ngok Bongo of Southern Kordofan have incorporated foreigners into their society wholly and completely only if the initiates complete a series of "tests."

According to Abyei Kon the Bongo "form one of the nine major clans of the Western Ngok today and absorbed many non-Nilotic Nuba" who commonly reside in the hills of the same name to the northeast of these Dinka. Additionally, the Western Nilotic Nuer (long time enemies of many Dinka in the South) who reside on the southeastern boundary of the Bongo have also been incorporated. Furthermore, some Islamic Baggara also became "Dinka" during the eighteenth century (see chapter 17). Within the Bongo, the actual mechanism for absorption of "foreign" peoples was by way of initiation ceremonies into age sets. Abyei Kon states:

> My great-grandfather, Lual Deng, brought a lot of Nuer under his control because he was a powerful *beny*. Only the Bongo adopted a lot of Nuer. . . . A few Nuer were absorbed by the Acak [also one of the nine major Ngok clans]. Some Nuer fought with their own people and came to the Dinka region. When the Nuer came, a Nuer family would put their young boy into

the age set. Now you demonstrate your ability [as a warrior] and get the Dinka cuts [on the forehead]. Within the age sets you have to demonstrate you are grown up and prove your valor. You have to create hundreds of songs [this is known in Dinka as *dip*]. . . . This is how people will know you. As you are being initiated into adulthood, as a group you go around the neighborhood singing. . . . We also go through a series of sports activities and if you cannot get through it they (the elders) deny you your name and say you are too young [to be initiated].

In the present day, when a young would-be initiate has completed his Bongo "qualifying exams" involving all of the activities required of the upcoming age set, he is then informed that his "head will be cut" with the distinct ethnic markings of the Bongo Dinka section, sometime within a year. It is difficult to find practitioners to perform the operation of cutting the markings into the forehead of young men. Few have the skill and it is now infrequently practiced; therefore, an expert (*ran ger*) must be booked well in advance and is paid well in cows. After being cut a young man stays in doors for two weeks whereupon he starts dancing (*ager*). This is the time of the big ceremony. After a young boy's head is cut it takes two months to fully recover because of the loss of blood. He requires a safe place to stay, preferably where there are trees and a food center because the whole community donates food.

Of importance within the Bongo community, however, is that any former non-Dinka male who becomes initiated into a Dinka age set must never be referred to again as a "foreigner." Abyei Kon states: "After going through this ceremony we [the Dinka community] are told not to tell the people [newly naturalized Dinka males] they are foreigners. We would have to pay a fine [to the chief] for calling someone a "Nuer" . . . When we are small we are taught this."

To a much lesser degree other Western Ngok Dinka clans have also absorbed non-Dinka peoples in this fashion. The Abyor clan, for example, who, in the nineteenth century onwards bordered the Baggara, absorbed a small number of these Islamic pastoralists. In modern-day parlance of the South the Islamic Baggara are often incorrectly referred to as "Arabs." They are, however, Muslim Africans from western and central Africa. Abyei Kon states:

The Abyor took captives. Arabs were taken to wealthy people or to the chief and they were adopted as actual kinsmen. In the 1930s we adopted a Baggara man as an artificial kinsman. He was called Mohammed and was later called Mamoth Bungjok. He was absorbed into an age set generation. He was a strong fighter and later in the 1960s he was fighting the Baggara, his own people [during the first civil war in Sudan]. The Abyor have absorbed a lot of Baggara in the same way. Some Baggara have joined us voluntarily. Aluel, a Baggara, who was fifty years [old] came to the Bongo area. He talked Dinka. He moved with his wife and his children and stayed but when they [his children] grew up they went back to the Baggara but he stayed with the Bongo. The Alei have also absorbed many Arabs as well as Nubans. But it is difficult to talk about it. My mother comes from Alei. The Alei have rulers whose ancestors were Nuba.

The above instances are the only cases that I have come across in which foreign peoples have historically been absorbed into a Dinka clan section, other than by marriage. For the most part, however, throughout Dinkaland in the sixteenth and seventeenth centuries, according to Dinka oral histories, the only official means by which a person could eventually acquire a Dinka ethnic identity and become socially, economically, and politically "accepted" into Dinka society was by marriage.

Dinka Marriage Customs and Economics

Before explaining why marriage led to ethnic expansion in Southern Sudan, I must briefly explain Dinka marriage customs. In Africa, wealth creates status, which then attracts further wealth. In patriarchal societies such as the Dinka and other Western Nilotes of the Southern Sudan, ownership and control of wealth rests with men and only with those who are married.[3] Like most African societies, the Dinka are polygynous. Today, as in the past, there are two methods by which a Dinka man acquires a wife. In the first, a prospective husband officially pays bridewealth, often in a bidding system controlled by the prospective father-in-law. The highest bidder usually acquires the woman and the bridewealth is made in a series of payments over an extended period of time. The second method is by raiding, which circumvents the complicated system of bridewealth payments between two clan families. Ultimately, the more wives a man possesses, the greater is his status in society at large.

The Importance of Acquiring Numerous Wives

For as long as the Dinka can remember they have believed that the acquisition of many extra wives strengthens the clan and section. The adage, until recently, according to Ciec Dinka Cagai Matet Guem, was that "many wives shall bring forth many daughters who shall be married with great numbers of cattle." While women and cows have represented and continue to represent wealth within Dinka clan families, it has also been important to have manpower for the defense of the section or clan in wars.[4] There have always been restrictions, however, as to whom a man may marry. These rules are governed by observation of "symbols of protection," or totems.

Exogamy, Incest (Totemism), and Ethnicity

John and Jean Comaroff suggest that totemism is an historically specific form of the universal process of classification. In this instance groupings define themselves as independent identities in contrast to one another.[5] This theory is exemplified in the marriage customs of the Dinka, who, like other pastoral peoples, are customarily patrilineal, polygynous, and exogamous (i.e., they marry nonrelated peoples). The identification with key totems (see chapter 10) dictates who is and who is not "related." In the case of the Dinka, for example, should it be found that two prospective marriage partners have clan totems in common, even generations ago, it is believed that the two are "related by blood" and that marriage would represent "incest" and be inauspicious for both partners. Thus, even today the prospective Dinka man and woman seeking marriage compare two things: family genealogy for several generations and family clan totems. Nyarruweng Dinka Lazarus Leek Mawut states: "Our blood relations are traced through a common deity. We trace our lineage back up to ten and that is how we determine it. If there is a common deity (totem) before ten on the male side you are related. However, if you go up to eight and there is no common deity it is possible for marriage." Pakam Agar Dinka Steven Anyaak Col states: "The minute you meet a girl she asks about your lineage. We will discuss what our great grandparents have and we can go up to twenty generations discussing totems before marriage. Even children as young as three years of age are inculcated to understand that lineage is extremely important." Hence, the Dinka believe that "we can only marry foreign people, we can never marry our relations." Because Dinka marriages have been the most expensive—for example, as many as two hundred cows— "cheaper" wives have always been sought, often among the peripheral Nilotic and non-Nilotic neighbors of the Dinka.

Bridewealth and Status/Rank in Dinka Society

Dinka society is stratified by wealth and status. In anthropological parlance Dinka pastoral society is termed "ranked." This denotes a society where

bridewealth is negotiable and never equal; thus the daughter of a prominent chief commands more bridewealth than one who has a nonprominent
father. Jane Fishburne Collier states that with "ranked" (hierarchical) societies, men marrying for the first time usually acquire a women of equal or
higher rank because status is determined by the initial marriage contracted.
Secondary wives, however, tend to be of lower rank and thus command a
lower brideprice. Conversely, low-ranking families often give sisters or daughters in marriage to higher ranking men to obtain patronage.[6]

Because the Dinka arrived in the Southern Sudan in the sixteenth
and seventeenth centuries as the people in possession of the most wealth
(cattle and grain), the brideprice for a Dinka wife today, as in the past, is
still higher than all of their surrounding non-Dinka neighbors. This includes the Shilluk, Anyuak, Atwot, Luo, Nuer, Maban, Murle, Mundari,
Yibel, Bongo, Azande, Balanda, and Fertit. Thus, the Dinka have often
preferred to acquire secondary wives from among their non-Dinka neighbors. Aliab Dinka Parmena Awerial Aluong asserts: "After we marry Bor
[Dinka] we marry more Mundari [non-Dinka], because these women are
cheaper; you may only pay five cows. To us a girl is like a toic or a river, you
keep taking water without stopping and you have to keep going every season." An Atwot, Andrew Anhiem Alit states: "the Aliab [Dinka] area is very
rich while most Mundari [non-Dinka] have a low income. Therefore more
Aliab men marry Mundari women." In regard to their Nuer neighbors,
who reside on their inner periphery, and who, in previous centuries, were
completely encapsulated, a Ciec Dinka Gordon Matot Tut states: "The
most expensive marriages are those Dinka from Yirrol [the Ciec] because
they have a lot of cattle [or used to, before the war] and they have good
grazing, excellent agricultural land, and the people are more wealthy there.
Therefore, their bridewealth is very high. On the other hand, Nuer marriages are very cheap because they don't have much cattle and we can marry
prestigious Nuer women with thirty cows." Eastern Twic Dinka informants
also comment on Nuer brideprice: "Our bridewealth is expensive. With
the Dinka it ranges from thirty to one hundred cows. However, for Nuer
women it is usually fifteen to twenty-five. Uniformly, throughout Dinkaland
a Dinka woman is worth thirty cows but if she is beautiful she commands
more and if she is from a large family, she is worth still more."[7]

Because the Dinka could acquire secondary non-Dinka wives more
cheaply after their arrival in Southern Sudan, they expanded ethnically
against many of their surrounding neighbors in the ensuing centuries. In
so doing they decreased the pool of marriageable non-Dinka women available to their male neighbors to maintain populations on their periphery.

For example, there has been so much intermarriage between the Agar Dinka and the Yibel (their non-Nilotic neighbors to the south) that it has decreased the numbers of the latter.[8] Not all peoples on the Dinka periphery, however, would allow their women to marry these Nilotes.

At the northwestern limits of the Dinka amalgam ethnic expansion slowed considerably in the latter eighteenth century. In this era the territory of what is now southern Kordofan and southern Darfur became home to Islamic cattle nomads from west and central Africa, known today as the *Baggara*. The meaning of *Baggara* in Arabic is cattle nomad (*bagr* is cows). By the mid to late eighteenth century the Islamic Baggara had arrived from the west, separating into a number of groups: the Humr and Zurug (now called Messiria or Missiriyya), Hawazma, and Rizeiqat. Unlike those in the South, Islamic society particularly in Central Sudan has an entirely different socioeconomic structure. In this instance endogamy prevails wherein men marry close kin to maintain the wealth within the family.[9] With the exception of the few Baggara who have been absorbed into Western Ngok society by way of initiation into an age set in the last two centuries, ethnic expansion by marriage between the Dinka and the Muslim Baggara has happened only rarely. In recent times, the Dinka rules of incest have changed to aid marriage within Dinka society.

A Relaxation of Incest Rules in the Present Day

In recent times Dinka ethnic expansion has slowed considerably, largely because the rules of incest are beginning to relax, possibly to facilitate marriage within Dinka communities. Among the Amol clan of the Western Twic in northwest Dinkaland, for example, a priest, Nyuol Bol, some generations ago, abolished incest laws altogether "so that his people could multiply more quickly." Bol Col states:

> In the old days we never intermarried. But when Nyuol Bol was dying he called the people and said . . . [in order] for you to multiply . . . the blood relations that previously inhibited intermarriage, I will take down with me [as he was buried]. Then he said "on my grave when I die bring a goat and a sieve and bury me with these things. I will be buried with the blood relations and you can marry people with the same totem and no harm will come to you." After that, the people of the Amol Western Twic subsection intermarried.

Similarly, and for the same reason, fifty years ago the Padhieu clan of the Rek Dinka in western Dinkaland also abolished their incest laws. Today on the east bank of the Nile some Bor-Atoc Dinka clans can marry even if they share the same clan totems, but the actual lineages of the prospective bride and groom are still discussed at great length.[10]

Among most other Rek groups today however, incest laws are still in place but another factor has become important: the comparison of diseases. Bona Acuil states: "Prospective couples looking to get married check the clans (lineage names), totems, which are our symbols of protection, and also check up the family line for diseases. Totems are only compared for about two generations and we remember totems on the father's side." Beyond paying lengthy and expensive bridewealth payments many pastoral groups in Southern Sudan have regularly raided their pastoral nonrelated neighbors, both Dinka and non-Dinka, for wives.

The Acquisition of Wives by Raiding

Many pastoralist communities around the world frequently acquire extra wealth in the form of animals and women by raiding each other and foregoing the official practice of paying bridewealth. Louise Sweet argues, for example, that pastoral peoples customarily rob and pillage their neighbors, since to continue long in a state of peace diminishes their wealth. Alois Musil also adds that the more geographically distant these groups are the more prolonged will be their hostile relations.[11] Among the Dinka a similar philosophy prevails and the raiding of one's neighbors, both to acquire cows as well as women, has been a time-honored activity. Thoi Dinka Philip Thon Marol states: "There has been a lot of raiding for greed. It has always been important to show we are good warriors and when you are strong you go and rob the weak. It was the formula for those days and everybody did it. If you defeated another clan you took their cows and women. We took the women to become wives while young girls could be married to other men and bring more cows. Small boys could raid for more cattle."

However, the Dinka have never been free to declare war on all their neighbors. They are constrained by the degree of close totemic ("incest") relations both within the various Dinka groups as well as with their neighbors, the Nuer, many of whom share similar totems. Thus, even if a neighbor is not Dinka but viewed as "related," one can neither declare war nor marry them, for "they are our brothers." One's totem, therefore, defines "enemy" versus "family." An Eastern Luaic Dinka, Malwal Can Gaac, and a Thoi Dinka, Philip Thon Marol, who form part of the Padang group on the northern and northeastern Dinka periphery, explain why they often tend to raid non-related Nuer communities: "Many of the Padang have the same totems so we tend only to have small skirmishes among ourselves and we never raid each other. Therefore we have to raid the Nuer and we all unite against them." On the other hand, those neighbors with fewer if any cattle such as the Nilotic neighbors of the Padang Dinka, the Shilluk, and even farther to the north, the Nuba, who are primarily agriculturalists, are, for the most part, not considered worth raiding.

In modern times intra-Dinka raiding is more intense geographically in some regions than others. For example, it occurs more frequently among the Bahr el-Ghazal Dinka in western Dinkaland than within the Padang in the north or the Bor Dinka groups in southeastern Dinkaland. This suggests that over the centuries the Bahr el-Ghazal Dinka have acquired far more non-kin neighbors, whom they can term "outsiders" who qualify for raiding, than the Bor and Padang, because they have undergone more rapid geographical expansion, historically. Thus, wars in the Bahr el-Ghazal have been more plentiful, because the clan taboos among these people, which would limit intra-Dinka raiding, do not exist.

Conclusion

Economics, culture, and religious mechanisms have historically dictated marriage laws and customs which, in turn, allowed the forefathers of the Dinka to expand ethnically against other groups in Southern Sudan. Within a few centuries these Nilotes had expanded geographically into a large part of the region encompassing, by the twentieth century, an ethnic circumference of over one thousand miles. They occupied, along with their inner neighbors, the Nuer, an area of about 113,000 square miles.[12] By the twentieth century they had become Sudan's largest ethnic group. Their economic advantages (grain and cattle) coupled with the fact that they were a polygynous, patrilineal, ranked society who observed incest laws led to this increased ethnic expansion in Southern Sudan as they sought to marry "foreigners on their periphery." Over time the Dinka acquired so many non-Dinka wives they decreased the pool of marriageable women in the societies on their inner and outer peripheries. Of all the peoples absorbed into the Dinka amalgam historically, their close neighbors, the Western Nilotic Luo, by all accounts, have become the most integrated.

14

SOVEREIGN NATIONS WITHIN THE DINKA

Today the Western Nilotic Luo form part of a great confederation of Nilotic-speaking peoples spread throughout eastern Africa from the modern countries of Sudan to Uganda, Kenya, and Tanzania. The cradleland of the Luo is believed to have been the Sudan, and their closest relations are the Shilluk of the White Nile and the Anyuak, who reside southeast of the Shilluk and extend into Ethiopia. These Nilotes contribute, along with the Dinka, Nuer, and Atwot, to the larger Western Nilotic-speaking peoples in Southern Sudan.[1]

Where Have All the Luo Gone?

Although the original homeland of the Luo is believed to be the Southern Sudan, a number of Luo oral histories, much like those of the Dinka, suggest that these Nilotes are not indigenous to this region. As mentioned in chapter 3, according to the grandparents of one Sudanese Luo, Albino Ukec Simon, all the Nilotes originated from the southern Gezira region: "We Shilluk Luo came from the far east in southern Blue Nile at a place called 'Tindil' close to the Ethiopian border." A Tanzanian Maasai (linguistically classified as Eastern Nilotes) also claims that his Nilotic ancestors "originated in North Africa" and that "[M]any centuries ago we migrated and followed the Nile River upward to where we are now."[2]

According to historical linguistics the Southern and Western Nilotic language groups split between the years 670 and 1070. Soon thereafter, numerous Nilotic peoples began to migrate into Southern Sudan. Oral histories of the Luo suggest that at one time they came to occupy large parts of the Southern Sudan prior to the arrival of the Dinka. From here they slowly dispersed southwards, with the forefathers of the Maasai, linguistically classified as Eastern Nilotes, moving into Kenya and beyond. As mentioned in chapter 9, further waves of migrations beyond the Southern Sudan took place because of famine. The famine of 1382 to 1409 broke up the remaining Luo settlements in Southern Sudan. Other droughts followed during the years 1436–63 and 1587–1652, during which many other Luo groups migrated south into what is now Uganda.[3] Kenyan Luo Dickson Ogolla Oroku states: "Of the Luo that moved south, the group that got to Kenya were the last to arrive after going through Uganda. We were cattle people but became fisherman and we grew millet and maize." But despite the drought, Luo oral histories, which also corroborate those of the Dinka, suggest that a number of Luo remained in Sudan. Dickson Ogolla Oroku states: "We never talk of our history without referring to the Dinka. We came from the Sudan and the Dinka pushed us south although some remained behind."

Many of the Luo still residing in Southern Sudan today were originally part of the greater Shilluk nation located at the White Nile and Sobat River junction in the north. During the early sixteenth century they split away from their parent group and forged south. Their routes into the Southern Sudan were two-fold. Some followed the east bank of the Nile in a southerly direction beyond the modern town of Bor. Here, according to the nineteenth-century missionary Father Kaufmann, the Luo of this region, often referred to as the Nilotic Beri, had come to reside in the mountains at Lokoya and Liry. But they were pressed westwards into the large islands of the Nile in the wake of the seventeenth-century Bari migration first from the north and then retracing their steps from the south.[4] Other Luo communities crossed the Nile westwards wending their way northwest, as did the Dinka a few generations later.

The second route of the Luo into Southern Sudan, followed by many, went directly southwest from the Shilluk homeland on the Nile. This led into the region known today as the Bahr el-Ghazal. Here the Luo met the residents of much of the South, the martial non-Nilotic Luel who militarily defended their homelands. Thus, many Luo (although not all) were forced to migrate to the far west to the boundaries of the powerful non-Nilotic nation of the Bongo, who halted further advancement. Here, the Luo settled along the edges of the ironstone belt, adopting agriculture and becoming blacksmiths because thick bush and tsetse fly discouraged pastoralism. It has been variously estimated that these Luo folk arrived in the Bahr el-Ghazal any time between 1500 and 1620.[5]

In the sixteenth and seventeenth centuries, approximately two generations after the Luo arrival in the Bahr el-Ghazal, the forefathers of the Dinka migrated south along the eastern banks of the Nile from the Sobat. They encountered small Luo communities on the eastern banks of the Nile, some of whom had apparently not migrated west after the arrival of the Bari but rather had retraced their steps a little farther to the north. Thus, east of the White Nile in southeastern Dinkaland the Nyarruweng Dinka and the Adul subsection of the Bor Dinka (located south of the Nyarruweng) comprises many Luo peoples. Eastern Twic Dinka Philip Aguer Panyang states that Bor Dinka oral histories remember that when they initially arrived in their present day settlements "there was a pastoral group called the Loki or Lau. . . . These Loki(o) people are now part of the Nyarruweng [Dinka]."

West of the Nile, after the Dinka successfully routed the resident Luel in the Bahr el-Ghazal, with help from some of their Luo allies, many were ethnically absorbed by marriage into the Dinka confederation. Since the sixteenth and seventeenth centuries and particularly in the nineteenth century many Luo have continued their integration into Dinka society. By the 1950s, for example, the chief of the Apuk, a large section of the Rek Dinka in the Bahr el-Ghazal in western Dinkaland acknowledged that half of his subjects were originally Luo.[6]

The ethnic incorporation of the Luo into the Dinka amalgam was initially propelled by economic stress caused by the ecological strain on the land. Many had previously been pastoralists and lost their animals. While it is evident that many Dinka men married Luo women, conversely, a number of Luo men married Dinka women and then reidentified themselves as "Dinka," passing this new identity on to their children. In this case the change of ethnic identity was connected to the desire for the acquisition of wealth in the form of cattle. Changing ethnic identity for economic reasons is common in many regions of the world and when the agricultural Fur, for example (who reside north of the Dinka in Darfur), buy cows, pastoralism being economically more lucrative than agriculture, they attach their newly acquired animals to the herds of the pastoral Islamic Baggara. By definition their agricultural/ethnic association is then altered and very shortly thereafter they identify themselves as Baggara.[7] This phenomenon is also evident among the Luo. One Malwal/Luo, Duang Deng Duang, states: "My maternal uncle is a Jur-col [Dinka term for black (*col*) stranger (*jur*)] and he married a Dinka woman. When you marry Jur-col people you pay less but with Dinka women you have to pay more to marry them. However, the Jur want to marry Dinka because they don't have much cattle and they want to become Dinka to acquire cows." Thus, intermarriage among the Dinka and the Luo, as well as the tendency of the Luo in the past to reidentify themselves ethnically as Dinka after marriage, has encouraged Dinka ethnic expansion against the latter's communities, particularly in the Bahr el-Ghazal. Not all communities of Luo in western and eastern Dinkaland, however, have been ethnically absorbed by marriage.

Unintegrated Luo Communities

Although many Luo have become ethnically integrated into the Dinka amalgam, others who previously resided in Southern Sudan prior to the Dinka arrival, and who today are not primarily pastoralists, have remained as unincorporated or discrete ethnic groups within the Dinka amalgam. In eastern Dinkaland these Luo are known by various names. The Luo of Jebel Lafon (mentioned above), for example, located east of the Nile and south of Dinkaland, are known as the Pari (Peri or Beri).[8]

Another small unintegrated group of probable Luo origin, who now refer to themselves as the Mon Thain "Dinka," reside on the banks and islands of the Nile. Oral histories of the Eastern Nilotic Bari recount that when they arrived in their present homelands from the north they drove a Nilotic people, the Beri (Peri or Pari) from the mountains at Lokoya and Liry, and militarily forced them into the large islands of the Nile. The Mon Thain still inhabited these islands in 1857. When missionary Kaufmann came to work in the area he noticed that within the Ciec, Twic, Bor, and Aliab Dinka, who live on both sides of the Nile, small settlements of poor nations supported themselves by fishing and blacksmithing. It is therefore likely that these Mon Thain are of Luo origin.[9]

There are also many Luo groups beyond the western banks of the Nile in the northern and southern Bahr el-Ghazal where even more discrete communities have come to be known variously as Shilluk-Luo, Jur-Col, Jur, Shilluk-Jur, Padimo, Pakir, Mananger, Shatt, Jur Wir, and so on. In recent times, these numerous Luo communities have resided independently under their own chiefs. For example, there is Chief Akol Unquac, whose Luo section is located in the Paliet-Malwal region, and Ajing Upia, whose community is located in the Palyoupiny Malwal region. They both continue to speak their own language, although others have adopted the Dinka custom of dental evulsion (removal of the lower teeth) and marking their heads in accordance with the designs of the major Dinka grouping in which they reside.[10]

In Southern Sudan there also remain many smaller unincorporated ethnic groups within Dinkaland who are not Luo. None are primarily pastoralists. Some own a few cattle and are primarily agriculturalists, fishermen, and blacksmiths.

Other Discrete Ethnic Groups Within the Dinka

In recent times many discrete non-Nilotic Luel communities, the original inhabitants of the Southern Sudan prior to the Luo and Dinka arrival, have continued to exist peacefully within the larger Dinka amalgam. As late as 1957 there was a Luel group residing among the Western Twic Dinka; their close relatives, the Patek, lived nearby in the Malwal Dinka region while others resided among the Rek Dinka of Thiet. Luel oral histories remember that Tek was their common ancestor who remained in the Twic Dinka country begetting numerous children. Another Luel group, the Gurmok and Ber, represented major Luel sections in Dinkaland; the former became known as the Girma among the Western Ngok Dinka in southern Kordofan. Others resided at Ber Ajou near the Nuer border in the country of Chief Ngok Lual Ayak. Another Luel group were located in Chief Benjamin Lang's territory on the borders of Nuerland. They lived as hunters of elephants and hippopotami, and some Ber (Luel) resided among the Mananger (Luo). As recently as the 1980s, there was a village within the Palyoupiny Malwal Dinka area northwest of Aweil called Makuac Lang. Here other groups of unintegrated Luel clans existed, among them the Panyang.[11]

The main body of the Eastern-Nilotic Mundari peoples (a group closely related to the Bari) now reside south of the Aliab Dinka on the White Nile. But much farther north discrete groups of this Eastern Nilotic ethnic culture remain today within the Western Nilotic Ciec Dinka amalgam, which suggests that centuries ago this region was originally part of their homeland. In recent years these Mundari within the Ciec had their own chiefs and actually identified themselves as Dinka although they were understood by all to be of Mundari ancestry. Today they are identified as non-pastoralist farmers and iron-working clans and known as the Nyonker and Gumbek, (or collectively the Adjong.) Historically, they sold their iron products to the Western Nilotic non-Dinka Atwot to their south and hunted elephants. These clans were endogamous, and because they lacked cattle found it difficult to integrate with the surrounding Dinka. In very recent times they have acquired some cattle and intermarried with the Aliab Dinka, the Atwot, and to a lesser degree the Ciec.[12]

Within the southeast confederation of the Dinka known as the Bor there are numerous group of unintegrated Nuer. The latter depart from the usual rule of unintegrated peoples being non-pastoralists. Their arrival corresponded with the early British colonial era (1898–1956) during which the Dinka and Nuer were forcibly separated by an artificial boundary to inhibit wars. A well-known Nuer leader, Malwal Riak, and his people, the Galuak Nyor Nuer, nevertheless settled among the Ghol Dinka, remaining unintegrated as a discrete group, speaking their own language until present times. Throughout the process of forcible separation this Nuer group refused to move and claimed to the British to be Dinka. Over time they came to preside over certain Ghol Dinka clans in the region. In the meantime Malwal Riak's leadership "continued down the line Dinka-style." It is surmised that Galuak had "burned his bridges with his Nuer kinsmen and was unable to return."[13]

Within the Nyarruweng there is a similar story. Lazarus Leek Mawut states: "The Nyarruweng are not a single group of people. Within this large section, some clans of Nuer have been there a long time. The Kumas clan was originally a Nuer group who secretly remained when the British expelled the Nuer peoples from the region in the early twentieth century. They have been under their own chiefs, and although these people are identified as 'Dinka' they continue to speak Nuer." Similarly among the Eastern Twic and Bor Dinka "Nuerized Dinkas," who migrated during the British colonial era, now exist in a region controlled by the Aborom clan. These peoples, it is claimed, are the remnants of a larger group of people who moved away during the British period. Today they are recognized as Dinka but actually speak Nuer.

Thus, numerous agricultural and fishing communities have maintained their sovereignty as discrete, largely unincorporated entities within the larger Dinka amalgam today. This has also included the pastoral Western Nilotic Nuer. These people are often recognized as "Nuerized Dinka"; nevertheless, they remain unintegrated within the larger Dinka amalgam. The existence of unintegrated communities of sovereign nations within the Dinka amalgam shows, on the one hand, the difficulties of acquiring Dinka identity, but also suggests that although the Dinka have been at war with a number of Southern peoples historically, they have also peaceably and successfully lived alongside other foreign cultures for centuries.

Conclusion

The group of people who, over time, appear to have most successfully integrated into the expanding Dinka amalgam are the Dinka's linguistic neighbors, the Western Nilotic Luo. Yet still other peoples, both Luo and non-Luo, have remained in small, discrete, ethnic communities, or sovereign nations primarily as agriculturalists and fishermen surrounded by the Dinka. The exception to the rule are the Nuer, who have come to live as discrete communities within the Dinka in the Bor region during the twentieth century and yet continue to live as pastoralists. In this case, the Dinka tend to recategorize them as "Nuerized Dinkas."

Having come to terms with their neighbors in the mid-eighteenth century, the various Dinka clans were not to rest long, however, for they were soon to be invaded from the north by raiders who would change their communities forever.

Foreign Intrusion and Its Consequences

━━━━━━━━━━━━━━━━━━━━━━━━━━━━━━━━━━━━━━━

15

EIGHTEENTH-CENTURY SLAVERS AND TRADERS

"Slavery probably came to the Malwal [Dinka] area sooner than elsewhere [in Dinkaland] because of our geographic continuity with the north."
Lawrence Lual Lual Akuey, Malwal Dinka

Little is formally recorded of eighteenth-century Southern Sudanese history, yet it was a critical period. It began with the intrusion of Islamic slave raiders from the north. Ironically, the event giving birth to this new era of intense strife had taken place a generation or more earlier when the former residents, the Luel, were forced off their land by the expanding Dinka arriving from the southeast.

The Dinka Wars with the Luel

Prior to the Dinka arrival the mound-building Luel had inhabited many parts of the Southern Sudan, particularly west of the Nile. Scholars believe them to be closely related to the Daigu (Daju or Dago) and the Beigi, who now reside in Kordofan and Darfur provinces in what is now west-central Sudan. The Dinka remembered them as dwarfs, light in color and short and stocky in appearance. They were armed with bows, arrows and poisoned hand darts and possessed many sheep and cattle of the non-humped variety.

The Shilluk-Luo had preceded the Dinka and been militarily beaten by the Luel until they collaborated with the newly arrived Rek Dinka and jointly attacked these hostile peoples—this time, successfully. Shortly thereafter the Malwal and Western Twic Dinka followed suit. From this point on many of the Luel were forced to live far in the north beyond the Kir/Bahr el-Arab River in ecologically harsher regions. They were not to rest long, however, for yet another series of Dinka clans, who later collectively came to be known as the Western Ngok, migrated into their territory. These folk arrived in the region from the east and settled onto the land known today as southwest Kordofan. The Abyor clan of the Western Ngok warred with the Luel and forced some from the land while other small pockets of these people remained.[1] Soon, however, the Dinka would encounter another militarily powerful people from the north.

The Coming of the Islamic Baggara Slavers

For a generation (at most) the Ngok resided in peace until the arrival of Islamic nomads, the stateless pastoral Baggara on their northern frontier (c. 1770). This event marked the beginning of permanent instability in the region, for these Islamic pastoralists were a slave-raiding society. The Baggara had previously resided northwest of Dinkaland in the region of Dar Burgo (Bagirmi) within the environs of the Islamic kingdom of Wadai in what is now Chad. This society formerly herded camels as well as cattle and forged east into what is now Muglad around 1770. They settled in modern-day southwest Kordofan province directly north of the various clans of the Western Ngok Dinka. Once in the region they followed typical pastoral lineage society politics and fissioned or splintered into various groups: the Humr and Zurug (now called Messiria), the Hawazma, and the Rizeiqat. After bitter fighting among each other, eventually only the Humr-Messiria remained and the others were forced northwest. Messiria oral histories recount that a leader, Hameidan Abu Hazla, arrived in Muglad and declared war on the Beigi King Dienga, a people believed to be closely related to the Luel. Easily defeated, the king fled south towards the Ngok Dinka territory. Following in hot pursuit, Baggara warriors came into contact for the first time with the Alei Dinka clan (of what was later to become the large Western Ngok Dinka section) who had settled along the Ngol River north of the modern-day town of Abyei. This river is not listed on maps as Ngol but may well be the Ragaba.[2]

The Alei Dinka clan were expanding northward when they met the Humr-Messiria and began a war that lasted for several years. Most of the fighting took place along the northern Ngol River area leading up to the modern town of Muglad, known to the Dinka as *Aguoth*. Initially the Alei defeated the Humr and continued moving north as far as what is now the Babanusa region. To their east were the Nuba (in Dinka *dhony*). The Alei Dinka resided in this region many years and then other Baggara joined the Humr so that the Alei were pushed south of the River Ngol once more. In the meantime, the Baggara met another Dinka clan group, one of whose leaders, Deng (Deing) of Torjok (the Abyor clan) resided at Debbat El Mushbak near the modern Dinka town of Abyei. Another prominent Dinka leader of the time, Moindong (son of Kwal Dit, chief of the Mannyuar), has settled his people near Hasoba.[3]

Soon after their arrival, pastoral politics and ethnic stresses associated with the struggle to acquire land among individual Baggara sections gave rise to an alliance between the Baggara and certain Western Ngok Dinka. Much of the following information was noted in the British period by District Commissioner Lampen who acquired it from an old man, Rihaima Kabbashi (a Mahri), who later passed it on to District Commissioner Henderson. A Seruri *feki* (holy man), Ali Abu Gurun, persuaded the leader of the Torjok Dinka (later the Abyor and also known as the Jok), as well as the Acak Dinka sections of the Western Ngok, to join him in battle against the Messiria Zurug leader, Abu Agbar, at a place called Fut. Other Ngok leaders, however, preferred to remain peripheral to the fray, returning south; these included the Alor chief of the Mannyuar clan. At some point these intra-Baggara feuds evolved into slave and cattle raids, first in the southern Nuba mountains and then south of the Kir/Bahr el-Arab River in Dinka territory. The motivation to move south came from the previous residents, the Luel, of what had recently become Dinka territory. They also had become peripherally involved in the Baggara fray and appealed to the latter for assistance in returning to their previous homelands. Now the Malwal and Western Twic Dinka became fair game for these new Islamic slave raiders.[4]

The First Penetration of Slavers into the Bahr el-Ghazal

The attempted return of the Luel to their former homelands, accompanied by the Baggara who were mounted on horseback, marked the genesis of a centuries-long destabilization of the northern Bahr el-Ghazal region. Having never before seen horses, the Dinka were terrified by what appeared to be "men with two heads and four legs running very quickly." There were two columns which forged south through Malwal Dinka territory during which the Baggara captured men, women, children, and large herds of cattle. Then both columns returned north with much booty. Of the two columns, one passed through Lewal Maturm's country and forged as far as Warait just north of Meding-Aweil. The other column passed through Chief Nuan Atoyon's country, penetrating the River Lol opposite today's town of Nyamlel.[5]

As it has been reasonably well established that the Baggara arrived in Kordofan north of Abyei about 1770, it can be argued that the first slave raids into Dinka territory occurred shortly after this time. Malwal informants, Kuol Lual Mou, Akot Ajuou Majok, Akec Macol Akec, Ater Bol Mayen, Piol Piol Adim, Ding Akuei Deng, and Paulino Akon Ken recount: "When we came to our present area we fought with people on horseback. [Because] we are tall, these people could see us from afar and when we ran the men on horseback overran us. Then Turtuk, a man, brought out a red bull and killed it and asked God to reduce the size of the red people."

Emboldened by the success of their initial attempts at slave raiding in the Dinka country the Baggara made further forays into the Malwal region of Meding-Aweil, capturing more cattle and slaves. Within the year, however, the Dinka discovered that horses and men constituted two different beings. Resisting further invasions, they annihilated the latest Baggara column. After their defeat the Baggara slavers created small parties of horsemen who lay further west, in forests just beyond the Dinka country, where they abducted the children of various non-Dinka southern peoples.[6]

By this time the Humr-Messiria Baggara had acquired enough cattle from the Dinka and their Nilotic neighbors to the east, the Nuer, by way of ongoing raids into the Bahr el-Ghazal, to switch from a former existence as camel and cattle pastoralists to primarily cattle-owners. Evidently many Baggara camels died of disease in the new homelands to which the latter migrated. Thus, these Islamic pastoralists were pressured to acquire the hardier breed of Dinka cattle. Other Baggara to their west, however, maintained a mix of camels and cattle, particularly the Zurug, the Salamat, and Rizeiqat.[7]

In the meantime, the Western Ngok Dinka as a whole, who were subjected to far fewer raids because of the Abyor and Acak alliances with their Baggara neighbors, returned with their herds to the Kir/Bahr el-Arab River region for grazing. This river and its vicinity is viewed by some scholars as a frontier representing an ideological and physical barrier between what is today the "Arab" Muslim north and the African non-Muslim south in the modern country of Sudan. Geographically, it leads westwards from the White Nile through southwest Kordofan and runs approximately between southern Darfur and Bahr el-Ghazal provinces. For a time both the Baggara and the Ngok Dinka sections maintained an uneasy but militarily matched peace. In the meantime the Baggara continued slave raids in the southern Nuba mountains as well as among more vulnerable groups in southwest Kordofan, including a Luo related group, the Shatt, who lived between the Rizeiqat Baggara and the Dinka.[8]

These initially successful Baggara raids encouraged others in the north to enter the slaving business and with the rise in economic power of the Islamic kingdom of Dar Fur, based directly north and northwest of Dinkaland, numerous itinerant traders (*jellaba*) forged south. Although the growing power of Dar Fur was concomitant to the increased slave raiding of peoples in the Southern Sudan, southern Nuba mountains, and other regions, it was also connected to events further west in the Islamic kingdom of Wadai.

The Islamic Kingdoms of Wadai, Dar Fur, and the Explosion of Slave Raiders

The region stretching from Lake Chad to the Nile and from the Sahara to the Bahr el-Ghazal comprises multiple states and societies. Of great significance to the entire eastern Sudan has been the presence of numerous itinerant traders (*jellaba*). Slave raids in this region were an extension of a mobile Sudanic state because any of the sultan's subjects could request permission to make a raid into southern non-Islamic territories for slaves.[9]

The Baggara, who initially resided within the southern environs of the Islamic kingdom of Wadai, were obliged to pay taxes to the sultan in the form of slaves and they evidently forged great distances to acquire their booty. By 1816, for example, traveler John Lewis Burckhardt was informed that a large Dinka slave society resided in this region. He noted "west of Darfur in the Islamic kingdom of Borgo (Wadai), slaves are acquired from pagan negro nations ten to fifteen days journey." The most noted slaving groups included the Dinka, as well as the Dargulla, Benda, Yemyem (Zande), and Ola.[10]

Some decades before 1816, however, many Baggara migrated from what is now modern-day Chad to the east to escape the tight monopoly exercised on slave raiding by the sultans of Wadai. Nevertheless, they continued the business of slave raiding in their new homelands of what became the provinces of southern Kordofan and Darfur. During this period the emerging free enterprise system of the nearby Islamic state of Dar Fur became more attractive for slave raiding societies such as the Baggara, largely because this sultanate held less control over its surrounding territories.[11]

From his new capital of El Fasher east of Jabal Marra the sultan every year gave permission for between sixty and seventy raids (*ghazwa*). Each expedition was given a particular route to follow and a particular people to raid.[12] Thus, the rise of a franchised private commerce in slaves in Dar Fur during the last quarter of the eighteenth century saw a concomitant increase in slave raiding into Southern Sudan.

The outlet for the new trade of this era was Egypt. Many raiders and *jellaba* (traders) based themselves in Kobe, north of El Fasher, a city where merchants both native and foreign conducted a direct trade with Egypt. The flourishing eighteenth- and nineteenth-century commerce between Egypt and Dar Fur along the *darb al-arba'in* (the forty-days road) from Kobe in Dar Fur to Assiut in Egypt was due, in large part, to increased slave raids into the southern Nuba mountains and Southern Sudan. Prior to the latter eighteenth century, the route may have been known but was little used.[13] The success of raids into Southern Sudan correlates with the travel accounts of the period.

Dinka and Other Southern Slave Settlements in Dar Fur and the Expansion of Slave Raiding

While there is little documentation of the exact number of ethnic groups who came to comprise the slave populace of the Sultanate of Dar Fur, travelers' accounts suggest that the Dinka and possibly their Western Nilotic neighbors, the Nuer, formed a sizeable segment of its slave population. Traveler W. G. Browne describes settlements of slaves located near the kingdom's slave markets. Concerning the slaves themselves he remarked that they "mark themselves on the face, and . . . one race of idolatrous negroes near Fur has a habit of extracting two or more of the front teeth of children before puberty."[14] To the best of my knowledge, in this region only the Nuer and Dinka simultaneously practice dental evulsion as well as distinguishing their major sections by facial markings. Therefore, adding to Burckhardt's note of Dinka settlements in Wadai, it is not unreasonable to argue that traveler Browne was observing early Dinka and/or Nuer slave settlements in the environs of Dar Fur.

Dinka informants today suggest that the Nuba rather than the Dinka were the first to be raided. Malwal Dinka Lawrence Lual Lual states: "We believe that the Nuba were enslaved first and then the idea caught on with the Dinka further south, because it is easier to get to Malwal territory than other parts of Bahr el-Ghazal and this region is adjacent to the Baggara." Other informants support this evidence. Western Ngok Dinka Abyei Kon states that around this time one of the nine major clan groups of the Western Ngok, the Alei, were migrating west and northwest from south of the Nuba mountains. Over time this Dinka clan adopted many Nuba refugees referred to by the Dinka as *dhony.* It is probable that these fleeing peoples were a product of recent Baggara slave raids.

That the Baggara enslaved sizeable numbers of Nuba peoples as well as Dinka and possibly Nuer is supported by other travelers' accounts. Mohammed El-Tounsy noted that in 1789–1800 Sultans Muhammad Tayrab and Abd al Rahman al Rashid established slave settlements known as *Turuj.* Located in Dar Daju in southeastern Dar Fur, near the Nuba territory, the inhabitants of these settlements were used as laborers and soldiers and included those from the Nuba Mountains, southern Kordofan, and the Malwal and Twic Dinka territories. Along with *Turuj* various other terms for slaves evolved, including *Fartit,* which was applied to the non-Islamic inhabitants below the ill-defined southern boundary of Dar Fur, living north and south of the Kir/Bahr el-Arab River and in the far western Bahr el-Ghazal region. Those south of the Sinnar Sultanate in the Gezira to the east were referred to as *Nuba* and those south of Wadai were *Kirdi.*[15]

A testament to the numbers of slaves procured and the extent to which slavery and the slave trade expanded in this region is noted by travelers of the period. In 1796 W. G. Browne was the first and only European to pass along the whole length of the *Darb el Arba'in.* He noted a caravan of one thousand slaves. By 1820, just prior to the Egyptian colonial invasion of Sudan, the German geographer Ritter observed that Dar Fur caravans numbered from five-to-twelve thousand slaves.[16]

In the meantime, relations between the Baggara in the north and all other Dinka in the south, except the Western Ngok, were reduced to constant raiding across the Kir/Bahr el-Arab River, giving rise, over the centuries, to a genetic racial mix in the region. Geographically, the Twic and Malwal are adjacent to each other and located at the northwestern extent of Dinka territory south of the Kir/Bahr el-Arab River and north of the town of Aweil. The Ngok are to their northeast, situated primarily north of the Kir/Bahr el-Arab River. The Messiria are the most easterly of the Baggara on the river and their northern neighbors are the Fellaita section of the Humr Baggara and the Ngok Dinka. Malwal informants claim: "We Malwal all war with the Rizeiqat and the Humr. A long time ago we contracted certain marriages between the Dinka and Baggara but since our grandfathers there has been no marriage. We raid the Baggara and capture girls and make them wives and they give birth to children and they do the same thing. This has been going on a long time across the [Kir/Bahr el-Arab]

River."[17] The Ruweng Dinka reside east of the Western Ngok and south of the Nuba mountains. John Biem Ngok Bilkuai states: "Before the British [colonial period] we captured Baggara and vice versa. If we captured men we killed them but we kept the women and children. A Baggara women may bring a brideprice of fifty cows, the same for a Dinka woman although the brideprice changes if she is good looking. A Dinka man cannot marry if he doesn't have cows." Along with slave raiding, different exchange relationships were developing in the Bahr el-Ghazal region, although southern peoples had always traded with each other.

Intra-Southern Trade and Early Foreign Traders

Prior to the penetration of Southern Sudan by external raiders from the north a lively intra-Southern trading network existed. The Dinka acquired hats from a distant people of Kekess (possibly Murle), exchanging them for cows. They refused to part with them when the European travelers offered them beads in exchange. During field research in South Sudan Dinka informants stated that they fought the Murle to acquire their hats.

Many Southern Sudanese exchanged iron goods, particularly east of the Nile. Iron ores are abundant in Africa, though in a variety of forms, qualities, and concentrations. Within the environs of the modern Sudan iron ore was first smelted in the Nile kingdom of Meroe, which was richly endowed with both iron ore and the hardwood timber needed for charcoal. Today, huge mounds of slag testify to the scale of iron production that powered this kingdom's rise. Peter Schmidt suggests that the production of iron goods in Africa encouraged trade with neighboring peoples. In the nineteenth century, for example, people often traded iron goods for ivory and during earlier times commodities such as salt and cattle were traded. The presence of iron ores in various regions of Southern Sudan also encouraged intra-Southern trading contacts. By far, most iron-working took place among the Eastern Nilotic Bari located east of the Nile and south of the Dinka. Kakwa informant, Ebe Enosa, whose mother was Bari, states more specifically that only certain small clans of the Bari were blacksmiths. They must have been prolific, however, for in the early nineteenth century European travelers noted that spears all over the region of the White Nile resembled those of the Bari. On the other hand, Nyarruweng Dinka Lazarus Leek Mawut adds: "Before the cash economy of today we had our own markets. We obtained iron tools from the Bahr el-Ghazal (west of the Nile) because iron-working was not done in our area. We only obtained finished products such as spears from the Ciec Dinka [west of the Nile] by way of the Bor and Twic Dinka [in the east]." The Thain fisherfolk, of former Luo or Mundari ancestry and now recognized as "Dinka" who reside on both sides of the Nile, also provided iron implements. The Dinka did not usually become blacksmiths, but the Thain [formerly Luo] were an exception, for within their polity were many who practiced this skill.[18]

West of the Nile, others also traded iron products with the Dinka. The Ciec Dinka exchanged iron for arrows with Mundari iron-making clans (today known as the Nyonker and Gumbek, or collectively the Adjong) who continued to live within their midst. The southern neighbors of the Agar Dinka, the Yibel, also traded with them and Ruben Macier Makoi adds that "a hundred years ago we paid the Dinka in iron products. We were iron-workers and we used to make spears and bows." The Luo, who migrated into the Bahr el-Ghazal (ca. 1500–1620) prior to the Dinka, had also been forced to change their mode of production when they were forced to migrate west to the boundaries of the powerful and numerous non-Nilotic nation of the Bongo. Here, as they settled on the edges of the iron-stone belt in the western Southern Sudan they became blacksmiths.[19]

In the far southwestern Southern Sudan the Azande arrived in the region from the south in the latter eighteenth century. They incorporated and ruled over avid iron-workers. Ephraim Sunguzagi states that the place for smelting iron in Azandeland was called Bigiwi: "We obtained the raw material, iron stones along the streams. . . . We found iron everywhere." The neighbors of the Azande, the Balanda, also produced iron implements. Bandindi Pascal Uru claims: "In blacksmithing we are excellent, we smelt iron. We call it *mugo* or in Azande, *vongbanzi*. These were the special stones that we collected from which we smelted the iron. We had ovens such as one would use for bread making."

Iron-working appears to have been practiced by almost all Southern Sudanese peoples at one time. Within the Dinka culture, however, the practice was considered too lowly. This perception has changed in the twentieth century with the coming of the money economy, as it afforded the opportunity to acquire more cattle. Western Twic Dinka blacksmith Marko Mabior Majok explains:

> My father's name was Majok Madut and I am from Gogrial. I learned this trade in Wau. My father was not a blacksmith but I saw some blacksmiths and learned from them years ago in 1970. I owned cattle and was cultivating and left all the cattle with relatives to do blacksmithing. There are many Dinka blacksmiths in Wau. I went into a garage and picked up metal and pieces from the railway and I made spears, knives, arrows, hoes and joints for

the doors. . . . If children want to learn the skill they will. In the old days it paid a lot of money.

An Agar Dinka blacksmith, John Majok Makoi, states:

> I learned the trade in Rumbek when I was very small from my uncle, Mathiang Nguan. I also learned from others who are very old; someone called Majok. There are many Dinka blacksmiths today and we get a lot of money to buy cows. I opened shops. Today my uncle has much cattle. He also cultivates. In winter we do the blacksmithing and stop during the rains to do the cultivating. Another member of my family looks after the cows. I make spears, hoes, pots and big bells for the bulls.

In modern times, more and more Dinka are acquiring the skills of blacksmithing, particularly west of the Nile. According to the Malwal there are numerous blacksmiths in their homeland. According to Nyarruweng Dinka Gabriel Col Can, "If you have no cows you can become a black-smith, and sell your items for goats and then buy cows. Many Dinka do this." Among the Western Twic there are also local Dinka blacksmiths who primarily make spears. They acknowledge, however, that blacksmithing is normally an inherited trade.

Other Dinka, however, specifically those east of the Nile, state that blacksmithing is still considered a lowly profession. Eastern Twic Philip Aguer Panyang states: "The attitude among the Bor Dinka has not been positive to blacksmithing. The art of blacksmithing among the Dinka of this area originated in Yirrol [west of the Nile] because there is a lot of iron in Rumbek and in Yirrol which is the Ciec Dinka area. They know how to produce spears and arrows [in reality it is the former Mundari clans who do this]. In the Bor-Twic area there is only one family who did this, Biar Shaw and his son, Deng Biar. Even today it is only this family who are black-smiths." Thus, the presence of iron in Southern Sudan has historically given rise to an intra-Southern trading system. While a thriving intra-Southern trade continued centuries ago, the coming of slave raiders introduced for-eign traders into the region.

Historically, it has often been assumed that the Southern Sudan was "totally isolated" and "free" of foreign influences until the Egyptian colo-nial era of the nineteenth century (1821) onwards. In reality this is not correct. Travelers' accounts suggest that prior to this time the Dinka ex-changed ivory with the Islamic Baggara, who sold it to itinerant traders from Northern Sudan (Danagla and Ja'alliyyin). During the same period the Abialang Dinka on the northeastern Dinka periphery sold or exchanged cut agates or flints of the desert and corals to the Selim Baggara in the Gezira. When the first European traders arrived in the Southern Sudan on the White Nile in the 1840s at Kuronjah, Ciec Dinka Chief Tchinkah already possessed strings of blue glass vermiglio or Venetian beads. Other Dinka on the Nile possessed strings of white beads which they claimed to have acquired from West African Takruri (Fellata) traders who peddled their wares in the Hofrat el-Nahas region in western Bahr el-Ghazal beyond the Dinka country. Soon the traders extended their commercial contacts and conducted business south and east of this territory as far as two days west of the White Nile. Traveler Ferdinand Werne deduced that these traveler/traders did not use the Nile River route, as nothing had been reported of them in the major town in the north, Khartoum. Rather, it appeared more likely that they joined the pilgrim caravans of Islamic Bornu in West Africa and then branched southeast into the Southern Sudan, particularly after the penetration of the Baggara slave raiders. This trading was well under way at the dawn of the Egyptian colonial era of 1821.[20] Thus, much intra-and extra-Southern Sudanese trade existed prior to the colonial period (1821), and iron products, in particular, fueled much of this exchange.

Conclusion

Between 1770 and 1780 Muslim Baggara slavers penetrated into both the Nuba and western Dinka territories, taking captives. The Southern Sudanese penetration was triggered by the attempted return of the Luel to their former homelands, supported by their newly acquired Baggara allies mounted on horseback. This era marked the beginning of wars in Southern Sudan that have continued to present times, including a centuries-long destabilization of the northern Bahr el-Ghazal region, particularly around the plains of the Kir/Bahr el-Arab River. This period, however, also saw the rise of much intra- and extra-Southern Sudanese trade, for merchants from West Africa appeared in the region at this time exchanging beads for numerous southern items. The arrival of the Baggara slave raiders, however, was to introduce an ethnic phenomenon, unique in Western Nilotic history.

16

NILOTIC CHAOS: DINKA, NUER, ATWOT, AND ANYUAK

> "The Nuers are the only group of people who are capable of assimilating Dinkas; no other group does this. The majority of Nuer are Dinka . . . but they won't admit they are Dinka."
>
> *Gordon Matot Tut, Ciec Ador Dinka*

Most scholars of the modern-day Sudan are aware that there has been a long historical conflict between the Dinka and their closely related Nilotic neighbors, the Nuer. However, the relationship between these two is an enduring mystery, particularly as the Nuer today comprise approximately 70 percent of peoples of former Dinka origin. For example, Evans-Pritchard estimated that as much as 75 percent of the Lou Nuer were of Dinka descent.[1] Yet, the question of the original forefathers of the Nuer is still open to debate. Even the Dinka and the Nuer do not agree on this issue. Further, the Luo have become very much involved in this discussion because many now believe that the original Nuer may, in fact, have been one of the several Luo groups previously resident in the region centuries ago, prior to the Dinka arrival. A subsidiary event also concerns the major body of the Atwot, considered to be closely related to the Nuer. This chapter covers this debate and catalogues the events that led many Dinka to change their ethnic identification to that of Nuer. Further, a discussion of the Anyuak, a number of whom were absorbed into the Nuer and Dinka amalgams, also follows.

The Origins of the Nuer: The Debates

Ray Kelly and Peter Newcomer suggest that the Nuer are an ethnic group born entirely of the Dinka. Much of their evidence comes from linguistic studies; glottochronological analysis yields a separation date between the Dinka and Nuer at around 85 A.D. Other scholars, however, strongly disagree. Mohamed Riad, for example, suggested that the Nuer, like the Shilluk, are of Luo origin. He cites oral histories of the Nuer who claim that they originated from a barren waterless country northwest of their present homeland in a region they identify as *Kwer-Kwong*. It is remembered that a leader, Gau, married Kwong, giving birth to Gaa, who became the most important Nuer leader, the Land Chief, acquiring the title of "Chief of the Leopard Skin." Studying Nuer oral histories Riad postulated that on or before 1700 they migrated south from a previous residence in a drought-ridden area of what is now southern Kordofan or Darfur, arriving at the junction of what is now the Bahr el-Homr and Bahr el-Ghazal Rivers. Furthering Riad's argument, Douglas Johnson adds that, although the Dinka and Nuer are connected linguistically, the latter's language contains much to suggest it is also of Luo origin. In social organization the Nuer share significant common traits with the Shilluk as well as with their closely related cousins, the Anyuak, both of Luo extraction. Lastly, John McLaughlin's linguistic figures indicate that, contrary to the arguments of Kelly and Newcomer, the Nuer share a higher percentage of cognates with the Anyuak, who are of Luo extraction, than do the Dinka.[2]

Muddying this puzzle, however, is that in modern times Nuer informants themselves believe that they were originally born from the Dinka and support it in myths. Nuer elder Abraham Riak Bum states:

> The cultural system and political system is what differs between the Dinka and Nuer. The Nuer and Dinka were all one. The Dinka was the older and the Nuer, the younger. When the father of both was ready to die there was only one cow left. He called the Dinka and he was given the cow and the Nuer was given the calf. When the father divided the property the mother called to the Dinka . . . who was loved by the mother more because the Nuer was the trouble-maker. So the Dinka son and the mother were together. When it was time to receive the share from the father, the father said to the Nuer you must take the calf because it will reproduce. So the older Dinka pretended to be Nuer and the next morning he deceived his father and received the calf. The next morning the Nuer son found he had the old cow. So his father said "you can go after the cow. If you get it good! It is up to you." So this is our problem today. The Nuers always have rotten cows and when we raid Dinka cattle, it is because they are ours. The Dinka will not deny this.

Nineteenth-century Nuer oral histories, however, gainsay these more recent Nuer beliefs of Dinka ethnic origination. Rather, they support the arguments of Riad and Johnson above. Missionary Giovanni Beltrame in 1858, for example, noted that "the Shilluk and Nuer speak one language and they state long ago [that] the Dinka invaded their land." On the other hand, some Dinka agree with Nuer Abraham Riak Bum above and also recount similar myths of a shared heritage. According to Agar informants: "Marol is the grandfather of our grandfathers. His various daughters gave birth to four groups. Amou Marol gave birth to the Rek [Dinka] people, Nyantoc gave birth to the Nuer, Acuei gave birth to two sons, one of which gave birth to the Gok [Dinka] and the other to the Luaic [Dinka]."[3]

Other Southern Sudanese, on the other hand, also believe that the Nuer were originally Luo. Sudanese and Kenyan Luo peoples today note linguistic connections between Nuer and their own language. Kenyan Luo Dickson Ogolla Oroku states: "I understand Nuer better than Dinka; it is linguistically closer to us. We believe we, the Luo, were in one place with the Nuer, the Shilluk, and the Anyuak."

The answer to the original identity of the Nuer may very well lie in the older histories of the Western Nilotic Luo and Atwot. Oral histories of the Luo claim that centuries ago they comprised a large series of contiguous disparate groups who lived in numerous parts of what is now southern Darfur, southern Kordofan, and the Southern Sudan. Thus it is not unreasonable to argue that the Nuer represented yet another mosaic of the multiple Luo (Lwo) groups who became disconnected from the larger Luo confederacy as the Dinka migrated into the Southern Sudan. According to Father Crazzolara, who collected these Luo oral histories, numerous Luo clans circulated around the Southern Sudan, perhaps for centuries, prior to the arrival of the Dinka.[4] Certainly this assertion is supported by linguistic studies (see chapter 14). If this is in fact the case, it would explain how the Nuer became encapsulated with the later arrival of the Dinka from the southeast. The question of the origins of the Western Nilotic Atwot may shed further light on the origins of the Nuer.

Who are the Atwot—Nuer, Dinka, or Luo?

Another Western Nilotic people who may also be of former Luo ancestry are the Western Nilotic Atwot. John Burton's research among the Atwot suggests that these Western Nilotes migrated into their modern-day homeland more than 360 years ago. A Chief Reel is claimed to be the ancestral figure who led the migration of the Atwot after parting company with the Nuer. This is supported by certain Atwot informants, including Akec Nyatyiel Nar who recounts: "The people came from the east. We are connected with the Nuer who were our brothers and the Nuer went east and the Atwot came south. This is remembered because my family goes back sixteen generations and Ror-Kec is the name of my grandfather."[5] Atwot Paul Mabor Aliab says it is remembered that the Nuer and Atwot quarreled over cows, which split the two apart: "We really call ourselves the Reel people. The other Nuer colluded against us. The name Akot was our great-great-grandfather and when we arrived here we settled peacefully, although we had sectional fights with the Agars [Dinka]."

Confusingly, many Ciec Dinka informants claim that their ancestors were with the Atwot during their migrations up the Nile into the Bahr el-Ghazal. It is recounted that both peoples then crossed the Nile at two places, one between Ganyliel and Shambe at Khor Liel and the other at Panhom.[6] This data is also supported by the Atwot. Napoleon Adok Gai notes: "The Atwot, Ciec [Dinka], and Aliab [Dinka] . . . are small groups and we arrived at the same time and settled peacefully becoming reasonably unified." Additionally, Atwot Akec Nyatyiel Nar states: "We settled in our present location and came together with the Aliab [Dinka], Agar [Dinka], and Atwot people."

On the other hand certain Atwot do not even adhere to the belief that they were of original Nuer stock or that they migrated to their present land with the Dinka. Rather, they believe their ancestry is more closely linked to that of the Luo. For example, Napoleon Adok Gai and Sudanese Luo Albino Ukec Simon believe: "The Atwot language is closer to the Luo than any other language and we speak a dialect of Nuer only because we were adjacent to these people for a period. But we were a people of separate identity."[7] Apak Atwot David Deng Athorbei suggests that Luo people resided in the area and did not leave the Atwot territory but rather were absorbed by the incoming people: "The legend is that the Luo left Atwotland or that the Atwot left the Nuer territory settling in this area. We ourselves believe the vast majority of Atwot today are descended from people who were always here and that many of us are of Luo origins."

If, indeed, four centuries ago the Atwot resided adjacent to the Nuer and the latter two groups were originally Luo (much like the Shilluk and Anyuak), it would explain why modern-day Sudanese and Kenyan Luo people perceive a close linguistic and cultural affinity with these two groups (and not with the Dinka). Thus, the Nuer and Atwot were likely yet another part of the older Luo mosaic that had resided in Southern Sudan some time before the arrival of the Dinka. The date of the Atwot split from the Nuer may also have been connected to the entrance of the Dinka into Southern Sudan and the actual reason that these two groups were geographically split in two. Regardless of the origins of the Nuer, their relations with the Dinka were fraught with tension since the earliest times.

Dinka/Nuer Relations Prior to the Eighteenth-Century Slave Raids

Dinka oral histories recount that they have been at war with the Nuer for at least three centuries. Western Ngok Dinka Maguith Deng Kuol and Agoth Alor Bulabek state that at least one conflict erupted between the Dinka and the Leik Nuer shortly after the various clans (which later became the large Western Ngok Dinka grouping) arrived in southwest Kordofan: "Ngok Chief Kuot Awut failed to deliver his daughter to a Nuer man who had paid a large bridewealth for her in marriage. The Nuer were in a fix and declared war on the Dinka."

Further, the Nuer homeland, which was within the inner periphery of the Dinka and closer to the *sudd* swamp, was often flooded. In the rainy season these Nilotes were forced to move west across the Ngol River. Tensions ensued with the newly arrived Acak Dinka clan in the eighteenth century. Soon the Alei Dinka clan under their chief, Deng Col, and the Acak Dinka under Chief Kuot Awet, as well as the Bongo Dinka under Chief Lual Deng (later all part of the Western Ngok Dinka) united to fight another war against the Nuer. Remembered as a great battle, *Dek Jor,* it took place at Panyayir.. The outcome of the war is uncertain, but relations between these three Dinka clans became consolidated because of ongoing conflicts with the Nuer, particularly as the Bongo and Acak had at one time been one clan family.[8]

The Nuer however, have also been ethnically absorbed into certain Western Ngok clans. According to Abyei Kon:

> My great-grandfather in the seventeen hundreds adopted a lot of people, big groups assimilate little groups. There are four sections within the Bongo. One of these . . . is the biggest in Paneru and is called the Awet-Ruweng. My grandfather, Lual Deng, brought a lot of Nuer under his control because he was a powerful *beny.* Only the Bongo adopted a lot of Nuer because of the power of Lual Deng. Both before and after the Turkish period [1821–85] this chief was absorbing Nuer. Lual Deng's son was Ayei. Until the British period [1898] the Nuer kept coming to this area because only the Bongo

treated the Nuer well. Because the Bongo and the Acak were the last to come they became familiar with each other and these Nuer became Dinka after a while by marriage. . . . A few Nuer were absorbed by the Acak; only a few. Some Nuer fought with their own people and came to the Dinka region.

Unsurprisingly, however, the increased stresses of the eighteenth-century Islamic Baggara raids further intensified ethnic conflict between the Dinka and the Nuer.

The Nuer Scramble Towards the East

Around the time of the Baggara slave raids into the Bahr el-Ghazal in the eighteenth century, the Bul Nuer, the eastern neighbors of the Western Twic Dinka, initiated a mass Nuer migration east. As they did so they came into conflict with their eastern neighbors the Jikainy Nuer.[9] Rather like dominoes, over time, all peoples suddenly forging east came into conflict with each other.

What followed was an ethnic phenomenon new to Southern Sudanese history. Up to this point the Dinka had steadily absorbed numerous non-Dinka on their inner and outer peripheries. In this period, however, various Nuer groups continued to thrust, often militarily, far to the east to the edge of the Upper Nile Basin. Within a century they had hewn a hundred-mile wide swath through the center of Dinka as well as Anyuak territory in the far east of Southern Sudan. In the process, because ethnic absorption into Nuer society occurred with great ease, by 1890 they had increased their territorial domain fourfold to a total of thirty-five thousand square miles.[10] During this often tumultuous migration many Dinka lying in the path of the Nuer were "digested" into the expanding Nuer culture. This took place when the land became over-populated and the resident Dinka were forced to change their mode of production in order to survive. This in turn affected their political structure. As Nuer Abraham Riek Bum argues, "between the Dinka and Nuer, it is the cultural system and the political system which differs." In time the Dinka, who became outnumbered by the Nuer, were more formally absorbed into the latter clans with a ceremony. This move may well have been motivated by the need for military support and protection. The dates of this initial Nuer advance to the east have been estimated by Riad to be around 1750, which correlate closely with the beginnings of Baggara slave raids into the heartlands of Southern Sudan.[11]

Up to this time in Southern history it was the Dinka who had primarily absorbed their Southern Sudanese neighbors. Now, for the first and only time, the reverse took place. Only a significant event, above and beyond drought and famine (which had plagued the south for centuries), could have caused such a phenomenon. The Dinka memories of this expansion recount violence; the Nuer remember accommodation. Either way, neither has forgotten this precolonial event.

Dinka and Nuer Oral Histories of the Nuer Expansion

The Nuer expansion ethnically absorbed many Dinka clan groups, but forced others to flee north or south of their former residences in Southern Sudan. Further, it completely split some large Dinka clan families. For example, the Ghol (now part of the Bor Dinka group in the southeast) and Dunghol (now part of the Padang group in the far north) claim at one time to have been geographically connected. The Ruweng and Nyarruweng make a similar claim. In terms of population two Dinka groups greatly affected by the Nuer expansion were the Rut and Thoi Dinka. It is probable that these groups were once far more numerous in the past than in modern times (approximately three thousand during the British period) and that they previously occupied an enormous area further south of their present homeland. However, many were killed or absorbed by the Nuer while others fled in all directions seeking refuge with other related Dinka clans. As the Thoi fled north to the Zeraf hills it forced the Ruweng and Abialang Dinka migrations to the northwest and northeast respectively.[12] A Thoi Dinka, Philip Thon Marol, states that his ancestors resided in Ayod and were militarily forced north to their present position:

> We were neighbors of the Bor who were based in Ayod but today it is a Nuer town. We were pushed by Lau, Gawaar, Lak, and Thiong Nuer north. They also displaced the Anyuak from the Nasir area. My great grandfather was born in Ayod and the Thoi people used to live further south and we were pushed north by the Nuer. The Ruweng and Nyarruweng used to be in the present-day Gawaar area in Ayod. However, the Nuer came and fought them, penetrating them and dividing them, sending the Nyarruweng south and the Ruweng north.

Other Dinka claim they too were militarily forced north by the Nuer. A Rut Dinka, Santino Malual Meet, notes that his people used to reside much farther south in Ayut and were expelled from their homelands: "After migrating south we settled in Ayut [today's Gawar territory] and the Nuer came in big numbers and we fought them and we were pushed north to our present position of Khor Fulus." Two Ghol Dinka, Samuel Majak Piok and Barnaba Wuor, state that the Nuer now reside in what used to be Padang territory: "The Padang used to be further south and got pushed north by the Nuer. The Nuer wars ended up with the Thoi and Luaic moving north and the Ghol remaining where they are now. So the present location of Nuer used to be a settlement of Padang."

On the other hand this Nuer expansion also forced many Dinka clans south of their former homelands. Solomon Leek Deng and Abdengokuer Adut note that "We were all along the Nile from Renk down to Bor and it was our area when the Nuer came and fought with us and cut us in two. Now the Nuer are in Waat, Ayot, and Fanjak. When the Nuer came and raided us they took cows, women, and children." An Eastern Twic Dinka Diing Akol Diing states: "In the early nineteenth century the Nuer pushed the Bor Dinka further south to their present region. We have songs remembering the places we used to live, and today they still have Dinka names, but these areas are now occupied by the Nuer."

On the other hand, certain Nuer view this period as one of war as well as accommodation. Abraham Riak Bum states:

> My ancestors were from Bentiu in Upper Nile. When we came there the settlers in these places were Dinka and there was tension between us until we expelled the Dinka from these places on the central Upper Nile. After a time there was a reconciliation between the Nuer and Dinka and we agreed to share the land. So the Dinka moved back to the Malakal border along the Sobat. This agreement was reached with the aid of Nuer elders Kuany Jang and Wal Nangjok, and on the Dinka side, Deng Pakak of the Thoi Dinka and Riak Yak of the Eastern Luaic. However, initially, the fighting was between the Nuer themselves; we fought over cattle and grazing; we are also farmers and we grew our own *dhurra*. However, as we migrated, our population increased and the Bentiu region became overpopulated, so we had to migrate into more marginalized areas. We found Dinka also moving into the region and we fought with them, partly because the Dinka and Nuer cultural and political systems differ.

Many Dinka, however, preferred not to flee and remained as the Nuer moved into their territories. Over time, they adapted to the culture and economic system of the invading group.

The Dinka Who Became Nuer: Ecology and Population Crises

It is known that substantial numbers of Dinka became Nuer in this era. For example, the Nyarruweng Dinka, now some few thousand, claim that at one time they held all the Lau Pali and comprised a much larger population (some hundred thousand).[13] Marshall Sahlins suggests that Nuer political organization represents a tool for military expansionism born from seasonal ecological scarcity and recurrent famines. E. E. Evans-Pritchard argues that ecological scarcity produces a high interdependence between members of the same Nuer villages and cattle camps, encouraging a "common economy" of "mutual assistance and consumption of food" within these groups. Adding the factor of Baggara slave raids into the western Nuer territories, which forced many to flee east, it is not difficult to comprehend how the recently encapsulated Nuer panicked as they sought a means of escape in the opposite direction. Further, much of the Nuer violence may have been a factor of increased militarism among those Dinka now forced to convert to the Nuer socioeconomic and political system as the land became stressed with the increasing number of fleeing peoples from the west. This crisis would have affected those living within the periphery of the Nuer and Dinka regions, for lacking sufficient arable land to accommodate an increasing population, these folk would have been forced from an economic system of agropastoralism, more typically Dinka, to one more heavily dependent on pastoralism and raiding (which evolved from a life in the wetter ecologically poor regions nearer the *sudd*), more typical of Nuer society.[14] I have argued earlier (in chapter 13) that a change of mode of production often extends to a change in ethnicity.

Thus, each generation of Dinka exposed to the expanding Nuer economic and political system initially had no choice but to readapt to the dominant mode of existence. The ease of "becoming Nuer" quickly facilitated a change of ethnic identification from that of Dinka to Nuer, for ethnic incorporation into Nuer society may be accomplished by means of a ritual of sacrifice. Gordon Matot Tut also states that "in occupied Nuer territory today the . . . Nuer have Lou and Ador sections much the same as the Ciec Dinka [next door]." This suggests that the Lou and Ador of both groups were of former Dinka origin.

Within the modern-day Nuer territory (bordering the Ciec Dinka to the north) are people who also claim their ancestors were part of the Cuei group who crossed the Nile with the Ciec Dinka from east to west centuries ago. This supports the idea that many Nuer and Dinka in this region actually share the same ancestry and were originally Dinka. Neither the Dinka nor Nuer forgot their ancestral backgrounds or genealogies, and those of newly acquired Nuer identity would have always remembered their Dinka roots. Further, their Nuer compatriots would also have remembered. This factor, nevertheless, did not alienate them in Nuer society, and indeed many former Dinka citizens absorbed into Nuer society subsequently became prominent leaders.[15] On the other hand, pertaining to modern-day Dinka boys abducted by the Nuer, Bor-Atoc Dinka Mom Kou Nhial Arou states: "I remember some stolen Dinka children coming back to Dinkaland. . . . One of my uncles came back. . . . He had the gar (Nuer markings) on his head. . . . He had to come back because the Nuer would not buy him a wife. Later he was killed by the Nuer in 1992. My uncle was welcomed back by his Dinka relatives who gave him cows to acquire a wife."

The Western Nilotic Anyuak

Another group of "Luo" origin is the Anyuak. These Nilotes have resided in the east along the Sobat River for centuries and today now also extend into Ethiopia. These Western Nilotes are most closely related to the Shilluk and trace their origin to the "country of Dimo" south of their present homeland. They were led north by a powerful chief, Gila, a brother of the Shilluk King Nyakang. A quarrel led to a split between the two groups prior to Nyakang's arrival at the present-day Shilluk homeland on the White Nile during which the Anyuak migrated east.[16]

Gila's grandchild, Cuwai, became their first king. The Anyuak political organization, like that of the Shilluk, is a factor of geography. Among the eastern Ethiopian Anyuak there is more dry ground available, giving rise to closely connected villages and a wider political organization than that afforded the autonomous villages of the western Anyuak in Sudan. The Ethiopian Anyuak historically have had a royal clan and a king while western villages have not.[17]

When the Ngok Dinka migrated eastwards back to the Sobat River during the sixteenth and seventeenth century droughts they encountered, along with the Shilluk, Anyuak peoples, some of whom they later absorbed. According to Eastern Ngok Dinka Simon Ayuel Deng: "Originally we were Anyuak and then the Dinka came from the west." This phrase suggests the Dinka moved into what was then Anyuak territory after they crossed the Nile from west to east, eventually incorporating a number of these closely related Western Nilotic residents into their amalgam.

In the eighteenth century, along with the Dinka, the Anyuak were also affected by the Nuer advance to the eastern banks of the Nile. They had lived on the Sobat River from the Pibor mouth down to Tawbai in the Tawj district to the northeast of Khor Machar, and on the Adura and Mokwai Rivers to the south. But they were driven out of all these places by the powerful Jikainy Nuer who came from, and still occupy, all of the swamp country inland from Shambe in the Bahr el-Ghazal. The Nuer also swept up the Sobat and Baro Rivers and drove the Anyuak east and southeast. In consequence, there has also been great enmity between these two Nilotic groups.[18]

Conclusion

The late eighteenth century saw the genesis of early Islamic Baggara slave raids into the western Dinka and Nuer country, which in turn gave rise to the genesis of eighteenth-century Nuer flight and expansion to the east. During this movement the Nuer dislodged and ethnically incorporated many Dinka and to a lesser extent Anyuak peoples. Eventually their population in the east increased fourfold. The ecological stress on the land explains why so many Dinka were forced to convert to the Nuer mode of existence. Forced to rely more heavily on pastoralism alone in the wake of ecological stress, population pressures, and difficulties involved in an agropastoral livelihood as populations rapidly expanded, many Dinka became Nuer. The massive absorption of Dinka into the Nuer amalgam reversed, temporarily, Dinka expansion in Southern Sudan. This anomaly however, soon became reversed again as the Dinka continued marrying and integrating with those on their peripheries.

Although certain scholars argue that the forefathers of the Nuer and Dinka were one, it appears likely that the Nuer were formerly a Luo group that became isolated from the larger Luo confederation that resided in much of Southern Sudan and southern Kordofan prior to the Dinka arrival. If, indeed, the Nuer were originally Luo, then their former close neighbors, the Atwot (today located south of the Agar Dinka), would also be part of the same mosaic. It is estimated the Atwot "migrated" away from the Nuer some four centuries ago, suggesting their geographical split from the Nuer coincided with the Dinka advance into the Bahr el-Ghazal. This correlates with Dinka oral histories of moving into regions of the Bahr el-Ghazal with or behind the Atwot. In sum, the Shilluk, Anyuak, Nuer, and Atwot are most obviously, along with many others groups in Southern Sudan today, members of the larger Luo confederation which resided throughout much of Southern Sudan prior to the Dinka arrival. With the exception of the Shilluk (and eastern Anyuak) the Dinka are the only other Western Nilotes who have historically tended towards a highly stratified society and political centralization.

17

POLITICS AND STRATIFICATION AMONG STATELESS PEOPLES

Although Dinka myths suggest certain key leaders attempted to centralize society, since the time these Nilotes arrived in Southern Sudan, they, and other pastoral stateless societies, have primarily pursued the typical pastoral lineage philosophy of decentralized politics. Lineage systems, generally, due mainly to lack of centralized and persistent political authority, tend to be in a condition of continual change and instability. For example, when a Dinka clan prospered and grew large, it tended to draw apart from the group of which it was a part, becoming distinct within itself. Thus, when the largest political entity, a cattle-camp (*wut*), increased in size due to the arrival of a group of latecomers, it often became overcrowded. Being less advantageously placed in the wet season camp, perhaps on water-logged land up to the very edges of the camping site, the late-comers often came to resent the superior geographical position of the first-comers. Thus, a prominent individual, usually a priest, gathered a group of his own kin, and perhaps others whose places in the *wut* did not satisfy them, and set off to form his own camp.[1] This political strategy was successful as long as there was sufficient land available to which one might further migrate.

Dinka political fissioning also sometimes took place for other reasons. British administrator G. W. Titherington noted that the Dinka nature is essentially free and independent, that they think nothing of transferring from one clan or family to another following a fight or grievance. Often new family groups (*gol*) are fissiparous as a result of fratricidal blood feuds. Many also follow the departing priest because Dinka males prefer to withdraw from the larger corporate society of their kinfolk to relieve themselves of the customary requirement of contributing towards marriage payments.[2]

Ultimately, in many pastoral stateless societies, including the Dinka, there developed a considerable scattering of lineages across large geographical areas as long as there was sufficient available land to which to migrate. Today, segments of the same Dinka clans, for example, can be found hundreds of miles from each other throughout Southern Sudan.[3] Increasing populations, land shortages, ecological stress, and the Dinka philosophy of political atomization therefore encouraged political fissioning and geographical expansion for centuries, giving Dinka politics an embedded centrifugal quality. When arable land suddenly became scarce, however, fission was forced to a halt, as was the case on the northern Dinka frontier.

The Political Centralization of the Western Ngok

The Western Ngok Dinka departed from typical Dinka politics in beginning a phase of political centralization in the late eighteenth and early nineteenth centuries. Around 1740 Chief Kwoldit, a prominent leader of a large and prominent Dinka clan, the Abyor (or Jok), moved his people north across the Kir/Bahr el-Arab River into what is now southern Kordofan, the region south of the modern-day town of Abyei. These Dinka represented those on the northernmost periphery of the Dinka confederation in the west.

Much like the Nilotic Shilluk of the White Nile, the Abyor can recount a long line of prominent priest/leaders and connect this to historical events. Their lineage, in descending order, includes Bulabek (the earliest remembered), Dongbek, Kwoldit (who guided the people to their modern homeland), Monydhang, Allor, Biong, Arob, Kwol, and Deng Majok, who presided over the Western Ngok in the 1960s. Father Santandrea differs in his list of the Ngok Abyor leaders and suggests that the leader Jok lived around 1640 east of the Nile at Ngok-luel-yat and that he was succeeded by the following leaders: Bulabek (1665), Donbek (1690), Kuol (1720, who crossed the Nile and settled along the Ngol), Monydan (1750, who lived along the Ngol), Alor (1785, who went to Abyei [c. 1810] and is buried near the Ngol), Biong (1815, who went south to Wunewei and died there), Arop (1840), Kuol (1865), and Deng Makwei (Deng Majok).[4]

After the Abyor clan's arrival in the eighteenth century in what is now Southern Kordofan, the Bongo, a less powerful Dinka clan, came to reside to their north. The problem, however, was that the Bongo, unwittingly, had settled on the richest land in the region. According to Western Ngok Abyor Dinka Paul Kok Bol, "land is very important because the Dinka are agro-pastoralists and while cattle represents wealth, grain (particularly *dhurra*) constitutes a major part of the diet." Thus, according to Abyei Kon, a Bongo, the first remembered intra-Dinka conflict in this region, remembered as the "Nainai war" (or Nayinai), ensued along the river between the Bongo and the Abyor when the latter attacked the former in a bid to acquire more arable land. Within a century other clans arrived in the area ; as "first-comers" to this region's south, the Abyor clan began to wrestle the best farming and grazing lands from other late-arriving intruders. By 1810 approximately nine distinct Dinka clan groups had settled on the very limited arable land in the region of southwest Kordofan in and around what is now the modern town of Abyei.

Notwithstanding the Abyor attempts to become masters of the land, they nevertheless were not the first to arrive in the entire region. Rather, the Alei had actually formerly migrated and come to reside along the River Ngol north of what is now the Western Ngok territory in the latter seventeenth and early eighteenth centuries. Over time these people spread so far north they came to reside near what is now Muglad. In the meantime the Abyor, followed by another powerful Dinka clan, the Mannyuar, had approached this region from the south a few decades later. These latter clans, however, were the most populous and thus were recognized by all in the region as the most militarily and politically powerful.[5] Soon a number of factors encouraged political centralization in the region.

There are many causes, historically, for the emergence of states and proto states. Marvin Harris argues that chiefdoms often evolve into states when the population is large and "circumscribed," or has limited fertile lands.[6] Of all the major Dinka groupings, the Western Ngok, who represent the far northcentral periphery of Dinkaland today, appear to have undergone an early phase of political centralization, largely because of the paradigm presented by Harris—a severe shortage of arable land.

Ecology, Land Shortages and Political Centralization

Located north of the Kir/Bahr el-Arab River in what is now Southern Kordofan province in the modern-town of Abyei, the land in which the newly arrived Western Ngok clans settled experienced the worst weather conditions in Southern Sudan. The climate included radical alterations between dry and wet seasons. In the summer it was a hot and parched semi-desert for some months; during the rainy season it became an isolated and muddy tropical swamp. Further, to the naked eye the region appeared to be flat, but this vast plain was deceptive in that it was laced with a meandering system of raised sandy ridges, which were connected. Crucial during the rainy agricultural season, the wide depression lacked adequate drainage to prevent water-logging of the Dinkas' sorghum plants. This situation was exacerbated by the extreme impermeability of the black clay soil, which limited agriculture to the low slopes between the ridges and the depressions. If the Dinka economy rested entirely on pastoralism, this ecological factor would have been less important, but as mentioned earlier, agriculture forms an important part of the Dinka economy and diet. It was only because of the Western Ngok's skill in farming historically that they had many successful harvests under the most difficult of conditions. The growth of sorghum and the quality of the soil in this region thus became an important factor in the political centralization of the various Ngok Dinka clans in the eighteenth century. This was because the land had only a limited series of connected ridges which were dry enough to allow a great deal of contiguous settlement.[7]

In the early years the various Dinka clans of this region came to be dependent on a limited number of sorghum crops that grew quickly. Paul Kok Bol states that of the ten varieties of *dhurra* which the Western Ngok grow, *ngai* grows the most quickly with a three to four-month growing season, followed by *ruth,* which is harvested later than the *dhurra.* These *caudatum* sorghum varieties are extremely hardy compared to other indigenous African crops and grow despite high water, drought, and parasites. Nevertheless, once cultivated, they become dependent on ecologically and culturally specialized areas which limited the direction and extent of migration of peoples cultivating them. Thus successful cultivation of crops in this region negated the possibilities of typical Dinka political expansion or fission and fusion into new areas, for there was no more arable land available. Thus, the Western Ngok Dinka began to emulate the Nilotic Shilluk of the White Nile, who arrived in the early sixteenth century. The latter had also developed a centralized political system due largely to the ecologically limited environment of sandy ridges, coupled with the limitation of movement for food crop cultivation. In the Western Ngok territory, therefore, the extreme ecological conditions of the land encouraged a different political philosophy among these Dinka clan groups as compared to those on their southern periphery.[8]

Initial political stratification took the form of a division in society between those who came first and those who came later. For example, there were the earliest settlers to the whole region, the *koic* (the "first-comers"), which included the Alei, Abyor Mannyuar, Acweng, Anyiel, Diil, and Mareng clans. Second, there were the "latecomers," the *pancieng*, which comprised the Acak and the Bongo who had migrated into the region from the north some decades or more after the Alei. Robin Horton suggests that this kind of nascent polity gains politically by incorporating weak immigrants.[9] However, shortly after the various Ngok clans had settled in Abyei and began a limited system of political stratification, a centralizing third factor came into play, solidifying pyramidal leadership among these Dinka clans—the arrival of the Islamic Baggara.

The Politicizing Effect of the Islamic Baggara

Prior to the arrival of all of the Western Ngok clans, the Alei Dinka clan had already been at war with the newly arrived Islamic Humr-Messiria Baggara north of the present-day Western Ngok homeland. As mentioned in chapter 5 war between these two groups lasted throughout the eighteenth century. In a few years, the Alei defeated the Humr and continued to move north. Over time, however, the latter were joined by other Baggara and pushed the Alei Dinka clan south of the River Ngol, back to their former homeland. Reinforcements then arrived in the form of another Dinka clan group, the Bongo, who had just migrated from the eastern region known as Paneru. Still later, the Acak Dinka clan joined in the war against the Humr-Messiria Baggara.

In the meantime, the Abyor, located to the south of the Alei, Bongo, and Acak clans was struggling with a neighboring clan, the Mannyuar, for possession of the best land. Led by Alor Adjing and his son Kuor Alor, a great military leader, the Mannyuar in the mid-eighteenth century were recognized as the greatest military power among all the Dinka clans in the region. Thus, the Bongo, less powerful militarily, paid homage to the latter. To this effect they offered gifts (cattle) to the Mannyuar leader in the hopes of acquiring political alliances and military protection. Geographically the Abyor were in Mirok, the Alei were in a place called Gokmou, and the Bongo located in Abyei, whose name derived from the presence of trees with a particularly sweet fruit (although others claim the name derived from steam coming from the ground).[10]

In the mid to late eighteenth century, the Abyor clan leader, Kwoldit, feeling outmaneuvered, in a bold political move initiated early alliances with the Baggara to the north, rather than suffer incessant war as had their Dinka neighbors to their north. Some of the alliances made by the succeeding

Abyor clan leaders with the Baggara have endured to present times. Thus, this event, in turn, encouraged the Bongo leader, Lual Deng, to approach the leader of the Abyor for a reconciliation; largely because the Alei and Bongo were now also threatened with a war on two fronts, one in the north with the Baggara and one in the south with the Abyor.[11]

Towards the end of the eighteenth century all of the Ngok clans discovered they had become peripheral to the environs of the increasingly powerful Islamic Sultanate of Dar Fur. Leading theorists suggest that the natural concomitant to military unification is political centralization. More specifically, state formation is encouraged when, along with limited territoriality, external pressures escalate and a chief is able to provide protection for the populace against enemy attacks. This is because the organizational capabilities demanded by warfare, its hierarchy, and central command spread from the military to society. Warriors then become kings and bring military discipline to government.[12]

Under the special circumstances of Baggara attacks and Dar Fur's expansion (notwithstanding recent alliances with members of this Islamic pastoralist group) the various Western Ngok Dinka clans found it necessary to make military changes. Initially age-sets came to play a far more significant role in Ngok warfare than in other contemporary Dinka groups. Over time they then altered their military institutions so as to create a standing army against Baggara attacks. In the past all young men, after initiation, joined the Dinka warrior class and protected their particular clan families from external aggression. Now all of the warrior clans consolidated to produce a more formidable military power. Further military adjustments were introduced to increase security by electing "war chiefs" for each individual village. Thus, the number of military leaders increased and a military hierarchy came into being under a prominent military leader who deferred to priests for spiritual guidance. Occasionally priests were also military leaders.[13]

The Rise of the Abyor

In this era, from the late eighteenth century onwards, the Abyor came to predominate over all other clans because their leaders began to provide military protection for many Dinka and non-Dinka alike. Concurrently, the powerful Mannyuar leader's son, Kuor Alor, began to behave as a "dictator" and disgusted so many of his own people that numbers moved to the Abyor area. Over time the Mannyuar, previously the most politically and militarily powerful, became generally unpopular. According to Abyei Kon:

"When you want to become a leader among the Dinka, collect the wealth and then open your house to everybody." Abyor clan leaders then gained further political respect among their neighbors by providing military protection against Baggara attacks. This was more easily accomplished because Abyor leader, Kwoldit, and his successors initially relied on diplomatic skills by making alliances with the Humr-Messiria section of the Baggara in a bid to save all of the Ngok.[14] Over time, the Abyor became recognized as the most powerful Dinka clan in the region.

Although these Dinka/Baggara alliances aided all the Western Ngok clans, they were also critical to the Baggara. The Western Ngok capital, Abyei, and the main town of the Baggara, El-Muglad, are separated by a harsh desert scrub of only 120 miles. Thus, relations with the various Ngok Dinka clans have always been marked by the need for precious water over that of slave raids. The Baggara, too, were plagued by a climate which was one of the harshest in the Sudan, for El Muglad suffered ecological limitations in that the arable land consisted of ridges of grey sandy soil in and around the Humr-Messiria towns. Like the Dinka, they came to cultivate sorghum and watered their herds from the pools which held water for only six to eight weeks after the yearly rainfall.[15]

Throughout the late eighteenth and nineteenth centuries, when the Humr-Messiria and Ngok Dinka clans needed water for their herds from the river systems south of the Ngok homeland, Abyei, military tensions erupted. However, according to Humr and Dinka oral histories a compromise between both groups over water rights and access to the rivers south of the Ngok was reached. Thereafter, each Baggara and Ngok section maintained the same specific route north and south from their rainy to their dry season camps. The need to maintain forage and fodder for the animals required that these routes not cross each other, and these migratory routes prevailed for centuries. Tensions intermittently resulted however, when, during certain years of drought, the Humr migrated south ahead of schedule while, conversely, the Ngok failed to move north away from the rivers for exactly the same reason.[16] Nevertheless, unlike the Dinka to their south, in precolonial times the Western Ngok had built a formidable military and political power within the region that countered the advance of the Baggara.

Although the Ngok underwent a phase of formal political centralization and stratification in the precolonial era, all those Dinka to the south and east of the Ngok have also been societally stratified. Many scholars believe that stateless societies, and in this case the Nilotic groups (with the exception of the Shilluk and Anyuak) in Southern Sudan, have been "egalitarian." Kathleen Gough, however, notes that the egalitarian ethic governing relations among Nuer kin groups, for example, are not extended to their dependent immigrant clients.[17] Dinka oral histories also suggest that they have embedded within their socioreligious culture key elements of political stratification and are far more stratified than the Nuer. For example, according to Ciec Dinka Gordon Matot Tut: "The Nuers have one thing when you are among them; you are not discriminated against. They take you wholly and even if others may discriminate against you they will protect you. This does not happen in Dinka society. We are more hierarchical. The Dinkas are often made into leaders of the Nuer. . . . The Dinka are like the English, the Nuer are like the Americans." Since the time the Dinka first entered Southern Sudan their society has distinguished between priestly and commoner clans.

Early Stratification in Dinka Society

As the Dinka were resident in the Gezira on the periphery of the Nilotic kingdoms of Meroe and Alwa for centuries, it is not surprising that they acquired elements of state culture and carried it with them as they migrated south. Since their arrival in Southern Sudan the Dinka have continued to be a highly structured society wherein "chiefly clans" are recognized as having more religious and political rights than "commoner clans." The aristocratic/commoner social and political division in society can be remembered as far back as Aiwel, the first known leader of the Dinka to guide his people into Southern Sudan. This power structure has been supported for centuries by Dinka myths and histories, dating back to Aiwel's migration into Southern Sudan, that recall how resident "commoners" yielded political power to this powerful priest and "chiefly" outsider and his people. Aiwel then passed on his priestly powers only to his descendants.

Thus, over the coming centuries two models of power distribution came to exist among the Dinka: *bany* (those with special "inherited" religious power and functions symbolized by the sacred fishing spear, *bith*) from which the priests, *bany-bith,* are derived; and *kic,* or "commoners," the members of Dinka society who had no special hereditary religious powers and, thus, no political rights or functions. Even today among the eastern Dinka the chiefly clans are regarded on the one hand as immigrants, but on the other as nevertheless possessing unquestionably great religious and political power. Within the large Malwal Dinka grouping in northwest Dinkaland, the *bany bith* are found only among particular clans: the Parek, Pahol, Pagong, Panguet, Pariath, and Patek, whose ancestors reputedly received the fishing spears from Longar Dit or Aiwel Longar "the Great."[18]

The Dinka system of societal stratification has been held in place for centuries, and one can very quickly determine who is "chiefly" versus "commoner" by heritage and history. Godfrey Lienhardt observed that among these Nilotes the genealogies of dominant or "authentic" clan groups are far longer than those of accessory groups. Or, as Paul Macuer Malok states, this genealogy is supported by "the essence of one's background [which] is the knowledge of one's totem and those of one's family tree for at least ten generations."[19] Thus, power distribution in Dinka society is controlled by a long knowledge of ancestral totems and family lineage. Those who cannot produce a long family lineage with remembered ancestral totems are automatically relegated to the class of commoners. In modern times elite Dinka society comprises those who claim to be direct ancestors of those who migrated into the Southern Sudan four to five centuries ago with a remembered ancestry, in some cases, of twenty generations. Thus, historically important blood lines have divided the Dinka into those tho have politico-religious power and those who do not.

Conclusion

Although many Southern Sudanese Western Nilotic peoples have been described by scholars as "egalitarian," the Dinka, and to a lesser degree the Nuer, have in fact been, and continue to be, a socially and politically stratified society. Since the earliest times, the Dinka have distinguished between priestly or "aristocratic" and "commoner" clans. These distinctions have historically bestowed political and economic power only on those whose genealogies can prove a long Dinka ancestry.

Other forms of economic and political stratification among the Dinka came about when arable land became scarce and populations intensified. This, therefore, limited the feasibility of the long practiced political fission and fusion which had encouraged so much Dinka geographic expansion in Southern Sudan. The best documented case of political centralization prior to the intrusion of the colonizing Egyptians in 1821 involved the various clans of what became the Western Ngok Dinka. Within this grouping, large Dinka clan groups defined themselves as "first comers" to the land to distinguish themselves from the "latecomers." In the process the former proclaimed a political right of dominance and representation over all other peoples. Situated in northern Dinkaland, near the environs of the Islamic Sultanate of Dar Fur, the Ngok were forced, because of limited arable land, increasing populations, and the threat of Islamic Baggara raids, to centralize politically under the leaders of the Abyor clan. At the dawn of the Egyptian colonial period (1821) the Dinka nation had become the largest in Southern Sudan and in key regions it was in a process of political and military centralization. As the new intruding colonizers forced their way into the heartlands of this tumultuous population, they were to bring about an end to this Southern Sudanese historical era and initiate an epic of centuries of wars and external domination, a process that continues into the modern day.

18

SUMMARY AND HISTORY

This chapter contains three parts: 1) a summary of the book's themes thus far, 2) a brief comparison of the various Western Nilotes of South Sudan, and 3) a brief history of precolonial Southern Sudan. In chapter 19 I examine the legacy of that history.

Thematic Summary

As I have shown, numerous themes have driven precolonial Southern Sudanese history from the fourteenth century onwards. These have included northern predation, the changing Nilotic frontier, migrations and expansion, ethnic conflict, the pastoral economy and raiding, a strong reliance on the communal religions of nature and power of the ancestors, slave raids, societal stratification and its concurrent tension, fission politics, and older forms of male dominance over females.

Northern Predation

The theme of northern predation is an historically long one in both oral histories and myths of Southern Sudan. The northernmost Western Nilotes, the Dinka, were under pressure from the Nubian Christian kingdom of Alwa in the thirteenth and fourteenth centuries. With the rise of the Islamic Sultanate of Sinnar after 1501 the Dinka, Shilluk, and numerous others faced predatory slave raids.[1] In the late eighteenth century, Islamic pastoral West African slave raiders, known as the Baggara, relocated east into the territory north of the Dinka and began to raid the Nuba Mountains. Soon thereafter, because of the attractiveness of Dinka and Nuer cattle (the cattle of the Nuba were miniature) as well as the need to raid for slaves, the northwest Dinka frontier came under severe pressure from this time onwards.

Migrations and the Changing Nilotic Frontier

The Nilotic frontier has been changing for centuries, moving in a southerly direction. The historical traditions of Nilotic migrations form an important aspect of East African history. Indeed, these migrations have concerned peoples (today broken linguistically into Western, Eastern, and Southern) who originated in central Sudan and, over a period of centuries, forged south into modern-day South Sudan, Ethiopia, Uganda, Kenya, and Tanzania. Those of South Sudan today fall into two groups: the Western and Eastern Nilotes. By far the most numerically powerful are the Western Nilotes, whose linguistic category includes the Dinka, Shilluk, Anyuak, Nuer, Luo, and Atwot. The Eastern Nilotes of South Sudan comprise the Bari, Mundari, Latuka, and others who today possess much smaller populations and reside primarily east of the Nile in the far south of South Sudan, with the exception of the close relatives of the Bari, the Mundari, who are on the Nile's western banks south of the Dinka. South Sudan's populations also include large communities of peoples who migrated from central and western Africa and include the Azande (who entered into southwestern Sudan in the latter nineteenth century, the Balanda, and Yibel peoples, who entered the region in the seventeenth and eighteenth centuries, as well as numerous smaller groups who migrated into western Southern Sudan as late as the early twentieth century. In modern times, the Dinka have the greatest population, numbering an estimated four to six million.

Historically, the most northern Nilotes, the Western Nilotic Dinka, claim to have lived throughout the Gezira on both the Blue and White Niles prior to the fourteenth century. Over time, they were forced to migrate in a more southerly and or southwesterly direction because of the fall of the thirteenth-century Nubian kingdom of Alwa. At this juncture, pressures from slave raiders and severe droughts encouraged the forefathers of these Nilotes to flee southwest to safer, more inaccessible regions.[2] Eventually from the sixteenth to the eighteenth centuries the forefathers of most Dinka peoples migrated far into what is now Southern Sudan, finding new homelands in the region surrounding the *sudd* swamps.

In sum, the theme of long-distance migrations, either because of bad weather conditions such as drought, or raids, wars and devastations, has predominated in Southern Sudanese history for centuries. Hence, the majority of South Sudanese today are not indigenous to the region but rather arrived only within the last two to four centuries. The original inhabitants, the Luel, exist in recent times only in small pockets in South Sudan. In the meantime severe droughts in Southern Sudan forced many Luo communities in the fifteenth century to forge even further south out of what is now Sudan into the Great Lakes region.

Ethnic Expansion, Marriage, and the Ethnic Formation of Southern Sudan

The theme of Dinka ethnic expansion in Southern Sudan has also played a prominent role in the region's history, as these Nilotes have absorbed numerous non-Dinka peoples from their inner and outer peripheries. Thus, over the centuries these Nilotes and their culture came to dominate numerically in the region. This historical factor was closely connected to economics and culture, for these Nilotes were polygymous, observed ranked marriage practices, and preferred to acquire as many wives as possible. Therefore, these sociocultural beliefs dictated that all Dinka must be exogamous and that their first wives should be a prominent Dinka women but that all subsequent wives should be obtained at the lowest possible bridewealth. Thus, Dinka men (after acquiring a prominent Dinka wife) subsequently married non-Dinka women on their periphery because their bridewealth was cheaper, to such an extent that this Nilotic culture expanded at the expense of all others. This advance was only checked on one occasion: when the Nuer fled east across the Nile in the eighteenth century, during the era of the first slave raids, and absorbed numerous Dinka and Anyuak in their wake. This phenomenon was easily accomplished, for with the Nuer one can change ethnic identification with a ceremony. After that event, however, ethnic expansion reversed once more and Dinka absorption of foreign women by marriage continued. This historical factor suggests that much Dinka ethnic expansion in Southern Sudan was non-violent.

Nevertheless, the arrival of the Dinka in Southern Sudan was followed by numerous conflicts that have continued to be well remembered by all parties in modern times. From the time the Dinka arrived at the Sobat/Nile River junction from the fourteenth to the seventeenth centuries, they warred initially with a people called the Funj who represented the farthest extent of the Nubian speaking world. Later, in the seventeenth century, the Funj Sultanate pressured many of those Dinka still resident in the Gezira to flee southwest. Some remained at the Sobat while others migrated across the Nile to the west and settled south of the Nuba mountains. Meanwhile in the same century there followed a series of wars with the Western Nilotic Shilluk, who had recently forged north out of the Southern Sudan and made their new home at the Nile/Sobat Rivers junction. The Shilluk represented one of the several Western Nilotic Luo groups who migrated southwest out of the Gezira into Southern Sudan centuries prior to the Dinka.

After a residence west of the Nile and south of the Nuba mountains in the sixteenth, seventeenth, and eighteenth centuries many Dinka returned to the east because of drought and forged south beyond the Sobat River and east of the Nile into the heartlands of Southern Sudan. In the eighteenth century they were displaced by a martial pastoral group, the Murle. These non-Nilotic peoples had recently migrated from what is now the Ugandan border region and forced the Dinka to relocate east. When the Dinka crossed the Nile westwards into what is now the Bahr el-Ghazal they also ran into the non-Nilotic Yibel and various Luo groups, all of whom they militarily displaced, partially absorbed, or eventually encapsulated. When the Dinka and other Nilotic peoples had initially forged into Southern Sudan, they also found an older indigenous people, the Luel. After a long series of formidable wars, these pastoralists were displaced; over the centuries they were either driven north, integrated both with the Dinka and their neighbors, or lived in discrete communities surrounded by the newcomers.

The people most successfully integrated into the Dinka amalgam have been the Western Nilotic Luo. Many other non-Dinka peoples, however, have remained in small, discrete or unincorporated sovereign ethnic groups surrounded by the Dinka, living primarily as agriculturalists and fishermen. They include the Mundari, Luel, and even isolated pockets of Nuer, though for the most part these Nilotes have maintained their pastoral lifestyle.

Economy and Raiding

The theme of economics is also very important in Southern Sudan's history. The Dinka came to predominate socioeconomically, politically, and numerically in the region largely because their arrival marked the introduction of a new and superior agro-pastoralist system hitherto unknown in the region. Specifically, the Dinka arrived during a period of droughts with hardier humped-backed cattle that could withstand ecological hardship and long-distance migrations. They also introduced hardier varieties of grain known as *caudatum* sorghum. Both of these items greatly facilitated Dinka migrations, allowing them to move into various points of Southern Sudan in a relatively short period.

In the meantime, the built-in mechanism of ethnic conflict has always predominated because of the predominance of stateless pastoralist peoples. Historically, typical pastoral systems worldwide commonly raid each other for animals and women. The conflict is directly related to socio-economic pastoral systems whose subjects customarily rob and pillage their neighbors, for to continue long in a state of peace diminishes their wealth. Further, the more geographically distant these groups are the more prolonged will be their hostile relations. This type of raiding has primarily concerned the pastoral peoples of Southern Sudan (the Dinka, Murle, Atuot, Nuer, and Baggara), who form a large percentage of the populace.

Slave Raids

It has often been assumed that external slave raids into Southern Sudan took place in the 1840s. But these events apparently occurred sixty to eighty years earlier, as evidenced by the existence of Dinka slaves in the northwestern Islamic Sultanate of Wadai in the early nineteenth century as well as in Dinka oral histories. It appears that during the late eighteenth century the pastoral stateless Islamic Baggara, who had recently moved east out of what is now Chad, began raiding the peoples to their east in the southern Nuba mountains for cattle and slaves. The Nuba cattle, however, were miniature and of little use to these cattle- and camel-pastoralists. The Dinka peoples to the south of the Baggara, however, were an attractive proposition, as they possessed the finest and hardiest cattle as well as dense, enslaveable populations. Thus, although the Nuba continued to be raided, over time the Dinka territories came under intense pressures. For the inhabitants of Southern Sudan these stresses encouraged a further dependence on Southern belief systems.

Religion and Politics

Most Southern Sudanese communities primarily observed a "communal" typology of religion where the powers of nature and the ancestors predominated. However, the observance of totems along with the practice of human and animal sacrifice also prevailed during times of stress. The Dinka and Shilluk practice of human sacrifice suggests that their religions were also of the Olympian typology most usually associated with early African states, such as Dahomey. It also suggests exposure to the older central Nile kingdoms of the Gezira.

Oral histories suggest that religious leaders, the Dinka priests, were always the lightning rods of culture and politics. These leaders spearheaded migrations, legitimized control over those foreign territories into which their people migrated, and made use of their knowledge of statecraft to gain control over those into whose territories the migrants came to reside. Hence, it appears that Dinka priests carried with them an understanding and appreciation of political centralization and administration. Among the other Nilotic groups in Sudan, it is only the Shilluk who resemble the Dinka in this tendency towards political centralism; to a much lesser degree the Anyuak and the Luo also possess a limited ability towards this endeavor. Priests, however, were heavily dependent on the superiority of the Dinka economic system, without which their political skills would have been useless. Thus, these historical figures held sway over a system of societal stratification.

Social Stratification and the Importance of Blood Lines

Although state societies are, by definition, stratified (the Shilluk, for example, and to a lesser degree the Eastern Anyuak in Ethiopia), it is often assumed stateless societies are egalitarian and possess no classes. Statelessness does not equal egalitarian society however, as certain scholars have argued in the case of these societies. Both the Dinka and Nuer, for example, accumulate wealth and cultural possessions and their leaders have, at times, commanded forms of tribute and possessed judicial authority and military power. Since the first Dinka migrations into Southern Sudan four and five centuries ago, these Nilotes have distinguished between priestly and commoner peoples. Larger clans are considered more prestigious than smaller ones. Further, the Western Nilotic societies are not egalitarian, for many are ranked and thus, by definition, some peoples have more stature than others. Dissatisfaction with one's position in society has led to constant fissioning or splintering, politically, among these stateless Nilotic groups.

Nilotic "Fission Politics" Versus Centralization

With the exception of the Shilluk, most other Nilotic groups in Southern Sudan have tended towards decentralization, or what I term "fission politics," which distinguishes itself by being centrifugal in nature. In earlier times the abundance of land made this choice possible. With the coming of severe external military threats, expanding population and land scarcity limiting the possibility of new population movements, however, large Western Nilotic clans began to stratify and centralize. The best documented example of this phenomenon can be seen in the history of the Western Ngok, who settled in the poorest land in the Dinka confederation. The process began when leaders of certain powerful clan groups preceded the arrival of other "latecomers" and proclaimed a political dominance over the region. With the arrival of the Baggara on their northern frontier these Nilotes were forced to militarily centralize and political centralization followed. Further south of the Ngok the "built-in" mechanism for war and raiding, as described above, has given rise to centuries of ethnic tension in Southern Sudan.

Ethnic Conflict and Ethnic Accommodation

The theme of ethnic conflict has been a prominent one in the history of Southern Sudan. The concomitant "blood memories," or long historical memories of wrong-doing by one people or clan against another, are rarely forgotten through the generations and have tended to dominate, particularly in Western Nilotic relations. With the Dinka and Nuer, for example, intra-ethnic strife dates back to the beginnings of the Dinka arrival in Southern Sudan and such wars are still remembered. Because of their encapsulation by the Dinka centuries ago when they first arrived, the succeeding slave-raiding era saw the initiation of eighteenth-century violent Nuer flight and expansion away from these raids eastwards as far as the eastern banks of the Nile. During this period the Nuer dislodged or ethnically incorporated many non-Nuer peoples (Dinka and Anyuak) into an amalgam that eventually equaled four times its original population. The violence of this period has never been forgotten by succeeding generations of Dinka or Nuer.

Although certain scholars argue that the forefathers of the Nuer and Dinka were one, and that the Nuer and their linguistically close relatives, the Atwot, were also closely related, the question of the original forefathers of the Nuer (and the Atwot) is still open to debate. By extrapolating the historical, oral, and linguistic evidence, it seems most obvious that the Nuer and Atwot originated from the mosaic of various Luo groups (which includes the Shilluk and Anyuak and numerous others who have different names today) residing in Kordofan and Southern Sudan prior to the Dinka arrival. I therefore suggest that much of the population of South Sudan today is of original Luo descent. According to linguistics, all of the Luo preceded the Dinka into South Sudan centuries ago.

Notwithstanding the long ethnic wars which have dominated Southern Sudan's history numerous non-integrated discrete communities have also existed within the Dinka amalgam. Many of these polities have resided as sovereign communities protected by the wider Dinka community since the latter's arrival. These have included, particularly, Mundari, Luo, and other Western Nilotic peoples, as well as the former residents of Southern Sudan, the Luel. The expansion of the Dinka in Southern Sudan was intimately connected to gender relations.

Gender, Ethnic Expansion, and Slavery

Among the Western Nilotes of South Sudan, a communal culture, rather than one based on the individual, has prevailed for centuries. Thus, levirate marriage has been the means by which the Western Nilotes, particularly the Dinka and Nuer, maintained their large populations. Within this sociocultural marital system, when a woman's husband dies, she is given automatically to his brother or nearest male relative. Hence, her reproductive capabilities are not "wasted" and she can continue bearing children in her husband's name. The Dinka and Nuer, particularly, have always aspired to acquire as many wives as possible. They are expected to bear many children to increase the size of the clan, which in turn helps build the military, economic, and political power of the larger section.

The groups with high bridewealth systems, such as the Dinka (and to a lesser degree the Nuer, except that they were historically surrounded by the Dinka), discovered that wives were more easily procured by raiding than by waiting long periods to accumulate the bridewealth. In fact, over time, raiding became a time-honored activity. Scholars have termed this practice "lineage slavery," for as an institution it brought about the same basic features as all types of slavery. Abducted women were forcibly cut off from kin, became property that was exchanged for cattle, and then represented an alien identity among their captors. And as in state-sponsored slavery, violence and the productive and sexual exploitation of women were intrinsic to these pastoral raiding systems.[3]

The Western Nilotes of Southern Sudan: Summary And Comparison

Since the Western Nilotes have dominated this volume, as indeed they numerically dominate South Sudan today, a brief summary and comparison of the various groups seems in order before considering their historic legacy.

Linguistic studies strongly suggest that the cradleland of all Nilotic peoples is the central Sudan, and archaeological studies support this evidence. Yet, with the exception of the Dinka, most other Western Nilotes can remember a residence only in Southern Sudan. The Shilluk recount that they were led north by their first king and culture hero, Nyakang, along with six families. They arrived at their present location at the junction of the Sobat and Nile Rivers around 1500 A.D. from a previous southern homeland remembered as Dimo. The Anyuak, closely related to the Shilluk, also trace their origin to the "country of Dimo" southeast of their present homeland. They were led northwards by a powerful chief, Gila, a brother of the Shilluk king, Nyakang. A quarrel led to a split between the Shilluk and Anyuak prior to Nyakang's arrival at the present-day Shilluk homeland at the Nile/Sobat confluence. Thus, the Anyuak migrated east. Gila's grandchild Cuwai became their first king. Today these Nilotes reside in both Ethiopia and Sudan. Historically, the Nuer claim they originated from a barren waterless country northwest of their present homeland in a region they identify as *Kwer-Kwong,* which geographically most closely resembles the modern-day province of southern Kordofan (now officially in Northern Sudan) just north of the South Sudan region. A leader Gau married Kwong, giving birth to two sons, Gaa and Kwok. As the eldest, Gaa became the land chief, and as the most important Nuer leader also acquired the title of "Chief of the Leopard Skin." A closely related group, the Atwot, can only trace their recent history to residence by a revered chief, Reel, adjacent to the Nuer about three to four hundred years ago. Today they are located south of the Dinka. As the last Nilotes to migrate to Southern Sudan, the Dinka still remember a homeland in central Sudan. These oral histories are supported by linguistic data that show loanwords from the classical language of Nubia, *Nobiin,* suggesting a cultural and religious connection with the Nubian kingdom of Alwa (c. 300–1300 A.D.). They remember that they migrated southward (c.1300–1600) into the upper Nile valley of Southern Sudan along the eastern bank of the Nile and then forged west across the river three hundred miles northwest. At this juncture they had fully surrounded the Western Nilotic Nuer.

The politics and religion of the Nilotes are not uniform. The Shilluk have been historically united in a single polity headed by a series of divine kings (*reths*) chosen by primogeniture. The Dinka have been less politically centralized than the Shilluk because of the vast geographical area they occupied, which has been fairly rich agriculturally, particularly in the southern

Dinka confederation. However, the Western Ngok, residing in the poorest soils of the Dinka confederation, were the first to centralize when they came under pressure from Islamic Baggara slave raiders on their northern frontier. The Dinka language is diverse and each group is internally segmented into small political units with a high degree of autonomy. During times of war, however, all Dinka have historically valued intragroup unity and tended towards temporary political and military centralization. Politically the Nuer form a cluster of autonomous communities within which there is little unity largely because in distant and recent centuries they have been confined to more watery homelands with less contiguous settlements. The basic social group is the patrilineal clan and in each community the men are divided into six age sets. The Atwot, closely related to the Nuer historically, follow a similar political philosophy. In Anyuakland, because more dry ground is available to the eastern Ethiopian Anyuak, their villages are more closely connected, giving rise to a wider political organization than that afforded by the autonomous villages of the western Anyuak in South Sudan. The Ethiopian Anyuak historically have had a royal clan and a king while western villages have not.

From a religious viewpoint there is much similarity among the Western Nilotes. Dinka priests and Shilluk kings (*reths*) were and are believed to be divine, and their physical and ritual well being has always been held to ensure the prosperity of the whole land. Among the Shilluk the large royal clan traces descent from the first king and culture hero, Nyakang (Nyakango). Among the Dinka, "aristocratic" patrilineal clans provide their priests who continue to be revered authority figures (rainmakers) known as the *bany bith* or masters of the fishing spear. Their positions continue to be validated by elaborate myths. The Dinka aristocratic clans trace their descent from their culture hero, Ayuel Longar. Dinka priests and Shilluk kings, as sacred leaders, can never die a natural death. If death or severe illness is imminent they are ritually killed, most commonly by burial alive for Dinka *bany bith,* and strangulation for Shilluk *reths.* Dinka priests have tended to live much longer than Shilluk kings, for there has been no special stress laid on the maintenance of high standards of sexual activity that the Shilluk have demanded of their royal leaders. Neither the Nuer, Atwot, nor Anyuak have ritually killed their priests or kings; they do not observe divine kingship.

Social stratification differs widely among these Nilotes. Along with several classes of royalty the Shilluk are divided into commoners, royal retainers, and slaves. The Dinka possess "aristocratic" and "commoner" clans, as do the Anyuak. The Nuer and Atwot, however, recognize only a limited aristocracy, tending towards less social stratification than the Dinka, Shilluk, and Anyuak.

All these groups are patrilineal and polygynous. Marriage is marked by the giving of cattle by the bridegroom's kin. Almost all are semi-nomadic. The young unmarried men and boys take their cattle to the rivers during the dry seasons while the older and married people stay behind in permanent villages. The Shilluk are sedentary agriculturalists with strong pastoral interests (cattle, sheep, and goats). Unlike the Dinka, Atwot, Nuer, and Shilluk, the Anyuak keep some cattle but rely heavily on fishing, hunting, and agriculture. Among the Shilluk and Anyuak, spears and sheep and to a lesser degree cattle have also come to represent bridewealth.

As by far the largest of the Western Nilotes in South Sudan today (four to six million), the Dinka are broken into three major geographical (and political) sections: the *Padang* in the North, the *Bor* on the eastern bank of the Nile in the southeast, and the *Bahr el-Ghazal* Dinka on the western banks of this river. Here they reside in an arc from the Nile three hundred miles northwest up to and a little beyond the Kir/Bahr el-Arab River. In all, the Dinka comprise twenty-six major groupings, each residing in its own well-defined territory distinctly separated from each other by history and geographical boundaries such as rivers.

The longer-term legacy of the trials and challenges of the Western Nilotes and the other numerous peoples who came to make up the community of Southern Sudan in the precolonial and colonial era has been a long and troubled one.

History from the Precolonial Era to the Present

This volume comes to a close at the dawning of the first colonial era in Sudan, which began in 1821 and is commonly referred to as the *Turkiyya* or the "Turco-Egyptian" era. By this period the Dinka confederation had become the largest in Southern Sudan. The new Egyptian conquerors, under their regent in Cairo, Mohammed Ali, made their way into the swamps of Southern Sudan and brought an end to the Southern Sudanese historical era in which intra-Southern events dominated peoples' lives. Now, externally generated traumas would equally, although not exclusively, consume the lives of Southern peoples. Slavery and raids, on a scale hitherto not experienced, dominated the nineteenth century. Turbulence increased when a Northern Sudanese Muslim nationalist, the Mahdi, "liberated" Sudan in 1885. To Southerners, however, this era represented another colonial slave-raiding period.

The second official colonial power to rule Sudan began when the British overthrew the Mahdists at Karari in 1898. Known as the Anglo-

Egyptian Condominium, this period in Sudan's history was calm compared to events in the nineteenth century. To the Southern Sudanese people the British era is best summed up by a Thoi Dinka elder, Philip Thon Marol, who declared: "When the British came they made borders; then they left!" The British militarily attempted to "pacify" those pastoral groups who continued to raid each other frequently. Most of the Southern Sudan was perceived as filled with stateless, warring societies and British district commissioners reigned over these peoples in paternalistic fashion. When independence came in 1956, Southern peoples were passionately unwilling to be governed by their former enemies beyond their northern frontier in Khartoum, to which the British hastily and unthinkingly bestowed all political and economic power. To quote the late South Sudanese politician, Samuel Aru Bol (an Agar Dinka), "We got sold to the North!"[4] War with the north began again.

Since 1955, with a brief interregnum from 1972, when the Addis Ababa (Peace) Agreement introduced temporary peace between North and South, the government of Sudan, located at the capital, Khartoum, at the junction of the Blue and White Niles, has been at war with its Southern counterpart. The second civil war, which continues to this time, began in 1983. In the early 1980s a series of events triggered the process of Southern re-militarization on a grand scale. Northern Sudanese president Jaafar Nimeiri was under severe political pressure after surviving his fifteenth coup attempt from pro-Muslim factions in Khartoum. Then in 1982 oil was discovered in Southern Sudan in the Nuer territory. At this juncture Nimeiri realigned himself with those who had hitherto opposed him the most, the political-religious forces in the Islamic North. Yielding to pressures from the Arab states, he elected to build the refinery for his newly discovered oil in Southern Kordofan, a Northern province.

In 1983 Nimeiri devised a final solution for controlling Southern wealth while simultaneously disenfranchising Southern peoples: he unilaterally abrogated the Addis Ababa Agreement by dividing the South into three regions. The dictator then promulgated the infamous "September Laws" of 1983, making Islamic law, the *Shari'a,* the law of the land. Sudanese law now prohibited non-Muslims from holding political office even in Southern Sudan. The imposition of *Shari'a* law in the justice system led most conspicuously to floggings and amputations of limbs, most of the victims of these new holy punishments being poor Muslims from the west and non-Muslim destitute Southerners. By aligning himself with the radical Muslim Brothers in Khartoum and adopting the Islamic law of *Shari'a* Nimeiri benefitted from the Muslim Brothers' close alignment with Saudi

Arabia, which ensured a constant cash flow into the now-impoverished Sudan government.[5] In the next decade, Osama Bin Laden was to invest in Sudan.

The country's political and economic difficulties led to the overthrow of Nimeiri by the army in 1985. A civilian government, elected by Northern Sudanese, took office in 1986 but was unable to end the civil war. Muslim fundamentalist army officers headed by General Omar Hassan Ahmad al-Bashir seized power in 1989 and punitive Islamic laws continued to be the basis of the political system. In 1996 Bashir claimed to have been reelected by popular vote but opposition parties were banned and the civil war continued. He signed a law restoring the multiparty system in 1998. Again in 2000 Bashir claimed to have been reelected by those in the North. To date the war continues.

19

LEGACY OF THE PRECOLONIAL ERA

The memory of war and blood over the centuries, remembered in myths and oral histories, has framed the psychology of much of the modern-day South Sudanese populace, particularly the Dinka. Indeed, this "blood memory" dominates the actions of all modern-day peoples in this part of Africa. The emotions, however, that accompany these memories are reserved for both those beyond their northern frontier as well as those within their homelands who have been enemies for centuries.

"Primordialism" is a scholarly term that presumes that cultures remain static over long time periods. South Sudanese society has not remained dormant, but rather has been vibrant over the centuries and undergone enormous changes. The British colonial era introduced Christianity (which was not successful until very recent years) and Western education into the region. In the 1970s a vibrant Western-educated middle class in Southern Sudan began to flourish. In modern times factors such as the means by which wars are fought, particularly the introduction of guns, and the inclusion of women into the military have changed society drastically.

Certain historical themes, however, have continued to dominate and play a critical role in the sociopolitical and religious cultures of South Sudan today, particularly among the Western Nilotic peoples who predominate numerically. The themes include the ongoing predatory attacks by the North, the southward moving Nilotic (and hence South Sudanese) frontier and migrations, intra-Southern fears of Dinka expansion, the economic and numerical predominance of the Dinka, the "raiding complex," social stratification, the importance of blood lines, Nilotic fission politics versus centralization, religion and politics, slave raids, gender dominance and lineage slavery, and, last but not least, the ongoing ethnic conflicts and "blood memories." In these instances emotions that are attached to the memories of previous wars, killings, and misdeeds die hard. Less prominent but equally important, however, both historically and in modern times, is that there has always been ethnic accommodation. Each of the above factors will be dealt with in turn below.

The Changing Nilotic Frontier and Long-Distance Migrations

Today the Nilotic frontier and the frontier of South Sudan has come to mean the same thing. What is clear by looking at the long history of the Nilotes in Sudan is that this boundary has been shifting southwards for centuries and has never been fixed. Recently one modern-day scholar of Sudan declared that "during the ancient Egyptian era the Southern Sudan began at the first cataract (in what is now Egypt)."

From the beginning of the Dinka flight from the Gezira in central Sudan in the fourteenth to fifteenth centuries the Nilotic frontier has been moving steadily from central Sudan into the south and southwest as well as into central and eastern Africa. In 2003, as the Sudan Peoples Liberation Movement/Army (SPLM/A) and the Sudan government sit in Kenya debating a peace proposal, both argue bitterly over the definition and possible legitimate border or boundary of a future "South Sudan." The Sudan government prefers to observe the boundaries laid out by the British government during the early twentieth century, which limited the region to that approximately just north of the Nile/Sobat River and north of the Kir/Bahr el-Arab River in the northwest. The SPLM/A however, prefers to observe those boundaries that still incorporate the older homelands of the Nilotic and other non-Muslim southern Gezira communities along with their closely related linguistic neighbors, the Ingessana, as well as those who have suffered perceived similar historical abuses at the hands of Islamic Northern Sudanese and Baggara aggressors, and who have staunchly supported the SPLM/A, namely the communities of the southern Nuba Mountains.

In the meantime, the historical trend of long-distance migrations has continued over the centuries. While the wealth of the communities of South Sudan have been extracted to enrich those to their north (in the precolonial era it was slaves while in modern times it is now slaves and oil) most who perceive persecution continue to flee south. Today, many South Sudanese, particularly the Nilotes, reside on the borders of Kenya and Uganda while others have moved into refugee camps within these countries. Before they reached these destinations, they had to flee, once again, much as in precolonial times, hundreds of miles east and south. Prior to 1991 many female informants had to escape by foot to refugee camps hundreds of miles away in Ethiopia, carrying all their possessions as well as their children. Over the course of hiking several hundred miles many died en route. For example, one female Malwal, Martha Nyedier Akok, stated:

> We fled to Ethiopia by foot. It took three months and we had six children. My husband came too. When the food was finished we ate groundnuts and grass in the road like animals. Then we ate the leaves off the trees and many people died. But we kept going. The lions came up to us but we had no energy to run or protect ourselves and the lions ate us. When the people slept under the trees they died. About four thousand of us left and two thousand made it to Ethiopia. When my child died in my arms I had to throw it away.

Many women interviewed recounted the horrors of having to escape from Ethiopia after the fall of Haile Mengistu Mariam in 1991 and struggling with their children to flee aerial bombings and attacks by Ethiopian troops and the Sudanese government to safe-havens in far South Sudan, Kenya, and Uganda. Many arrived without clothes or shoes or other possessions, for they were forced to exchange them for food to keep their children alive. Thousands of others died of thirst en route. By the time many women reached Kakuma Refugee Camp in Kenya on the borders of South Sudan they showed serious signs of stress. For example, among the Dinka, songs and singing have a sociocultural, religious, and political place in society, particularly for women. It is one of the few socially acceptable means by which a woman can vent her emotions. According to a female Agar elder, Mary Acuoth, who is a famous song composer: "We advertise loudly when we feel we have been or that society has been wronged. Singing is a means by which to channel one's emotions constructively and also to make sure a wrong is remembered throughout time. It is a means of social protest." But according to the Catholic sisters working in the camp: "They have been through so much trauma they can no longer express their emotions by singing."[1]

Slave Raids

Although slave raids into Dinka country have seen a resurgence in the last two decades, this practice also represents an age-old phenomenon dating back to the earliest memories and myths of the Dinka. For as long as these Nilotes can remember, their enemies have always been those "Arabs" in the "north." Along with drought, slave raids by Nubian slavers comprised the major reason the Dinka fled from their ancient central Sudanese homelands centuries ago. In the sixteenth and seventeenth centuries the increasingly powerful Islamic Sinnar Sultanate enslaved numerous Nilotic peoples on its southern frontier in the Gezira. In the eighteenth century slave raids conducted by the Islamic Baggara (people of West African descent also referred to as "Arabs" by South Sudanese) in the Dinka territories represented, once again, "northern" hostilities. These raids were to continue intermittently for centuries. As the Dinka were the most prized of slaves during the Egyptian colonial era (1821–85), hostile penetration into their villages in northwest Dinkaland was unceasing. Since this time, the main economic activity of the slave-raiding pastoral Baggara has been the acquisition, use, and sale (in points north of the Southern Sudan including the Middle East and north Africa) of slave labor acquired from those Dinka folk on their southern borders beyond the Kir/Bahr el-Arab River. Widespread and systematic enslavement of men, women, and children reemerged during the second civil war after 1983. Militias known as *Murahaliin* were initially consolidated by Prime Minister Sadiq Al Mahdi, who utilized his historical politico-religious connections with these Islamic pastoralists. He recruited from among those on the Kir/Bahr el-Arab River in southern Kordofan and southern Darfur as well as those in the western and southern Gezira, the northern Upper Nile, and the northern and northwestern Bahr el-Ghazal. More recently government troops and the government-backed Popular Defense Forces (PDF), made up of the Baggara, have regularly raided African communities for slaves and other forms of booty.[2]

Rape has become commonplace along with the abuse of children, and many Malwal Dinka women and children have suffered the brunt of *Murahaliin* attacks. Informants note that their husbands and other male family members in the vicinity are killed, their babies are seized, and their young female children violently raped.[3] One anonymous informant notes:

> If you are a young woman or girl the Baggara Rizeiqat take you and rape you. If you are old they shoot you. The Rizeiqat take leaves and cover the genitals to conceal the rape of young children. I remember two young girls of age eight and ten years. The Rizeiqat came to our area and seized the small girls and raped them. After that the eight year old died. They took leaves and put them in the vagina of the child that died. The other was still alive and they took her but my relatives rescued her the same day. After some years she still has not given birth.

Many mothers suffer the trauma of having their children seized by Northern Sudanese troops. An anonymous Malwal states: "One Northern Sudanese soldier tried to take my child and run away with it so I left town and went to the village at Adon. The soldiers [*Murahaliin*] caught up with me and attacked. They were Rizeiqat Baggara and they took my son. I have no information of my child up to now. I have not recovered. After that I ran to Ethiopia and then eventually into Kakuma in Kenya."

Another anonymous Malwal informant discussed the death of most of her family members: "The daughter of my aunt was taken by the *Murahaliin*. Then they took my brother by force to put into the Khartoum army. My sister was killed after chasing after her stolen child. They killed my husband also. I was left with five children and ran to Itang in Ethiopia." In the meantime those victims who are caught by the Baggara in South Sudan, most of whom are children and young women, are taken north where they are forced to provide domestic and agricultural labor and sexual services.[4]

Military Slaves

During the rise of the precolonial Islamic Funj Sultanate in the sixteenth century Gezira, much of their military force comprised Western Nilotic and Nuban peoples recently captured in slave raids. This theme was revisited in the nineteenth century and in more recent decades as South Sudanese people are forcibly conscripted into Northern armies to fight the civil war in the South. Thus, although the Islamic government persists in characterizing the current civil war as an "Islamic holy war" or *jihad,* the vast majority of young men drafted into the Northern forces are non-Islamic Southerners or those who have professed adherence to Islam under duress. *Kashas* or forced military recruitment began with the creation of the Southern militias after 1983, and many children captured or abducted from the South have been brought north and forced into military service. In Khartoum, within the marginalized Southern refugee communities, teenagers are rounded up, abducted, put into camps, and trained for the army. Some comply, for they can acquire a salary; they are hungry and it is a means of survival.[5]

Religion and Cultural Hegemony of the North

Many in the international community today believe that the primary reason for the civil war in Sudan has been religious differences between the north and south—that is, an Islamic north versus a Christian South. Neither Islam nor Christianity, however, were particularly popular religions among many in Southern Sudan until very recently. Abdul Monheim Younis, a Southern Sudanese Fertit Muslim, argues that decades ago Southern Muslims attempted to proselytize the Dinka without success: "My grand-father was a Muslim holy man based in the Bahr el-Ghazal and was con-verted by the Tijaniyya during the Condominium period. We had many Dinka friends and my grandfather tried to teach them about Islam. But most Dinka would not embrace Islam or Christianity. They were animists and would only go to the kujur."

Islam has been described as a religion that was born from an urban environment and that assumes, for the most part, that its practitioners exist in a politically stable (noncentrifugal) and geographically fixed set-ting. On the other hand, the communal religion of many South Sudanese, including the Dinka, appeals to the power of nature, the land and its ani-mals, and is ideally designed to support cultures in nonurban, politically and geographically unstable environments. According to Pajulu South Sudanese Reverend Elioba: "Our religion is part of life itself; it is a tradi-tion that has been incorporated into holistic life. Our laws are evolution-ary, drawn from nature [as] are our everyday experiences and challenges." Thus, monotheistic religions such as Islam and Christianity have devel-oped as part of adaptations to different ecological environments.

Although most South Sudanese prefer their communal religions, the religion of Islam, itself, is not the key reason for the war between North and South Sudan. Muslim Southerners support this assertion. For example, Muslim Dinka claim a closer alliance with their non-Muslim Southern brothers and say that religion is not the issue. According to one Muslim Aliab: "The Southerners, they are my people! And I am pro-Dinka over any other ethnic group. If Southerners want to achieve anything in Sudan they should stay together." Other Southern Muslims interviewed, both those born into Islam and those who converted, reiterated this viewpoint. Fur-ther, since the inception of the second civil war, there have been Islamic *qadi's* (Muslim holy men) within the ranks of the SPLA, and in 1992 Tahier Bior Ajak was the spokesman and head of the Muslim faction within the Southern military. Thus, according to Fertit Muslim South Sudanese as well as Dinka Muslims, *qadi's* administer to those who are Muslim while Protestant and Catholic pastors and fathers administer to those who are Christian. Further, the South Sudanese leadership has had no problems allying themselves with Muslims. A staunch supporter and colleague of the present-day leader of the SPLM/A, John Garang, since 1983 was the late Muslim leader and Commander of the Nuba Mountains, Yusuf Kuwa.

On the other hand, the reason for war—and Muslim Southerners support this assertion—is the Northern Sudanese government's blatant contempt and racist attitudes towards the culture of all South Sudanese, including their religions. This approach has had the effect of encouraging mass conversion to Christianity, a religion that was not particularly popular or successful until this postcolonial era, despite the presence of Christian missionaries in the region for over a century. The acquisition (alongside the communal religion) of Christianity for the Southern Sudanese masses dates to November 1958 when the Northern Sudanese army took control in Khartoum and the commander-in-chief who headed the coup, Major General Ibrahim Abboud, announced the military's assumption of power. That very year the dictatorship launched a crude attempt at forced Islamization in Equatoria and Bahr el-Ghazal provinces in Southern Sudan. Islamic training centers (*khalwas*) and mosques suddenly appeared everywhere, particularly in Azandeland. Abboud was convinced that the English language and its concomitant culture were increasing because of the separatist influences of Christian European missionaries. However, according to Malwal Dinka elder Kawac Makuei Mayar, it was in fact the Southern Sudanese Anya Nya guerrilla movement of the 1960s that was the most influential in spreading English usage. All commands were given in English and many Dinka who did not speak the language learned to do so. Nevertheless, Abboud passed the Missionaries Act of 1964, which expelled all European missionaries from the South. Then he executed all Southern Christian pastors and, when possible, their congregations.

Abboud's methods for "eradicating Christianity" from the South were very crude. For example, according to Yibel Bishop Ruben Macier Makoi, during a Sunday service in Rumbek, Reverend Saturlino was dragged out of his church, shot, and then thrown back in, and the church burned to the ground; the congregation was then beaten. The same year in the nearby Agar Dinka town of Akot, government troops attacked and burned Reverend Ruben Macier's church, which was filled with his Dinka congregation. Although he was on a list of people to be executed he narrowly escaped. Hence from the Southern Sudanese viewpoint civil war with the North is less a product of religious disagreement than the factor of civil and political rights and racism.

The Southern reaction to the violent prohibition of Christianity was, thus, to suddenly embrace it, for it now represented the religion of resistance. According to Nuer Reverend Steven Ter, Yibel Bishop Ruben Macier Makoi, Zande Bishop Daniel Manase Zindo, and Bor Dinka Reverend Nathaniel Garang, the South Sudanese now took the place of European missionaries, "spread the word of God," and gained many adherents. Nathaniel Garang had returned to the south in 1975 and ordained large numbers of Christian pastors in the Bor territory. He was later ordained a Bishop by the Anglican church shortly after the second civil war in 1983. From a religious viewpoint, therefore, South Sudanese have undergone a religious revolution that is closely connected to politics. Since this time Christianity has been the means by which to tie the South into a unified block as well as to connect it to the Western world. It has also become a powerful weapon to resist the last several decades of the Northern Sudan government's policy of forced Islamization in the South.

Notwithstanding the adoption of Christianity, the older religions are also keenly adhered to and observed simultaneously. For example, the Dinka religion is very predominant today, as evidenced by ongoing human sacrifice of prominent priests and the close observance of the powers of nature and totems. Thus, South Sudanese simultaneously practice their own religions as well as Christianity or Islam, wearing the last two as an overcoat.

Further, in the midst of all the violence, African and European church leaders have played key roles in peacekeeping. For example, according to Kakwa Ebe Enosa, after the Chukudum Conference in 1994, Kakwa church leaders were distressed by the level of SPLA atrocities against the general population. They appealed to John Garang to "please put chaplains in the army." Garang complied and in recent times violence against local citizens has decreased. Three Azande religious leaders—Catholic Father and Doctor Michael Katawa, Reverend Murangi Salatiel, and Reverend Botrus Bandaka—argue that their Christian institutions can maintain peace and that the church is one of the most important instruments for reunification of the South. Throughout the war they claim church leaders have mediated between all the rival ethnic parties both in Sudan and in Kenya. Thus, modern-day church leaders have been acquiring the religious and political tasks historically performed by priests. They claim that to a great degree they have been successful.

Northern Predation and Contempt, and the Southern Desire for an Independent State

Throughout the history of the Southern Sudanese people and particularly the Western Nilotes, those on their northern frontier have always represented a realm of predators. Along with the numerous precolonial slave raids, in the nineteenth century the entire Southern Sudan was pillaged and torn apart by Egyptian, Northern Sudanese, Baggara, and Mahdist troops in slaving expeditions. Two million people were affected by war, disease, and slave raids.[6] Baggara slave raids continue into the present day. Thus, today South Sudanese people uniformly view "the North" (or those beyond their northern frontier) as the ongoing predatory "enemy."

Those Muslim peoples in the central and Northern Sudan have historically also viewed Southerners with contempt; as peoples who are "primitive" and "inferior." As early as the fourteenth century this perception was clearly described by geographer Abi Talib as-Sufi Ad-Dimishqi, who wrote: "Beyond the 'Alwa country there is a land inhabited by a race of Sudan who go naked like the Zanj and who are like animals because of their stupidity; they profess no religion." Half a millennium later in 1994 Comboni Father Mattia was in Khartoum and stated: "I was sitting next to an African sister · in a bus and a small Northern Sudanese boy behind kept playing with the strap on her shoulder. After the fourth time she asked the boy to stop and the boy tore her bag off her shoulders and bellowed 'you slave of the south go back to your country.' The boy was no more than twelve years but in Northern Sudanese families this is the mentality! These ideas will not change!"

Little marriage, historically, has taken place between the Islamic Northern Sudanese and non-Islamic Southerners. Western Twic Dinka Dominic Akeg Mohammed argues that "marital integration between North and South will always be difficult. There has always been an unwritten law that among Muslim Sudanese, you do not marry a 'slave.' On the other hand, the unwritten law of the Dinka is that you do not marry a 'slave trader.'" Ultimately, Agar Dinka Gordon Muortat Mayen's assertion represents the thoughts of many in the South: "Could we ever one day become equal with the Arab? They don't respect us and it will never happen! It is clear that the heart of the matter is that Southern Sudanese will be second-class citizens forever!"

In light of the belief that "Northerners" will never respect Southern rights, the universal call in South Sudan since 1983 (and in fact, even before 1972) has been for permanent separation from Northern Sudan. Southerners claim they want their own separate state with a firm nation-state boundary forever protecting it. Benedict Anderson argues that "nationness is the most universally legitimate value in the political life of our time" and that it is inseparable from political consciousness."[7] Thus, in the midst of civil war many South Sudanese insisted that an official state structure within their homelands should be implemented. Thus, in April 2, 1994, under intense pressure from much of the populace, a new South Sudanese nation was conceived in Chukudum in Equatoria. At the first national

convention organized by the primarily Dinka-led Sudan Peoples Liberation Movement/Army (SPLM/A) fighting the civil war with the north, this
new proto-nationalist entity was called "New Sudan." Its flag was represented by one star and five stripes, representing a united nation under five
"states" or regions: Bahr el-Ghazal, Equatoria, Upper Nile, Southern
Kordofan, and Southern Blue Nile provinces. The convention created two
new legislative bodies known as the National Liberation Council (NLC)
and the National Executive Council (NEC). Civil authorities were therefore separated from the military. The new state was based loosely on the
Eritrean and Ethiopian models; the chairman and commander of the SPLM/
A, John Garang, was elected by the convention to head this new governing
body. The SPLA chief of staff commander and Rek Dinka Salva Kiir
Mayardit was elected as his deputy. For its legal system the "New Sudan"
government adopted the British legal code.[8]

Yet, in South Sudan today, beyond the externally induced traumas,
are unresolved internal troubles that date back many centuries.

Ethnic and Political Expansion: Dinkaphobia

When the Dinka migrated into Southern Sudan centuries ago they quickly
expanded ethnically against all the other peoples in the region. Dinka expansion is today still feared by many who complain that these Nilotes are
the new "colonizers" of the South. When Northern Sudanese president
Jaafar Nimeiri appointed Bor Dinka Abel Alier as the first president of the
Southern High Executive Committee in 1972 the Dinka came to represent
the new political power in the South. Now large numbers of Bor Dinka
moved with their cattle to Juba, the Southern Sudanese regional headquar-
ters in Equatoria. Some over time referred to this town as "New Bor" and
this event became a particular focus of resentment by the Eastern Nilotic
Bari, into whose homeland the former relocated.[9]

In the 1970s the increasingly powerful Dinka were perceived as dominating many of the Southern civil and administrative posts. Acholi and
Azande peoples believed they were overlooked for jobs in the various min-
istries in favor of "less qualified Dinka" because of "nepotism and patronage." Tensions further increased with the fall of Ugandan leader Idi Amin
in 1979. Equatorians (a term used for the Eastern Nilotic Bari and the
non-Nilotic peoples of Southern Sudan in the far south) returned to the
Southern Sudan from Uganda and felt their opportunities for public em-
ployment were being blocked by Nilotes who, taken together, formed the
majority of the region. Pressures due to the perceived Nilotic expansion

among the numerically smaller non-Western Nilotic communities peaked in 1981 when a Dinka minister left this passionate and unforgettable remark on the records of the Regional Assembly body: "It took the Sudan fifty years to get rid of the British; it took the Southerners seventeen years to get rid of the Arabs; it will take you (Southerners) one hundred years to get rid of the Dinka."[10]

With the coming of the second civil war in 1983 the perception and fear of Dinka ethnic expansion, particularly by marriage, has continued. It was by this practice that, centuries ago, the Dinka became the largest ethnic group in the region. Today, Dinka bridewealth is still the highest in South Sudan and, as one Bari woman stated: "The Dinka don't want their girls to be married to other people . . . [yet] why do they want to marry ours? They do not pay the equivalent for us as for Dinka women. They get us very cheaply." An Azande man complained: "You cannot talk to a Dinka girl. If you do you will be speared! But they can touch any Azande girl without a problem!"

Because of Southern Sudanese fears of Dinka expansion and power in the midst of war the government of Sudan has been able to manipulate the situation considerably. In 1988 the Sudan government extended its operations by creating and supporting Southern militias among all those ancient "enemies" of the Dinka including the Mundari, Murle, Toposa, Acholi, Latuka, Madi, Azande, and Fertit. According to an Acholi informant: "They built on the pre-existing Acholi discomfort with the Dinka. . . . Then the government argued that the Dinka were moving into all parts of the South and were going to take jobs away from Acholi people. When they offered us weapons and training to defend ourselves, the Acholi accepted and we formed a militia against the Dinka in 1983." To the Azande, the Dinka appeared as an alien race. One informant noted: "All Nilotics suffer from a 'raiding complex.' They gather together in herds and are defensive towards outsiders. Others find them clickish. Because they are cattle owners they do not mix with social centers of dancing. They lack the sensitivity of other cultures because they do not mix with others."[11]

Other Azande informants, however, noted that the Sudan government, which was present in the Azande territories until 1991, propagandized the Azande people by building on their fear of Dinka domination. Northern officials reminded the Azande that the Dinka did not know how to interact with other peoples. Because there had been isolated cases of rape and the stealing of property by SPLA troops when the latter took the Azande area of Yambio in 1991, many Azande, believing Northern propaganda, fled into the Congo or Central African Republic.[12]

The irony here is that even though many people call themselves "Dinka" today, most can actually trace their origins to other ethnic groups, some as far away as the Kakwa who presently live on the Uganda/Sudan border. In fact the size of the Dinka confederation today, attributed to the absorption of many other South Sudanese peoples, suggests that these Nilotes are the best representation of a genetically mixed homogeneous mass in South Sudan.

The Economic Predominance of Raiding

A large proportion of South Sudanese today are those who have practiced a precolonial economy and culture of pastoral lineage societies. These societies function as communal or family entities and not as "individuals." Typical of these types of polities is the need to raid one's neighbors for economic reasons, for the larger the clan family, the more powerful it becomes. Thus, for centuries, the Western Nilotic Dinka, Nuer, and Atwot as well as the Murle and Baggara have resided in a state of regular conflict with those on their peripheries. Since the precolonial era, raiding has continued to be a very popular means of acquiring wealth in the form of cattle and women. These conflicts are closely tied to economics, and those raided are actually determined by the level of close totemic observances of their neighbors and not by ethnicity alone. Thus, certain sections of the Dinka have historically raided each other, such as the Agar and Luaic and the Apak Atwot and Agar, for they do not have close totemic alliances and therefore are "free" to raid each other.

The rise of small businesses during the twentieth century in Southern Sudan did, on occasion, actually put a dent in this popular economic practice of raiding. For example, during the British colonial era in the Dinka town of Akot one marginalized, cattleless Nuer became a very wealthy merchant and a prominent member of the community. As a child Benjamin Bil Lual suffered a Murle attack in his town of Waat during which his father was killed. He was then sent to his maternal uncle in Duk Fadiet, who sent him to school. Reverend Arnold of the Episcopal church brought him to the Ciec Dinka territory at Yirrol, where he eventually became a teacher. However he was later excommunicated. Meanwhile his wife, Roda Atiel, an Agar Dinka from Akot, had begun bartering grain for clothes, salt, and tobacco. She then bought cattle. In the 1940s with the emerging cash economy of Southern Sudan Roda Atiel was joined by her husband, Benjamin, who reinvested in her business (which was growing rapidly) by buying iron doors and corrugated iron. Later they bought trucks (lorries) to transfer goods west to Wau. By 1955 the couple had built a brick shop and had both became so rich that Benjamin had to "give up the Dinka life of raiding," as his business was encompassing so much of his time. He later opened a school. According to his daughter Julia Benjamin (Duany) and son Lual Benjamin Bil, his children today are identified as Agar "Dinka." He acquired another eight wives and ended his life with fifty-eight children. Thus, Benjamin Bil Lual and Roda Atiel had unwittingly undergone the transition from a corporate or family to an individual economy. With the return of war and the reversal of the individual economy to the family economy, pastoral raiding has increased. This in turn has exacerbated long-standing ethnic tensions, but it has also made victims out of South Sudanese women; in this case the persecutors are their own citizens.

Raiding and Women

Gayle Rubin argues that women in many societies are the key currencies of exchange; they are given in marriage, taken in battle, exchanged for favors, sent as tribute, traded, bought, and sold. During the precolonial era the raiding for and abduction of women throughout Southern Sudan by various pastoralist communities has translated into wealth, for females became important commodities for these economies. On both sides of the Kir/ Bahr el-Arab River in the northwest, for example, for centuries the Baggara abducted Dinka women for agricultural and household help and concubines.[13] The Dinka did likewise. Throughout the British colonial era the agro-pastoral Dinka and their pastoral neighbors, the Nuer, the Murle, the Atwot, and the Baggara continued to raid each other to acquire cows as well as women. As late as 1912 the Rizeiqat Baggara mounted on fast horses and well equipped with firearms raided the Dinka territory. When the British introduced money for bridewealth payments it also became even more lucrative for the Dinka to abduct Baggara women. Previously, cattle formed the primary currency of exchange in Dinka society and the high cost of bridewealth meant many could not afford a wife. With the new money economy, bridewealth debt could be offset by abducting Baggara women for economically minded Dinka men in need of a wife. This was because the extended Dinka family was expected to help in making contributions to bridewealth payments. Hence, many Dinka accumulated lifelong debts. Instead of cows, the bridewealth for a Baggara women often involved money; thus, her bridewealth yielded cash to her surrogate Dinka family, allowing them to buy more cattle and increase their wealth. Girls of unknown parentage were usually adopted by a Dinka and brought up as one of the family. According to Luo John Lueth Ukec, who grew up in Western Twic territory with a Baggara nanny, if a Baggara woman was not married she often remained in the Dinka household and aided in household chores.[14] Although most South Sudanese perhaps do not view this very ancient practice as a mode of slavery, it continues to represent another aspect of an unfree social and labor system in South Sudan today. These wars of economics have evolved into violent ethnic struggles and dissention.

Gender Dominance and Marital Stress

Gender studies and ethnicity in precolonial Africa cannot be understood in isolation and the factor of marriage and ethnic expansion are critically important aspects of Southern Sudanese history. Today, the Dinka represent the largest ethnic group in South Sudan, and yet, unlike the Nuer, for example, conversion to Dinka "citizenship" has always been difficult. It is virtually impossible to become ethnically integrated into this community except through marriage. On the other hand, it is clear that Dinka marriage practices, centuries ago, provided the mechanism for vast Dinka ethnic expansion against all other Southern Sudanese.[15]

Despite the two million killed since 1983 the Dinka and Nuer have maintained large populations. One factor that has always enhanced population growth has been the reverence extended to women who have given birth to many children. In 1996 one such Dinka lady, who was also a founder of a womens' self help organization in the Rek territory near Tonj, was hailed for having given birth to eighteen children. The other practice which has encouraged massive population increases has been the levirate marriage system. Today this is specifically observed among the Western Nilotic Dinka and Nuer but not among the Eastern Nilotes or others in South Sudan. The interminable civil war, however, is causing the levirate marriage system to break down. One female informant stated recently: "In April 1986 the Nuer killed my husband. When my husband died my father-in-law assigned a brother-in-law to me. He stayed for six years but I had no children. After this I was assigned to another brother-in-law. But I still had no more children. Now my brother-in-law will not take care of me and my children. The system is breaking down. In the rainy season I will cultivate as best as I can." Thus, the levirate marriage system which was designed to care for Dinka widows on the one hand, and to make full use of their reproductive years on the other, is not functioning as it has in the past.

From the perspective of many young Western Nilotic women today, however, as they acquire a sense of individual rather than corporate identity because they have had to fend for themselves without the support of their corporate families, they no longer wish to follow older marital rules. Many have expressed anger at the prevailing sociocultural system that forces women to be locked into endless marriage (to their brothers-in-law) and yet offers little in financial or emotional support. According to one Nuer informant who recently lost her husband: "You cannot divorce in our culture and if I meet another man he would be killed by my brother-in-law. We are bought like clothes. If your husband dies you go to another male relative. The woman does not choose but is informed. Women are often forced to be with their brothers-in law. Ladies get beaten if they are disobedient because bridewealth has been paid for you."

The modern-day observance of levirate marriage customs within the Dinka and Nuer communities has also exacerbated ethnic tensions. Some South Sudanese women of other cultures have been unaware, upon marrying Dinka men, that these customs still existed. One such unsuspecting Bari women married a Dinka man and claimed: "I met my husband at the Malakiyya [multi-ethnic communities] in Juba in 1978. My parents said 'do not marry a Dinka,' but I insisted. Traditionally there are a lot of things about the Dinka that differ from our people. . . . We see the Dinka as uncultured cattle keepers, not cultivators [such as the Bari]. They live in the forests and cattle camps. They have these extended families. This is hated by our people." Troubles fell on the Bari woman during the second civil war when her husband was killed and she discovered that she was now to be forcibly held to the Dinka levirate marriage system against her will. She chafed bitterly that she was now forbidden from acquiring another husband, as her Dinka children would suffer and, in essence, that she was continually raped: "I am forced to give sexual service to the brother of my dead husband. The wife [widow] has no say in the matter. The family de-cides she has to comply and the man presses himself on the woman. Some [non-Dinka/Nuer] women really object violently but can do nothing. There is no support from anywhere. . . . In our culture we do not have this. I learned later about this custom after I was married. It is not possible to deny sex to my brother-in-law—my children would suffer. There are other Bari women in the same position. . . ." Thus, the older prevailing marital customs of the Western Nilotes, specifically the Dinka and Nuer, have caused and continue to cause much ethnic stress in the larger South Sudanese community. These practices will not help South Sudanese society to inte-grate.

Nilotic Fission Politics

In contrast to the fixed political systems of modern nation-states, the historical political organization of many pastoral stateless societies, particularly those of the Western Nilotic Dinka and Nuer, is best described as one that "fissions and fuses." In precolonial times, at any point when the cattle camp reached a certain size, a prominent and ambitious man of chiefly lineage gathered a group of his own kin and others who were dissatisfied, and set off to form his own camp. This happens even today. In Dinka and Nuer political culture, each man wants to found his own descent group, a formal segment of the subclan that will long be remembered by his name. In the past these would-be leaders were easily able to find followers because many Dinka males preferred to withdraw from their more distant agnatic kin in order to relieve themselves of the customary requirement of contributing towards marriage payments. British administrator G. W. Titherington asserted that the Dinka nature was essentially free and independent, that they thought nothing of transferring from one clan or family to another following a fight or grievance. These examples are indicative of the centrifugal political quality of most South Sudanese Nilotes today. This philosophy is in direct opposition to the fixed, stable, and unified model espoused by many nation-state societies today. Further, modern-day nation state leaders possess a state authority which is historically little experienced by the Western Nilotic peoples. Historically, most Nilotic societies have contained minimal political authority in precolonial times. Leaders rarely commanded tribute; their ritual authority enabled them to arbitrate only in cases of witchcraft accusation and homicide. Nor did they command judicial authority in the settlement of disputes.[16]

On the other hand the other communities in the far southwestern and far northwestern South Sudan, the Eastern Nilotic Bari, the non-Nilotic Azande, and Fertit, were all at one time eighteenth- and nineteenth century-kingdoms and empires. Thus, the political culture of the far more numerous Western Nilotes in the center stands out in stark contrast to that of the once-unified Southern Sudanese states that existed on the periphery.

The centuries old preference for "fission politics" among Western Nilotic peoples has predominated in recent times, seriously hindering the prospect of ending the present civil war and increasing the number of casualties. Further, this lack of unity has represented centuries of manipulation of these Western Nilotes by outside forces. An early example of the inability to remain unified was recorded in 1868 by the traveler Georg

Schweinfurth, who noted that "the Dinka have all the material of national unity; but where they fail is that they not only make war upon each other, but submit to be enlisted as the instruments of treachery by intruders from outside."[17] Another example of this phenomenon in the twentieth century has been that of the Western Ngok, who had begun a process of centralization in the precolonial era. These Nilotes live at the northern limits of Southern Sudan in southern Kordofan and were the first to self-destruct in the postcolonial era in a series of clan struggles over political control of the region. John and Jean Comaroff argue that once upward mobility is seen as a possibility and energies are expended to achieve it, ethnic groups must inevitably become internally stratified. Similarly, Immanuel Wallerstein argues that ethnic consciousness becomes a reality when groups feel it is an opportune moment politically, to overcome long-standing denial of privilege. These theories explain why war erupted within the emerging Ngok Dinka proto-state of Kordofan, for no sooner had the British departed in 1955 than the Ngok political leadership was torn apart by internal clan rivalries. Historically, the British supported the Pajok (Abyor) political clan of Paramount chiefs, including Arob Biong, Kwol Arob, and later Deng Majok, over the other eight Ngok sections, including their political rival, the Dhiendior clan. The Dhiendior's population, however, was greater than the clans of the Paramount chiefs. Smoldering for decades during the British period, at independence the Dhiendior chiefs forged alliances with the Northern government in an attempt to alter the balance of power within the Ngok leadership. In 1965 Deng Majok's controversial involvement in Messiria Baggara politics increased clan rivalry when the Ngok leader was elected president of the Messiria Council of Chiefs. This political move increased the power of the Ngok Dinka in Kordofan but led to eruptions of violence between the two major political clans. Strongly objecting to Deng Majok's politics, many rebelled, resulting in a civil war where thousands of Ngok citizens were wounded or died. Meanwhile, in a continued attempt to end the old system implemented by the former colonial power, members of other rival Ngok clan families continued to undermine the Abyor/(Pajok) political leadership by cooperating with the Khartoum government. The death of the powerful Ngok leader Deng Majok in 1969, and subsequent events during that year, signaled the demise of the emerging proto-state power and centralization in Abyei and its Ngok-Pajok chieftaincy. The words of Georg Schweinfurth a century later had prevailed.[18] This event marked the end of the Ngok political power in Southwest Kordofan. In microcosm, their demise augured future stress within a larger political Southern Sudan as centralization and elite struggles for power started to take hold.

In 1991 another example of fission politics and "submission to manipulation" took place within the SPLM/A itself and politically destabilized South Sudan to such a degree that it nearly lost the war. A combination of certain members of international relief agencies and U.S. and British representatives pressed for a change in the SPLA leadership. Until this time John Garang and the SPLA had quelled several internal efforts at dissent with the help of Ethiopian leader Mengistu's army along with his internal security apparatus. With the Ethiopian leader's fall in 1991 the SPLA leadership became instantly vulnerable to more division.[19] In June of 1991 two of Garang's senior commanders in the SPLA, Riek Machar, a Nuer, and Lam Akol, a Shilluk, were offered international support if they would be willing to take over the leadership of the SPLA. Hence, the two plotted a coup. They announced to the international press that they had taken over as the new leaders of the SPLA and that the new movement would be democratic and aim for total independence of the South. Scholars suggest this international support was offered only with a keen eye on the oil reserves of the South; however, the "coup" never took place because no senior Dinka commander joined Riek Machar and Lam Akol. Garang now renamed his force SPLA-Torit or SPLA-Mainstream and the two rebel commanders gathered up their adherents and renamed themselves SPLA-Nasir.[20] Prior to the attempted coup the Sudan government had offered John Garang a position as First Vice President of the Sudan, which, however, he refused. Then the government approached the two rebel SPLA commanders. The meeting was rumored to be facilitated by the British investor, "Tiny" Rowland. At this time the government sought short-term advantages in this rift between the Southern rebel forces, and shortly thereafter Riek Machar received unmarked shipments of food and weapons to fight John Garang and the SPLA. From the perception of a number of Dinka: "We feared the British were now trying to reassert control."[21] The actions of Riek Machar destabilished the South for years. By 2003 he had ceased working with the Khartoum government and his loyalties were back in the South Sudanese fold. But his actions ultimately allowed the Northern Sudanese government to seize the South Sudanese oil fields. The denouement of all this action is that the South's wealth, in the form of oil, is used by the North to buy weapons to fight the civil war.

Ethnic Conflict

Ethnic conflict has been fueled by long blood memories in South Sudan. The worst intra-South Sudanese ethnic conflicts in recent times have taken place between the Dinka and the Nuer. In the 1990s this hostility over-shadowed all other conflicts in the South, including the North/South civil war.[22] The long memory of the Nuer eighteenth-century flight because of slave raids from the north, followed by violent wars, and absorption and displacement of large numbers of Dinka in the east, initiated unceasing conflict between these two groups. The Dinka have harbored very negative memories about the Nuer conquest and seizure of "their" territories centuries ago. The Nuer, however, have tended to recount these ancient events as more of an accommodation. But wars after this time have also been long remembered.

Even among Dinka whose ancestors were formerly Nuer this tension, fed by the ongoing "blood memory," has continued to fuel intense violence. Among the most noted Dinka/Nuer wars of the Turco-Egyptian period was that initiated by the Pakam Agar Dinka leader, Wuol Athian, whose clan was originally of partial Nuer descent. He called his people together and invited the Nuer to join him in battle against the Turco-Egyptian intruders. In a speech he urged that "our hostility with the Nuer should be suspended and let us [the Dinka] befriend each other against the Turks." According to the great-grandson of Chief Wuol, Lual Wuol Nhiak, "The Nuer agreed to join Chief Wuol against the Turks in battle. However, unknown to the Nuer, Wuol Atiang had deceived them for a secret agreement among the Pakam resolved that after uniting with the Nuer and winning in battle against the Turks, the Dinka chief would call out 'Kedian Wien' [let's attack; the secret password to first kill the Turks and then to immediately turn on the Nuer]. We carried out the plan and the Nuer were unprepared. The Turks were killed and only a few Nuer escaped. Today this battle-ground is called Wath Kawata, and it is located east of present-day Rumbek."[23] According to Agar Dinka Simon Adel Yak, the great grandfather of the modern-day Nuer leader, Riek Machar, Dhorgon was killed by Wuol in this battle. In the meantime Dinka and Nuer raids and ethnic wars continued into the British colonial era.

By the 1980s the historically long ethnic malaise between the Dinka and Nuer was manipulated by aspiring leaders. Crawford Young argues that aspiring politicos learn that a personal clientele is most easily built upon cultural affinities. Those whose ascension is blocked within one political organization are sorely tempted to launch another with the cry of "ethnic solidarity." As the stakes of acquiring leadership increased along with the concomitant necessity to prove to outsiders that one had a following in order to acquire foreign finance, South Sudanese elites in the 1980s amplified and even created "ethnic divisiveness." Abel Alier suggests that many of those opposing SPLA leader Garang were former Dinka who later reidentified themselves as Nuer for the purposes of acquiring new recruits. For example, Anya Nya II leader William Abdulla Chuol was originally Dinka but became Nuer by residence and naturalization. Then to gain legitimacy he claimed spiritual powers to maintain a hold over his Nuer followers and to attract other constituents to his campaign. He went barefoot and wore the more "traditional" Nilotic *lau,* though he did not wear the leopard skin associated with Nuer prophets. In this way he attempted to emulate earlier Nuer leaders and prophets.[24] Thus, to acquire support and military hardware from the Sudanese government in the north and elsewhere, these Southern military leaders needed to resuscitate popular support by manipulating age-old ethnic rivalries.

Then in 1991 one of the worst massacres of the civil war took place between the Dinka and the Nuer. Shortly after his failed coup attempt of the SPLA, Nuer leader Riek Machar went on a rampage. The Dinka town of Bor was bigger than that of Riek Machar's base in Nasir, and had a good airstrip. Thus the United Nations delivered much food there and nearby villages were rich in long-horned cattle. On the other hand, heavy rains had destroyed crops in much of Riek's territory of eastern Upper Nile. Aided and encouraged by the Sudan government, Riek Machar's forces, accompanied by sections of the Gaajak, the Lou, and the Gawar, attacked the Dinka areas of Panaru, Bor, and Kongor, the last being SPLA leader John Garang's home region. Accompanying those who attacked the area was a Nuer prophet, Wut Nyang, and hundreds of his ash-covered white-robed followers. What transpired was an event of unprecedented brutality: raping, burning, and looting cattle and other property. In some instances Dinka children were roasted alive on open fires in front of their parents. Women and children were abducted and later divided as war booty. Observers later noted disembowelled women, children tied and shot through the head, and people hanging from trees. Amnesty International estimated that two thousand were murdered over a period of two weeks but other informants suggest the number was closer to five thousand.[25] One of those who accompanied Riek's attack on the Dinka asserts that "we were mobilized to help ourselves to Bor property. It was also Khartoum's idea to undermine ethnic alliances and therefore the attack was made to look like a Nuer/Dinka conflict. In reality the brutality was about acquiring aid supplies and land." According to one Shilluk present at the battle, "the Nuer soldiers were ruthless. . . . At one place, they killed a suckling mother and left her eight-months-old child crawling over her corpse. The Nuer attitude was 'Well that was war, the vultures will find that child alive and they will feed on both.'" The Nuer explained themselves by arguing that the Dinka had been just as violent with the Nuer civilian population. This raid came to be known as the "Bor Massacre" and in a matter of days Southerners had wreaked greater havoc on each other than they had jointly against their common enemy in the north. One Eastern Twic whose mother was murdered by having her throat cut by the Nuer in 1991 asked: "Why did they need to kill an old woman in such a manner?"[26]

The enormous tension that arose between the Dinka and Nuer after this event had a massive impact on other Dinka/Nuer communities that were more integrated ethnically such as the Pakam. As presented in chapter 7, ethno-history of this particular Agar section is very different from that of other Dinka, since they were originally Nuer. In 1991 a crisis flared. The prominent priest/chief of this Pakam Dinka section, Kulong Marial Wuol, who was also the great-grandson of the famous religious and military leader of the nineteenth and early twentieth centuries, Wuol, was arrested by the Sudan People's Liberation Army. His charge was that he was a traitor to the mainstream Dinka leadership for allowing Nuer peoples to reside within his community; yet the original Pakam were of Nuer ancestry, unknown to the SPLA. According to one Pakam: "The SPLA took all of the Nuer cattle and arrested Wuol. . . . But the lineage of Wuol is respected by the [Pakam] Dinka as sacred. So the Pakam asked 'who is this John Garang . . . is he bigger than Kulong Marial?' . . . The Pakam did not believe that Garang was bigger. If Garang had done something to this chief the Pakam would have [ultimately] joined Riek Machar."

In the meantime Dinka/Nuer violence in various points of South Sudan continued; in 1993 it was reported that approximately 1.3 million people had died in the first ten years of the second civil war, a great many at the hands of South Sudanese themselves. With the increasing number of deaths there developed, according to Dinka informants, a disturbing new trend of brutality, which also manifested itself along ethnic lines. For example, it became commonplace for the "the Nuer and Dinka to cut off women's breasts with pangas and slit old women's throats."[27]

However, tensions between the Dinka and Nuer are only one ethnic problem; there has also been severe intra-Dinka strife in recent years.

THE MALWAL/BOR CONFLICT

Noting that Southern leaders tended to fission from his movement and soon thereafter were easily "bought" by the Northern Sudanese government, John Garang began a campaign of arresting and incarcerating anyone deemed suspicious. The beginnings of serious intra-Dinka tensions began when Garang and Malwal leader Kawac Makuei Mayar clashed over the meaning of military discipline. While Garang has not been interviewed, the Malwal side of this episode was relayed by Kawac Makuei; the following represents his views and perceptions.

The initial problem between Garang and Kawac arose because of fears of the large numbers of Malwal who joined the SPLA campaigns in Ethiopia. In modern times it is claimed that 80 percent of the ethnic composition of the SPLA is Dinka. Of this percentage, however, 45 percent comprises Malwal recruits alone. To complicate matters, numbers of Malwal remained part of a splinter group from the SPLA, known as the Anya Nya II, whose members disapproved of John Garang as military leader. Initially the Malwal leader Kawac Makuei, a Lieutenant Colonel, was appointed fifth in line of succession to the SPLA leadership and made a commander of the Bahr el-Ghazal. His battalion was named "Jamuse" (buffalo).

Serious tensions erupted, however, when Garang tested Kawac Makuei's loyalty. The SPLA leader ordered his Malwal commander to eliminate numbers of Anya Nya II generals still based in the Malwal territory in the Bahr el-Ghazal. This order posed a dilemma for Kawac Makuei, whose father had been a prominent Paramount religious priest/chief. Further, Kawac Makuei had been a Southern politician of the 1970s and a Dinka elder who felt responsible for his former Malwal constituents in the Bahr el-Ghazal regardless of modern political affiliations. He refused the order. He stated: "I was a parliamentarian and wouldn't consider such a thing!" When he arrived in Ethiopia accompanied by thousand, who had formerly broken away from the SPLA but now had agreed to rejoin the SPLA under Kawac, Garang arrested the Malwal leader. He became one of John Garang's longest prisoners-of-war, remaining in various SPLA camps for ten years.[28] This action has caused enormous stress between the Malwal and Bor Dinka troops up to the present time.

On the other hand important intra-ethnic alliances have also been made between the Dinka and their neighbors.

ALLIANCES

Dinka and Nuer ethnic tensions in recent times have existed most often at the level of elite politicians and military leaders. At the village level, on many occasions, the two groups have united in a common cause. In the early 1980s numbers of Ngok Dinka came to base themselves with the Bul Nuer south of Abyei. During this time the chiefs frequently met to talk about how they could protect themselves and present a united front against the Baggara.[29]

Further, the Dinka have periodically also made alliances with their centuries-long enemies, the Baggara. R. Brian Ferguson argues that it is quite common for a mutual interest in trade to lead to a special relationship of peace within an environment of war.[30] During the first civil war in the 1960s, alliances had been created between the Islamic Baggara and Dinka who resided in the region of the Kir/Bahr el-Arab River. In 1991 a substantial number of Messiria Baggara allied with the Dinka to gain access to pasture during the dry seasons. The Rizeiqat Baggara militia split in two and one signed an agreement with the SPLA Dinka Commander Aleu Akacak. This agreement created a "buffer zone" on the Kir/Bahr el-Arab River so that all parties could graze their cattle. As it is a "hunger area" the Baggara frequently bought *dhurra* (grain) from the Dinka, and because of a series of centuries-long Rizeiqat and Malwal marriage alliances the agreement continues to the present time. Other agreements between the Abiem Malwal and the Messiria Baggara in 1991 and 1993, however, were created but did not last. Nevertheless, for a brief period a Messiria leader, Buryi Bushara, joined the SPLA and became a Commander. Malwal informants state that relations with the Messiria are worse than with the Rizeiqat largely because of the lack of long-term alliances. The Malwal and Rizeiqat trade items; the latter bring sugar, clothes, salt, and oil in exchange for *dhurra* and cows. The Malwal state their cows are more hardy than the Rizeiqat's but the latter have more milk. While it hardly constitutes an alliance, some Baggara have also made a living in the Bahr el-Ghazal by providing a safe haven for former Dinka slaves, repatriated back to the South, and selling them back to their relatives. (In recent times the practice of buying the freedom of slaves by Christian Solidarity International has been severely criticized by numerous non-governmental and governmental agencies as it has encouraged more raids and corruption.) Thus on the Arab/African frontier key historical alliances have prevailed within the larger civil war. Long recognized as an "African/Arab" frontier, the Kir/Bahr el-Arab region in reality is an ethnic kaleidoscope. Hence relations have not so much been dictated by external events as by local necessity.[31]

Leroy Vail argued that ethnicity and parochial loyalties within the borders of nation states are likely to continue and that condemning them as "reactionary" or "divisive" will accomplish little. Rather, it is necessary for politicians and scholars to work towards accommodating "ethnicity" within these nation states, for it will continue as a potent force. Hence, Africans will have to produce political solutions derived from African experience in order to solve African problems.[32]

As to ameliorating perceptions of Dinka expansion and insensitivity, the former Southern Sudanese president of the 1970s, Bor-Atoc Dinka Abel Alier Wal Kwai (known in his home village as Alier Kwai), stated:

In a post war situation we have now seen we can work together much like other African countries. I have two visions. One, grass roots development; we should go the long way towards helping people help themselves. We need to be sensitive about the division of limited resources; between urban and rural and between one rural area to another because there are some areas in the South which are more undeveloped than others. We must maintain workable decentralization of authority and give the responsibility to the people for their local government and services. Civil associations should be encouraged to do things, such as women's associations, non-governmental organizations, etc. In other words, we must make use of human resources and let the people be busy and do things for themselves. The Southern Sudan has resources such as tourism and we need to develop our folklore. We need to develop physical athletics and put our people on the map quickly. We need a conscious exchange of visits between the different ethnic groups so that we can learn about each other and the limitations of others. Leaders must have a sense of justice. We have to weld our society into a neutral body and the people have to feel we are being just.

To some degree the 1994 SPLA Convention ameliorated ethnic and political tensions. The Equatorian fear and distrust of the Dinka has began to decline. In 1996 many still noted that the Dinka dominated the South politically. However, there appeared to be an increased respect for the SPLA leader, John Garang. Azande leader Samuel Abujohn Kbashi, the 1960s Anya Nya commander and Governor of Equatoria Province (in 1996), stated: "Garang works tirelessly, he works throughout the night. He's had breakaways but he has held on. He's a true nationalist." Other non-Dinka informants I interviewed claimed they were less critical of the SPLA than in the past. Residents of the Azande and Balanda town of Yambio in Equatoria note: "First the SPLA was known only as a Dinka movement; today we know it as a national movement." The Balanda view the SPLA as having given them a measure of liberation. According to Bandindi Pascal Uru : "In the early 1990s John Garang allowed the Balanda to separate politically from the Azande . . . and Garang established Balanda chieftainships. We wanted to be politically represented by our own people." Equatorian scholar Yongo Bure Jame, a Kuku, stated: "The South needs the Dinka: we cannot do without their numbers, and Garang is the Dinka that can attract the other groups. He has had so much exposure and he has become enlightened. He has an international appeal."

NOTES

Chapter 1

1. J. Vansina, "Is Elegance Proof?: Structuralism and African History," *History in Africa* 10 (1983) 307–348 and "Once Upon a Time: Oral Traditions as History in Africa," *Daedalus* Spring (1971) 442–468; T. Beidelman, "Myth, Legend and Oral History," *Anthropos* 65 (1970) 74–97; J. Miller, ed. *The African Past Speaks,* (Kent, England: Wm. Dawson and Sons, Ltd., 1980); R. Harms, "The Wars of August: Diagonal Narrative in African History," *The American Historical Review* 88, 4 (1983) 809–843; R. Horton, "African Traditional Thought and Western Science," *Africa* 37 (1967) 50–71; T. Spear, "Oral Traditions: Whose History?" *History in Africa* 8 (1981) 165–181.

2. Francis Mading Deng, *The Man Called Deng Majok* (New Haven: Yale University Press, 1986), 8. Burton

3. Fernand Braudel, *On History* (Chicago: University of Chicago Press, 1980), 25–53; A. Bernard Knapp, ed., "Archaeology and Annales: Time, Space, and Change," in *Archaeology, Annales, and Ethnohistory* (Cambridge: Cambridge University Press, 1992), 1–21; Peter R. Schmidt, *Historical Archaeology A Structural Approach in an African Culture* (Westport, CT: Greenwood Press, 1978).

4. John Middleton and David Tait, eds., "Introduction," in *Tribes without Rulers* (London: Routledge and Kegan Paul, 1958), 1–31.

5. Henri J. M. Claessen and Peter Skalnik eds., "Introduction," in *The Early State* (New York: Mouton Publishers, 1978), 22–23.

Chapter 2

1. U. S. Department of State, Bureau of African Affairs, Background Note, March 2003; John Garang de Mabior, "Identifying, Selecting and Implementing Rural Development Strategies for Socio-Economic Development in the Jonglei Projects Area, Southern Region, Sudan" (Ph.D. diss., Iowa State University, 1981), 31–41; K. M. Barbour, *The Republic of the Sudan: A Regional Geography* (London: University of London Press, 1961).

2. James Bruce, *Travels to Discover the Source of the Nile* 2nd ed. (Edinburgh: Constable, 1805) 265–75; A. Kaufmann, *Schilderungen aus Centralafrica oder Land und Leute im obern Nilgebiete am Weissen Flusse* (Brixen & Lienz: A. Weger, 1862), 68.

Chapter 3

1. Also PI#76–80; PI#82; PI#196; M. Pumphrey, "The Shilluk Tribe," *Sudan Notes and Records* 24 (1941): 1–45; Mohamed Riad, "The Divine Kingship of the Shilluk and its Origin," *Archiv Fur Volkerkunde* Band XIV (1959): 219, 266; Gabriel Jiet Jal, "The History of the Jikany Nuer Before 1920" (Ph.D. diss., School of Oriental and African Studies, University of London, 1987), 110; John W. Burton, *A Nilotic World: The Atuot Speaking Peoples of the Southern Sudan* (New York: Greenwood Press, 1987), 10.

2. Also PI#292; PI#255; PI#196.

3. Merrick Posnansky, "East Africa and the Nile Valley in Early Times," in Yusuf Fadl Hasan, ed., *Sudan in Africa* (Khartoum: Khartoum University Press, 1968), 58; A. J. Arkell, *A History of the Sudan to A.D. 1821* (London: Athlone Press, 1955), 49; C. G. Seligman and Brenda Z. Seligman, *Pagan Tribes of the Nilotic Sudan* (London: George Routledge & Sons, 1932); John Lewis Burckhardt, *Travels in Nubia,* 2nd ed. (London: John Murray, 1822), Appendix III, 453.

4. PI#113; PI#142; PI#213, PI#196, PI#299; O. G. S. Crawford, *The Fung Kingdom of Sennar* (Gloucester: John Bellows Ltd., 1951), 61–3; Ali Salih Jaiballa, *Mudhakirat Al-Oumda Al-Sabiqa: Al Haj Ali Salih Jaiballa* (Memories of the Former Omda), (Khartoum: Mahmoudiyya Press, 1974), 10.

5. Also PI#136, PI#160–163.

6. For a history of the Funj Sultanate see Jay Spaulding, *The Heroic Age in Sinnar* (East Lansing, Michigan State University Press, 1985) and R. S. O'Fahey and J. L. Spaulding, *Kingdoms of the Sudan* (London: Methuen, 1974).

7. PI#182–183. Also, PI#112, PI#208, PI#213.

8. G. Beltrame, *Brevi Cenni Sui Denka e Sulla Loro Lingua* (Rivista Orientale, 1867), 792, and *Le rive del Fiume bianco da Chartum a Seilak* (Venice, 1881), 843.

9. Damazo Dut Majak Koejok, "The Northern Bahr al-Ghazal: People, Alien Encroachment and Rule, 1856–1956" (Ph.D. diss., University of California, Santa Barbara, 1990), 23–6.

10. Tepilit Ole Saitoti, *The Worlds of a Maasai Warrior* (Berkeley: University of California, 1988), xxv.

11. Also PI#62; PI#66; PI#72–3, PI#153, PI#213; PI#276.

12. M. Lionel Bender, "Sub-Classification of Nilo-Saharan," in *Proceedings of the Fourth Nilo-Saharan Conference, Bayreuth, Aug. 30–Sept. 2, 1989,* ed. M. Lionel Bender (Hamburg: Helmut Buske Verlag, 1989), 20–21, 177; Christopher Ehret, "Nilo-Saharans and the Saharo-Sudanese Neolithic," in *The Archaeology of Africa* (New York; Routledge, 1995), 104, 115, and *Southern Nilotic History* (Evanston, Ill.: Northwestern University Press, 1971), 30, 35, and "Population Movement and Culture Contact in the Southern Sudan, c. 3000 B.C.E. to A.D. 1000: a Preliminary Linguistic Overview," in John Mack and Peter Robertshaw, eds., *Culture History in the Southern Sudan Archaeology, Linguistics and Ethnohistory* (Nairobi: British Institute in East Africa, 1982), 27; Nicholas David, "The B.I.E.A. Southern Sudan Expedition of 1979: Interpretation of the Archaeological Data" (unpublished paper) and "Prehistory and Historical Linguistics in Central Africa: Points of Contact," in Christopher Ehret and Merrick Posnansky, eds., *The Archaeological and Linguistic Reconstruction of African History* (Berkeley: University of California Press, 1982), 83; William Y. Adams, "The Coming of Nubian Speakers to the Nile Valley," in *The Archaeological and Linguistic Reconstruction of African History* 13.

13. Christopher Ehret, *The Civilizations of Africa: A History to 1800* (Charlottesville: University Press of Virginia, 2002), 92, 126, 217–20, 391.

14. Also PI#61; PI#208; Robin Thelwall, "Lexicostatistical Relations Between Nubian, Daju and Dinka," unpublished paper presented at the Third International Colloquium of Nubian Studies, Chantilly, 1975, 5. In a published version of his findings ("Lexicostatistical Relations Between Nubian, Daju and Dinka," *Extrait des Etudes Nubiennes,* Colloque de Chantilly, 2–6 Juillet 1975, 273), Thelwall changed the interpretation of his evidence to suggest that all the similarities in vocabulary between Dinka and Nobiin could be attributed to cognate descent of these terms from an ancestral proto-language. Since this proto-language has never yet been reconstructed this interpretation remains speculative at best, and in view of the plausibility of historical interaction between medieval Dinka speakers and medieval Nubian speakers, it is unnecessary; Bender, "Sub-Classification of Nilo-Saharan," 20–21; Jay Spaulding, "The Old Shaiqi Language in Historical Perspective," *History in Africa* 17 (1990): 283–292; Adams, "Nubian Speakers," 13.

15. Crawford, *The Fung,* 1; A. C. R. Hownam-Meek, "On the Culture History of Tooth Mutilation in Africa," cited in David, "Nilotic Expansion," 64–5; S. Cole, *The Prehistory of East Africa* (London: Weidenfeld and Nicolson, 1963), 282; F. Addison, *Jebel Moya* (Oxford: Oxford University Press, 1949), 53–5.

16. Else Johansen Kleppe, "Towards a Prehistory of the Riverain Nilotic Sudan: Archaeological Excavations in the Er Renk District," *Nubian Letters* 1 (1983), 14–20.

17. Peter Robertshaw and Ari Siiriainen, "Excavations in Lakes Province, Southern Sudan," *Azania* 20 (1985): 89–161; Nicholas David, "The Archaeological Context of Nilotic Expansion," in Rainer Vossen, Marianne Bechhaus-Gerst, eds., *Nilotic Studies: Proceedings of the International Symposium on Languages and History of the Nilotic Peoples Cologne, January 4–5, 1982* (Berlin: Dietrich Reimer Verlag, 1983), 72, and "Historical Linguistics," 78–103 and "Southern Sudan Expedition."

18. Robertshaw and Siiriainen, "Excavations in Lakes Province, Southern Sudan," 108–9, 138, 146; David, "Nilotic Expansion," 72, "B.I.E.A. Southern Sudan," and "Archaeological Context," 68.

19. David, "Nilotic Expansion," 72, and "B.I.E.A. Southern Sudan" and "Prehistory," 87–8; Santandrea, *Ethno-Geography,* 141–149.

20. Fr. Giovanni Vantini, *Oriental Sources Concerning Nubia* (Heidelberg and Warsaw, Polish Academy of Sciences and Heidelberger Akademie der Wissenschaften, Frg., 1975), 4–6, 179, 400, 449, 465; Mohi el-Din Abdalla Zarroug, *The Kingdom of Alwa* (Calgary: University of Calgary Press, 1991).

21. Jay Spaulding, "The Funj: A Reconsideration," *Journal of African History* 13, 1 (1972): 39–53.

22. H. A. MacMichael, *A History of the Arabs,* Vol. 2 (London: Frank Cass & Co., 1967), 194–201; Crawford, *The Fung,* 156.

23. Although MacMichael claims this document dates from the 1500s, scholars take issue with this claim as the account documents the 1821 invasion of the Turco-Egyptians into the Sudan; see Jay Spaulding, "The Chronology of Sudanese Arabic Genealogical Tradition," unpublished paper presented at the workshop "Ideologies of Race, Origins and Descent in the History of the Nile Valley and North East Africa," 12 July 1994, St. Anthony's College, Oxford, 5; MacMichael, *A History of the Arabs,* 27–28.

24. MacMichael, *A History of the Arabs,* 12–13; 194, 209; J. Spaulding, "The Fate of Alodia," *Transafrican Journal of History* 2 (1977): 39–53; al-Shatir Busayli' Abd al-Jalil, *Makhtutat*

Katib al-Shuna fi tárikh al-sultana al-sinnariya wa'l-idara al-misriya (Cairo, 1961); J. Beaven, *Renk District Notes, Upper Nile Province Handbook* (1931), chap. 3; SAD 212/14/1.

25. Dakhlia 112/16/102, "Buruns and Allied Tribes," J. W. Robertson, "Sillak, Maghagha & Abu el Dugu," (15/12/31).

Chapter 4

1. These sentiments were also echoed by PI#61, PI#208.

2. William Y. Adams, *Nubia Corridor to Africa* (London: Lane, 1977), 43, 471, 505, 537; Margaret Shinnie, *A Short History of the Sudan Up to A.D. 1500* (Sudan Antiquities Service, [n.d.].), 4–5; Harold MacMichael, *A History of the Arabs*, vol. 1 (London: Frank Cass & Co. Ltd., 1967), 48.

3. Fr. Giovanni Vantini, *Oriental Sources Concerning Nubia* (Heidelberg and Warsaw: Polish Academy of Sciences and Heidelberger Akademie der Wissenschaften, FRG., 1975), 457.

4. Vantini, *Oriental Sources,* 47, 205–6.

5. R. S. Herring, "Hydrology and Chronology: the Rodah Nilometer as an Aid in Dating Inter-Lacustrine History," in J. B. Webster, ed., *Chronology, Migration and Drought in Inter-Lacustrine Africa* (London: Longman and Dalhousie University Press, 1979), 39–86; J. B. Webster, "Noi! Noi! Famines as an Aid to Interlacustrine Chronology," in *Chronology, Migration and Drought,* 5; Peter Robertshaw and David Taylor, "Climate Change and the Rise of Political Complexity in Western Uganda," *Journal of African History* 41 (2000): 1–28; Sharon Elaine Nicholson, "A Climatic Chronology for Africa: Synthesis of Geological, Historical, and Meteorological Information and Data" (Ph.D. diss., University of Wisconsin-Madison, 1976), 96–7, 130; O. G. S. Crawford, *The Fung Kingdom of Sennar* (Gloucester: John Bellows Ltd., 1951), 28.

6. Of the two principal cattle types of the Sudan today, the Sanga is the older of the hump-backed variety and bred mainly by the Southern Sudanese Dinka, Nuer, Shilluk, and Mundari, H. Epstein, *The Origins of the Domestic Animals of Africa* (New York: Africana Publishing Corp., 1971), 415, 417, 517, 556; Nicholas David, "The Archaeological Context of Nilotic Expansion," in Rainer Vossen, Marianne Bechhaus-Gerst, eds., *Nilotic Studies: Proceedings of the International Symposium on Languages and History of the Nilotic Peoples Cologne, January 4–5, 1982* (Berlin: Dietrich Reimer Verlag, 1983), and "The B.I.E.A. Southern Sudan Expedition of 1979: Interpretation of the Archaeological Data" (unpublished paper).

7. PI#60–63, PI#66, PI#70–71, PI#88–89, PI#97, PI#105, PI#136, PI#213, PI#223–224, PI#256, PI#261; A. Triulzi, *Salt, Gold and Legitimacy* (Napoli: Istituto Universitario Orientale, 1981), 61–7.

8. Stefano Santandrea, *The Luo of the Bahr el Ghazal Sudan* (Verona: Editrice Nigrizia, 1968), 132, and *Ethno-Geography of the Bahr el Ghazal Sudan* (Bologna: Editrice Missionaria Italiana, 1981), 126–27.

9. Also PI#183; Jay Spaulding, "The Funj: A Reconsideration," *Journal of African History* 13, 1 (1972): 39–53; Else Johansen Kleppe, "The Debbas on the White Nile, Southern Sudan," in John Mack and Peter Robertshaw, eds., *Culture History in the Southern Sudan Archaeology, Linguistics and Ethnohistory* (Nairobi: British Institute in East Africa, 1982), 59–71; O. G. S. Crawford, "People without a History," *Antiquity* 22 (1948): 8–12.

10. SAD GIIS1124/438; Herring, "Hydrology and Chronology," 39–86.

11. Also PI#60, PI#144, PI#145, PI#146, PI#147, PI#150, PI#151.

12. PI#60, PI#182, PI#183; Diedrich Westermann, *The Shilluk People: Their Language and Folklore* (Philadelphia: The Board of Foreign Missions of The United Presbyterian Church of N.A., 1912), LV.

13. Al-Shatir Busayli' Abd al-Jalil, *Makhtutat Katib al-Shuna fi ta'rikh al-sultana al-sinnariya wa'l-idara al-misriya* [The Funj Chronicle] (Cairo: United Arab Republic Ministry of Culture and Information, 1961), 17. "Umm Lahm" in Arabic translates to the "mother of meat"; Biography of Dayf Allah b. Al-Shaykh Muhammad Abu Idris, see Yusuf Fadl Hasan, ed., *Kitab al-Tabaqat ta'lif Muhammad al-Nur b. Dayf Allah* (Khartoum, University of Khartoum Press), 210, 357.

14. Kathy Ann Yunger, "Nyikang The Warrior Priest: Shilluk Chol Imagery, Economics and Political Development" (Ph.D. diss., State University of New York at Stony Brook, 1985), 131; P. W. Hofmayr, *Die Schilluk* (St. Gabriel, Modling bei Wien: Administration des Anthropos, 1925); M. E. C. Pumphrey, "Shilluk 'Royal' Language Conventions," *Sudan Notes and Records*, vol. 22, pt. 2 (1937), and "The Shilluk Tribe," in *Sudan Notes and Records*, vol. 24 (1941).

15. PI#257; PI#258; PI#111; C. A. Willis, "The Cult of Deng," *Sudan Notes and Records* 11 (1928): 195–207.

16. There is some discrepancy in the Shilluk dating system, for Fazugli was invaded around 1685 and the Shilluk king, Duwat, is listed as reigning somewhat earlier. See Westermann, *The Shilluk People*, LV; Triulzi, *Salt, Gold and Legitimacy* , 61–7; Hofmayr, *Die Schilluk*, 66; R. Hartmann, "Skizzen aus Aethiopen, *Globus* 4 (1861): 433, 449, and *Reise des Freiherrn Adalbert von Barnim durch Nord-Ost-Afrika in den Jahren 1859 und 1860* (Berlin: G. Reimer, 1863), 473, 547, 559; A. E. Brehm, *Reiseskizzen aus Nord-Ost Afrika; Egypten, Nubien, Sennahr, Roseeres und Kordofahn, 1847–1852* (Jena: F. Mauke, 1855) I: 246; F. Cailliaud, *Voyage a Meroe* (Paris: Imprimerie Royale, 1823) III: 84–5; James Bruce, *Travels to Discover the Source of the Nile,* 2nd ed. (Edinburgh: Constable, 1805), 265–75; R. S. O'Fahey and J. L. Spaulding, *Kingdoms of the Sudan* (London: Methuen, 1974), 61–66. Crawford, *The Fung Kingdom of Sennar,* 82.

17. PI#62; Westermann, *The Shilluk People,* LV; Yunger, "Nyikang The Warrior Priest," 131; Herring, "Hydrology and Chronology," 39–86; Webster, "Noi! Noi!," 5.

18. Hofmayr, *Die Schilluk,* 66; Westermann, *The Shilluk People,* LV; Yunger, "Nyikang The Warrior Priest," 8, 159–66.

19. PI#67; W. G. Browne, *Travels in Africa, Egypt, and Syria From the Year 1792 to 1798* (London, 1799), 452–53; Mohamed Riad, "The Divine Kingship of the Shilluk and its Origin," *Archiv Fur Volkerkunde* Band XIV (1959): 144–79; Yunger, "Nyikang The Warrior Priest," 131–49; Westermann, *The Shilluk People,* XLIX, 144; Spaulding, "The Funj," 43, and "Farmers, Herdsmen and the State in Rainland Sinnar," *Journal of African History* 20 (1979): 329–347; G. Lienhardt, "The Shilluk of the Upper Nile," in D. Forde, ed., *African Worlds* (London: Oxford University Press, 1954), 144 and "Nilotic Kings and Their Mother's Kin," *Africa* 27, (1955): 341–55.

20. Gabriel Giet Jal, "The History of the Jikany Nuer Before 1920" (Ph.D. diss., School of Oriental and African Studies, University of London, 1987), 94.

21. PI#76–82; PI#88–89, PI#278, PI#285; Bender, 2; SAD 104/16/1–13.

22. PI#285; Louise E. Sweet, "Camel Raiding of North Arabian Bedouin: A Mechanism of Ecological Adaptation," *American Anthropologist* 67, no. 5 (1965): 1132–50; Alois Musil, *The Manners and Customs of the Rwala Bedouins* (New York, American Geographical Society, 1928), 504.

23. PI#107–108, PI#111, PI#255.

24. PI#255; G. Beltrame, *Il Fiume Bianco E I Denka* (Verona: 1881), 263.

25. They may also be of Luo origin. Peter Robertshaw and Ari Siiriainen, "Excavations in Lakes Province, Southern Sudan," *Azania* 20 (1985): 148; PI#255; also informal discussion with Gary Jones, Lutheran World Federation, Nairobi, Kenya, who worked among the Yibel (Jurbel) for two years.

26. PI#202, PI#206.

27. A. Kaufmann, A. *Schilderungen aus Centralafrica oder Land und Leute im obern Nilgebiete am weissen Flusse* (Brixen: A. Weger, 1862), 153; and "The White Nile Valley and Its Inhabitants," in Elias Toniolo and Richard Hill, eds., *The Opening of the Nile Basin* (London: C. Hurst, 1974), 140–95; R. S. O'Fahey, "Fur and Fartit: The History of a Frontier," in John Mack and Peter Robertshaw, eds., *Culture History in the Southern Sudan Archaeology, Linguistics and Ethnohistory* (Nairobi: British Institute in Eastern Africa, 1982), 75–87; Waltraud and Andreas Kronenberg, *Die Bongo* (Wiesbaden: Franz Steiner Verlag, 1981).

28. Godfrey Lienhardt, *Divinity and Experience* (Oxford: Clarendon Press, 1961), 187.

29. SAD 465/3 H. C. Jackson.

30. Also PI#278.

31. PI#160–167; David, "B.I.E.A. Southern Sudan," Santandrea, *The Luo*, 131–2 and *Ethno-Geography*, 126–27; Lienhardt, *Divinity*, 177; P. P. Howell, *The Equatorial Nile Project and its Effects in the Anglo-Egyptian Sudan Being the Report of the Jonglei Investigation Team*, vol.1 (London: Waterlow and Sons, 1954), 116.

32. David, "B.I.E.A. Southern Sudan," and "Prehistory and Historical Linguistics in Central Africa: Points of Contact," in Christopher Ehret and Merrick Posnansky, eds., *The Archaeological and Linguistic Reconstruction of African History* (Berkeley: University of California Press, 1982), 87–8, and "Nilotic Expansion," 72; Santandrea, *Ethno-Geography*, 133, 138–49 and *The Luo*, 86 ; Majak, "Northern Bahr al-Ghazal," 23–6, J. M. Stubbs and C. G. T. Morrison, "The Western Dinkas, Their Land and Their Agriculture," *Sudan Notes and Records* 21 (1938): 251–68.

33. Stephanie Beswick, "The Ngok: Emergence and Destruction of a Nilotic Proto-State in Southwest Kordofan," in Michael Kevane and Endre Stiansen, eds., *Kordofan Invaded: Peripheral Incorporation and Sectoral Transformation in Islamic Africa, 1785–1995* (Leiden: Brill, 1998), 145–64; and S. Beswick, "Violence, Ethnicity, and Political Consolidation in South Sudan: A History of the Dinka and their Relations with their Neighbors, 1200–1994" (Ph.D. diss., Michigan State University, 1998); K. D. D. Henderson, "A Note on the Migration of the Messiria Tribe into South-West Kordofan," *Sudan Notes and Records* 22 (1939): 58.

34. David Cole and Richard Huntington, "African Rural Development: Some Lessons from Abyei," unpublished manuscript, Cambridge, Mass., Harvard Institute for International Development, October 1985, chap. 7, 1, 10 and 2, 3; Santandrea, *Ethno-Geography*, 126; and *The Luo*, 129, 191; Henderson, "A Note on the Migration of the Messiria Tribe," 58.

Chapter 5

1. PI#65, PI#182–183.

2. PI#60, PI#65.

3. Ibid., Jal, 94.

4. PI#60, PI#182–183; SAD 212/15/4.

5. PI#62–64, PI#257–258, PI#294, PI#300, PI#302; SAD GIIS1124.

6. PI#62–64, PI#257–258.

7. PI#66, PI#252–3.

8. PI#60, PI#62–64, PI#185–186, PI#257–258, Raymond C. Kelly, *The Nuer Conquest: The Structure and Development of an Expansionist System* (Ann Arbor: University of Michigan Press, 1985), 24; SAD 764/12/21.

9. PI#67–69, PI#72–73, PI#75, PI#184, PI#285.

10. PI#257–258, PI#68–69.

11. PI#192–193.

12. PI#179–180, PI#294, PI#300, PI#302; Francis Mading Deng, *The Man Called Deng Majok* (New Haven: Yale University Press, 1986); Stefano Santandrea, *The Luo of the Bahr el Ghazal Sudan* (Verona: Editrice Nigrizia, 1968), 190; Cole and Huntington, "African Rural Development, ch. 7: 2–3.

Chapter 6

1. PI#70–71; SAD 212/15/4; G. Beltrame, *Il Fiume Bianco E I Denka* (Verona: 1881), 263; A. Kaufmann, A. *Schilderungen aus Centralafrica oder Land und Leute im obern Nilgebiete am weissen Flusse* (Brixen: A. Weger, 1862).

2. PI#70–73, PI#285.

3. PI#61, PI#76–82, PI#85–87, PI#93, PI#97, PI#285; Per Sofholm, "The River-Lake Nilotes: Politics of an African Tribal Group" (Ph.D. diss, Uppsala University, 1973), 58, 116–31; SAD 212/15/4.

4. PI#95.

5. PI#61; PI#85, PI#105–108; PI#111, PI#120, PI#196, PI#278; SAD104/16/1–13; Kaufmann, *Schilderungen,* 153.

6. Kaufmann, *Schilderungen,* 55, 134–8; SAD 639/12/1.

Chapter 7

1. PI#136–41, PI#255, PI#282; Captain V. H. Fergusson, "The Nuong Nuer," *Sudan Notes and Records* 4 (1921): 146–54. Beltrame, *Il Fiume Bianco E I Denka* (Verona: 1881), 263; SAD 212/15/4; conversation with Gary Jones, Lutheran World Federation, Nairobi, Kenya.

2. PI#107–108, PI#136–143, PI#190, PI#284.

3. Stephanie Beswick, *Slavery in Southern Sudan,* forthcoming; J. M. Stubbs and C. G. T. Morrison. "The Western Dinkas, their Land and their Agriculture," *Sudan Notes and Records* 21 (1938): 251–68.

4. PI#51, PI#136, PI#209–210, PI#214, PI#221, PI#230, PI#252; John W. Burton, *A Nilotic World: The Atuot Speaking Peoples of the Southern Sudan* (New York: Greenwood Press, 1987), 5.

5. PI#136, PI#209–210, PI#221, PI#230, PI#252, PI#256; Burton, *A Nilotic World,* 5, 12–13.

6. PI#202, PI#213.

7. SAD 767/11/28; PI#202, PI#144, PI#145, PI#146, PI#147, PI#150, PI#151.

8. PI#144–147, PI#150–151, PI#194, PI#202, PI#205, PI#213, PI#265, PI#276, Nicholas David, "The Archaeological Context of Nilotic Expansion," in Rainer Vossen,

Marianne Bechhaus-Gerst, eds., *Nilotic Studies: Proceedings of the International Symposium on Languages and History of the Nilotic Peoples Cologne, January 4–5, 1982* (Berlin: Dietrich Reimer Verlag, 1983), 68; Bol Yuol, "The Agar of Rumbek," unpublished paper, written for Oxfam South Sudan, March 1996; SAD 767/11/28.

9. PI#196, PI#212.

10. PI#148–149, PI#202, PI#206–208, PI#215, PI#251, PI#260, PI#265; Waltraud Kronenberg and Andreas Kronenberg, *Die Bongo* (Wiesbaden: Franz Steiner Verlag, 1981).

Chapter 8

1. PI#66, PI#152, PI#222–224, #253.

2. PI#153–156, PI#181, PI#223–225, PI#292–3, PI#301, PI#303; SAD 465/3; G. Schweinfurth, *The Heart of Africa*, 2 vols. (London: Sampson Low, Marston, Low, and Searle, 1874).

3. PI#152, PI#170–176, PI#220, PI#261–264, PI#266, PI#278, *Ethno-Geography of the Bahr el Ghazal Sudan* (Bologna: Editrice Missionaria Italiana, 1981), 126–27, 133, 138–49.

4. PI#6, PI#14, PI#61, PI#76–82, PI#86–87, PI#97, PI#160–167, PI#191, PI#218, PI#222–224; Stefano Santandrea, *The Luo of the Bahr el Ghazal Sudan* (Verona: Editrice Nigrizia, 1968), 132, and *Ethno-Geography*, 126–27, and Godfrey Lienhardt, *Divinity and Experience* (Oxford: Clarendon Press, 1961), 177, and P. P. Howell, *The Equatorial Nile Project and its Effects in the Anglo-Egyptian Sudan Being the Report of the Jonglei Investigation Team*, vol.1 (London: Waterlow and Sons, 1954), 116.

Chapter 9

1. R. S. Herring, "Hydrology and Chronology: the Rodah Nilometer as an Aid in Dating Inter-Lacustrine History," in J. B. Webster, ed., *Chronology, Migration and Drought in Inter-Lacustrine Africa* (London: Longman and Dalhousie University Press, 1979), 39–86; A. B. L. Stemler, J. R. Harlan, and J. M. J. Dewet, "Caudatum Sorghums and Speakers of Chari-Nile Languages in Africa," *Journal of African History* 16, no. 2 (1975): 161–83.

2. Stemler, "Caudatum Sorghums," 161–83; John Garang de Mabior, "Identifying, Selecting and Implementing Rural Development Strategies for Socio-Economic Development in the Jonglei Projects Area, Southern Region, Sudan" (Ph.D. diss., Iowa State University, 1981), 38, 40; Peter Robertshaw and Ari Siiriainen, "Excavations in Lakes Province, Southern Sudan," *Azania* 20 (1985): 144; J. B. Webster, "Noi! Noi! Famines as an Aid to Interlacustrine Chronology," in *Chronology, Migration and Drought*, 5–11; Herring, "Hydrology and Chronology," 39–86; E.I. Steinhart, "The Kingdoms on the March: Speculations on Social and Political Change," in *Chronology, Migration and Drought*, 415–556.

3. Steinhart, "The Kingdoms on the March," 415–556.

4. R. A. L. Bayoumi, S. D. Flatz, W. Kiihnau, and G. Flatz, "Beja and Nilotes: Nomadic Pastoralist Groups in the Sudan with Opposite Distributions of the Adult Lactose Phenotypes," *American Journal of Physical Anthropology* 58 (1982): 173–78.

5. PI#185; Cagai Matet Guem; Robertshaw, "Excavations," 144

6. Bayoumi et al., "Beja and Nilotes," 173–78.

7. PI#251.

8. PI#223–224; Kathy Ann Yunger, "Nyikang The Warrior Priest: Shilluk Chol Imagery, Economics and Political Development" (Ph.D. diss., State University of New York at Stony Brook, 1985), 112–19.

9. PI#66, PI#138, PI#148–9, PI#152, PI#154; PI#166, PI#170–6, PI#185, PI#196, PI#223–4, PI#284; Robertshaw, "Excavations," 144.

10. Nicholas David, "The Archaeological Context of Nilotic Expansion," in Rainer Vossen, Marianne Bechhaus-Gerst, eds., *Nilotic Studies: Proceedings of the International Symposium on Languages and History of the Nilotic Peoples Cologne, January 4–5, 1982* (Berlin: Dietrich Reimer Verlag, 1983), 94, and "The B.I.E.A. Southern Sudan Expedition of 1979: Interpretation of the Archaeological Data" (unpublished paper).

11. Nicholas David, "Prehistory and Historical Linguistics in Central Africa: Points of Contact," in Christopher Ehret and Merrick Posnansky, eds., *The Archaeological and Linguistic Reconstruction of African History* (Berkeley: University of California Press, 1982), "The B.I.E.A.," and "Nilotic Expansion," 64–95; Robertshaw, "Excavations," 89–161.

12. Robertshaw, "Excavations," 144; Herring, "Hydrology and Chronology," 39–86; David, "Nilotic Expansion," 72, "The B.I.E.A.," and "Prehistory," 87–8; Stemler, "Caudatum Sorghums," 161–83.

Chapter 10

1. PI#179–180; Dagmar Freuchen, ed, *Peter Freuchen's Book of the Eskimos* (New York, The World Publishing Company, 1961), 25; A. R. Radcliffe-Brown, "Notes on Totemism in Eastern Australia," *Journal of the Royal Anthropological Institute* 59 (1929): 399–415, and *Structure and Function in Primitive Society* (London: Cohen & West, 1952), 126; David C. Conrad, ed., *A State of Intrigue* (Oxford: Oxford University Press, 1990), 46.

2. Also PI#60.

3. PI#170–176, PI#294.

4. PI#121–122.

5. See also R. T. Johnston, "The Religious and Spiritual Beliefs of the Bor Dinka," *Sudan Notes and Records* 17 (1934): 124–28.

6. PI#121–122; Paper presented by Reverend Marc Nikkel at the International Sudan Studies Association, Cairo, May 1997.

7. PI#138.

8. PI#44, PI#301.

9. PI#113.

Chapter 11

1. C. G. Seligman, "Some Aspects of the Hamitic Problem in the Anglo-Egyptian Sudan," *Journal of the Royal Anthropological Institute* 43 (1913): 665–66; A. J. Arkell, *A History of the Sudan to A.D. 1821* (London: Athlone Press, 1955); Timothy Kendall, "Ethnoarchaeology in Meroitic Studies," in Sergio Donadoni and Steffen Wenig, eds., *Studia Meroitica 1984* (10) (Berlin: Akademie-Verlag 1989), 625–745; R. Oliver and J. D. Fage, *A*

Short History of Africa (Baltimore: Penguin, 1962), chap. 4; R. Oliver, ed., *The Dawn of African History* (London: Oxford University Press, 1961), chap. 8; Jan Vansina, *Kingdoms of the Savanna: A History of Central African States until European Occupation* (Madison: University of Wisconsin, 1966); see also Laszlo Torok, *The Kingdom of Kush: Handbook of the Napatan-Meroitic Civilization* (Leiden: Brill, 1997).

2. Marvin Harris, *Our Kind* (New York: Harper and Row, 1989); Edward R. Tylor, *Primitive Culture* (London: J. Murray, 1871); James Frazer, *The Golden Bough: A Study in Magic and Religion* , vol. 3 (London: Macmillan CoLimited, 1914), 9; Jay Spaulding, "Toward a Demystification of the Funj: Some Perspectives on Society in Southern Sinnar, 1685–1900," *Meroitica* 7–8 (1984): 505–21.

3. SAD 767/9/92–3; Seligman, "the Hamitic Problem," 665–66.

4. SAD 767/10/94–5.

5. George A. Reisner, *Harvard African Studies* 5–6 (1923); William Y. Adams, *Nubia Corridor to Africa* (London: Lane, 1977), 203–4.

6. C. G. Seligman and Brenda Z. Seligman, *Pagan Tribes of the Nilotic Sudan* (London: George Routledge & Sons, 1932), 195–205.

7. G. W. Titherington, "Burial Alive Among Dinka of the Bahr el-Ghazal Province," *Sudan Notes and Records* 8 (1925): 196–97.

8. Adams, *Nubia*, 203–4; Titherington, "Burial Alive," 196–97.

9. PI#300–301.

10. Triulzi, 54; E. E. Evans-Pritchard "Ethnological Observations in Dar Fung," *Sudan Notes and Records* 15, Part I (1932): 46–57.

11. Mohamed Riad, "Of Fung and Shilluk," *Wiener Volkerkundliche Mitteilungen* 3 (1955): 138–66, and "The Divine Kingship of the Shilluk and its Origin," *Archiv Fur Volkerkunde* Band XIV (1959):184.

12. Stephano Santandrea, *The Luo of the Bahr el Ghazal Sudan* (Verona: Editrice Nigrizia, 1968), 48, 82–4.

13. Tomasz Habraszewski "A Brief Account of Evliya Celebi on a Violent Death Practised in the Southern Sudan (1672)," *Folia Orientalia* 9 (1969): 139–45; J. von Russegger, *Reisen in Europa, Asien und Afrika, unternommen in den Jahren 1835–1841*, vol. 2, fasc. 2 (Stuttgart: E. Schweizerbart, 1843), 603; R. Lepsius, *Briefe aus Aegypten, Aethiopien und der Halbinsel des Sinai geschrieben in den Jahren 1842–1845* (Berlin: 1852), 212.

14. Ibrahim Bedri, "More Notes on the Padang Dinka," *Sudan Notes and Records* 29, Part 1 (1948): 40–57.

15. Also PI#284.

16. SAD 764/12/17, SAD GIIS1124; P. P. Howell, "'Pyramids' in the Upper Nile Region," *Man* 55, 56 (1948): 52–53.

17. PI#222–224.

18. Arthur E. Robinson, "Abu El Kaylik, The Kingmaker of the Fung of Sennar," *American Anthropologist* 31 (1929): 232–64; A. Triulzi, *Salt, Gold and Legitimacy* (Napoli: Istituto Universitario Orientale, 1981), 54; Seligman, "Hamitic Problem," 665–66; Riad, "Of Fung and Shilluk," 163; Spaulding, "Toward a Demystification," 513; Russegger, *Reisen in Europa,* 603; Habraszewski, "A Brief Account of Evliya Celebi," 139–44.

19. PI#44; SAD 767/10/38.

20. Emil Ludwig, *The Nile: The Life-Story of a River* (New York: Viking Press, 1937), 84.

21. SAD GIIS1124/437.

22. PI#170–176, PI#261.

23. Account acquired by Mom Kou Nhial Arou.

24. Lord Prudhoe, "Extracts from private Memoranda kept by Lord Prudhoe on a Journey from Cairo to Sennar, in 1829," *Journal of the Royal Geographical Society* 5 (1835): 38–58; Bedri, "More Notes on the Padang Dinka," 40–57; E. A. Ritter, *Shaka Zulu* (New York: Penguin Books, 1985), 333.

25. SAD 767/11/51–52; SAD 767/9/92–3; P. W. Hofmayr, *Die Schilluk* (St. Gabriel, Modling bei Wien: Administration des Anthropos, 1925), 176–80 and Adams, *Nubia.*

26. Godfrey Lienhardt, *Divinity and Experience* (Oxford: Clarendon Press, 1961), 315.

27. Sudan Interior Mission, uncatalogued document entitled "Death of a Bany,"; Titherington, "Burial Alive," 196–97; SAD 28/2/45.

28. Seligman, *Pagan Tribes,* 196–98.

29. Lienhardt, *Divinity,* 2.

Chapter 12

1. See Kathy Ann Yunger, "Nyikang The Warrior Priest: Shilluk Chol Imagery, Economics and Political Development" (Ph.D. diss., State University of New York at Stony Brook, 1985), 204; Max Weber, *Economy and Society: An Outline of Interpretive Sociology,* ed. Guenther Roth and Claus Wittich, vol. 3 (New York: Bedminster Press, 1968), 430; J. Goody *Technology, Tradition and the State* (Cambridge: Cambridge University Press, 1971), 21–38

2. PI#153; Godfrey Lienhardt, *Divinity and Experience* (Oxford: Clarendon Press, 1961), 41, 179, 204–18, 311, and "The Western Dinka," in John Middleton and David Tait, eds., *Tribes Without Rulers Studies in African Segmentary Systeos* (London: Routledge & Kegan Paul, 1958), 97–135; Per Sofholm, "The River-Lake Nilotes: Politics of an African Tribal Group" (Ph.D. diss, Uppsala University, 1973), 58, 63, 116–31; SAD 761/6/3–4; Damazo Dut Majak Koejok, "The Northern Bahr al-Ghazal: People, Alien Encroachment and Rule, 1856–1956" (Ph.D. diss., University of California, Santa Barbara, 1990), 41.

3. Lienhardt, *Divinity,* 179, 204.

4. Personal communication with Jay Spaulding; SAD 767/11/50–51.

5. Dr. Georg Schweinfurth, *The Heart of Africa,* vol. 1(London: Sampson Low, Marston, Low, and Searle, 1874), 131.

6. Anthony Wallace, *Religion: An Anthropological View* (New York: Random House, 1966), 83–100; Schweinfurth, *The Heart of Africa,* 145; Lienhardt, *Divinity,* 2, and "Western Dinka," 131.

7. Lienhardt, *Divinity,* 179, 204, 210; Kenneth Honea, "The Deng Cult and its Connections with the Goddess Aciek Among the Dinka," *Wiener Volkerkundliche Mitteilungen* 2, no. 1(1954): 16–20; E. E. Evans-Pritchard, *Nuer Religion* (Oxford: Clarendon Press, 1956), 31; John W. Burton, "Nilotic Women: A Diachronic Perspective," in *The Journal of Modern African Studies* 20, no. 3 (1982): 478.

8. Christopher Ehret, *An African Classical Age* (Charlottesville: University Press of Virginia, 1998), 248.

9. Lienhardt, *Divinity,* 41, 216–18, 311; SAD 767/11/44–5.

10. A. Southall, *Alur Society* (Cambridge, W. Heffer and Sons, Ltd , 1956), 261; Weber, *Economy and Society* , 3:430; Yunger, "Nyikang The Warrior Priest," 204; Lienhardt, *Divinity,* 41, 216–18, 311.

11. Sofholm, "The River-Lake Nilotes," 116–31, 58; SAD 767/11/44–5.

12. PI#182–183; SAD 767/11/44–5; Sofholm, "The River-Lake Nilotes," 63; Lienhardt, *Divinity,* 41; SAD GIIS1124.

13. SAD 761/6/3–4; Lienhardt, *Divinity,* 41, 210, 311; Sofholm, "The River-Lake Nilotes," 63.

14. P. P. Howell, "'Pyramids' in the Upper Nile Region," *Man* 55, 56 (1948)): 52–53; Lienhardt, *Divinity,* 245.

15. P. W. Hofmayr, "Religion der Schilluk," *Anthropos* 6 (1911): 120–31; Mohamed Riad, "The Divine Kingship of the Shilluk and its Origin," *Archiv Fur Volkerkunde* Band XIV (1959); Damazo Dut Majak Koejok, "The Northern Bahr al-Ghazal: People, Alien Encroachment and Rule, 1856–1956" (Ph.D. diss., University of California, Santa Barbara, 1990), 41; E. E. Evans-Pritchard, "The Nuer: Tribe and Clan," *Sudan Notes and Records* 16, Part 1 (1933): 40–53.

Chapter 13

1. Douglas H. Johnson, "History and Prophecy Among the Nuer of the Southern Sudan" (Ph.D.diss., University of California, Los Angeles, 1980), 84; Sandra E. Greene, *Gender, Ethnicity, and Social Change on the Upper Slave Coast: A History of the Anlo-Ewe* (Portmouth, NH: Heinemann, 1996), 1.

2. E. E. Evans-Pritchard, "The Nuer: Tribe and Clan," *Sudan Notes and Records* 16, Part 1 (1933), 1–53.

3. Francis M. Deng, "The Family and the Law of Torts in African Customary Law," *Houston Law Review* 4, no. 1 [n.y.]: 1–50.

4. Cagai Matet Guem.

5. John and Jean Comaroff, *Ethnography and the Historical Imagination* (Boulder, Co.: Westview Press, 1992), 51.

6. Jane Fishburne Collier, *Marriage and Inequality in Classless Societies* (Palo Alto, Cal.: Stanford University Press, 1988), 147.

7. PI#76–82.

8. Gary Jones, Lutheran World Federation, 1996.

9. Stephano Santandrea, *The Luo of the Bahr el Ghazal Sudan* (Verona: Editrice Nigrizia, 1968), 195; D. D. Henderson, "A Note on the Migration of the Messiria Tribe into South-West Kordofan," *Sudan Notes and Records* 22 (1939): 58; Stephanie Beswick, "The Ngok: Emergence and Destruction of a Nilotic Proto-State in Southwest Kordofan," in Michael Kevane and Endre Stiansen, eds., *Kordofan Invaded: Peripheral Incorporation and Sectoral Transformation in Islamic Africa, 1785–1995* (Leiden: Brill, 1998), 145–64; SAD GIIS1124/446.

10. PI#44, PI#293.

11. Louise E. Sweet, "Camel Raiding of North Arabian Bedouin: A Mechanism of Ecological Adaptation," *American Anthropologist* 67, no. 5 (1965): 1132–50; Alois Musil, *The Manners and Customs of the Rwala Bedouins* (New York, American Geographical Society, 1928), 504.

12. Johnson, "History and Prophecy," 84.

Chapter 14

1. M. Lionel Bender, "Sub-Classification of Nilo-Saharan," in *Proceedings of the Fourth Nilo-Saharan Conference, Bayreuth, Aug. 30–Sept. 2, 1989,* ed. M. Lionel Bender (Hamburg: Helmut Buske Verlag, 1989), 20–21.

2. Tepilit Ole Saitoti, *The Worlds of a Maasai Warrior* (Berkeley: University of California, 1988), xxv.

3. B. Blount and R. T. Curley, "The Southern Luo Languages: A Glottochronological Reconstruction," *Journal of African Languages* 9 (1970): 1–18; Stephano Santandrea, *The Luo of the Bahr el Ghazal Sudan* (Verona: Editrice Nigrizia, 1968), 155; Webster, "Noi! Noi! Famines as an Aid to Interlacustrine Chronology," in J. B. Webster, ed., *Chronology, Migration and Drought in Inter-Lacustrine Africa* (London: Longman and Dalhousie University Press, 1979), and R. S. Herring, "Hydrology and Chronology: the Rodah Nilometer as an Aid in Dating Inter-Lacustrine History," in *Chronology, Migration and Drought,* 5–11.

4. A. Kaufmann, *Schilderungen aus Centralafrica oder Land und Leute im obern Nilgebiete am Weissen Flusse* (Brixen & Lienz: A. Weger, 1862), 153.

5. Nicholas David, "The Archaeological Context of Nilotic Expansion," in Rainer Vossen, Marianne Bechhaus-Gerst, eds., *Nilotic Studies: Proceedings of the International Symposium on Languages and History of the Nilotic Peoples Cologne, January 4–5, 1982* (Berlin: Dietrich Reimer Verlag, 1983), 72, and "The B.I.E.A. Southern Sudan Expedition of 1979: Interpretation of the Archaeological Data" (unpublished paper), 64–95; Santandrea, *The Luo,* 86 and *Ethno-Geography of the Bahr el Ghazal Sudan* (Bologna: Editrice Missionaria Italiana, 1981),130–32; Damazo Dut Majak Koejok, "The Northern Bahr al-Ghazal: People, Alien Encroachment and Rule, 1856–1956" (Ph.D. diss., University of California, Santa Barbara, 1990), 23–6; SAD 465/3; J. M. Stubbs and C. G. T. Morrison, "The Western Dinkas, their Land and their Agriculture," *Sudan Notes and Records* 21 (1938): 251–68.

6. Santandrea, *The Luo,* 155.

7. Fredrik Barth, ed., *Ethnic Groups and Boundaries* (London: Allen and Unwin, 1969), introduction.

8. Santandrea, *The Luo,* 131, and *Ethno-Geography,* 148.

9. Kaufmann, *Schilderungen,* 55, 134–38, 153; SAD 639/12/1.

10. PI#220, PI#223–224, PI#261; Santandrea, *The Luo,* 131, and *Ethno-Geography,* 139–48.

11. PI#278; Santandrea, *Ethno-Geography,* 133, 138–49, and *The Luo,* 129–33, 177.

12. PI#255.

13. PI#70–71.

Chapter 15

1. PI#179–180; Stephano Santandrea, *The Luo of the Bahr el Ghazal Sudan* (Verona: Editrice Nigrizia, 1968), 129.

2. SAD 660/11/147; D. D. Henderson, "A Note on the Migration of the Messiria Tribe into South-West Kordofan," *Sudan Notes and Records* 22 (1939): 49–79; Santandrea, *The Luo,* 195; G. Nachtigal, *Sahara and Sudan,* vol. 4: *Wadai and Darfur,* trans. Allen G. S. Fisher and Humphrey J. Fisher (London: C. Hurst, 1974); Heinrich Barth, *Travels and Discoveries in North and Central Africa* ,vol. 2 (London: Longmans Green & Co. 1857; reprinted, Frank Cass & Co. Ltd. 1965), 652.

3. PI#302; SAD 660/11/154; Henderson, "A Note on the Migration of the Messiria," 61–62.

4. PI#179–180, PI#294; SAD 465/3; SAD 660/11/146–156; Francis Mading Deng, *The Man Called Deng Majok* (New Haven: Yale University Press, 1986); Santandrea, *The Luo,* 190. Henderson, "A Note on the Migration of the Messiria," 58.

5. SAD 465/3.

6. SAD 465/3; SAD 660/11/147; Henderson, "A Note on the Migration of the Messiria," 49–79; Santandrea, *The Luo,* 195.

7. SAD 660/11/151.

8. SAD 465/3; Stephano Santandrea, *Ethno-Geography of the Bahr el Ghazal Sudan* (Bologna: Editrice Missionaria Italiana, 1981),149, 152, 155; Mohammed el-Tounsy, (al-Tunisi, Muhammad b. Umar), *Voyage au Ouaday* (Paris: B. Duprat, 1851), 467–95.

9. R. S. O'Fahey, "Slavery and the Slave Trade in Dar Fur," *Journal of African History* 14, no. 1 (1973): 29–43.

10. Barth, *Travels and Discoveries in North and Central Africa* , vol. 3, 657; John Lewis Burckhardt, *Travels in Nubia,* 2nd ed. (London: John Murray, 1822), 441.

11. El-Tounsy, *Voyage au Ouaday,* 481; R. S. O'Fahey and J. L. Spaulding, *Kingdoms of the Sudan* (London: Methuen, 1974), 37–9; R. S. O'Fahey, "Fur and Fartit: The History of a Frontier," in John Mack and Peter Robertshaw, eds., *Culture History in the Southern Sudan Archaeology, Linguistics and Ethnohistory* (Nairobi: British Institute in Eastern Africa, 1982), 75–88, and "Slavery and the Slave Trade in Dar Fur," 41; Watkiss Lloyd, "Some Notes on Dar Homr," *The Geographical Journal* 29 (January to June 1907): 653; Nachtigal, *Sahara and Sudan,* 4: 98, 165; G. K. C. Hebbert, "The Bandala of the Bahr el-Ghazal," *Sudan Notes and Records* 22 (1939): 187–94; W. G. Browne, *Travels in Africa, Egypt, and Syria From the Year 1792 to 1798* (London, 1799), 226, 298.

12. El-Tounsy, *Voyage au Ouaday,* 481.

13. El-Tounsy, *Voyage au Ouaday,* 467–95; O'Fahey and Spaulding, *Kingdoms of the Sudan,* 122; Nachtigal, *Sahara and Sudan,* 4: 353–54; Browne, *Travels in Africa* , 267, 272; SAD 660/11/152.

14. Browne, *Travels in Africa* , 347–49.

15. O'Fahey, "Slavery," 36–38; El-Tounsy, *Voyage au Ouaday,* 173; Na'um Shuqayr, *Jughrafiya wa-ta'rikh al-Sudan* (Cairo: Dar al-Kutub, 1902), 455.

16. Quoted in Thomas Fowell Buxton, *The African Slave Trade and its Remedy* (London: J. Murray, 1840), 65; W. B. Shaw, "Darb el Arba'in," *Sudan Notes and Records* 12 (1929): 63, 71; Browne, *Travels in Africa,* 226, 267–98, 347–49.

17. PI#170–176; Godfrey Lienhardt, *Divinity and Experience* (Oxford: Clarendon Press, 1961); N. Yunis, "Notes on the Baggara and Nuba of Western Kordofan," *Sudan Notes and Records* 6 (1922): 203; and Ian Cunnison, *Baggara Arabs* (Oxford: Clarendon Press, 1966), 7.

18. Ferdinand Werne, *Expedition to Discover the Sources of the White Nile in the Years 1840–1841* (London: R. Bentley, 1849) vol. 1: 257, 268–69, 295, vol. 2: 162–72; Peter R.

Schmidt, *Historical Archaeology A Structural Approach in an African Culture* (Westport, Ct: Greenwood Press, 1978), 40; A. Kaufmann, *Schilderungen aus Centralafrica oder Land und Leute im obern Nilgebiete am Weissen Flusse* (Brixen & Lienz: A. Weger, 1862), 55, 134–38; SAD 639/12/1.

19. PI#255; S. Beswick, "Violence, Ethnicity, and Political Consolidation in South Sudan: A History of the Dinka and their Relations with their Neighbors, 1200–1994" (Ph.D. diss., Michigan State University, 1998), appendix; PI#202; Nicholas David, "The Archaeological Context of Nilotic Expansion," in Rainer Vossen, Marianne Bechhaus-Gerst, eds., *Nilotic Studies: Proceedings of the International Symposium on Languages and History of the Nilotic Peoples Cologne, January 4–5, 1982* (Berlin: Dietrich Reimer Verlag, 1983), 72, and "The B.I.E.A. Southern Sudan Expedition of 1979: Interpretation of the Archaeological Data" (unpublished paper), 64–95; Santandrea, *The Luo,* 86 and *Ethno-Geography,* 130–32; Damazo Dut Majak Koejok, "The Northern Bahr al-Ghazal: People, Alien Encroachment and Rule, 1856–1956" (Ph.D. diss., University of California, Santa Barbara, 1990), 23–26; SAD 465/3; J. M. Stubbs and C. G. T. Morrison, "The Western Dinkas, their Land and their Agriculture," *Sudan Notes and Records* 21 (1938): 251–68.

20. R. C. Stevenson, "Old Khartoum, 1821–1885," *Sudan Notes and Records* 47 (1966): 15; Werne, *Expedition,* vol. 1: 268, 335–38; vol. 2: 172, 311.

Chapter 16

1. See, E. E. Evans-Pritchard, "The Nuer: Tribe and Clan," *Sudan Notes and Records* 16, pt 1 (1933): 53.

2. Peter J. Newcomer, "The Nuer are Dinka: An Essay on Origins and Environmental Determinism," *Man* 7, no. 1 (1972): 5–11; Raymond C. Kelly, *The Nuer Conquest: The Structure and Development of an Expansionist System* (Ann Arbor: University of Michigan Press, 1985), 166; Maurice Glickman, "The Nuer and the Dinka: A Further Note," *Man* 7, no. 4 (1972): 586–94; M. Lionel Bender, "Sub-Classification of Nilo-Saharan," in *Proceedings of the Fourth Nilo-Saharan Conference, Bayreuth, Aug. 30–Sept. 2, 1989,* ed. M. Lionel Bender (Hamburg: Helmut Buske Verlag, 1989), 7; Karen Sacks, "Causality and Chance on the Upper Nile," *American Ethnologist* 6, no. 3 (August 1979): 437–48 (Sacks connects the Nuer expansion east with the nineteenth- rather than the eighteenth-century slave raids); John McLaughlin, "Tentative Time Depths for Nuer, Dinka, and Anuak," *Journal of Ethiopian Studies* 5 (1967): 13–27; Evans-Pritchard, *The Nuer;* Douglas H. Johnson, "History and Prophecy Among the Nuer of the Southern Sudan" (Ph.D.diss., University of California, Los Angeles, 1980), 85–98, 568; J. P. Crazzolara, "The Lwoo People," *Uganda Journal* 5 (1937) and "Lwoo Migrations," *Uganda Journal* 25 (1961): 136–48; Mohamed Riad, "The Divine Kingship of the Shilluk and its Origin," *Archiv Fur Volkerkunde* Band XIV (1959), 256–66.

3. PI#144–147, PI#150–51; G. Beltrame, *Fiume Bianco Nell'Africa Centrale* (Verona, 1864), 843.

4. Crazzolara, "The Lwoo People," 1–21; *The Lwoo Migrations* (Verona: Missioni Africane, 1950), and "Lwoo Migrations," 136–48.

5. PI#221, PI#230; Burton, *God's Ants* and *A Nilotic World: The Atuot Speaking Peoples of the Southern Sudan* (New York: Greenwood Press, 1987), 5 and "Some Observa-

tions on the Social History of the Atuot Dialect of Nilotic," in Thilo C. Schadeberg and M. Lionel Bender, eds., *Nilo-Saharan: Proceedings of the First Nilo-Saharan Linguistics Colloquium, Leiden, September 8–10, 1980* (Dordrecht, Holland: Foris Publications, 1981), 134.

6. PI#137–141.

7. See also, Johnson, "History," 84.

8. PI#302.

9. C. A. Willis, "The Cult of Deng," *Sudan Notes and Records* 11 (1928): 195–207; Johnson, "History," 29, 95–6.

10. SAD G11S1124; Kelly, *The Nuer Conquest*, 1; Evans-Pritchard, *The Nuer*; Riad, "Divine Kingship," 223–24, 238, 241.

11. Riad, "Divine Kingship," 223–24, 238, 241.

12. SAD 212/15/4.

13. Willis, "The Cult of Deng," 199.

14. PI#255; Marshall Sahlins, "The Segmentary Lineage: An Organization of Predatory Expansion," *American Anthropologist* 63 (1961): 322–45; Evans-Pritchard, *The Nuer*, 81–93.

15. PI#255; Newcomer, "The Nuer are Dinka," 5–11; Godfrey Lienhardt, *Divinity and Experience* (Oxford: Clarendon Press, 1961), 41, 216–18, 311, and "The Western Dinka," in John Middleton and David Tait, eds., *Tribes Without Rulers: Studies in African Segmentary Systems* (London: Routledge & Kegan Paul, 1958), 97–135.114; Evans-Pritchard, *The Nuer*; Captain V. H. Fergusson, "The Nuong Nuer," *Sudan Notes and Records* 4 (1921): 154.

16. Conradin Perner, *The Anyuak Living On Earth In The Sky* (Basel, Switzerland: Helbing and Lichtenhahn, 1997), 138–60; E. E. Evans-Pritchard, *The Political System Of The Anuak Of The Anglo-Egyptian Sudan* (London: London School of Economics, 1940).

17. Perner, *The Anyuak*, 138–60

18. C. R. K. Bacon, "The Anuak," *Sudan Notes and Records* 5, no. 3 (1922): 115.

Chapter 17

1. John Middleton and David Tait, eds., "Introduction," in *Tribes without Rulers* (London: Routledge and Kegan Paul, 1958), 25; Godfrey Lienhardt, "The Western Dinka," in Middleton and Tait, *Tribes Without Rulers*, 114–15.

2. G. W. Titherington, "Burial Alive Among Dinka of the Bahr el-Ghazal Province," *Sudan Notes and Records* 8 (1925): 167; Lienhardt, "Western Dinka," 109, 112–17, 134.

3. Middleton and Tait, "Introduction," 9

4. PI#302; Stephano Santandrea, *Ethno-Geography of the Bahr el Ghazal Sudan* (Bologna: Editrice Missionaria Italiana, 1981), 126, and *The Luo of the Bahr el Ghazal Sudan* (Verona: Editrice Nigrizia, 1968), 129, 191–93; Francis Mading Deng, *The Man Called Deng Majok* (New Haven: Yale University Press, 1986), 43–45; D. D. Henderson, "A Note on the Migration of the Messiria Tribe into South-West Kordofan," *Sudan Notes and Records* 22 (1939): 58; SAD GIIS1124/450.

5. PI#302.

6. Marvin Harris, *Our Kind* (New York: Harper and Row, 1989); Edward R. Tylor, *Primitive Culture* (London: J. Murray, 1871), 383–88.

7. David Cole and Richard Huntington, "African Rural Development: Some Lessons from Abyei," unpublished manuscript, Cambridge, Mass., Harvard Institute for Inter-

national Development, October 1985, ch. 7: 9, 47, ch. 10: 14–5; Francis Deng, "Property and Value-Interplay Among the Nilotes," *Iowa Law Review* 51, no. 3 (1966): 546; J. M. Stubbs, and C. G. T. Morrison. "The Western Dinkas: Their Land and their Agriculture," *Sudan Notes and Records* 21 (1938): 251; A. B. L. Stemler, et al., "Caudatum Sorghums and Speakers of Chari-Nile Languages in Africa," *Journal of African History* 41 (1975): 165–66, 177.

8. Cole and Huntington, "African Rural Development," ch 7: 1, 2–3, 10, ch 10: 14–5; Stemler, et al., "Caudatum Sorghums," 171; Aidan Southall, "Nuer and Dinka are People: Ecology, Ethnicity and Logical Possibility," *Man* 11, no. 4 (Dec. 1976): 469–70.

9. PI#302; Henderson, "A Note on the Migration of the Messiria," 58; SAD GIIS1124/450; Robin Horton, "Stateless Societies in the History of West Africa," in J. F. A. Ajayi and Michael Crowder, eds., *History of West Africa* (New York: Columbia University Press, 1972), 78–119.

10. PI#302.

11. PI#302; Stephanie Beswick, "The Ngok: Emergence and Destruction of a Nilotic Proto-State in Southwest Kordofan," in Michael Kevane and Endre Stiansen, eds., *Kordofan Invaded: Peripheral Incorporation and Sectoral Transformation in Islamic Africa, 1785–1995* (Leiden: Brill, 1998), 145–64.

12. F. O. Gearing, "Priest and Warriors," *American Anthropological Association Memoir* No. 93 (1962); Keith Otterbein, *The Evolution of Warfare* (New Haven, Ct.: HRAF Press, 1970), 23–28; Elman R. Service, *Origins of the State and Civilization* (New York: Norton, 1975), 259, 271, 299; Herbert Spencer, *Principles of Sociology* (New York: Appleton-Century-Croft, 1897).

13. Daniel Deng Farim Sorur, "A Dinka Priest Writing on his Own People," in Elias Toniolo and Richard Hill, eds., *The Opening of the Nile Basin* (London: C. Hurst & Company, 1974), 199; Francis Mading Deng, *The Dinka and Their Songs* (Oxford: Clarendon Press, 1973), 68; "Property and Value-Interplay Among the Nilotes," *Iowa Law Review* 51 (1966): 544; *The Man Called Deng Majok*; and *Africans of Two Worlds: The Dinka in Afro-Arab Sudan* (New Haven: Yale University Press, 1978), 130–38; P. P. Howell, "Notes on the Ngork Dinka of Western Kordofan," *Sudan Notes and Records* 32 (1951): 258.

14. Francis M. Deng, *Recollections of Babo Nimir* (London: Ithaca Press) 1982, 59.

15. Beswick, "The Ngok," 145–64; Cole and Huntington, "African Rural Development," ch 7: 1–10.

16. PI#302; David Decker research notes from Southern Kordofan, May 1987; Cole and Huntington, "African Rural Development," ch 7: 7.

17. Kathleen Gough, "Nuer Kinship: A Re-examination," in T. O. Beidelman, ed., *The Translation of Culture: Essays to E. E. Evans-Pritchard* (London: Tavistock Publications, 1971), 79–121.

18. PI#153; SAD 761/6/3–4; Per Sofholm, "The River-Lake Nilotes: Politics of an African Tribal Group" (Ph.D. diss, Uppsala University, 1973), 58, 63, 116–31; Godfrey Lienhardt, *Divinity and Experience* (Oxford: Clarendon Press, 1961), 41, 216–18, 311, and "Western Dinka," 97–135; Majak, "The Northern Bahr al-Ghazal: People, Alien Encroachment and Rule, 1856–1956" (Ph.D. diss., University of California, Santa Barbara, 1990), 41.

19. Lienhardt, *Divinity,* 41, 216–18, 311; Majak "The Northern Bahr al-Ghazal," 42.

Chapter 18

1. See also, Stephanie Beswick, *Slavery and its Trade in Southern Sudan from the Sixteenth Century to the Present* (forthcoming).

2. Ibid.

3. Paul E. Lovejoy, *Transformations in Slavery: A History of Slavery in Africa* (New York: Cambridge University Press, 1983), 19.

4. For a British view of colonial history in Southern Sudan, see Robert O. Collins, *Land Beyond the Rivers The Southern Sudan, 1898–1918* (New Haven: Yale University Press, 1971), and *Shadows in the Grass* (New Haven: Yale University Press, 1983).

5. *Africa Confidential* 14, no. 5 (March 2, 1973): 2.

Chapter 19

1. Personal interviews: anonymous Bari and Bor-Atoc informants; Catholic Sister Nikki, Catholic Sister Mary Ellen, and Catholic Sister Carolyn Buhs, Kakuma, Kenya.

2. Baroness Cox, *Slavery in Sudan* (Christian Solidarity International U.S. Congress House Committee on International Relations, Wednesday March 13, 1996), 1; *All Africa Press Service APS Bulletin* 15/96 (April 15, 1996): 8.

3. Anonymous Malwal female informants; G. Obat, "The Jebellein Massacre," *Information Africa Faith and Justice Network* (Washington, D.C., Jan. 1990), 2; Abel Alier, *Southern Sudan: Too Many Agreements Dishonored* (Exeter: Ithaca Press, 1990), 255–57.

4. Cox, *Slavery in Sudan* 1; *All Africa Press Service APS Bulletin* 15/96 (April 15, 1996): 8.

5. John Prendergast, *Sudanese Rebels at a Crossroads* (Washington, D.C.: Center of Concern, 1994), 10.

6. See Beswick, *Slavery in Southern Sudan.*

7. Benedict Anderson, *Imagined Communities* (London: Verso, 1995), 3, 135.

8. "This Convention is Sovereign," Opening and Closing speeches by Dr. John Garang de Mabior to the first SPLM/A National Convention, April 2, 1994 (SPLM Secretariat of Information and Culture (n.d.), 1; *SPLM/SPLA Update* 3/94, no. 14 (April 18, 1994): 1.

9. *Sudanow* (December 1977): 15; *Africa Confidential* (March 2, 1973): 2.

10. Personal interviews: Anonymous informants; *Africa Confidential* 20, no. 6 (March 14 1979): 5; Douglas H. Johnson, "The Southern Sudan," *The Minority Rights Group Report* No. 78 (1982): 5–6; Othwonh Dak, "Southern Region: Decentralisation orRecentralisation?" Paper presented at the "Conference on the North-South Relations Since the Addis Ababa Agreement," Khartoum, March 6–9, 1985, 3.

11. Anonymous personal interviews; Alier, *Southern Sudan,* 247, 255; *Sudan Times* (January 10, 1988); Human Rights Watch/Africa, *Civilian Devastation Abuses by All Parties in the War in Southern Sudan,* 25.

12. Personal interviews: Anonymous Azande informants.

13. Gayle Rubin, "The Traffic in Women: Notes on the "Political Economy of Sex," in Rayna R. Reiter, ed., *Towards an Anthropology of Women* (New York: Review Press, 1975), 174.

14. Also personal interviews: Andrew Mayen (Bor Dinka), Helen Amako (Agar Dinka), Musa Adam (Agar Dinka), Martin Koshwal (Atwot), Mom Kou (Bor Dinka), Isaiah

Deng (Ciec Dinka), and Lueth Ukec (Luo); John W. Burton, "Nilotic Women: A Diachronic Perspective," in *The Journal of Modern African Studies* 20, no. 3, (1982): 488; Sharon Hutchinson, "The Cattle of Money and the Cattle of Girls Among the Nuer, 1930–83," *American Ethnologist* 19, no. 2 (May 1992): 294.

15. Stephanie Beswick, "'We Are Bought Like Clothes:' The War Over Polygyny and Levirate Marriage in South Sudan," forthcoming in special volume on "Women in Sudan," *Northeast African Studies*.

16. Godfrey Lienhardt, "The Western Dinka," in Middleton and Tait, *Tribes Without Rulers*, 112–17, 131; G. W. Titherington, "The Raik Dinka of Bahr el Ghazal Province," *Sudan Notes and Records* 10 (1927): 159–210.

17. G. Schweinfurth, *The Heart of Africa*, vol. 1 (London: Sampson Low, Marston, Low, and Searle, 1874), 167.

18. Stephanie Beswick, "The Ngok: Emergence and Destruction of a Nilotic Protostate in Southwest Kordofan," in Endre Stiansen and Michael Kevane, eds., *Kordofan Invaded* (Leiden: Brill, 1998); Francis M. Deng, *The Man Called Deng Majok* (New Haven: Yale University Press, 1986), 23–45; SAD 768/2/28–9; John and Jean Comaroff, *Ethnography and the Historical Imagination* (Boulder, Co.: Westview Press, 1992), 63; Immanuel Wallerstein, *The Capitalist World Economy* (Cambridge: Cambridge University Press, 1979), 184.

19. Human Rights Watch/Africa, *Civilian Devastation Abuses by All Parties in the War in Southern Sudan* (New York, 1994), 25; Personal interviews: Anonymous informants.

20. Francis M. Deng, *War of Visions* (Washington D.C., The Brookings Institute, 1995), 230–34. The British wife of Riek Machar, Emma McCune was also accused of being a British spy and having influenced her husband in the "creeping coup" against the SPLA. Personal interviews: Anonymous Dinka informants and *Sudan Update* 3, no. 9 (December 16, 1991): 6; Deborah Scroggins, "Emma," *Granta* 60 (Winter 1997): 103, 109, 119.

21. Personal interviews: Anonymous Dinka informants; Deborah Scroggins, "Emma," 99–145; Deng, *War of Visions,* 233–34.

22. Stephanie Beswick, "The Dinka as 'Northern Sudanese,' the Nuer as 'Luo' and the Genesis of Intra-Southern Sudanese Conflict," in Mohamed Mahmoud, ed., *Sudan: Dilemmas and Prospects, Northeast African Studies,* forthcoming 2004.

23. Also personal interviews: Simon Adel Yak (Agar-Rub) and Joseph Mathiang Dhalbeng (Agar Dinka); Captain V. H. Fergusson, "The Nuong Nuer," *Sudan Notes and Records* 4 (1921): 146–54. Fergusson describes this battle, although his suggestion of the date 1886 appears rather late.

24. Alier, *Southern Sudan,* 253.

25. *Sudan Update* 3, no. 9 (December 16, 1991): 1. *Sudan Democratic Gazette* (December 1991): 6; Scroggins, "Emma," 129. PI#15.

26. Personal interviews: Anonymous Shilluk informants; John Prendergast, *Crisis Response: Humanitarian Band Aids in Sudan and Somalia* (London: Pluto Press, and Washington, D.C.: Center of Concern, 1997), 26–8, 51; *Sudan Democratic Gazette* (January 1992): 2; Peter Adwok, "Rights of Vulnerable Groups in Conditions of Conflict: the Link Between Traditional Values and International Humanitarian Principles in South Sudan in Respect to Rights of Children," unpublished paper acquired from UNICEF, Nairobi 1996, 7–9.

27. Anonymous personal interviews: Ayuel Parmena Bul (E. Twic Dinka), Kakuma, Kenya, and Catholic Father Mattia, Nairobi, Kenya; Human Rights Watch/Africa, *Civilian Devastation,* 11; Scroggins, "Emma," 99.

28. Stephanie Beswick, "Violence, Ethnicity and Political Consolidation in South Sudan" (Ph.D. diss., Michigan State University, 1998).

29. Correspondence, Rev. J. Roger Schrock, former Executive Secretary of the New Sudan Council of Churches, Nairobi, Kenya, Nov. 1995. In early 1980 he was based among the Bul Nuer of South Sudan.

30. R. Brian Ferguson, "Explaining War," in Jonathan Haas, ed., *The Anthropology of War* (Cambridge: Cambridge University Press, 1990), 26–55.

31. Personal interviews: Monica Nyibol Aleu, Simon Ngor Ngor, Lawrence Lual Lual Akuey, and Bol Akok Akok; Prendergast, *Crisis Response,* 82; S. F. Beswick, "A Religious and Ethnic Kaleidoscope or a North/South Frontier? Dinka/Baggara Relations Across the Kir/Bahr el-Arab River," in Mel Page et al., eds., *Personality and Political Culture in Africa* (Boston: African Studies Center, Boston University, 1998).

32. Leroy Vail, ed. "Introduction: Ethnicity in Southern AfricanHistory," in *The Creation of Tribalism in Southern Africa* (Berkeley: University of California Press, 1991), 1–19.

GLOSSARY

Alwa	Large Nubian kingdom in the central Sudan, with its capital at Soba near the Nile Confluence
Anyuak	A Nilotic language; the people who speak it
Anya Nya	Southern-based opposition movement born of the First Civil War (1955–1972)
Baggara	(Or *Baqqara*) Arabic-speaking cattle pastoralists; penetrated the Sudan from the west during the eighteenth century
Bahr el-Ghazal	A major western tributary of the White Nile; name of a province during the colonial periods and following
Bahr al-Arab	See "Kir;" A western tributary of the White Nile, significant in Dinka history; sometimes interpreted as a boundary between northern and southern peoples of the Sudan
beny	Dinka priest
Burun	Epithet applied to the small non-Muslim communities of the southern Gezira and adjoining Ethiopian borderlands. Some "Burun" are Nilotic-speakers, and because these small Nilotic tongues differ rather widely among themselves and between themselves and their historically more successful fellow-Nilotes, comparative linguists designate this area as the probable location of Nilotic dispersion, based on the principle of greatest linguistic diversity
caudatum	Several varieties of *dhurra* suitable for brewing, and unusually well adapted to the exegencies of a cattle-oriented way of life in which labor-intensive cultivation is not always possible
Chukudum	Site of 1994 constitutional convention in South Sudan; proclaimed "New Sudan"

clan	An exogamous lineal descent group, normally with political significance
Condominium	The second colonial period, from 1898 to 1956, in which Great Britain and Egypt were said to rule the "Anglo-Egyptian" Sudan jointly; Sudanese called the arrangement "the Second Turkiyya"
Damadim	(Plural forms, *Damdama* or *Damadim*), the fearsome "Tatars of the Sudan" during the thirteenth century, who invaded the southern Christian Nubian kingdom of Alwa from the south. Probably emergent Nilotes, and quite possibly the Dinka
Dar Fur	Western kingdom [and empire], c.1500–1916; based on the Fur-speaking community of Jebel Marra, during the later eighteenth century it acquired a fixed capital at the site presently called "the capital," al-Fashir.
dhurra	sorghum; a vital staple of the Southern Sudanese [and particularly the Nilotic diet], often consumed as porridge or beer
Dinka	A Nilotic language; the *jiang*, the community who speak it
Fellata	Muslim immigrants to the Sudan who spoke Hausa, Kanuri, or a geographically adacent language
Funj	The hereditary ruling elite of Sinnar
hump-backed cattle	Imported breeds of cattle which adapted to hardship, migrations, and resistant to disease; Sanga, Zebu
jebel	(Arabic *jabal)* "Mountain;" in the Sudan, a rather flat place, virtually any elevation will be perceived as a *jebel.*
jellaba	Private traders (as opposed to official state merchants of precolonial kingdoms) who travelled to seek profit, conspicuously in the slave trade. Usually Muslims, northern Sudanese, and often of formerly West African heritage such as the Tokruris (Fellata); during the nineteenth century became armed functionaries of the *zariba* system
jiang	Term of self-identification preferred by the Dinka; not commonly used by modern outsiders

jur	Dinka: "aliens," non-Dinka
kec	An exceptionally palatable variety of *dhurra*, whose cultivation is limited to certain favored soil conditions
kic	Dinka commoners; not from a clan capable of producing priests
Kir	Dinka for "river," especially the Bahr al-Arab
koic	Of "original" Dinka heritage with chiefly leadership potential, including priests
Kush	Northern Nile-Valley state, before c. 700 BCE
lineage	A sub-group of a clan
Luo	A Nilotic language; the people who speak it
Maban	A Nilotic language; the people who speak it
Mahdiyya	From about 1885 to 1898 the Sudan expelled the colonizers under the leadership of a man whose followers recognized him as the "Mahdi," or "Rightly-Guided One" of Islamic eschatology
Makuria	Northern Nubian kingdom with its capital at (Old) Dongola; for most of its history, also included Nobatia, in modern Egyptian Nubia
Meroe	Northern Nile-Valley state, c.300 BCE-c.300 CE
Meroitic	The language of Kush, Napata and Meroe; probably Nilo-Saharan and possibly Eastern Sudanic; undeciphered, but not Nubian
Murahaliin	Paramilitary armies [usually Baggara] licensed by recent Northern regimes; see also "People's Defense Forces"
naath	Term of self-identification preferred by the Nuer; not commonly used by modern outsiders
Napata	Northern Nile-Valley state, c.600–c.300 BCE.
Nilotes	Speakers of any of several related languages belonging to the Eastern Sudanic branch of Nilo-Saharan
Nubia	Northern Nile-Valley, c.300–c.1300 CE: see Alwa, Makuria, Nobatia, Sinnar
Nubian	One of several related Eastern Sudanic languages; includes Classical Nubian, the written language of the medieval Christian Nubian kingdoms, its modern descendant Nubiin, and Kenzi-Dongolawi, the most widely-spoken Nubian language today. Not Meroitic.

Nubiin	The modern Nubian language of Mahas; living descendant of Classical Nubian
Nuer	A Nilotic language; the people who speak it
pancieng	Dinka: "latecomers," assimilated Dinka
People's Defense Forces	Paramilitary armies licensed by recent Northern regimes; see also *murahaliin*
reth	Shilluk: "king"
Sanga	See "humped cattle"
Shari'a	Islamic law; under the *shari'a,* no non-Muslim may exercise political authority over any Muslim; this has made the introduction of democracy difficult in a land where some people are Muslims and others are not
Shilluk	A Nilotic language; the people who speak it
Sobat	An eastern tributary of the White Nile; figures prominently in Dinka legend and regional *Realpolitik*
Sinnar	Islamic Nubian kingdom, c.1500–1821 CE; its eponymous capital, after about 1650 a city. See also "Funj"
SPLM/A	Sudan People's Liberation Movement/Army; southern-based opposition movement born of the Second Civil War (1983–present)
toic	Dinka: "grasslands"
Tokruri	A Muslim who entered the Nile-Valley Sudan from the west; often referred to as Fellata, usually of humble estate, and included natives of Dar Fur and Wadai and as well as people from the Kanuri and Hausa-speaking world. Typical motives for travel included the Pilgrimage to Makka and private trade, but many settled permanently in the Sudan
totem	A symbol of clan identity; among the Dinka, a common totem prohibits marriage and encourages peaceful interactions
Turk	In the Sudan, anyone associated with either of the colonial governments, particularly but not exclusively if pale-skinned, was classified as a Turk, irrespective of native language and ethnic or religious preferences

Turkiyya   The first colonial period, from 1820 to about 1885, when the Ottoman elite who ruled Egypt annexed and exploited the Sudan also. In the beginning they spoke Turkish; by midcentury the language of colonial administration was Arabic, and by the 1870s, English. See also Condominium

Wadai   Western kingdom, c.1500–1909; based on Boro Mabang-speaking community of eastern Chad. Two comparatively fixed capitals of the nineteenth century were Wara, and then Abesher

Zebu   See "humped cattle"

BIBLIOGRAPHY

Personal Interviews

The interview number is followed by the name, the ethnic identity, and the place of the interview. (* = interviewed as part of a group.)

United States and Britain 1990–1994

SOUTHERN SUDANESE

PI#05   Revend Elioba, Pajulu, New York City, NY
PI#06   Dominc Akeg Mohammed, W. Twic Dinka, Miami, Fla.
PI#07   John Lueth Ukec, Luo, Ames, Iowa
PI#08   Andrew Mayen, Bor Dinka, Alexandria, Va.
PI#09   Helen Amako, Agar Dinka, Alexandria, Va.
PI#10   Abdul Monheim Younis [Fertit Muslim], Boston, Mass.
PI#11   Damazo Dut Majak, Malwal/Luo, Los Angeles, Calif.
PI#14   Archangelo Ayuel Mayen, W. Twic Dinka, Glendale, Md.
PI#15   Margaret Deng, Bor Dinka, Fairfax, Va.

Canada 1991–1996

SOUTHERN SUDANESE

PI#44   Mom Kou Nhial Arou, Bor-Atoc Dinka, Hamilton, Ont.
PI#45   Musa Adam, Agar Dinka, Hamilton, Ont.
PI#46   Isaiah Deng, Ciec Dinka, Hamilton, Ont.
PI#47   Martin Koshwal, Atwot, Hamilton, Ont.
PI#51   Ambros Beny, Atwot, Toronto, Ont.

Kakuma Refugee Camp, Kenya, 1996

PI#52   Peter Malwal*   Nuer
PI#53   James Gatluak*   Nuer (E. Jikainy)
PI#54   Thok Top Liem*   Nuer (E. Jikainy)
PI#55   Peter Nyang Khat*   Nuer (E. Jikainy)

PI#56	John Gatwec Turial*	Nuer
PI#57	Peter Gai Lual*	Nuer
PI#58	Steven Ter*	Nuer
PI#59	Abraham Riek Bum	Nuer (Gawar)
PI#60	Philip Thon Marol	Thoi Dinka
PI#61	Ayuel Parmena Bul	E. Twic Dinka
PI#62	Simon Ayuel Deng	E. Ngok Dinka
PI#63	Sarah Nyanek Daac	E. Ngok Dinka
PI#64	John Deng Pur	E. Ngok Dinka
PI#65	Musa Ajak Liol	Abialang Dinka
PI#66	Malwal Can Gaac	E. Luaic Dinka
PI#67	John Biem Ngok Bilkuai Ruweng	(Kwil) Dinka
PI#68	Daniel Dok Manyang	E. Ruweng Dinka
PI#69	Chol Macar Dau	E. Ruweng (Paweng) Dinka
PI#70	Barnaba Wuor	Ghol Dinka
PI#71	Samuel Majak Piok	Ghol Dinka
PI#72	Solomon Leek Deng*	Nyarruweng Dinka
PI#73	Abdengokuer Adut*	Nyarruweng Dinka
PI#74	Malwal Riak	Ghol Dinka
PI#75	Gabriel Col Can	Nyarruweng Dinka
PI#76	Alier Arok Akuein*	E. Twic Dinka
PI#77	Mayen Jok Majok	E. Twic Dinka
PI#78	Kuc Manyang Kuany	E. Twic Dinka
PI#79	Deng Dut*	E. Twic Dinka
PI#80	Dau Tor*	E. Twic Dinka
PI#81	Kuir Jok*	E. Twic Dinka
PI#82	Atem Ayiik*	E. Twic Dinka
PI#83	Marko Mabior Majok	W. Twic Dinka
PI#84	John Majok Makoi	Agar Dinka
PI#85	Philip Aguer Panyang	E. Twic Dinka
PI#86	Atem Garang Deng	E. Twic Dinka
PI#87	Deng Kuek Atem	E. Twic Dinka
PI#88	Tor Deng Lual*	E. Twic Dinka
PI#89	John Majok Deng*	E. Twic Dinka
PI#90	Thieu Atem Aleu	E. Twic Dinka
PI#91	Ajok Akei	E. Twic Dinka
PI#92	Kuir Deng Biar (female)	E. Twic Dinka
PI#93	Deng Malwal Mabur Mahboub	Ghol Dinka
PI#94	Samuel Bulen Alier	Bor Dinka
PI#95	Diing Akol Diing	E. Twic Dinka
PI#96	Dau Atem Yong	E. Twic Dinka
PI#97	Bul Awuol Ayuel	E. Twic Dinka
PI#98	Kuer Dut	E. Twic Dinka
PI#99	Kur Bol Aleu	E. Twic Dinka
PI#100	Ajith Bul	E. Twic Dinka
PI#101	Abuor Gordon Nhial	Bor Dinka
PI#102	Maria Abuk Bol	Malwal Dinka
PI#103	Suadony Awok	Malwal Dinka

PI#104	Rebecca Abuk Deng	Malwal Dinka
PI#105	Abed Nego Aciek	Bor-Gok Dinka
PI#106	Michael Majok Bor	Bor-Gok Dinka
PI#107	Wuut Mac*	Bor-Gok Dinka
PI#108	Wec Col*	Bor-Gok Dinka
PI#109	Deng Acuoth	Bor-Gok Dinka
PI#111	Abdulla Ayom Kuany*	Bor-Athoc Dinka
PI#112	Magot Majok Anyieth*	Bor-Athoc Dinka
PI#113	Col Mayen Kur*	Bor-Athoc Dinka
PI#114	Gideon Gai Deng*	Bor-Athoc Dinka
PI#115	Makere Yuang Malual*	Bor-Athoc Dinka
PI#116	Kuol Ayuen Biar*	Bor-Athoc Dinka
PI#117	Thon Deng Kuany*	Bor-Athoc Dinka
PI#119	Michael Alier Agou*	Bor-Gok Dinka
PI#120	Johnson Kuol Kur*	Bor-Gok Dinka
PI#121	Makuac Jok Deng*	Bor-Gok Dinka
PI#122	Makere Chol Adol*	Bor-Gok Dinka
PI#123	Akec Mayom Mac (female)*	Bor-Gok Dinka
PI#124	Deng Yai Deng*	Bor-Gok Dinka
PI#125	Pac Deel Deng*	Bor-Gok Dinka
PI#126	Martha Athou	Bor-Atoc Dinka
PI#127	Roda Yar Alier	Bor-Gok Dinka
PI#128	Deborah Yar Anyok	Bor-Gok Dinka
PI#129	Rebecca Amur Mac	Bor-Gok Dinka
PI#130	Martha Nyedier Akok	Malwal Dinka
PI#131	Susana Sum	E. Twic Dinka
PI#132	Teresa Gayo Jatluak	E. Twic Dinka
PI#133	Aluel Ayiel Chet	Gnol Dinka
PI#134	Diing Majak	Agar Dinka
PI#135	Nyanjur Ajong	W. Ngok Dinka
PI#136	Akec Nyatyiel Nar	Atwot Apak
PI#137	Emanuel Kot Kuany	Ciec Dinka
PI#138	Zande Cuor Yol	Ciec Dinka
PI#139	John Luk Majok	Ciec Dinka
PI#140	Martin Makur Beny	Ciec Dinka
PI#141	Zakaria Col Kot	Ciec Dinka
PI#142	Edward Ngong Deng	Aliab Dinka
PI#143	Philip Thokluel Kuol	Aliab Dinka
PI#144	Paul Manhom Mading*	Agar Dinka
PI#145	Isaac Makoi Majur*	Agar Dinka
PI#146	Kana Acol Dak (female)*	Agar Dinka
PI#147	Mabor Morwel Lok*	Agar Dinka
PI#148	Lual Wuol Nhiak*	Gok Dinka
PI#149	Deng Nhial Diek*	Gok Dinka
PI#150	Manasseh Keluel Cindut*	Agar Dinka
PI#151	Joseph Mathiang Dhalbeng*	Agar Dinka
PI#152	Makuac Majok Mangeng	W. Luaic Dinka

PI#153	Gabriel Awec Bol*	Rek Dinka
PI#154	Mayar Mayar Mareng*	Rek Dinka
PI#155	Mel Anyar Aduol*	Rek Dinka
PI#156	Aramthai Kur Deng (female)	Rek Dinka
PI#158	Susanne Gordon Kuol	Bor-Gok Dinka
PI#159	Grace Isaiah Piel	Bor-Gok Dinka
PI#160	Joseph Agel Ring*	W. Twic Dinka
PI#161	Paul Mangok Maror*	W. Twic Dinka
PI#162	Deng Agak Duot*	W. Twic Dinka
PI#163	Michael Angok Malong*	W. Twic Dinka
PI#164	Bol Bol Col*	W. Twic Dinka
PI#165	Maniem Maluak Mawien*	W. Twic Dinka
PI#166	Dhieu Deng Dhieu*	W. Twic Dinka
PI#167	Santino Nhom Acot*	W. Twic Dinka
PI#168	Paterno Imoi Lokoria	Dongotono
PI#169	Kasimoro Ohisa Odongi	Lotoka
PI#170	Kuol Lual Mou*	Malwal Dinka
PI#171	Akot Ajuou Majok*	Malwal Dinka
PI#172	Akec Macol Akec*	Malwal Dinka
PI#173	Ater Bol Mayen*	Malwal Dinka
PI#174	Piol Piol Adim*	Malwal Dinka
PI#175	Ding Akuei Deng*	Malwal Dinka
PI#176	Paulino Akon Ken*	Malwal Dinka
PI#177	Massimino Allam	Latuka
PI#179	Maguith Deng Kuol*	W. Ngok Dinka
PI#180	Agoth Alor Bulabek*	W. Ngok Dinka
PI#181	Fidele Majok Mabior	Rek Dinka
PI#182	Cok Kuek Ywai*	Dunghol Dinka
PI#183	Majak Col Mayiik*	Dunghol Dinka
PI#184	Mary Akuol Bith (female)	Ruweng Dinka
PI#185	Santino Malual Meet	Rut Dinka
PI#186	Paul Dak Kacuol	Rut Dinka
PI#190	Abraham Mayuom Mangok	Aliab Dinka
PI#191	Deng Dau Deng	E. Twic Dinka
PI#192	Mary Awien Nyok	Alor Dinka
PI#193	William Mayar Dau	Alor Dinka

Akot, South Sudan 1996

PI#194	Manasseh Mayen Malok	Agar Dinka
PI#195	Mourthon Marial Mourthon	Agar Dinka
PI#196	Stephen Anyaak Col	Pakam-Agar Dinka
PI#198	Dut Malual Arop	Agar Dinka
PI#199	Paul Kok Bol	Western Ngok Dinka
PI#200	Gabriel Makuac Nyiak Agrey	Agar Dinka
PI#201	Lilian Reuben Marmour	Moru
PI#202	Paul Macuer Malok	Agar Dinka

PI#205	Mabet Mabum Arop	Agar Dinka
PI#206	Jok Ayom Majak	Gok Dinka
PI#207	Col Gurke Door	Gok Dinka
PI#208	Joseph Lueth Ater	Gok Dinka
PI#209	Pur Ciengan	Apak Atwot
PI#210	Nek Martin Majok	Apak Atwot
PI#212	Simon Adel Yak	Agar Dinka
PI#213	Michael Manyiel Col	Agar Dinka
PI#214	Andrew Anheim Alit	Atwot

Bar Pakeny, South Sudan, 1996

| PI#215 | Ruben Madol Arol | Gok Dinka |
| PI#216 | Paul Mayom Akec | Agar Dinka |

Lokichoggio, Kenya, 1996

| PI#218 | John Mangok Kuot | W. Twic Dinka |

Nyabagok, South Sudan, 1996

PI#219	Dickson Ogolla Oroku	Luo (Kenyan)
PI#220	Albino Ukec Simon	Luo (Sudanese)
PI#221	Napoleon Adok Gai	Atwot
PI#222	Wilfred Ring Aduer	W. Luaic Dinka
PI#223	Victor Majok Amecrot	Rek Dinka
PI#224	Matthew Mathem Daw	Rek Dinka
PI#225	Bol Malek Jok	Rek Dinka

Agany, South Sudan, 1996

| PI#230 | Paul Mabor Aliab | Atwot |

Yambio, South Sudan, 1996

PI#231	Bangasi Joseph Bakosoro	Zande
PI#232	Ephraim Sunguzagi	Azande
PI#233	Pascal Bandindi Uru*	Balanda
PI#234	Michael Katawa	Azande
PI#235	Murangi Salatiel	Azande
PI#236	Botrus Bandaka	Azande
PI#244	Vincent Zangabeyo Windio	Zande
PI#245	Jerome Barikue*	Balanda
PI#246	Romano Gasi*	Blanada
PI#247	Daniel Manase Zindo	Azande
PI#248	Samuel Abujohn Kbashi	Kbashi
PI#249	Said Mohammed Arthur	Zande

Nairobi, Kenya, 1996

PI#251	Andrew Mayak Maloksu	Gok Dinka
PI#252	David Deng Athorbei	Apak-Atwot
PI#253	Telar Deng	Atwot-Luaic
PI#254	Lual Benjamin Bil	Agar Dinka
PI#255	Gordon Matot Tut	Ciec Dinka
PI#256	Andria Acin-Nyin Maketh	Apak Atwot
PI#257	Reuben Abiel Cuang	E. Ngok Dinka
PI#258	John Aben Deng	E. Ngok Dinka
PI#260	Ruben Macier Makoi	Yibel
PI#261	Kawac Makuei Mayar	Malwal Dinka
PI#262	Simon Ngor Ngor	Malwal Dinka
PI#263	Bol Akok Akok	Malwal Dinka
PI#264	Duang Deng Duang	Malwal Dinka/Luo
PI#265	Simon Malual Deng	Yibel
PI#266	Monica Nyibel Aleu (female)	Malwal Dinka
PI#267	Athieng Deng Acier (female)*	Malwal Dinka
PI#268	Arek Akot Awutier (female)*	Malwal Dinka
PI#269	Arek Akot Awutier (sister of above)	Malwal Dinka
PI#270	Ayuen Akot Awutier (female)*	Malwal Dinka
PI#271	Raphael Dut Atak	Malwal Dinka
PI#272	Mary Acuoth Dhel	Agar Dinka
PI#276	Samuel Aru Bol	Agar Dinka
PI#277	Comboni Fr. Mattia	Italian
PI#278	Lawrence Lual Lual Akuey	Malwal Dinka
PI#279	Gabriel Jiet Jal (telephone)	Nuer
PI#280	Pagan Amun	Shilluk
PI#281	Peter Adwok Nyaba (telephone)	Shilluk
PI#282	Cagai Matet Guem	Ciec Dinka

London, England, 1996

PI#284	Parmena Awerial Aluong	Aliab Dinka
PI#285	Lazarus Leek Mawut	Nyarruweng Dinka
PI#287	Gordon Muortat Mayen	Agar Dinka

Cairo, Egypt, May 1997

PI#290	Ebe Enosa Kakwa	
PI#291	Mourwel Ater Mourwel	Agar Dinka
PI#292	Asunta Mario (female)	Rek Dinka
PI#293	Mawien Kual Ariik	Rek Dinka
PI#294	Ring Deng Biong	W. Ngok Dinka
PI#295	Isaac Lat	Hol (Ghol) Dinka
PI#296	Gabriel Mathiang Rok	Agar Dinka
PI#297	Lomumba Tito Eman	Atwot

PI#298　Abel Alier Wal Kwai　　　　　　Bor-Atoc Dinka
PI#299　Meriam Al-Batool (female)　　　Jaali/Baggara N. Sudanese

United States 1995–2000

SOUTHERN SUDANESE

PI#300　Raphael Abiem, W. Ngok-Manyuar Dinka, Medford, Mass.
PI#301　Bona Acuil, Rek Dinka, Tacoma Park, Md.
PI#302　Abyei Kon, Bongo Western Ngok Dinka, Alexandria, Va.
PI#303　Kuot Mawien, Rek Dinka, Tacoma Park, N.J.
PI#304　Wal Duany, Nuer, Bloomington, Ind.
PI#305　Julia Ager Benjamin, Dinka, Bloomington, Ind.
PI#306　Yongo Bure Jame, Kuku, Flint, Mich.

Archives

Sudan Archives Durham, University of Durham, England

SAD GIIS1124
SAD 28/2/45
SAD 104/16/1–27
SAD 212/14/1–3, 168–170, 198
SAD 212/15/4
SAD 465/3
SAD 660/11/146–156
SAD 639/12/1
SAD 761/6/3–4
SAD 764/12/17–21
SAD 767/9/92–93
SAD 767/10/38, 94–95
SAD 767/11/28–52

Sudan Interior Mission Archives, Charlotte, North Carolina

Uncatalogued document of the Sudan Interior Mission (no date, no name, probably dating to the 1940s). Obtained from the SIM Archives, Charlotte, N.C. (Document regarding Chiefs in the Padang territory)

Archives for the Center for Development Studies, University of Bergen, Bergen, Norway

David, Nicholas. "The B.I.E.A. Southern Sudan Expedition of 1979: Interpretation of the Archaeological Data." Unpublished paper obtained from the Center for Development Studies, University of Bergen, Norway.

Cole, David and Richard Huntington, African Rural Development: Some Lessons from Abyei. Unpublished manuscript. Cambridge, Harvard Institute for International Development, October 1985. (Obtained from the Center for Development Studies, University of Bergen, Norway.)

Miscellaneous Documents, Letters and Presentations

Dak, Othwonh. "Southern Regions: Decentralisation or Recentralisation?" Paper presented at the Conference on the North-South Relations since the Addis Ababa Agreement; convened in Khartoum 6–9, March 1985.

Dakhlia 112/16/102, "Buruns and Allied Tribes," J. W. Robertson, "Sillak, Maghagha & Abu el Dugu" (15/12/31). (Obtained from the personal library of Dr. Jay Spaulding.)

Dr. David Decker research notes from Southern Kordofan May 1987.

Written document received from Bor Dinka Manyok Akuak Geu (resident in Kakuma Refugee Camp) about his family life and history.

Unpublished Works

Guem, Cagai Matet. "Orientation to Southern Sudan, Informal Introduction to Southern Sudan, Its History, Culture and Politics," Lokichoggio, Nov. 15–18, 1993.
———. "Position of the Girl among the Dinka Community and in Relationship with the Geneva Convention on the Rights of the Child." Unpublished paper presented to the South Sudan Law Society (n.d.).

Kir, Lino, and John Duerkson. *Language Learning Dinka Rek*. Unpublished volume by the Dinka Literature Production Team, Summer Institute of Linguistics, Nairobi, July 1996.

Spaulding, Jay. "The Chronology of Sudanese Arabic Genealogical Tradition." Unpublished paper presented at the workshop "Ideologies of Race, Origins and Descent in the History of the Nile Valley and North East Africa," 12 July 1994, St. Anthony's College, Oxford.

Thelwall, Robin. "Lexicostatistical Relations between Nubian, Daju and Dinka," Prepared for the Colloque de Chantilly, 2–6 July 1975, 273. Unpublished text, obtained from the library of Dr. Rex O'Fahey.

Published Sources

Adams, William Y. *Nubia Corridor to Africa*. London: Lane, 1977.
———. "The Coming of Nubian Speakers to the Nile Valley." In *The Archaeological and Linguistic Reconstruction of African History*, edited by Christopher Ehret and Merrick Posnansky, 11–38. Berkeley: University of California Press, 1982.
———. "Toward a Comparative Study of Christian Nubian Burial Practice." *Archeologie du Nil Moyen* 8 (1998): 13–41.

Addison, F. *Jebel Moya*. Oxford: Oxford University Press, 1949.

Arkell, A. J. *A History of the Sudan from Earliest Times to 1821*. London: University of London, 1955.

Bacon, C. R. K. "The Anuak." *Sudan Notes and Records* 5, no. 3 (1922): 113–29.

Barth, Heinrich. *Travels and Discoveries in North and Central Africa*. Vol. 3. London: Longmann, Brown, Green, Longmans and Roberts, 1857–58.

Baum, Robert M. *Shrines of the Slave Trade: Diola Religion and Society in Precolonial Senegambia*. Oxford: Oxford University Press, 1999.

Bayoumi, R. A. L., S. D. Flatz, W. Kiihnau, and G. Flatz. "Beja and Nilotes: Nomadic Pastoralist Groups in the Sudan with Opposite Distributions of the Adult Lactose Phenotypes." *American Journal of Physical Anthropology* 58 (1982): 173–78.

Beach, David. *The Shona and Their Neighbours*. Oxford: Blackwell 1994.

Beaven, J. *Renk District Notes, Upper Nile Province Handbook*. Khartoum: Sudan Government, 1931.

Bedri, Ibrahim. "More Notes on the Padang Dinka." *Sudan Notes and Records* 29 (1948): 40–57.

Beidelman, T. "Myth, Legend and Oral History." *Anthropos* 65 (1970): 74–97.

Beltrame, G. *Fiume Bianco nell'Africa centrale*. Verona, 1864.

———. *Brevi cenni sui Denka e sulla loro lingua*. Florence: Rivista Orientale, 1867.

———. *Il rive del Fiume Bianco da Chartum a Seilak*. Venice, 1881.

———. *Il Fiume Bianco e i Denka*. Verona, 1881.

Bender, M. Lionel. "Sub-Classification of Nilo-Saharan." In *Proceedings of the Fourth Nilo-Saharan Conference, Bayreuth, Aug. 30–Sept. 2, 1989*, edited by M. Lionel Bender, 1–36. Hamburg: Helmut Buske Verlag, 1989.

Bere, R. M. "An Outline of Acholi History." *Uganda Journal* 11 (1947): 1–8.

Beswick, Stephanie. "The Addis Ababa Agreement, 1972–1983: Harbinger of the Second Civil War in the Sudan." *Northeast African Studies* 13, no. 2 (1991): 191–215.

———. "Islam and the Dinka of the Southern Sudan from the Pre-Colonial Period to Independence (1956)." *Journal of Asian and African Studies* 29, no. 3–4 (1994): 172–85.

———. "Violence, Ethnicity, and Political Consolidation in South Sudan: A History of the Dinka and Their Relations with Their Neighbors (1200–1994)." Ph.D. dissertation Michigan State University, 1998.

———. "The Ngok, Emergence and Destruction of a Nilotic Proto-State in Southwest Kordofan." In *Kordofan Invaded Peripheral Incorporation and Sectoral Transformation in Islamic Africa, 1785–1995*, edited by Michael Kevane and Endre Stiansen, 145–164. Leiden: Brill, 1998.

———. "Nilotes of Eastern Africa: Western Nilotes: Shilluk, Nuer, Dinka, Anyuak." *Encyclopedia of African History*. London: Fitzroy Dearborn Publishers, forthcoming.

———. "The Dinka as 'Northern Sudanese,' the Nuer as 'Luo' and the Genesis of Intra-Southern Sudanese Conflict." Northeast African Studies, forthcoming.

———. "Women, War, and Leadership in South Sudan (1700–1994)," in *White Nile Black Blood: War, Leadership, and Ethnicity from Khartoum to Kampala*, ed. Jay Spaulding and Stephanie Beswick, 93–111 (Lawrenceville, N.J.: Red Sea Press, 2000).

Blount, B., and R. T. Curley. "The Southern Luo Languages: A Glottochronological Reconstruction." *Journal of African Languages* 9, no. 1 (1970): 1–18.

Braudel, Fernand. *On History.* Chicago: University of Chicago Press, 1980.

Brehm, Alfred Edmund. *Reiseskizzen aus Nord-Ost Afrika: Egypten, Nubien, Sennahr, Roseeres und Kordofahn, 1847–1852.* Vol. 1. Jena: F. Mauke, 1855.

Browne, W. G. *Travels in Africa, Egypt, and Syria From the Year 1792 to 1798* London, T. Cadell, 1799 2nd ed. London: T. Cadell, 1806.

Bruce, James. *Travels to Discover the Source of the Nile in the Years 1768–1772.* Vol. 6. 2nd ed. Edinburgh: Constable, 1805.

Burckhardt, John Lewis. *Travels in Nubia.* 2nd ed. London: John Murray, 1822.

Burton, John W. *God's Ants: A Study of Atuot Religion.* St. Augustine, West Germany: Anthropes Institute, 1981.

———. "Some Observations on the Social History of the Atuot Dialect of Nilotic." In *Nilo-Saharan: Proceedings of the First Nilo-Saharan Linguistics Colloquium, Leiden, September 8–10, 1980,* edited by Thilo C. Schadeberg and M. Lionel Bender, 134–38. Dordrecht, Holland: Foris Publications, 1981.

———. "Nilotic Women: A Diachronic Perspective." *Journal of Modern African Studies* 20, no. 3 (1982): 467–93.

———. "Living with the Dead: Aspects of the Afterlife in Nuer and Dinka Cosmology (Sudan)." *Anthropos* 73 (1978): 141–60.

———. *A Nilotic World: The Atuot Speaking Peoples of the Southern Sudan.* New York: Greenwood Press, 1987.

Buxton, Jean. "The Mundari of the Southern Sudan." In *Tribes without Rulers Studies in African Segmentary Systems,* edited by John Middleton and David Tait, 67–96. London: Routledge & Kegan Paul, 1958.

Buxton, Thomas Fowell. *The African Slave Trade and Its Remedy.* London: J. Murray, 1840.

Cailliaud, M. Frederic. *Voyage à Meroe, au Fleuve Blanc, au-delà de Fazoql.* 4 vols. Paris: Imprimerie Royale, 1826–27.

Cleaveland Timothy. *Becoming Walata.* Portsmouth, N.H.: Heinemann, 2001.

Collier, Jane Fishburne. *Marriage and Inequality in Classless Societies.* Stanford, CA: Stanford University Press, 1988.

Collins, Robert O. *Land beyond the Rivers: The Southern Sudan, 1898–1918.* New Haven, CN: Yale University Press, 1971.

———. *Shadows in the Grass.* New Haven, Conn.: Yale University Press, 1983.

Comaroff, John, and Jean Comaroff. *Ethnography and the Historical Imagination.* Boulder, CO: Westview Press, 1992.

Conrad, David C., ed., *A State of Intrigue the Epic of Bamana Segu According to Tayiru Banbera.* Oxford: Oxford University Press, 1990.

Crawford, O. G. S. "People without a History." *Antiquity* 22 (1948): 8–12.

———. *The Fung Kingdom of Sennar.* Gloucester: John Bellows Ltd., 1951.

Crazzolara, J. P. "The Lwoo People." *Uganda Journal* 5 (1937): 1–21.

———. *The Lwoo.* Part 1. *Lwoo Migrations.* Verona: Missioni Africane, 1950.

———. *The Lwoo.* Part 3. *The Clans.* Verona: Editrice Nigrizia, 1954.

———. "Lwoo Migrations." *Uganda Journal* 25 (1961): 136–48.

Cunnison, I. *The Baggara Arabs.* Oxford: Clarendon Press, 1966.

David, Nicholas. "Prehistory and Historical Linguistics in Central Africa: Points of Contact." In *The Archaeological and Linguistic Reconstruction of African History*, edited by Christopher Ehret and Merrick Posnansky, 78–103. Berkeley: University of California Press, 1982.

———. "The Archaeological Context of Nilotic Expansion." In *Nilotic Studies: Proceedings of the International Symposium on Languages and History of the Nilotic Peoples Cologne, January 4–5, 1982*, edited by Rainer Vossen and Marianne Bechhaus-Gerst, 64–95. Berlin: Dietrich Reimer Verlag, 1983.

Deng, Francis M. "The Family and the Law of Torts in African Customary Law." *The Sudan Law Journal and Reports* (1965): 587–605.

———. "Property and Value-Interplay among the Nilotes." *Iowa Law Review* 51, no. 3 (1966): 541–60.

———. *Africans of Two Worlds: The Dinka in Afro-Arab Sudan*. New Haven, CT: Yale University Press, 1978.

———. *Recollections of Babo Nimir*. London: Ithaca Press, 1982.

———. *The Dinka and Their Songs*. Oxford: Clarendon Press, 1983.

———. *The Man Called Deng Majok*. New Haven, CT: Yale University Press, 1986.

———. *War of Visions*. Washington D.C.: The Brookings Institute, 1995.

Diamond, Sigismund. *Primitive Law Past and Present*. London: Methuen & Co., 1971.

Ehret, Christopher. *Southern Nilotic History*. Evanston, IL: Northwestern University Press, 1971.

———. "Population Movement and Culture Contact in the Southern Sudan, c.3000 B.C. to A.D. 1000: A Preliminary Linguistic Overview." In *Culture History in the Southern Sudan Archaeology, Linguistics and Ethnohistory*, edited by John Mack and Peter Robertshaw. Nairobi: British Institute in East Africa, 1982, 19–48.

———. *An African Classical Age*. Charlottesville: University Press of Virginia, 1998.

———, and Merrick Posnansky, eds. *The Archaeological and Linguistic Reconstruction of African History*. Berkeley: University of California Press, 1982.

Epstein, H. *The Origins of the Domestic Animals of Africa*. New York: Africana Publishing Corp., 1971.

Evans-Pritchard, E. E. "Ethnological Observations in Dar Fung." *Sudan Notes and Records* 15, Part I (1932): 46–57.

———. "The Nuer: Tribe and Clan. *Sudan Notes and Records* 16, Part I (1933): 40–53.

———. *The Nuer*. Oxford: Clarendon Press, 1940.

———. *The Political System of the Anuak of the Anglo-Egyptian Sudan*. London: London School of Economics, 1940.

———. *Nuer Religion*. Oxford: Clarendon Press, 1956.

Fergusson, Captain V. H. "The Nuong Nuer." *Sudan Notes and Records* 3, no. 4 (1921): 146–54.

Frazer, James. *The Golden Bough: A Study in Magic and Religion*. Vol. 3. London: Macmillan Co., 1914.

Dagmar Freuchen, ed. *Peter Freuchen's Book of the Eskimos*. New York: World Publishing Company, 1961.

Garang de Mabior, John. "Identifying, Selecting and Implementing Rural Development Strategies for Socio-Economic Development in the Jonglei Projects Area, Southern Region, Sudan." Ph.D. diss., Iowa State University, 1981.

Gearing, F. O. "Priest and Warriors." *American Anthropological Association Memoir* No. 93, 1962.

Glickman, Maurice. "The Nuer and the Dinka: A Further Note." *Man* 7, no. 4 (1972): 586–94.

Goody, J. *Technology, Tradition and the State.* Cambridge: Cambridge University Press, 1971.

Gough, Kathleen. "Nuer Kinship: A Re-examination." In *The Translation of Culture: Essays to E. E. Evans-Pritchard,* edited by T. O. Beidelman, 79–121. London: Tavistock Publications, 1971.

Greene, Sandra E. *Gender, Ethnicity, and Social Change on the Upper Slave Coast: A History of the Anlo-Ewe.* Portmouth, N.H.: Heinemann, 1996.

Habraszewski, T. "A Brief Account of Evliya Celebi on a Violent Death Practiced in the Southern Sudan 1672. *Folia Orientalia* (Krakow) 11 (1969): 139–44.

Harris, Marvin. *Our Kind.* New York: Harper and Row, 1989.

Hebbert, G. K. C. "The Bandala of the Bahr el-Ghazal." *Sudan Notes and Records* 8 (1925): 187–94.

Henderson, K. D. D. "A Note on the Migration of the Messiria Tribe into South-West Kordofan." *Sudan Notes and Records* 22 (1939): 49–79.

Herring, R. S. "Hydrology and Chronology: The Rodah Nilometer as an Aid in Dating Inter-Lacustrine History." In *Chronology, Migration and Drought in Inter-Lacustrine Africa,* edited by J. B. Webster. London: Longman and Dalhousie University Press, 1979, 39–86.

Hofmayr, P. W. "Religion der Schilluk." *Anthropos* 6 (1911): 120–31.

———. *Die Schilluk.* St. Gabriel, Modling bei Wien: Administration des Anthropos, 1925.

Honea, Kenneth. "The Deng Cult and Its Connections with the Goddess Aciek among the Dinka." *Wiener Volkerkundliche Mitteilungen* 2, no. 1 (1954): 16–20.

Horton, Robin. "Stateless Societies in the History of West Africa." In *History of West Africa,* edited by J. F. A. Ajayi and Michael Crowder, 78–119. New York: Columbia University Press, 1972.

Howell, P. P. "Notes on the Ngork Dinka of Western Kordofan." *Sudan Notes and Records* 32 (1951): 239–93.

———. *The Equatorial Nile Project and Its Effects in the Anglo-Egyptian Sudan, Being the Report of the Jonglei Investigation Team.* Vol. 1. London: Waterlow and Sons, 1954.

———. "Pyramids in the Upper Nile Region." *Man* Nos. 55/56 (1948): 52–53.

Hutchinson, Sharon, "The Cattle of Money and The Cattle of Girls Among the Nuer, 1930–83." *American Ethnologist* 19 No. 2 May 1992, 294–316.

Jaiballa, Ali Salih. *Mudhakirat Al-Omda Al-Sabiqa: Al Haj Ali Salih Jaiballa.* Memories of the Former Omda. Sudan: Mahmoudiyya Press, 1974. Obtained from the personal library of Meriam Albatool Alkandri.

Jal, Gabriel Giet. "The History of the Jikany Nuer before 1920." Ph.D. Thesis, School of Oriental and African Studies, University of London, 1987.

Al-Shatir Busayli' Abd al-Jalil. *Makhtutat Katib al-Shuna fi ta'rikh al-sultana al-*

sinnariya wa'l-idara al-misriya [The Funj Chronicle]. Cairo: United Arab Republic Ministry of Culture and Information, 1961.

Johnson, Douglas H. "History and Prophecy among the Nuer of the Southern Sudan." Ph.D. diss., University of California, Los Angeles, 1980.

———. "The Southern Sudan." *The Minority Rights Group Report* No. 78 (1982): 1–10.

———. *The Root Causes of Sudan's Civil Wars.* Oxford: James Currey, 2003.

Kaufmann, A. *Schilderungen aus Centralafrica oder Land und Leute im obern Nilgebiete am weissen Flusse.* Brixen: A. Weger, 1862.

———. "The White Nile Valley and Its Inhabitants." In *The Opening of the Nile Basin,* edited by Elias Toniolo and Richard Hill, 140–95. London: C. Hurst & Company, 1974.

Kelly, Raymond C. *The Nuer Conquest: The Structure and Development of an Expansionist System.* Ann Arbor: University of Michigan Press, 1985.

Kendall, Timothy. "Ethnoarchaeology in Merotic Studies." In *Studia Meroitica 1984* (Meroitica 10), edited by Sergio Donadoni and Steffen Wenig, 625–745. Berlin: Akademie-Verlag 1989.

Kleppe, Else Johansen. "The Debbas on the White Nile, Southern Sudan." In *Culture History in the Southern Sudan Archaeology, Linguistics and Ethnohistory,* edited by John Mack and Peter Robertshaw, 59–71. Nairobi: British Institute in East Africa, 1982.

———. "Towards a Prehistory of the Riverain Nilotic Sudan: Archaeological Excavations in the Er Renk District." *Nubian Letters* 1 (1983): 14–20.

Koejok, Damazo Dut Majak. "Resistance and Cooperation in Bahr el-Ghazal." In *Southern Sudan: Regionalism and Religion,* ed. Mohamed Omer Beshir, 88–126. Khartoum: University of Khartoum, 1984.

———. "The Northern Bahr al-Ghazal: People, Alien Encroachment and Rule, 1856–1956." Ph.D. diss., University of California, Santa Barbara, 1990.

Kronenberg, Waltraud, and Andreas Kronenberg. *Die Bongo.* Wiesbaden: Franz Steiner Verlag, 1981.

Lepsius, R. *Briefe aus Aegypten, Aethiopien und der Halbinsel des Sinai geschrieben in den Jahren 1842–1845.* Berlin, 1852.

Lewis, B. A. *The Murle: Red Chiefs and Black Commoners.* Oxford: Oxford University Press, 1972.

Lienhardt, Godfrey. "The Shilluk of the Upper Nile." In *African Worlds,* edited by D. Forde, 138–63. London: Oxford University Press, 1954.

———. "Nilotic Kings and Their Mother's Kin." *Africa* 27 (1955): 341–55.

———. "The Western Dinka." In *Tribes without Rulers: Studies in African Segmentary Systems,* edited by John Middleton and David Tait, 97–135. London: Routledge & Kegan Paul, 1958.

———. *Divinity and Experience.* Oxford: Clarendon Press, 1961.

Lloyd, Captain Watkiss. "Some Notes on Dar Homr." *The Geographical Journal* 29 (January to June 1907): 649–54.

Lovejoy, Paul E. *Transformations in Slavery: A History of Slavery in Africa.* New York: Cambridge University Press, 1983.

Ludwig, Emil. *The Nile: The Life-Story of a River.* New York: Viking Press, 1937.

MacMichael, Harold. *A History of the Arabs.* 2 vols. London: Frank Cass & Co. Ltd., 1967.

McLaughlin, John. "Tentative Time Depths for Nuer, Dinka, and Anuak." *Journal of Ethiopian Studies* 5 (1967): 13–27.

Middleton, John, and David Tait. Introduction in *Tribes without Rulers,* John Middleton and David Tait, 1–31. London: Routledge and Kegan Paul, 1958.

Musil, Alois. *The Manners and Customs of the Rwala Bedouins.* New York: American Geographical Society, 1928.

Nachtigal, Gustav. *Sahara and Sudan.* Vol. 4, *Wadai and Darfur.* Translated by Allen G. S. Fisher and Humphrey J. Fisher. London: C. Hurst, 1974 [First published in German under the title *Sahara und Sudan.* 3 vols., 1879–1889.]

Nebel, Father A. *Dinka Dictionary with Abridged Grammar* (Rek/Malwal dialect). Verona: Missioni Africane, 1936.

Newcomer, Peter J. "The Nuer Are Dinka: An Essay on Origins and Environmental Determinism." *Man* 7, no. 1 (1972): 5–11.

Nicholson, Sharon Elaine. "A Climatic Chronology for Africa: Synthesis of Geological, Historical, and Meteorological Information and Data." Ph.D. diss., University of Wisconsin-Madison, 1976.

O'Ballance, Edgar. *Sudan, Civil War and Terrorism, 1956–99.* New York: Palgrave Macmillan, 2000.

O'Fahey, R. S. "Slavery and the Slave Trade in Dar Fur." *Journal of African History* 14, no. 1 (1973): 29–43.

———, and J. L. Spaulding. *Kingdoms of the Sudan.* London: Methuen, 1974.

———. "Fur and Fartit: The History of a Frontier." In *Culture History in the Southern Sudan Archaeology, Linguistics and Ethnohistory,* edited by John Mack and Peter Robertshaw, 75–88. Nairobi: British Institute in East Africa, 1982.

Oliver, R., and J. D. Fage, *A Short History of Africa.* Baltimore: Penguin, 1962.

Oliver, R., ed. *The Dawn of African History.* London: Oxford University Press, 1961.

Otterbein, Keith. *The Evolution of Warfare.* New Haven, CT: HRAF Press, 1970.

Perner, Conradin. *The Anyuak Living on Earth in the Sky.* Basel, Switzerland: Helbing und Lichtenhahn, 1994.

Peterson, Scott. *Me against My Brother at War in Somalia, Sudan, and Rwanda.* New York: Routledge, 2001.

Posnansky, Merrick. "East Africa and the Nile Valley in Early Times." In *Sudan in Africa,* edited by Yusuf Fadl Hasan. Khartoum: Khartoum University Press, 1968.

Prudhoe, Lord. "Extracts from Private Memoranda Kept by Lord Prudhoe on a Journey from Cairo to Sennar, in 1829." *Journal of the Royal Geographical Society* 5 (1835): 38–58.

Pumphrey, M. E. C. "The Shilluk Tribe." *Sudan Notes and Records* 24 (1941): 1–45.

Radcliffe-Brown, A. R. *Structure and Function in Primitive Society.* London: Cohen and West, 1952.

Rahhal, Suleiman Musa, ed. *The Right to be Nuba.* Princeton, N.J.: Red Sea Press, 2001.

Reisner, George. *Harvard African Studies.* Vols. 5–6. Cambridge, Mass.: Harvard African Studies, 1923.

Riad, Mohamed. "Of Fung and Shilluk." *Wiener Volkerkundliche Mitteilungen* 3 (1955): 138–66.

————. "The Divine Kingship of the Shilluk and Its Origin." *Archiv Fur Volkerkunde* 14 (1959): 141–284.

Robertshaw, Peter, and Ari Siiriainen. "Excavations in Lakes Province, Southern Sudan." *Azania* 20 (1985): 89–161.

Robertshaw, Peter, and David Taylor. "Climate Change and the Rise of Political Complexity in Western Uganda." *Journal of African History* 41 (2000): 1–28.

Robinson, Arthur, E. "Abu El Kaylik: The Kingmaker of the Fung of Sennar." *American Anthropologist* 31 (1929): 232–64.

Russegger, J. von. *Reisen in Europa, Asien und Afrika, unternommen in den Jahren 1835–1841* Vol. II, Fasc. 2, Stuttgart: E. Schweizerbart, 1843.

Sacks, Karen. "Causality and Chance on the Upper Nile." *American Ethnologist* 6, no. 3 (August 1979): 437–48.

Sahlins, Marshall. "The Segmentary Lineage: An Organization of Predatory Expansion." *American Anthropologist* 63 (1961): 322–45.

Saitoti, Tepilit Ole. *The Worlds of a Maasai Warrior.* Berkeley: University of California Press, 1988.

Salam, A. H. Abdel, and Alex de Waal, eds. *The Phoenix State Civil Society and the Future of Sudan.* Princeton, N.J.: Red Sea Press, 2001).

Santandrea, Stephano. *A Tribal History of the Western Bahr el Ghazal.* Verona: Nigrizia, 1964.

————. *The Luo of the Bahr el Ghazal Sudan.* Verona: Editrice Nigrizia, 1968.

————. *Ethno-Geography of the Bahr el Ghazal Sudan.* Bologna: Editrice Missionaria Italiana, 1981.

Schmidt, Peter R. *Historical Archaeology: A Structural Approach in an African Culture.* Westport, CT: Greenwood Press, 1978.

Schweinfurth, G. *The Heart of Africa.* 2 vols. London: Sampson Low, Marston, Low, and Searle, 1874.

Seligman, C. G. "Some Aspects of the Hamitic Problem in the Anglo-Egyptian Sudan." *Journal of the Royal Anthropological Institute* 18 (1913): 665–66.

————, and Brenda Z. Seligman. *Pagan Tribes of the Nilotic Sudan.* London: George Routledge & Sons, 1932.

Service, Elman R. *Origins of the State and Civilization.* New York: Norton, 1975.

Shaw, W. B. "Darb el Arba'in." *Sudan Notes and Records* 12 (1929): 63–72.

Shinnie, Margaret. *A Short History of the Sudan Up to A.D.1500.* Khartoum: Sudan Antiquities Service, n.d.

Shuqayr Na'um. *Jughrafiya wa-ta'rikh al-Sudan.* Cairo: Dar al Kutub, 1902.

Sofholm, Per. "The River-Lake Nilotes: Politics of an African Tribal Group." Studia Sociologica Upsaliensia #8. Uppsala: Ph.D. thesis, Uppsala University, 1973. Subsequent unpublished document derived from the dissertation: "The Dinka: The River-Lake Nilotes." Uppsala. 1973.

Sorur, Daniel Deng Farim. "A Dinka Priest Writing on his Own People." In *The Opening of the Nile Basin,* edited by Elias Toniolo and Richard Hill, 196–203. London: C. Hurst & Company, 1974.

Southall, A. *Alur Society.* Cambridge: W. Heffer and Sons, Ltd., 1956.

————. "Nuer and Dinka are People: Ecology, Ethnicity and Logical Possibility." *Man* 11, no. 4 (December 1976): 463–91.

Spaulding, Jay. "The Funj: A Reconsideration." *Journal of African History* 13, no. 1 (1972) 39–53.

————. "The Fate of Alodia." *Transafrican Journal of History* 2 (1977): 39–53.

————. "Farmers, Herdsmen and the State in Rainland Sinnar." *Journal of African History* 20 (1979): 329–47.

————. "Toward a Demystification of the Funj: Some Perspectives on Society in Southern Sinnar, 1685–1900." *Meroitica* 7–8 Berlin (1984): 505–21.

————. *The Heroic Age in Sinnar.* East Lansing: Michigan State University Press, 1985.

————. "The Old Shaiqi Language in Historical Perspective." *History in Africa* 17 (1990): 283–92.

————, and Stephanie Beswick, eds. *White Nile, Black Blood: War, Leadership and Ethnicity from Khartoum to Kampala.* Princeton, N.J.: Red Sea Press, 1999.

Spear, T. "Oral Traditions: Whose History?" *History in Africa* 8 (1981): 165–81.

Spencer, Herbert. *Principles of Sociology.* New York: Appleton-Century-Croft, 1897.

Steinhart, E. I. "The Kingdoms on the March: Speculations on Social and Political Change." In *Chronology, Migration and Drought in Interlacustrine Africa,* edited by J. Webster, 189–214. London: Longman and Dalhousie University Press, 1979.

Stemler, A. B. L., J. R. Harlan and J. M. J. Dewet. "Caudatum Sorghums and Speakers of Chari-Nile Languages in Africa." *Journal of African History* 16, no. 2 (1975): 161–83.

Stevenson, R. C. "Old Khartoum, 1821–1885." *Sudan Notes and Records* Vol. 47 (1966): 1–38.

Stubbs, J. M., and C. G. T. Morrison. "The Western Dinkas, Their Land and Their Agriculture." *Sudan Notes and Records* 21 (1938): 251–68.

Sweet, Louise E. "Camel Raiding of North Arabian Bedouin: A Mechanism of Ecological Adaptation." *American Anthropologist* 67, no. 5, part 1 (1965): 1132–50.

Thelwall, Robin. "Lexicostatistical Relations between Nubian, Daju and Dinka." In *Extrait des Etudes Nubiennes, Colloque de Chantilly, 2–6 Juillet 1975,* 265–86. Cairo: Institut Français d'Archéologie Orientale du Caire, 1978.

Titherington, G. W. "Burial Alive among Dinka of the Bahr el-Ghazal Province." *Sudan Notes and Records* 8 (1925): 196–97.

————. "The Raik Dinka of Bahr El Ghazal Province," *Sudan Notes and Records* 10 (1927): 159–210.

Torok, Laszlo. *The Kingdom of Kush Handbook of the Napatan-Meroitic Civilization.* Leiden: Brill, 1997.

El-Tounsy, Mohamed (al-Tunisi, Muhammad b. Umar). *Voyage au Ouaday.* Paris: B. Duprat, 1851.

Triulzi, A. *Salt, Gold and Legitimacy.* Napoli: Istituto Universitario Orientale, 1981.

Tucker, A. N. *Dinka Orthography.* Khartoum: Institute of African and Asian Studies, 1978.

Vansina, J. *Oral Tradition.* Chicago: Aldine, 1965.

————. *Kingdoms of the Savanna: A History of Central African States until European Occupation.* Madison: University of Wisconsin Press, 1966.

————. "Once upon a Time: Oral Traditions as History in Africa." *Daedalus* (Spring 1971): 442–68.

Vantini, Fr. Giovanni. *Oriental Sources Concerning Nubia.* Heidelberg and Warsaw: Polish Academy of Sciences and Heidelberger Akademie der Wissenschaften, FRG., 1975.

Wallace, Anthony F. C. *Religion: An Anthropological View.* New York: Random House, 1966.

Weber, Max. *Economy and Society: An Outline of Interpretive Sociology.* Edited by Guenther Roth and Claus Wittich. Vol. 3. New York: Bedminster Press, 1968.

Webster, J. B. "Noi! Noi! Famines as an Aid to Interlacustrine Chronology." In *Chronology, Migration and Drought,* edited by J. B. Webster, 1–110. London: Longman and Dalhousie University Press, 1979.

Welsby, Derek A. *Soba II Renewed Excavations within the Metropolis of the Kingdom of Alwa in Central Sudan.* London: British Museum Press, 1998.

Werne, Ferdinand. *Expedition to Discover the Sources of the White Nile in the Years 1840–1841.* Vols. 1 and 2. London: R. Bentley, 1849.

Westermann, Diedrich. *The Shilluk People: Their Language and Folklore.* Philadelphia: The Board of Foreign Missions of The United Presbyterian Church of N.A., 1912.

Willis, C. A. "The Cult of Deng." *Sudan Notes and Records* 11 (1928): 195–207.

Yunger, Kathy Ann. "Nyikang The Warrior Priest: Shilluk Chol Imagery, Economics and Political Development." Ph.D. diss., State University of New York at Stony Brook, 1985.

Yunis, N. "Notes on the Baggara and Nuba of Western Kordofan." *Sudan Notes and Records* 5 (1922): 200–207.

Zarroug, Mohi el-Din Abdalla. *The Kingdom of Alwa.* Calgary: University of Calgary Press, 1991.

INDEX

Stephanie Beswick is a professor of history at Ball State University in Muncie, Indiana. She was born in Khartoum, Sudan.